From Pictland to Alba
789–1070

Alex Woolf

Edinburgh University Press

Edinburgh University Press Ltd
22 George Square, Edinburgh

Reprinted 2008, 2009, 2010, 2011, 2014 (twice)

Typeset in 11/13 Ehrhardt
by Servis Filmsetting Ltd, Manchester, and
printed and bound in Great Britain by
CPI Antony Rowe, Chippenham, Wilts

A CIP record for this book is available from the British Library

ISBN 978 0 7486 1233 8 (hardback)
ISBN 978 0 7486 1234 5 (paperback)

Publisher's acknowledgement
Edinburgh University Press thanks Mercat Press, publishers of
the *Edinburgh History of Scotland*, for permission to use *The New
Edinburgh History of Scotland* as the title for this ten-volume series.

Contents

Maps and Genealogical Tables

Acknowledgements

I was first asked to write this book, volume two in a projected series, shortly after I had arrived in Scotland nearly a decade ago. As the new boy on the block, and a foreigner, I felt both flattered and overawed by the commission. Since then I have taught myself the history of Scotland in the early and central middle ages through the process of teaching others, principally undergraduates first in the University of Edinburgh and, since 2001, in the University of St Andrews. I owe a great deal to the generosity and professionalism of my immediate colleagues in both these universities. Above all, however, I owe my introduction to and education in early Scottish history to my friends Dauvit Broun, Thomas Clancy, Stephen Driscoll, Katherine Forsyth and Simon Taylor who have encouraged and helped me at every stage of the way. Over the years all of them have been drawn, one by one, into the employ of the University of Glasgow. To this list of 'usual suspects' can be added my successor at Edinburgh, James Fraser. Since moving to St Andrews I have gained a great deal from the friendship and support of Barbara Crawford of the Strathmartine Centre, whose knowledge of Scandinavian Scotland is second to none and who, perhaps unusually for an academic, finds it easy to agree to differ. Furth of Scotland, mention must be made of Catherine Swift and Colmán Etchingham who for some years have been the main organisers of the Irish Conference of Medievalists at which many of the ideas presented in this volume were first aired; as both facilitators and critics Cathy and Colmán deserve thanks. Conversations with Lesley Abrams and David Parsons have, over the years, greatly enhanced my understanding of many aspects of the early middle ages but especially those relating to Scandinavian settlement.

In the closing stages of the work mention must be made of the Arts and Humanities Research Council, who funded a period of leave during which much of the final draught of the book was completed. My colleagues Roger Mason, the general editor of the series, and Michael Brown, author of the only volume in the series to have appeared at the time of writing, have given invaluable guidance as to the final shape of the book. Dauvit Broun and Simon Taylor have read the entire text in manuscript and contributed enormously to the finished product. Finally, I must make mention of two people who were involved at the beginning of the project. John Davey, lately retired, conceived the project and persuaded Edinburgh University Press to take it up. Throughout his career in publishing he was a great supporter of serious works on Scottish history and cultural heritage. The late Patrick Wormald was one of the original publisher's readers for my initial proposal for this volume. His support and encouragement at this time and at another very difficult point in my career deserve my enduring gratitude. I am truly sorry that he did not live to see this book.

General Editor's Preface

The purpose of the New Edinburgh History of Scotland is to provide up-to-date and accessible narrative accounts of the Scottish past. Its authors will make full use of the explosion of scholarly research that has taken place over the last three decades, and do so in a way that is sensitive to Scotland's regional diversity as well as to the British, European and transoceanic worlds of which Scotland has always been an integral part.

Chronology is fundamental to understanding change over time and Scotland's political development will provide the backbone of the narrative and the focus of analysis and explanation. The New Edinburgh History will tell the story of Scotland as a political entity, but will be sensitive to broader social, cultural and religious change and informed by a richly textured understanding of the totality and diversity of the Scots' historical experience. Yet to talk of the Scots – or the Scottish nation – is often misleading. Local loyalty and regional diversity have more frequently characterised Scotland than any perceived sense of 'national' solidarity. Scottish identity has seldom been focused primarily, let alone exclusively, on the 'nation'. The modern discourse of nationhood offers what is often an inadequate and inappropriate vocabulary in which to couch Scotland's history. The authors in this series will show that there are other and more revealing ways of capturing the distinctiveness of Scottish experience.

Of no period is this more true than of the three centuries between 789 and 1070 tackled in this volume by Alex Woolf, a period when Scotland as we know it did not exist, when Northern Britain was peopled by at least five distinct linguistic groups, and when Viking invasions sparked intense and often violent competition between rival ethnic groups for political and territorial dominance. Moreover, the scarcity of contemporary sources makes all the more challenging the task of constructing a political narrative that makes sense of the demise of a once-powerful Pictish kingdom and the emergence of the Gaelic-speaking Scots of Dál Riata as Kings of Alba and the dominant power in North Britain. This truly is the 'dark age' of Scottish history. Alex Woolf rises to this challenge with style, not only guiding the reader through the available sources, but also reinterpreting them, drawing on available archaeological evidence and a wealth of comparative European perspectives to interrogate them as never before. The result is a remarkably innovative account of the history of Northern Britain that, ignoring modern 'national' preconceptions, and reading history forwards rather than backwards, provides a ground-breaking explanation of the formation and development of the Scottish kingdom of Alba in terms of its complex interactions with contemporary Anglo-Saxon, Gaelic and Scandinavian polities and cultures. Authoritative and illuminating, this is an up-to-date and compelling account of what is undoubtedly the most obscure period of Scotland's history.

Note on Spelling and Pronunciation

In the period covered by this book at least five different languages were spoken as vernaculars in the territories that now make up Scotland and many of the written records of the age were produced in a sixth language, Latin. In the representation of personal names (and a handful of technical terms) I have tried to adopt a consistent policy.

GAELIC

Names which were current in Gaelic are represented in the standard Middle Irish form which represents the established written forms of the age. This rule has been adopted partly because it is the closest we can come to a true representation of the names as they would have sounded to the people who bore them, and partly because the vast majority of the source materials for Scottish Gaels in this period were written in Ireland and deal largely with Irish affairs. Since Irish historiography has long since abandoned the use of modern anglicised forms for early medieval names, such as Angus and Donald for Óengus and Domnall, and since we are dependent upon editions of chronicles and other medieval texts undertaken by students of Irish history it is only sensible to follow their practice in representing medieval names.

Early Gaelic orthography is not simple but what follows presents a basic guide.

At the beginning of words most consonants have the same value as in modern English with the caveat that 'c' is pronounced as 'k'. In the middle or at the end of words, however, the following consonants tend to have modified values as indicated:

c = g
p = b
t = d
b = v
d = ð [where 'ð' = the sound at the end of English 'with']
g = y [as in 'youth']
m = v
f = [ ] [that is, it becomes silent]

In some compound names the initial consonant of a name is preceded by a lower case consonant, for example, *Cenél nGabráin* meaning 'kindred of Gabrán', in such cases the 'true' initial is replaced by the lower case prefix so, in this case we pronounce 'Kenél Navráin'. The digraph 'th' is voiced much as in modern English and 'ch' as in 'loch'. 'S' is sounded as 'sh' before 'i' and 'e'.

Accents on vowels signify their length and also give some indication of where to lay stress in the word. If the letter 'e' appears at the end of a name, following a consonant it should be pronounced (*unlike* English 'stone' or 'lime').

Some common names:

Domnall = Dovnal
Oengus = Oinyus
Cinaed = Kineyð
Aed = Eyð
Mael Sechnaill = Malshechnal

There is also something called an 'epenthetic' vowel which appears between an 'l' or 'r' and an immediately following consonant. It is little more than a pause for breath and is perhaps best represented by an apostrophe: Alba = Al'ba, Colmán = Kol'maan.

BRITISH/CUMBRIC/WELSH

The British Celtic language was widely spoken across Britain and in northwestern France during the early middle ages. This language is the ancestral language of modern Welsh, Cornish and Breton, although at this period most its dialects were not distinct enough to be classed as separate languages. Some historians of Scotland and northern England have, in recent decades, begun the habit of describing the British spoken in the north as 'Cumbric' but this is not really justified or necessary and one suspects that it is to some extent motivated by nationalistic concerns that the Welsh of today might claim northern British history and literature for themselves. Almost all the records of medieval British, barring a few names here and there, survive in manuscripts made in Wales in the central or later middle ages and thus it is sensible to keep in line with modern Welsh historiography, as we have kept in line with Irish historiography, to make cross-referencing easier. Unfortunately the Welsh tradition, in contrast to the Irish, has been to modernise name forms. Thus, in this book I have followed different conventions for the representation of British and Gaelic. In doing so, however, I have been maintaining the policy followed by the *Scottish Historical Review*, Scotland's premier periodical in this field.

Modern Welsh orthography is extremely consistent. Most letters are sounded as in English with the following exceptions:

c = k [without exception]
f = v
ff = f
ll = the sound in the middle of the word 'an*t*ler'
dd = ð
u = 'i' as in 'linen'
w = the vowel sound in 'cook' unless followed by a vowel in which case
    it has the English value
y = ə [the neutral vowel, or 'schwa', found at the end of 'snook*er*']
    unless there are two 'y's in a word in which case the second is the
    vowel in 'with' [thus *Aberystwyth* = 'Aberəstwith']
ch = 'ch' in loch
rh = 'hr'

Some common names:

Dyfnwal = Dəvnooal [the Gaelic name Domnall is probably a bor-
    rowing of this name]
Owain = O + 'wine'
Rhydderch = Hrəðerch

PICTISH BRITISH

English and Irish writers of the early middle ages seem to have believed that the Picts had their own language which was distinct from British. Unfortunately, no extended texts written in the language of the Picts survive and the place-names, personal names and a handful of loanwords which do survive are indistinguishable from British. In the 1950s Kenneth Jackson suggested that there had been two Pictish languages, one a dialect of British and the other of non-Celtic origin. This view is not as popular as it once was, although it is not entirely without supporters. In this book I have chosen to describe the British spoken in Pictavia as 'Pictish British', on the analogy of 'Scottish Gaelic', thus stressing both its common heritage with British and its distinctive character. The possible relationship between Pictish British and other British dialects is discussed at length in Chapter 8, here it is only necessary to discuss briefly its orthography. Our understanding of Pictish British orthography is based almost exclusively on the Pictish version of the Pictish king-list. The one liberty I have taken in this book is to represent the common letter cluster 'uu' as 'w'. Below are some Pictish names in the three Celtic orthographies:

Pictish British	British (Welsh)	Gaelic
Onuist	Ungust	Oengus
Wrguist	Gwrwst	Fergus
Wen	Owain	Eogan(án)
Bridei	Brydw	Brude
Naiton	Neithon	Nechtan

OLD ENGLISH

Most of the sound values in Old English, the language of the Anglo-Saxons, were similar to those in modern English. It is generally the case that historians of the Anglo-Saxon period standardise name forms to the Late West Saxon spelling system and that pattern has been followed here. It should be noted, however, that when names end in 'e', like Oswine, the final 'e' should be voiced and does not effect the preceding 'i' – this is 'Os' + 'win' + 'e' not 'Os' + modern English 'wine'. The major differences lies in the existence of certain characters not retained in modern English:

ð = 'eth' and represents the consonant at the end of 'with'

þ = 'thorn' and represents the sound at the beginning of that word (yes, it is different from ð)

æ = 'ash' and represents the vowel in that word (although it eventually became an 'eh' sound).

The pronunciation of the letter 'c' varies according to its 'environment'. Before or after 'i' and before 'e' this is sounded like 'ch' in English 'church'. Thus, the town now called Sandwich was originally spelt Sandwic. The cluster 'cg' is sounded like modern English 'dg' – thus Ecg- = 'edge'.

Some common names:

Ceolwulf = 'Cheolwolf'
Æðelstan = Athelstan
Ecgfrið = Edgefrith

OLD NORSE

The Scandinavians learned to write from the English and thus for the most part used the same spelling system with the exception that they used 'k' rather than 'c' and this character consistently represented a hard 'k' sound.

Introduction
Land and People: Northern Britain in the Eighth Century

In or around the year 1140 Henry, Archdeacon of Huntingdon and Cambridge, composed a history of the English. He took as his model and inspiration the *Ecclesiastical History of the English Nation* written some 400 years earlier by the Northumbrian monk Bede. As part of his introductory material Bede had described Britain as being inhabited by four nations speaking five tongues: the Britons; the English; the Gaels; and the Picts; each of whom had their own language. The fifth language was Latin which united the four nations in their study of the Christian scriptures. Henry of Huntingdon copied this passage into his own introduction but then added: 'but we see that the Picts have now been wiped out and their language also is totally destroyed so that they seem to be a fable we find mentioned in old writings.'[1] The purpose of the present book, volume two of the *New Edinburgh History of Scotland*, is to explore the changes that had taken place between the time Bede wrote and the time at which Henry wrote. Central among the issues to be investigated will be the mystery of Pictish ethnonemesis, their disappearance as a distinct people, a phenomenon which Henry of Huntingdon was the earliest observer to note. The narrative will take us from the middle of the eighth century to the middle of the eleventh century, and will encompass the Viking Age when Scandinavian warriors and settlers transformed so much of northern Britain, and which saw the emergence of the kingdom of Alba which the English called Scotland. It is in the course of this period that a kingdom that can unambiguously be said to be ancestral to modern Scotland first emerges, although the kingdom of the Scots would not reach its present extent until the 1460s, about four hundred years after our narrative closes.

[1] D. Greenaway, ed., *Henry Archdeacon of Huntingdon: Historia Anglorum* (Oxford, 1996), I.8, 24–5.

A REAL DARK AGE: THE PROBLEM OF THE SOURCES

The period with which we are concerned is an extremely obscure period in the history of northern Britain. No historical texts or documents survive intact that were written in Scotland during this time. We are almost entirely dependent upon external sources, mostly English and Irish, and upon later medieval Scottish texts whose authors seem to have had earlier Scottish works before them while they wrote. Assessing the value of these sources, in which information is passed on to us by inter-preters foreign in time or space to northern Britain, is a difficult task and one in which it is impossible either to avoid controversy or to reach a unanimous consensus. In this volume I shall endeavour to present alter-native explanations of events where necessary and, although I shall not disguise my own preferred interpretations, the reader should be aware that new information identified or insights made by scholars working in the field may upset the balance that I have sought to achieve.

Using Bede and Henry of Huntingdon as bookends reflects the fact that their respective generations mark the end and the beginning of far better documented periods than that which intervenes. Bede published his history in 731 and died in 735; our other major source for northern history also dries up at about this time. This source is preserved in manu-scripts of various Irish chronicles which survived the middle ages, such as the *Annals of Ulster*, the *Annals of Tigernach*, as well as in some early-modern manuscripts, such as *Chronicon Scotorum*.[2] These chronicles all started out life as continuations of a great chronicle which no longer sur-vives but which modern historians have labelled the 'Chronicle of Ireland' or the 'Irish World Chronicle'. This chronicle was being kept from at least the end of the ninth century in a monastery connected to Armagh but probably located a little further south in the Irish east mid-lands. The surviving Irish chronicles all originated as continuations of this prototype and seem to diverge from each other significantly after about 911. We are not sure when the 'Chronicle of Ireland' first started being kept, but whenever that was the people who produced it decided that they wanted their coverage to extend further back in time and they used previously existing texts as source material for their early sections. It has been demonstrated that for the period before the mid-740s the main source for this material was a chronicle kept at the monastery on the

---

[2] In future footnotes these three chronicles will be identified by the abbreviations *AU*, *AT* and *CS*, respectively.

island of Iona in the southern Hebrides.[3] This 'Iona Chronicle', which survives only within the Irish chronicles, seems to have been a contemporary witness to events in northern Britain and Ireland from at least the middle of the seventh century and perhaps from a little earlier (the question of when the annalistic entries become contemporary is hotly debated). The material surviving from the 'Iona Chronicle' breaks off presumably not because the monks of Iona ceased to keep their own annals but because it was at about this date that a copy of their chronicle was sent to some centre on the mainland of Ireland from which it found its way into the 'Chronicle of Ireland'. With the death of Bede and the despatch of this copy of the 'Iona Chronicle' to Ireland the light was effectively switched off in northern Britain. A relatively terse, and far more parochial, chronicle was maintained somewhere in northern England, probably York, but from Scotland itself we have nothing.

The lights were switched on again in the early twelfth century when a generation of English historians appeared including not simply Henry of Huntingdon but also Symeon of Durham, John of Worcester, William of Malmesbury and Orderic Vitalis. These men all belonged to the first generation born after the Norman conquest and were mostly, perhaps all, of mixed Norman and Anglo-Saxon descent. The England in which they had grown up had been sharply divided between conquerors and conquered, but for them the world was not so black and white and their desire to define their own identity, both Norman and English, was probably a major factor contributing to the flourishing of history writing in their generation. Theirs was also the generation which included the secular magnates who were to transform Scotland, men like Walter son of Alan, founder of the House of Stewart, Robert Brus, Lord of Cleveland and Annandale, and above all David, Earl of Huntingdon and, from 1124, King of Scots. David's earldom coincided with Henry's archdeaconry and William of Malmesbury's history was dedicated to David. Even though these writers were mostly based in the south of England Scotland was definitely on their radar and the transformation of Scotland under David, his followers and his descendants began to create a wealth of documentation, both within Scotland and from interested observers in England, that allows Scottish history to be told in any detail for the first time since the 'Iona Chronicle' was shipped off to Ireland.

---

[3] J. Bannerman, 'Notes on the Scottish entries in the early Irish annals', *Scottish Gaelic Studies* 11:2 (1968), 49–70, K. Hughes, *Early Christian Ireland. Introduction to the Sources* (London, 1972), 115–22.

THE POLITICAL LANDSCAPE

Bede wrote at Jarrow on Tyneside in the northeast of England at a time when the English were divided into many kingdoms. His own kingdom, Bernicia, had as its southern border the River Tees in the east and the Lake District massif in the west. The northern frontier lay on the Forth and the kingdom included at least East Lothian and possibly the whole of Lothian as far west as the River Avon which flows through Linlithgow. To the west the northern frontier of Bernicia appears to have been the Lowther Hills which separate Nithsdale from Clydesdale and within twenty years of Bede's death Kyle, in Ayrshire, had been added to their territory. It is possible that the annexation of Kyle by King Eadberht in 750 represented a reconquest of territory lost following the great defeat of the Bernicians by the Picts in 685 for we know from Bede that there was at some point in the seventh century a district called *Cuneningum* within Bernicia and this may have been Cunninghame in Ayrshire.[4] To the south of Bernicia lay Deira, another English kingdom which was broadly co-extensive with the modern counties of Yorkshire and Lancashire. For about a century Deira and Bernicia had been experimenting with a union of the crowns and, although the last known king of Deira had been slain in battle in 679 the two provinces remained culturally and politically distinct. From 735 the bishop of Deira, based in York, was recognised as metropolitan or archbishop for the whole of Northumbria (the term, possibly coined by Bede, used for the two kingdoms together). Bernicia was by the mid-eighth century divided into three dioceses with bishops based at Lindisfarne, Hexham and Whithorn. The boundary between Lindisfarne and Hexham lay up the River Aln and then along the watershed of the Cheviots but we do not know for certain where the boundary between Hexham and Whithorn lay. When the see of Whithorn was revived in the twelfth century it was roughly co-extensive with the modern counties of Kirkcudbright and Wigtown but we cannot be sure that this reflected the eighth-century arrangement. It should be clear, however, that at least two of these dioceses were largely within Scotland and it cannot be emphasised enough that Bernician history is as much Scottish history as it is English history.

For the most part Bernicia's northern frontier abutted on territories occupied and ruled by the Britons. So far as we know there was only one

---

[4] Bede's form *Cuneningum* might be dative of the population group name *Cuneningas*, 'descendants of *Cunen*'. *Cunen* would appear to be the British name Cynan.

Map I.1 Northern Britain and Ireland c. 750

British kingdom surviving in the north at this period and its kings are usually named for the royal citadel at Dumbarton, then known as *Al Clut* – 'Clyde Rock'. Its territory comprised, it seems, Clydesdale, the Lennox (around the shores of Loch Lomond), Renfrewshire, Peebles and at least parts of Ayrshire and Stirlingshire. It may also have extended into parts of Lothian and Cowal but this is far from clear. Apart from the obituaries of some of its kings and the occasional notice of conflict with its neighbours we know very little of the kingdom of Dumbarton. In language and culture it represented part of a British cultural continuum which extended via the Isle of Man and Wales through Cornwall to Brittany on the Continent. Dumbarton was attacked and forced to accept terms by a joint expedition mounted by the Pictish king Onuist son of Wrguist and the Northumbrian Eadberht son of Eata in 756, and after the death of its then king Dyfnwal son of Teudebur in 760 it is not heard of again for over a century. This may mean that the kingdom had been partitioned between Northumbria and Pictavia, and that Dyfnwal died in retirement or exile, or it may simply reflect the paucity of our sources.

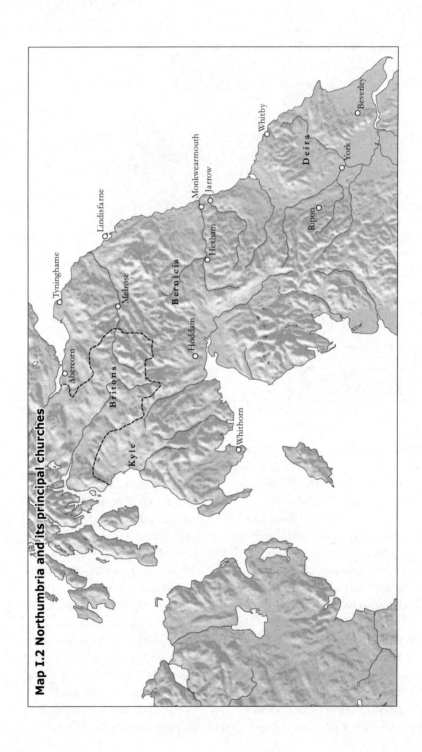

Map I.2 Northumbria and its principal churches

All of the territory of Bernicia had been conquered from British kingdoms, though not all from Dumbarton, and there were probably communities of Britons still living within Bernicia interspersed with the
English communities (early medieval Britain was probably more like
Bosnia or Kosovo in this respect than like modern nation-states). The
size, distribution and degree of autonomy of such communities is open
to debate.

To the west of the Britons of Dumbarton lay the Gaelic-speaking
kingdom of Dál Riata. Dál Riata seems to have originally comprised territory on both sides of the North Channel in Ireland and in Scotland.
Modern historians have tended to think that this arrangement had come
to an end by the middle of the seventh century but recent re-examination
of the evidence for this has thrown this into doubt. The text which John
Bannerman published under the title *Senchus Fer nAlban*, in part a sort of
census document that seems to have been drafted originally in the later
seventh century, may lack an Irish section due to much later editing rather
than because the Irish territories had gone their own way at the time of
composition.[5] Irish Dál Riata comprised the far north of County Antrim
with a royal centre at Dunseverick, not far to the east of the Giant's
Causeway, and an ecclesiastical centre at Armoy on the upper reaches of
the River Bush. In Scotland Dál Riata comprised Kintyre and Arran,
parts of Cowal, Lorn, Morvern and the islands south of Ardnamurchan,
principally Mull, Islay, Jura and Colonsay. It may also have extended at
times to the Small Isles (Rhum, Muck and Eigg), Sleat, Knoydart,
Moidart and Lochaber, though this is far less certain. To a large degree
Dál Riata was dominated by the Cenél nGabráin dynasty based in
Kintyre, and perhaps Arran, although in the decades around 700 their
dominance had been challenged by the Cenél Loairn kindred who may
have had their base at Dunollie near Oban. The leading ecclesiastical
site in Dál Riata as a whole was undoubtedly Iona although it was, in
territorial terms, quite marginal to the kingdom. It is unclear whether
there was an established episcopal see in Dál Riata in the middle
eighth century. Armoy had hosted bishops at an early date, as had
Kingarth in Bute (originally a British church), and some bishops had
certainly died on Iona, but we cannot say for certain whether Dál Riata
had several episcopal sees (like Bernicia), one which was peripatetic,

[5] J. Bannerman, *Studies in the History of Dalriada* (Edinburgh, 1974), 27–156, and
D. N. Dumville, 'Ireland and north Britain in the earlier Middle Ages: contexts for the
Miniugud Senchusa Fher nAlban', in *Rannsachadh na Gàidhlig, 2000* (Aberdeen, 2002),
185–212.

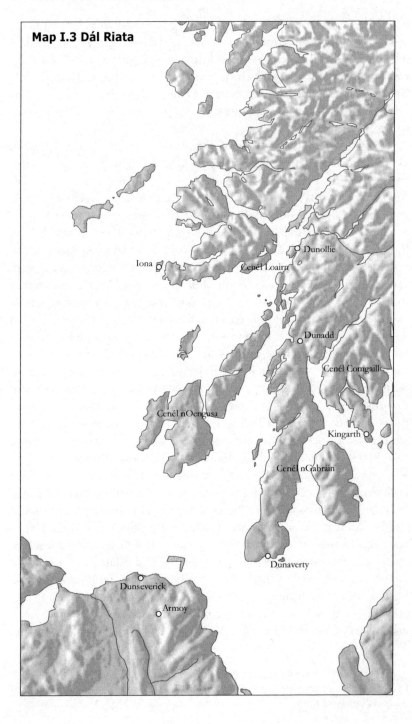

Map I.3 Dál Riata

Dunollie

Iona   Cenél Loairn

Dunadd

Cenél Comgaill

Cenél nOengusa

Kingarth

Cenél nGabráin

Dunaverty

Dunseverick

Armoy

or perhaps a single see which had changed its location over time moving from Armoy to Kingarth to Iona.[6] At precisely the period at which we take up our narrative, however, Dál Riata seems to have been conquered by its eastern neighbour, the Pictish king Onuist son of Wrguist whom the Irish chronicles describe as having 'smitten' Dál Riata in 741.[7] After this we do not hear of a king of Dál Riata for a generation.

King Onuist belonged to the fourth and final one of the peoples of Britain listed by Bede and Henry, the Picts. The term Pict seems to have originated inside the Roman province of Britain in the course of the third century AD. The Romans themselves had not originally distinguished northern and southern inhabitants of Britain from one another, instead using either much more local tribal names or referring to all the inhabitants of Britain as *Britanni* or *Brittones*. As the southerners began to think of themselves as Roman provincials, however, they needed to distinguish between 'tame' and 'wild' Britons and stereotyped their uncivilised kinsmen as 'painted ones' (Latin *Picti*). It has recently been argued by James Fraser that the acceptance of this term as an ethnic label by the Picts themselves, and with this a clear definition of where the boundary lay between Picts and Britons, was relatively recent, probably of late seventh-century date.[8]

By the 740s, however, our sources seem to indicate that a single strong Pictish kingdom existed comprising most of Scotland north of the Forth. At some point, probably in the mid-eleventh century, a list of Pictish kings, giving their names, their fathers' names and the number of years that each had reigned was added to the front of the list of the Scottish kings of Alba. This Pictish king-list names individuals going back into prehistory but from about the middle of the sixth century most of them can be cross-referenced to the obituaries which make up the largest part of the 'Iona Chronicle' as preserved in the later Irish chronicles. In the chronicle record most of these kings are referred to as kings of the Picts but some as are styled '*rex Fortrenn*' – 'king of Fortriu'. Fortriu is a Gaelicised form of the

---

[6] We cannot overlook the possibility that Kingarth had remained in British hands throughout this period.

[7] *AU* 741.10. This point may be as good a point as any to hypothesise a split between the Gaelic territories in Argyll and Dál Riata in Co. Antrim. It is unlikely that any *imperium* exercised by Onuist over the Irish mainland would have gone without comment. For a poem celebrating the taking of *Alba*, perhaps 'Scottish Dál Riata', see T. O. Clancy, ed., *The Triumph Tree. Scotland's Earliest Poetry AD 550–1350* (Edinburgh, 1998), p. 144.

[8] See vol. 1 of this series *From Caledonia to Pictland*.

name of a Pictish province which was in its turn derived from the Roman period tribe known as the Uerturiones. The earliest king to be styled *rex Fortrenn* in his obituary was Bridei son of Beli (†693), and it is likely that in the wake of his victory over the Bernician King Ecgfrith in 685 he extended a hegemony over many of the neighbouring tribes and provinces. He or his successors may then have appropriated the originally pejorative term *Picti* as a more inclusive, less overtly domineering, label for this Verturian hegemony (much as the term *Northumbria* was coined to make the Bernician yoke rest more lightly upon the shoulders of the Deirans).[9] This raises two important questions: what was the original location of the province or kingdom of Fortriu; and what was the nature of Pictish identity beyond its bounds? In the nineteenth century W. F. Skene, the pioneer of early Scottish history, suggested tentatively that Fortriu was located in Strathearn and Menteith and this identification subsequently became less tentative with every retelling.[10] The case for this identification was, however, very slight and recently a far stronger case has been made that Fortriu, in fact, lay on the shores of the Moray Firth at the far end of the Great Glen from Dál Riata.[11]

The Pictish king-list mentioned above has appended to its start a short origin legend of the Picts, *Do Bunad Cruithnech*, written by a Gaelic speaker, probably in the second half of the ninth century, though possibly as late as the mid-eleventh century. This legend names the founder of the kingdom as Cruithne (the Gaelic word for Pict) and then goes on to list his seven sons, who followed him in the kingship. The names of these sons (Cait, Ce, Círig, Fíb, Fidach, Fotla and Fortrenn) have long been recognised to derive from provincial or tribal names – Fortrenn (genitive of Fortriu), Fíb (Fife) and Fotla (Atholl < Ath Fotla) give the game away – and it has been assumed that this legend represents something in the nature of a claim to dominion and thus charts the extent of the Pictish kingdom. Unfortunately, not all these provinces can be located, nor can we be certain that the moment frozen in this list represents a particular time period or was even accurate (it was, after all, written by a Gael rather than a Pict). In fact, the alliterative pattern seems inherently implausible and the list probably represents a quite drastic literary reshaping of

---

[9]   J. E. Fraser, *From Caledonia to Pictland* (Edinburgh, 2007).

[10]   This is often the case with historical hypotheses. Before long they evolve into 'factoids'; fact shaped objects. These are the things which everybody knows to be true but for which there is little or no evidence.

[11]   Alex Woolf, 'Dún Nechtáin, Fortriu and the geography of the Picts', *Scottish Historical Review* 85 (2006), 182–201.

reality.[12] None the less, it probably gives us the right idea if, without getting too fixated upon geographical details, we recognise that Pictavia, as the Verturian hegemony was called in the learned Latin of the day, was made up of a core province or kingdom, Fortriu, surrounded by other, broadly similar, provinces over which it exercised dominion of fluctuating effectiveness depending upon a number of factors. The pertinent factors might include the intelligence and energy of any individual king of Fortriu, external threats or interference, religious schisms and, of course the weather and topography. Bede and the Irish chronicles give us to believe that the fundamental observed division within Pictavia was twofold between the Picts north and south of the Mounth, the eastward extension of the central highlands that slopes down to the North Sea between Stonehaven and Aberdeen. Bede also seems to have believed that the Forth marked the southern frontier of Pictish rule. North and south of the Mounth it is likely that the Pictish territories were divided into provinces roughly corresponding in size to medieval earldoms or modern counties.

One question that cries out for an answer but which seems beyond us at present is the nature of these other provinces. Should we imagine them as each also having their own king, as in southern England or Ireland where regional hegemonies like that of Fortriu also existed? The evidence for Pictish kings other than the kings of Fortriu is limited to one notice in the Irish chronicles of Talorcan son of Drostan, king of Atholl, being drowned by Onuist son of Wrguist in 739. An alternative model to that of the tiered kingship, in which lesser kings recognise the overlordship of greater kings, practised in Ireland and England, can be found in Scandinavia, and particularly in Sweden. Sweden was, in the early and central middle ages, made up of a number of tribal provinces which were governed by annual assemblies, each of which had a fluctuating oligarchy of self-styled chieftains who competed for influence among the free farmers. Only one cluster of these provinces, around the shores of Lake Mälar in the east of the country, -known as Svealand, had an established hereditary monarchy. These kings of the Svear competed with Danish and Norwegian kings for recognition of a very light level of overlordship over the other provinces, such as Jämtland, Värmland, Gotland, East and West Götland, Jarnberaland, etc.[13] Such a model may work well for understanding Pictavia if we imagine

---

[12] D. Broun, 'Alba: Pictish homeland or Irish offshoot?', in P. O'Neill, ed., *Exile and Homecoming: Papers from the Fifth Australian Conference of Celtic Studies* (Sydney, 2005), 234–75, at 250–52.

[13] For Sweden see P. H. Sawyer, *The Making of Sweden* (Alingsås, 1988).

Fortriu, strategically placed at the northern end of the Great Glen and on the 'mediterranean' of the Moray Firth, as possessing a precocious monarchy, while other regions had not evolved much from the, certainly kingless, societies that the Romans had encountered in northern Britain. The absence of information concerning the other Pictish provinces in the Irish chronicles might thus be open to a twofold explanation. First, Fortriu lying in the region of Inverness, Moray and the Black Isle, may have been substantially closer to Iona in terms of communications networks than the other major Pictish provinces. Secondly, if these provinces were, like Swedish provinces, acephalous, then they may have produced few great men whose obituaries or victories might be recorded in the bare record of the annals. Talorcan king of Atholl may simply have been a Verturian dynast who had gained support from the men of Atholl for a putsch against Onuist as Swedish princes often gained support for their kingship of the Svear from the Götar. Recognition that Pictavia was, in fact, a loose hegemony centred on a northern kingdom also allows us to accept what place-name scholars have been aware of for some time: that the linguistic and cultural frontier between the Britons and the Picts was far less clear cut than between any of the other peoples of early Scotland.[14]

The real blank on our map of Scotland for the eighth century lies along the Atlantic littoral from Ardnamurchan to Shetland. It is frequently assumed that the inhabitants of this region were Picts on the grounds that the natives of northern Scotland were all Picts (in the Romano–British sense of the word) and, therefore, they must have been included in the Pictish kingdom. It is far from clear that this was the case. Our texts make almost no references to anywhere in this region, save the occasional passing notice of Orkney, and this paucity of data led Professor Leslie Alcock in his recent book on northern Britain in the period 550 to 850 explicitly to exclude the northwest from his study on the grounds that it was, as yet, still prehistoric and its experiences, and the sources available for studying them, were not directly comparable with those of the rest of the study area.[15] By stopping his study in 850 Alcock was able to afford this luxury but in the century or so after 850 these very parts of Scotland underwent a radical transformation which cannot be ignored in this volume. Between the ninth and the eleventh centuries the whole area

---

[14] Place-names and other linguistic issues will be dealt with in far more detail in Chapter 8.
[15] L. Alcock, *Kings and Warriors, Craftsmen and Priests, in Northern Britain, AD 550–850* (Edinburgh, 2003), at xiv.

from Muckle Flugga to the Dornoch Firth and Ardnamurchan became entirely Scandinavianised in as clear-cut a case of ethnic cleansing as can be found in the entirety of British history. We cannot ignore this so we must endeavour to say something, however little, about the conditions that prevailed prior to the Scandinavian incursions of the Viking Age.

Orkney seems, fairly certainly, to have been within the Verturian hegemony, albeit perhaps somewhat more loosely than some other provinces. The appearance of sculpture and art typical of the Pictish heartlands throughout the islands would seem to indicate that Orkney was in some sense Pictish.[16] The same cannot be said for Shetland, Skye, the Outer Hebrides and the northwest mainland. Although there are examples of Pictish art from all these regions they are few and far between and might reflect sporadic links rather than full engagement with the Verturian hegemony. The extent to which the natives of these regions were culturally, linguistically or religiously linked to the other regions of northern Britain is also open to question. While place-names allow us to recognise that in much of Pictavia dialects of British Celtic were spoken which were not so different from those used in the Kingdom of Dumbarton, the Scandinavian ethnic cleansing eliminated almost all the pre-Norse names from the landscape of the northwest. It is possible British Celtic dialects were spoken here too and it is equally possible that dialects of Celtic belonging to or closely resembling the Gaelic language were spoken in parts of these areas, either as a result of colonisation from Dál Riata or evolving as part of a longer tradition of cultural links down the western seaways towards Ireland. The possibility must also be recognised that the elusive non-Celtic language which some of the early inscribed stones and a handful of the place-names of Pictavia may contain had survived on in these remote areas. We can be fairly certain that, Orkney aside, these regions did not contain kings or highly developed chiefdoms. If they had done so they would not have escaped the notice of the Iona chroniclers.

Scottish Nature in the early middle ages

Dark Age Scotland did not contain vast expanses of virgin wilderness. The country had been heavily settled for at least two thousand years by the time our narrative begins. The landscape was, however, far richer in biodiversity than it is today. Most striking, perhaps, would be the

---

[16] For a textual assertion of this view see D. N. Dumville, 'A note on the Picts in Orkney', *Scottish Gaelic Studies* 12 (1976), 266.

Scottish Nature in the early middle ages (*continued*)

extent to which woodland and scrub covered much of the uplands. While the Cairngorms and some of the other higher peaks would already have had their Alpine appearance, many of Scotland's hills and mountains would have been heavily wooded with the dominant species being Scots pine and oak. These woodlands would have hosted a variety of wildlife including species which still survive today, such as red and roe deer, capercaille, black and red grouse, pine martens and wildcats, along with others now absent from the wild in Britain, such as beavers, wolves, wild cattle, wild pigs, probably lynx and perhaps bear (these last two species had certainly been present in the Roman period and probably survived for some time afterwards). The suggestion from *Orkneyinga saga* that reindeer were present in Scotland in this period is almost certainly an error on the part of its author.

Marine and riverine species would probably have been much the same as today but far more abundant and we might imagine that when the salmon were running Scotland's firths and sea-lochs would have been patrolled by pods of killer whales, much as the coast of British Columbia and Alaska are today. Rats and rabbits had not yet come to these shores and this might suggest that ground and cliff-nesting birds would have been more numerous and widespread than they are today. We should, for example, imagine all the islands of the Forth to have been as rich as May Isle and the Bass Rock alone remain.

THE CHRISTIAN EXPERIENCE

Despite their political, linguistic and ethnic divisions all the people of northern Britain had a great deal in common with one another. For a start they were all by this time Christians. This does not necessarily mean that they were all good Christians or that they did not do things which to us, or to the church hierarchy of their own day, would seem decidedly pagan, but they will all have believed themselves to have been Christians and had the rudiments of a Christian education. Historians have become increasingly interested in the distinction between conversion to Christianity, which simply requires an act of faith, and what they call 'Christianisation', the adoption of a Christian way of life. While conversion can happen fairly rapidly the Christianisation of a community may take many generations and is in effect a negotiated settlement between two belief systems. Belief in the fairies, for example, originated as part of pagan practice but survived in Scotland into recent times. Although the fairies were, in origin, minor gods of the pagan religion it would be wrong to presume that Robert Kirk, the Presbyterian minister of Aberfoyle at the end of the seventeenth century, was a pagan because he believed in them.[17] Missionaries, despite their reputation, have to be relatively tolerant of heterodox practices among their flocks in order to persuade any to convert at all and they themselves may not always have been aware of the extent to which pre-Christian practice informed the rituals of daily life. In the eighth century papal legates visiting Britain complained that the English ate horses 'which no Christian does in the East', yet one can easily see why such a practice was not at the top of the list of 'don'ts' which early missionaries introduced.[18] Equally some pagan practices informed the subsequent development of Christianity – even the cult of saints, the central point of most medieval people's experience of Christianity, seems to have been the pagan Hero cult in origin adapted to Christian subjects.

Although the seventh and early eighth centuries had seen bitter divisions among the churches of Britain and Ireland regarding the method used for calculating the date of Easter, the correct way to wear the tonsure and other practices (though not significantly over doctrinal issues), these had all been resolved by the mid-eighth century. The last of the British Churches accepted the Roman Easter in 768 but the churches in the Kingdom of Dumbarton had probably changed long before this and the Picts and Dál Riata had conformed before 720.[19] This new found unity in the church allowed for much exchange of ideas and skills at the higher ecclesiastical level and this period saw the flowering of Insular Art exemplified by the Lindisfarne Gospels and the Book of Kells but also manifesting itself in sculpture and metalwork, almost all of which was probably produced at church-settlements for ecclesiastical patrons.[20] It would be interesting to know what proportion of the craftsmen and women, sculptors and smiths as well as scribes and illuminators were in holy orders.

What is less clear-cut is the degree of pastoral provision for the laity. Although they were Christian they were probably not expected to attend

[17] L. Henderson and E. J. Cowan, *Scottish Fairy Belief: a History* (East Linton, 2001).
[18] Translated extracts from the legates report of their visit to the English and the Britons can be found D. Whitelock, ed., *English Historical Documents, vol. 1, AD 500–1042* (2nd edn, London, 1979), 836–40.
[19] The Easter controversy and its ramifications for Scotland are dealt with in greater detail in Fraser, *Caledonia to Pictland*.
[20] In the study of this late pre-Viking period the term 'Insular' is increasingly used by scholars to emphasise the common traits, particularly those associated with ecclesiastical culture of Britain and Ireland.

church with the regularity that later medieval custom would require. We do not know if there were local churches in every community but if there were they would certainly have been too small to hold the full congregation. It is equally unclear how common secular clergy were. Though we often think of the terms monk and cleric as synonymous when dealing with the earlier middle ages this was certainly not the case. There were priests and deacons who were not monks and monks who were neither priests nor deacons. In formal theoretical terms monks were supposed to be enclosed and separated from the laity and so could not, and should not, engage in pastoral care. Provision for the laity was in the hands of the bishop who ruled a defined territory, often, perhaps usually, corresponding to a secular kingdom or former kingdom. In this duty he would be assisted by priests and deacons who had not taken monastic vows. In northern Britain, however, where a literate secular class and urban infrastructure were unknown the episcopate had retreated into monasteries (most bishops were or had been monks) and was surprisingly alienated from the laity. Bede, in a letter written to Bishop Ecgbert the year before he died, estimated that even the most pious of the laity probably only partook of the Eucharist three times a year (at Easter, Christmas and Epiphany), in contrast to the regular Sunday attendance and additional celebration of saints' days which he believed was normal in the Mediterranean world. He also complained of secular clergy who were unable to read Latin and, therefore, unable to explain the scriptures and the liturgy to the laity. He argued for the translation of scriptures and liturgy into the vernacular so that the uneducated, lay and clerical alike could have access to them (not through private reading but through hearing others read aloud).[21] It seems likely that those lay-folk who lived close to a major church-settlement, most of which would have been at least partly monastic, would have been reasonably well provided for by the clergy from that establishment, but that the further afield one dwelt the less contact one would have with the formal structures of the Church.

THE AGRICULTURAL EXPERIENCE

What all the people of northern Britain had in common was the fact that they were farmers. Kings and abbots lived on big farms but they were farms none the less. It should also be recalled that farming everywhere in the middle ages was mixed farming. Our own expectations that different

---

[21] Whitelock, *English Historical Documents*, 799–810.

regions and districts are good for different kinds of agriculture, sheep on the Highlands, grain in Angus, cattle in Galloway, etc., reflects the fact that modern farmers work within a global market in which transport infrastructure and refrigeration puts them in competition with farms around the world. Before the infrastructure and technology that supports the global market evolved, and it did so gradually over the centuries, most local communities had to be self-sufficient in the majority of their needs, particularly with regard to perishable foodstuffs. Thus, throughout Scotland in the pre-modern era the vast majority of farms produced meat, dairy products and cereals. This is not to say that the balance between these sectors may not have varied from district to district and that other natural resources such as hunting and fishing and foraging for berries and nuts will not have played a part, but the vast majority of people lived on mixed arable and pastoral farms. So far as we can tell, on the basis of the very limited archaeological evidence available, most of these farming settlements consisted of a single homestead or a cluster of up to four houses together. It is often difficult to assess precisely the size of these settlements because the evidence for dating individual structures on settlement sites is rarely refined enough for us to be certain how many of the buildings were occupied contemporaneously.[22] A site with two broadly contemporary houses upon it may represent two households living together but it may equally represent an old and a new house for the same household, particularly if, as on many modern farms, the older house remained in use while it decayed as a store or overspill activity area after the family had moved into the new one.

Although the surviving textual evidence for social history in Scotland is appallingly slight until the very end of the middle ages we can probably make some basic generalisations on the basis of what we know of the similar early medieval societies of England, Ireland and Wales. In all these societies the vast majority of land, the basis for wealth and sustenance in any rural society, was passed on through inheritance, usually in the male line. In all these societies all recognised sons[23] would share their father's lands equally between them, and in some circumstances daughters also seem to have got a share although they could rarely transmit land to their offspring. If a man were not survived by sons (or in some cases daughters)

[22] This is a particular problem in Scotland where the dearth of actual excavation means that we are particularly dependent upon aerial photography and the surveying of 'humps and bumps' in the landscape for our understanding of such settlements.
[23] While the sons of formal marriages were automatically assured a claim to their paternal inheritance it seems also to have been the case that a father could publicly recognise illegitimate sons thus giving them a share of the inheritance as well.

then the claim to his land would pass to his nearest paternal kinsmen, his brother(s) (if still living) or his nephew(s), and so on. Inheritance of this sort was only clear-cut, however, if the potential heir was descended from someone who had held the land. Thus, if the dead man had acquired the land, perhaps through purchase or as a gift from the king or a tenancy from a great church, then his sons could inherit it but not collaterals. In the absence of living sons such a man's heir was the original donor or his heirs. To inherit land one had to be descended from someone who had previously held or possessed it.[24] In Welsh and Irish law the recommended course of action with potential heiresses was that they should be married to the male collaterals who would inherit if their gender were held to exclude them. This would often have led to unions which were contrary to Canon Law but this does not seem to have actually resulted in any serious problems in our period.[25]

Such an inheritance system affected society in a number of ways. First, communities were largely viripatrilocal. This means that couples lived on the land that had been occupied by the husband's father (Latin *vir* 'husband', *pater* 'father', and *locus* 'place'); thus, most women were probably buried in different communities from those into which they had been born. Most men, on the other hand, would have as their male neighbours members of their own patrilineage. These neighbours would also have a potential claim to their land if they themselves were to die without leaving sons. Such neighbours could be relied upon to provide support against external aggrandisement of their property; from cattle-raiders, squatters or parties with a rival claim to the land (perhaps the descendants of alleged donors or previous tenants of another lineage), but they might not have been the best choice as babysitters or fosterers of one's children!

Regular division of land between co-heirs also carried with it the constant threat that portions would decrease in size until they were no longer able to sustain a functioning family. This was, in fact, the ever present

---

[24] The distinctions between secure and insecure tenancies and between leasehold and freehold which we observe seem not to have been so clear-cut in the early middle ages. It is often said that leaseholds became freeholds after three or four generations had inherited them. This may relate less to legal rights than to the realities of largely non-literate societies in which the local communal memory was the only guide to the history of tenure. Once no-one was alive who could remember the original leasing of the land it was hard to be certain that it had happened at all; the incumbents had lived on, or farmed, that land since time immemorial.

[25] Despite occasional complaints by reform-minded churchmen, enforcement of such regulations only became widespread in Europe in the course of the eleventh and twelfth centuries.

threat which drove much of early medieval society. It explains the endemic warfare and livestock raiding and, to some extent, explains the ubiquity of slavery in societies which practice partible inheritance (sometimes called 'gavelkind' from the Kentish dialect term!). The underlying equation of farming is the ratio of labour requirement to consumption requirement. Probably well over ninety per cent of people's food and drink was produced by the farms on which they lived and worked. It was thus essential that enough labour was available to provide food for all the mouths living on the farm. Unlike a production line, agricultural work is geared to a series of seasonally fluctuating cycles. Cattle, sheep, goats, pigs and crops all require differing intensities of labour in their management through the year. A mixed agricultural regime thus helps farmers either overstaffing their farms or becoming too reliant on itinerant seasonal labour. Since these farming settlements were also dependent on domestic production for most of their material culture needs (furniture, tools, clothing, etc.), slack periods in the agricultural cycle could be filled by craft production. The core of any household would have been a nuclear family not unlike our own ideal: a primary couple with their children. Early medieval Scotland was a high fertility, high mortality society, like much of the developing world today. There would have been lots of babies but fewer teenagers. Girls will have been considered ready for marriage from about the age of thirteen or fourteen and boys legally competent from about the same age. The problem with this kind of demographic profile is that there will always be more mouths to feed than hands to work, even when one considers that even quite young children would probably be expected to contribute to the economy of the farm.[26]

Unlike children, who tend to leave home at precisely the point at which they might have become truly useful, slaves will have, for the most part, come into households as older children or young adults. Most slaves probably originated as the spoils of war but they were probably sold on to their 'end-users'. Slavery is one of the few trades for which there is no natural gradient, no imbalance of natural resources effecting supply and demand. Since both owner and slave are human beings the slave trade can flourish between any two areas both occupied by people. In reality most successful slave trades require intermediate parties as well, for slaves will have found it harder to work for their captors, those who actually slew

---

[26] An old man on South Uist once told me that barbed wire was responsible for the vandalising of bus shelters. When I asked for clarification he remarked that before the widespread use of barbed wire the children were too busy making sure the cattle didn't wander into the crops to get into mischief.

their kin and stole or destroyed their property, than for a third party, who provided a stable home, sustenance and companionship that must have come as a great relief after the traumas of capture and transportation. Slavery in the early medieval world, particularly in entirely rural societies such as those found in Britain, Ireland and Scandinavia, did not resemble the institution with which we are familiar from the ante-bellum American south or Hollywood's interpretation of the Ancient Mediterranean. For a start, slave ownership penetrated a long way down the social scale and the slaves and masters were probably racially indistinguishable. Most rural households probably included some slaves.[27] Since these households mostly dwelt in one- or two-room dwellings the slaves would have lived side by side with the family, shared their experiences and eaten from the same pot (though they would probably have been last in the queue for second helpings). The best literary accounts that we have of such slavery come from Icelandic sagas and these represent slaves and their owners working alongside one another in a generally companionable way.[28] Since most slaves were probably very young when they were taken into captivity, and since they were alienated from their natal community, culture and in many cases language, then, to some extent, they grew into their new homes much as brides or children did. The concept of a freedman or woman was common and these individuals were mostly men and women who, being lucky enough to survive into middle age, had established real emotional and social bonds with their owners which were recognised through manumission. The advantage of slaves within a system of partible inheritance was that they provided labour without being co-heirs. Wealthy farmers might endow a freedman or woman with a small holding of their own on the edge of his farm, the rights over the farm if they died heirless remaining with him or his heirs.[29] Freedmen and women possessed partial legal status (not unlike the adult sons of living fathers) but their own offspring, if all went well, might acquire full membership of the group.[30] Because such freedmen were entirely dependent upon their

[27] The west Norwegian *Gulatingslog*, dating from the twelfth century, estimates the average peasant's property as comprising eight cows, two horses and three slaves, and broadly comparable figures would probably apply to many Scottish communities in our period.

[28] Ruth Mazo Karras, *Slavery and Society in Medieval Scandinavia* (New Haven, CT, 1988).

[29] Place-names like Leysington and Lazenby originally designated farms held by a *leysing* or freedman.

[30] As with the security of tenancy discussed above freedmen became freemen over several generations, at whatever point their servile origins became an uncertain memory.

former masters for their livelihood and tenancy they could be relied upon as clients much as poorer kinsmen might be. It may be that, as such formerly servile lineages bedded down into a community, the master who had granted their ancestor freedom may himself have come to be thought of as an ancestor.

To some extent slave labour provided ballast to the nuclear families at the heart of each farming household. If more land were acquired through inheritance, purchase or gift, more slaves could be bought in. If times were hard, through famine, livestock epidemic or a blight on the crop, slaves could be sold on or given away. The same might occur if a farm were subdivided between co-heirs and two or more nuclear families had to support themselves upon the same amount of land. In some cases, perhaps where brothers got on particularly well, shared inheritance probably resulted in two or three households living side by side and working the farm together, and this may be the explanation of the small clusters of dwellings we sometimes see in the archaeological record. Freedmen and other tenants may also have been the slack that could have been taken in. In times of hardship, they might be forced to give up all or some of the smallholding or to re-integrate back into a communal farming operation. Poorer neighbours upon whom the co-heirs had no hereditary claim may also have found themselves under pressure, for co-heirs were, by their very nature, several and in a world in which masculine physical strength counted for much in both labour and coercion a band of brothers may have brooked little resistance. The seventeenth-century Irish scholar Dubhaltach Mac Firbhisigh explained this aspect of traditional Gaelic society thus:

> It is customary for great lords that, when their families and
> kindreds multiply, their clients and their followers are oppressed,
> injured and wasted.[31]

It is very likely that 'Mac Firbhisigh's Law' applied across the whole Britain and Ireland in the earlier middle ages as a natural consequence of the system of partible inheritance. Those who were driven off their land in this fashion would be compelled to negotiate less favourable tenancies elsewhere, to enter into service, little better than slavery, with kinsman or neighbours, or to seek their fortune through commendation to some great lord.

---

[31] Cited and discussed in T. M. Charles-Edwards, *Early Irish and Welsh Kinship* (Oxford, 1993), at p. 121.

LORDS AND MEN

For great lords did exist, though they were neither so great nor so lordly as they would be in later ages. The kinds of lordship that we know most about are ecclesiastical lordship and royal lordship. The evidence for the nature of secular lordship below the level of king is very poor for any part of Britain and only really unambiguous for Ireland where the extensive legal material surviving from around AD 700 is unrivalled. Hints from various parts of Britain suggest, once again, that in broad terms the situation was similar. At the bottom end of the scale the relatively poor farmer who leased a corner of his land to a freedman is, in some sense, a lord. The Irish lawyers countered this kind of reasoning by claiming that to be legally recognised as a lord a man must have five landholders recognising his superiority. Clearly this is a legalistic rule of thumb but it gives one a sense of the scale of lordship and superiority. The same Irish legal texts tell us that it is preferable that a man's lord should be his kinsman. Lords in this period were not merely, nor even usually landlords (that is to say people with a superior claim to the land occupied by their men) but were often simply richer and better connected neighbours. The function of the lord was to act as an advocate and a provider of welfare to his men in time of need, much like an insurance company, but as with modern insurance companies the regular dues, payable in this case either in kind or labour, must often have seemed to outweigh the perceptible benefits. When it came to lordship, it would have been the luck of the draw whether one was blessed with a friend and patron or cursed with an oppressive tyrant. There is a stark contrast here, however, with the stereotypical lordship that we associate with later medieval and early modern society (although in Scotland that kind of lordship was never as well developed as it was in some other parts of Europe), in which the whole countryside is presented as occupied by peasants barely able to hold body and soul together labouring for oppressive landlords with whom they have nothing in common. The ubiquity of slaves and the fundamental divide in society being between free and unfree meant that all relations established between householders were at their core 'honourable', and if local lords were lords of only five or six households then it is likely that they were not too far removed, economically or culturally, from their men. Once again the practice of partible inheritance would probably militate against a growing gap between the rich and the poor. A lord may have been the richest man in the locale but that status would not necessarily have been inherited by his sons if they had to divide the inheritance. This may be particularly the case for rich men who were perhaps more likely to have had multiple sexual partners and whose children, with better access to resources, may have had a greater chance of reaching adulthood.[32]

Services paid to lords were of two broad kinds, which we may term 'base' and 'honourable'. Honourable services were performed in the lord's company, riding with him to court or war, attending his house when he entertained his lord, entertaining the lord in one's own house and so forth. Base services were essentially dirty jobs, working alongside the lord's slaves rather than the lord himself; hedge cutting, ditch digging and reaping, for example. In reality there may well have been many grey areas. Many of the lesser lords may have worked in the fields themselves at the busiest times of the year. The vision we get of early medieval society from the Irish and Welsh legal codes are probably far too rigidly codified. They present a model, and like all models they misrepresent the complexity of reality. Before he took his monastic vows at Melrose, St Cuthbert (†687) watched over sheep in Lauderdale, but he also rode on horseback and served in the army.[33] Was his condition base or honourable? In small-scale societies of this sort, so long as he was a householder, a man's personality and talents may have counted for as much as his acreage or the number of head of cattle or sheep he owned.

KINGS AND KINGSHIP

At the apex of all lordship stood the king. He toured the kingdom staying sometimes with his own clients, who might be local lords or great church-settlements, and sometimes on his own estates. Royal estates were in essence simply large farms not so different in many ways from those found elsewhere in the countryside. Beyond scale the main difference would probably be that most royal farms would have had a resident steward who would, for most of the year, live as if he were the householder. Indeed, he may well have maintained his own house and family within the villa while serving in a janitorial capacity with regard to a royal hall where the king and his household would stay while visiting. Royal villas of this sort would probably have been handsomely provided with storage facilities, for kings may have had the right to demand universal

[32] For lordship and clientage see Fergus Kelly, *A Guide to Early Irish Law* (Dublin, 1988), 26–35.
[33] *Anonymous Life of St Cuthbert* I.v, vi and vii, in B. Colgrave (ed. & tr.), *Two Lives of Saint Cuthbert* (Cambridge, 1940 and 1985).

Food renders

No detailed records of food renders from early Scotland survive but an idea of the character and extent of such renders can be gauged from a list surviving in a southern English legal tract from around 690, *Ine's Law Code*. Here we are told what the West Saxon king expected as tribute from ten hides of land (about 1,200 acres or 486 hectares):

> 10 vats of honey
> 300 loaves
> 12 ambers of Welsh ale (by the thirteenth century an amber was reckoned at 4 bushels, each of 8 gallons, this would make this 384 gallons of beer!)
> 30 ambers of clear ale (960 gallons?)
> 2 full grown cows *or* 10 wethers (castrated sheep)
> 10 geese
> 20 hens
> 10 cheeses
> a full amber of butter (32 gallons?)
> 5 salmon
> 20 pounds of fodder
> 100 eels

Obviously such renders would vary from district to district depending upon the local produce but it gives a fair sense of the priorities of lordship. If the volume of the amber was the same then as later, then there were 2,688 pints of beer to every side of beef! It should be emphasised that the proportions here represent the demands of lordship and not necessarily the productive capacity of the land.

renders from the whole kingdom as well as from those neighbouring farmers who looked to the king, through his steward, as their local lord. This question of the development of universal renders is extremely vexed, however, particularly with regard to Scotland.

Because of the dearth of historical texts from early medieval Scotland, historians have tended to reconstruct the early medieval social landscape on the basis of twelfth- and thirteenth-century accounts. During this period, widely termed the 'Anglo-Norman era', Scottish society, and particularly the structures of lordship and government, was radically transformed, largely through the introduction of institutions which had evolved in southern England and northern France.[34] The plethora of documentation that chart these transformations also shows us something of the structures that were in place before the transformation began, and which, in some parts of the kingdom, co-existed with the new practices for much of the rest of the middle ages. The paradigm that has governed our understanding of the 'Anglo-Norman era' is one of revolution in which what was overturned and replaced was an *ancien régime* which had its roots in a timeless Celtic past. Central to the *ancien régime*, it is argued, were the universal royal dues of *cáin* and *coinnmed* (Scots 'kane' and 'conveth'), which roughly translate as 'right' and 'hospitality' and are generally understood to have originally referred to food renders (largely cheese by the later middle ages), respectively those delivered up to a point of collection and those consumed by the king and his household in person on a visit. It remains open to question, however, whether these dues were, first, universally imposed across whole kingdoms and, secondly (if they were), whether this would have indeed been an ancient arrangement. Recent research done on the Irish material, where the same dues seem to have been in place in much of the country by the middle of the twelfth century, suggests that this state of affairs reflects a very recent development.[35] In an earlier era the distinction between *cáin* and *coinnmed*, as renders (*cáin* has a very wide semantic range), seems to have reflected the varied nature of an over-king's rights. *Coinnmed*, it seems, was the due that he would receive as he toured around his own kingdom while *cáin* was the tribute, usually cattle on the hoof, delivered to him across the frontier by those kings who recognised his overlordship (and it was this kind of *cáin* that the King of Scots received from Galloway in the twelfth century).[36] Only as over-kingship gradually transformed itself into a unitary monarchy (the argument goes), with local kings being eliminated or redesignated with less overtly royal titles, did *cáin* come to be regarded as a universal due within the kingdom, if indeed it ever did. *Cáin*, in the sense of cattle-tribute, in the earlier period, was probably paid sporadically and grudgingly, and viewed by those who paid it as a form of extortion, while *coinnmed* was probably recognised as a price worth paying for the king's company and his ear.

[34] See G. W. S. Barrow, *The Anglo-Norman Era in Scottish History* (Oxford, 1988). This period and these transformations are discussed in detail by Richard Oram in vol. 3 of the *New Edinburgh History*.

[35] T. M. Charles-Edwards, 'Submission to Irish Kings, 700–1212: Continuity and change', paper presented to the Conference of Irish Medievalists, June 2005.

[36] Robin Chapman Stacey, *The Road to Judgment: From Custom to Court in Medieval Ireland and Wales* (Philadelphia, 1994), 82–111.

It is also possible, indeed perhaps probable, that *cáin* and *coinnmed* were not solely royal dues but simply reflected the dues of lordship. Welsh law codes, surviving in thirteenth-century recensions, but largely reflecting somewhat earlier conditions, also divide tribute into two kinds which, like *cáin* and *coinnmed*, seem to be those consumed in the king's company and those delivered to a collection point. In these texts, however, the correlation between these renders and the according of honourable or base status is made explicit. The food render, *gwestfa*, on all land was the same and thus a given portion of land was capable of sustaining the king for one night. If a single household had the resources to pay this *gwestfa* in total then the householder was accorded honourable status, if, however, multiple households (the heads of which were usually members of a single patrilineage) had to combine to pay the *gwestfa* and were thus, actually or notionally, not able to entertain the king at their table, then they were accorded base status. What is perhaps most important for us here is that the apparent development which led to the conditions observed by historians of twelfth- and thirteenth-century Scotland were, if they happened at all, products of the Viking Age and almost certainly not in place before hand. Instead, we might ask whether, for example, the kings of the Picts in the eighth century regularly itinerated throughout Pictavia or whether they enjoyed hospitality only within Fortriu, supplementing their revenue with occasional cattle tribute from other provinces, much of which would doubtless have been redistributed to their Verturian clients and kinsmen?[37]

In many ways the fundamental question to be asked about early kingship is how it differed from other kinds of lordship. Was it simply a matter of scale? Probably not. Kingship, in the early medieval period at least, seems to be fundamentally linked to ethnicity. Kings were, by and large, kings of a people.[38] They presided at national assemblies and provided the final court of appeal. In the sixth and seventh centuries kings had negotiated the conversion to Christianity of their peoples *en masse* and they remained the main point of interaction between secular power and the Church hierarchy into the eighth century. Kings were also, first and foremost, leaders in war.

---

[37] D. Broun, 'The property-records in the Book of Deer as a source for early Scottish society', in K. Forsyth ed. *That Splendid Little Book: Studies in the Book of Deer* (Dublin, forthcoming). I am grateful to Dr Broun for letting me see this paper ahead of publication.

[38] Although such kingships were ethnically defined it was, of course, possible for the king*dom*, the jurisdiction of the king, to include people of other ethnic backgrounds but their consent was not necessary to legitimise the kingship.

The qualification for kingship was twofold. First, kings seem to have been drawn from a recognised royal dynasty and any aspirant to the kingship had at least to claim descent from the established apical figure (the ancestor standing at the apex of the dynasty). Among the English, Gaels and Britons royal dynasties were counted in the male line only; they were synonymous with patrilineages. Conquest or usurpation by neighbouring dynasties was sometimes legitimised by marriage to a female of the ousted dynasty but descent through the female line was not generally enough to legitimise a claim to the kingship. Thus, the Northumbrian King Alhred (765–74) and his son Osred (788–90) claimed the kingship through their patrilineal descent from a sixth-century royal ancestor even though Alhred was the son-in-law and Osred the grandson of the recently deceased King Oswulf (758–9). Most kings were the sons of previous kings, though not necessarily their immediate predecessor, but occasionally dynastic accidents or mortality made this difficult. For example, all the kings of the Bernician dynasty had claimed descent from Æðelfrith (†617) but his direct line seems to have died out with the murder of Osred son of Aldfrith in 716. Subsequent kings claimed not to be descended from Æðelfrith but from his supposed grandfather Ida who, with twelve sons (six legitimate and six bastards) seems more likely to have originated as an ancestor figure for the whole *gens* of the Bernicians.[39] Extending the notion of legitimacy to all the descendants of Ida, however, opened up competition for the kingship to a very wide pool indeed, and for much of the eighth and ninth centuries Northumbrian kings found themselves facing constant challenges from very distantly related rivals. Of course, the expansion of the definition of royal descent to include the whole *gens* was only possible in the context of the creation of a unified Northumbrian kingdom. When the Bernicians stood alone in the years around 600 they needed to distinguish quality among themselves. In their new empire, in the eighth century, they cohabited with the probably far more numerous Deirans and Britons and simply to be Bernician was enough to mark one out.[40]

[39] If the number of patrilineal descendants of Ida were imagined to have doubled in each generation then they might have numbered over 6,000 by the mid-eighth century. If they had trebled in each generation then they would have numbered in excess of 157,000. A figure somewhere between these two is entirely credible for heads of household among the Bernicians in the mid-eighth century. The distinction between the legitimate and illegitimate sons may have reflected a notional division of the *gens* into six base and six noble kindreds.

[40] These observations on Bernician dynastic ideology have benefited greatly from discussions over the years with James Fraser, who deals with these matters in greater depth in vol. I of the *New Edinburgh History, From Caledonia to Pictland*.

Thanks to Bede we can chart the history of the Bernician dynasty in some detail and thanks to the chroniclers on Iona we can observe the kings of Dál Riata and their kinsmen at a similar level of resolution. Up until 695 the kingship of Dál Riata had been dominated by the dynasty descended from Domangart Réti (retired 507) based in Kintyre and Cowal, but, after the death of Domnall Donn in that year, the Cenél Loairn kindred, whose name is preserved in Lorne, challenged their supremacy and, following a period of confused internecine strife, seem to have secured the kingship by 700. It was probably in an attempt to legitimise this putsch that the apical figure of the kindred, Loarn, was first described as the brother of Domangart's father Fergus. Interestingly the Pictish king Onuist's attack on and conquest of Dál Riata in the 730s and 740s coincided with this period of Cenél Loairn supremacy and it may be that to a king of Fortriu a ruler based on the Firth of Lorne presented a clear and present danger in a way that kings in Kintyre never did.[41]

For the kings of Dumbarton we have only their obituaries in the Irish and Welsh chronicles and a single unilineal pedigree for a king named Rhun son of Arthgal who lived in the late ninth century. Many, but not all, of the kings mentioned in the annals appear in Rhun's pedigree, which suggests that their dynastic politics worked in a similar way to that of the Gaels and the English. The kings not appearing in the pedigree were for the most part probably collaterals; uncles, brothers and nephews of Rhun's ancestors. For the Picts we are not so lucky. Onuist son of Wrguist (729–61) was succeeded by his brother Bridei (761–3) and by the end of the century a dynasty descending from one Wrguist (not Onuist's father) was in place and would rule for fifty years, but in between various kings appear who cannot be linked to any known dynasty. Prior to Onuist's time Pictish kings had often been brothers of previous Pictish kings but were rarely if ever the sons of previous kings. Why this happened is not clear, although this factor has undoubtedly contributed to the widely held view that some form of matrilineal succession was in place among the Picts. The evidence for this is not as good as it might be. The only contemporary witness to note Pictish succession practice, Bede, says that royal succession ran through the female line only 'whenever the case was in doubt'.[42]

---

[41] Dunollie, the Cenél Loairn royal centre, is almost equidistant between Inverness and the South End of Kintyre.

[42] *HE*, I.i. *Ut ubi res ueniret in dubium*. See A. Woolf, 'Pictish matriliny reconsidered', *Innes Review* 49 (1998), 147–67, and A, Ross, 'Pictish matriliny?', *Northern Studies* 34 (1999), 11–22.

Although kingship was hereditary, succession was not, like landhold-ing, governed by partible inheritance. Kingship was very occasionally divided or shared but this was very much the exception rather than the rule and when brothers ruled they tended to do so serially, as with the sons of Der-Ilei in Fortriu who ruled from 697 to 706 and 706 to 729, respectively. Men did not become kings solely by virtue of their descent, although membership of a recognised royal dynasty was a prerequisite. The other factor was what the Gaels called *febas*, which might be trans-lated 'worth'. This intangible quality was what led one royal prince rather than another to be elected to the kingship. In many cases it must have been clear during the closing months or years of the preceding reign who was the prince most likely to succeed, but not always. Kings may have ideally desired that their sons should succeed them but, to their followers, a mature and seasoned adult who had a proven record on the battlefield and could be trusted to make judicious decisions in court was infinitely preferable to a youth still wet behind the ears. So far as we know there was only one attempt at minority rule in our area during the eighth century and this was the peculiar case of Osred son of Aldfrith, the last survivor of the original Bernician dynasty, who became king at the age of eight in 705. His succession was challenged and his reign unhappy and relatively brief.

The contrast between the rules governing royal succession and the practice of partible inheritance of land raises the interesting and under-researched topic of royal estates. Were the farms that the kings visited as they itinerated around their kingdoms attached in some way to the office of kingship or were they simply inherited family estates? We know that there were some royal sites that were intimately associated with kingship – Bamburgh in Bernicia, Dumbarton among the Britons, Dunadd in Dál Riata and probably others elsewhere – but these were largely sites of ceremonial and ritual importance and strongholds into which kings could retreat in times of war. Thus, the *Annals of Ulster* record Onuist's 736 attack on Dál Riata:

> Onuist son of Wrguist, king of the Picts, wasted the territories of Dál Riata and seized Dunadd and burned Creic and bound in chains the two sons of Selbach, i.e. Donngal and Feredach.[43]

These sites were mostly fortified rocky outcrops impressive to look at, as Dumbarton Rock still is, but not very spacious and not located, generally speaking, amidst particularly fertile lands. Such citadels may have been

[43] *AU* 736.1

used for inaugurating kings, as the rock-cut footprint at Dunadd suggests, but they are usually mentioned only as places besieged or
attacked.[44] It is unlikely that kings spent much time in these fundamentally uncomfortable places. Low lying halls in rich farmland may have
been the most likely place to find them. Unfortunately such places are
much harder for archaeologists to locate. In Dál Riata and parts of
Pictavia and the kingdom of Dumbarton, many of the richer farms,
including royal villas, may have had their main buildings located on *cran-
nóga* (sg. *crannog*) or artificial islands. Scotland is filled with such artificial
islands but as a type of site they originate back in the Neolithic, several
thousand years before our period, and it is only by excavation that individual sites can be assigned to a specific era. For our period the best excavated examples are probably Loch Glashan, near Dunadd in Dál Riata,
and Buiston, in Ayrshire, which was probably British.

Some historians and archaeologists interpret the fragmentary evidence
for royal itineration and villas as indications of an entrenched govern-
mental system. This view regards royal villas as part of a permanent
demesne which was evenly distributed throughout the core areas of the
kingdom. Each royal villa, in this model, sat in the middle of its *regio*, or
district, like a spider in the centre of its web, extracting tribute and labour
services from the surrounding farms. This model is drawn from the
thirteenth-century law codes which describe Welsh kingdoms as being
divided into *cantrefi*, ancient territories usually clearly defined by topography and whose population possessed a long established sense of identity. Each *cantref* was further divided into two or more *cymydau* and it is
the lawyers' description of royal exploitation of each such *cwmwd* (anglicised as 'commote') which lies behind our model. At the heart of each
cwmwd lay a *maerdref* – 'steward farm' – which provided the venue for
royal itineration and the consumption of food renders. That the concept
of the *maerdref* itself, our royal villa, is old is not open to dispute. What
is, however, is the idea that each royal villa lay at the centre of a standard
local government unit analogous to the *cwmwd*.

The existence throughout Britain of deeply entrenched local population groups, whose territories were constrained in part by topography and
in part by traveling time, is not inherently unlikely, though some landscapes may have lent themselves to this kind of embedded geographical
determinism more easily than others; in Scotland we can think of islands,
glens and peninsulas as obvious examples of such landscapes. What is
open to question is whether there was a royal villa at the centre of each

---

[44] A. Lane and E. Campbell, *Dunadd, an Early Dalriadic Capital* (Oxford, 2000).

such area. An alternative view might suggest that a king's own personal patrimony was likely to be relatively discretely located in whichever district his patrilineage hailed from, and that, beyond this, he, or perhaps his predecessors, might accrue additional estates through a piecemeal process of conquest, confiscation, as marriage portions or through purchase. In any given traditional district a king might consolidate his lands and administer them through a single villa but in some districts he may possess no estates or too few to warrant regular visitation. Since kings were constantly under pressure from their followers and churches to redistribute lands, an immutable patchwork of evenly distributed villas might have been difficult to maintain. Within regional hegemonies, such as Northumbria and Pictavia, the reliance of kings upon their own ethnic following, Bernicians and Wærteras[45] in these cases, for their core support may have meant, paradoxically that it was in the least committed parts of their hegemony that they were able to accrue the greatest access to land through conquest and confiscation. In Sweden this phenomenon led, by the thirteenth and fourteenth centuries, to the kings having very few lands in Svealand proper and to be largely reliant upon estates built up in the less committed provinces occupied by the Götar to the south. Some of these lands would be redistributed to core supporters, a process which, while it might offend some locally at first, and even provoke resistance to royal authority, would cumulatively, in the long run, bind the hegemony into something approaching a unified kingdom.[46]

Kings, then, came to spend much of their time at the margins of their kingdoms, enjoying acquired landed wealth and making the most of the less equitable relations which they enjoyed with the locals.[47] The frontier also put them close to potential enemy territory, raids from which they might be required to repel, and into which they themselves might raid.

Leadership in warfare was one of the main functions of the king and certainly the main quality determining the success of any individual

---

[45] We do not know the name that the inhabitants of Fortriu gave to themselves but the Old English borrowing of it, *Wærteras*, does survive. Since we habitually use the Gaelic name for the kingdom, Fortriu, then no impediment prevents us from using Wærteras.

[46] One of the recurring themes of the Norwegian 'Kings' sagas', found in the compendia *Morkinskinna*, *Fagrskinna* and *Heimskringla*, is the history of the relations between the kings and the province of Trondheim which from an initially marginal and hostile position within the kingdom is alternately wooed and bullied into becoming a core region.

[47] In southern and eastern England it is noticeable that the royally sponsored trading settlements which archaeologists have labelled *emporia* were mostly located on acquired land rather than in core territories.

aspiring to the kingship. Many kings were slain in battle, either by domestic rivals or by foreign enemies. Raiding for moveable wealth, largely, but not exclusively, cattle, horses and slaves, if successful gave the ruler the ability to exercise patronage through the redistribution of plunder. Such redistribution could be used to reward faithful service or to woo the less committed.[48] Slaves might also be sold overseas for profit. Neighbouring kingdoms too weak to resist yet too strong to conquer, might be persuaded to buy off attacks with negotiated tribute. The king's military following was made up of his household retainers, the *comitatus*. One reason why kings needed to itinerate was that their *comitatus* was too large to be supported from a single estate. Thus, they circulated around the kingdom, consuming and then moving on. The *comitatus*, for the most part, will have been made up of young fit men in their teens or twenties who performed military and other services for the king, both in his presence and on detachment. These men might be drawn from the kingdom or from abroad, although it is perhaps less likely that the major ethnolinguistic boundaries would often be crossed by such *comites* for reasons of both practicality and prejudice.[49] While many such retainers may have been of royal blood the opportunity to become a king's man was also open to the relatively humble so long as they could secure an introduction (often through a friend of a friend or through their father's lord), and impress on first being admitted to the court. Thus, from the king's perspective the institution of the *comitatus* provided not merely a military guard and expeditionary force but also an opportunity to keep an eye on potentially over-ambitious young kinsmen and to talent spot 'new men' who might rise to greatness purely through royal patronage.

Royal service, in its turn, offered the *comites* not only a few years of adventure and over-indulgence before settling down to the endless agricultural cycle, but also the opportunity to accrue moveable wealth that could be used to pay a bride price or to win friends and influence people back home. Also important was the opportunity that successful royal service provided for access to landed wealth. In a world where a man's status and survival depended entirely upon his access to land, the sons of living fathers could be consigned to a living limbo, unable to marry or

[48] See T. Reuter, 'Plunder and tribute in the Carolingian empire', *Transactions of the Royal Historical Society*, 5th series 35 (1985), 75–94.

[49] While the Britons, English and Gaels were clearly ethnolinguistically discrete groups, the position of the Picts is less clear. Although they seem to have enjoyed particularly close relations with the Gaels it is hard for modern scholars to distinguish the British spoken in Pictavia from that spoken south of the Forth. These aspects of Pictish identity will be discussed in greater depth in a subsequent chapter.

establish their own independent identity until their share of the family farm came to them. Landed estates, held either in free tenancy or in stewardship, were in the gift of the king and receipt of such estates at the end of his term of service allowed the retainer to marry and begin to establish himself even if his father yet lived. These estates were also lands that he would not need to share with any co-heirs. Presumably if the retainer was settled far from home on a free tenancy he might even sell his share of the family lands to his co-heirs in return for investment capital in stock, seed or slaves. One southern English law code from the reign of King Ine of Wessex (688–726) describes the situation of a former retainer leaving an estate he has been holding in stewardship, presumably because he has decided to return to his patrimony. We are told that he may take his grieve, his smith and his children's nurse with him, the implication being that the other slaves stay with the land, and that he must make sure that three-fifths of his arable land is sown so that the new tenant will be assured of a harvest (the other two-fifths were presumably being left fallow).[50] For the king such landed retainers provided a reserve force of experienced men who could be called upon for military expeditions and also agents scattered across the kingdom of whose loyalty he could be fairly certain.

The *comitatus* also helped to bind the kingdom together by providing a milieu in which up and coming young men from across the kingdom and beyond could cement friendships and relationships which would endure through their subsequent lives. Thus, being a king's man tied the individual not just into a relationship with the king but also with his contemporaries at court, settled across the kingdom, creating a powerful counterbalance to the demands and draws of the viripatrilocal society into which he had been born. Such external links both formally and informally created the structures and conditions which allowed king's men to build up a position of influence in the locale which exceeded anything that they might have achieved on the basis of their patrilineal heritage alone. Such men were taking the first steps towards the creation of an aristocracy but these were early days and this was still an aristocracy of service. Their own heirs may have been in a position to start life with some advantages but they were not immune from the burdens of partible inheritance and the viripatrilocal claims upon them. Within such a society a key tension in the localities lay between king's men and those who had become leaders of their kindreds purely through local connections and activities. The resolution of our sources, however, does not allow us to see

[50] Whitelock, *English Historical Documents*, p. 406.

which group was more successful in providing the local leaders such as Northumbrian *ealdormen* and Gaelic heads of *cenéla*. The most success-ful local leaders must, one would imagine, have been those who managed to play both hands simultaneously.

THE CHURCH IN THE WORLD

One group of recipients of royal largesse was immune from the burdens of partible inheritance. These were the church-settlements that grew up around the monastic and other ecclesiastical foundations. Lands granted to God and His saints were lands granted to the immortals and thus did not undergo partition in every generation. Kings and other laymen granted lands to churches for a variety of reasons both spiritual and worldly. Monks and nuns may well have brought their share of their pat-rimony with them when they took their vows. Over time even quite modest endowments could accumulate and in some areas kings seem to have given some churches the right to whatever universal dues or services were owed them barring, in most cases, the *trinodas necessitas* – 'the three necessities' – military service, bridge building and the maintenance of roads. The exemption of Church property from partible division in every generation rapidly turned the church-settlements into the richest estate centres to be found anywhere. Not only did they possess more land than any of the laity but their security of tenure meant that long-term strate-gies of exploitation could be developed.

The essential role of these churches was twofold: to provide a monas-tic retreat for cœnebitic clergy who spent their days contemplating the Godhead and singing their way through the Psalter; and to provide a base from which more effective pastoral care and missionary work could be carried out and supported. Although individual monks had taken a vow of poverty and may, in many cases, have lived truly ascetic lives, the church-settlements as institutions found it necessary to engage in quite complex economic activities. While an eremitic lifestyle may have required little more agricultural labour than the monks themselves were able to provide there were other needs to be catered for. On the most basic level divine office required regular access to wine, which had to be imported from the Continent, and the ordination of clergy (and, increasingly, kings) required *chrism* made from olive oil. To acquire these essentials for ecclesiastical routine, church-settlements had to channel the surplus production from their lands into consumer durables which could be directed towards an export market. Cloth was an obvious product and its production in much larger measures than the subsistence needs of rural society must have radically altered the agricultural cycle of those farms engaged in the husbandry of sheep which produced the wool for it. In some areas local mineral resources, from metals and coal to quern stones, may have provided the basis for market-oriented production and in others timber or salmon runs may have contributed. Effective missionary work and pastoral care also required extensive book production and this also led to specialised animal husbandry directed towards the production of parchment and vellum. Book production might also have entailed the import of dyes and paints for illumination and illustration. The desire to emulate Mediterranean church architecture also led to some church-settlements importing window glass and to the development of craft specialisations on site. The larger church-settlements were inhabited, *inter alia*, by masons, sculptors and smiths and wrights of all kinds. Some of these craftsmen may have been in holy orders, secular or monastic, while others may have been laymen, free or unfree. It is from this point, in the early- to mid-eighth century, that we begin to see the spread of the remarkable ecclesiastical sculpture for which early medieval Scotland is rightly famous. To some extent these church-settlements resembled tumours, comprised of the same basic components as their host society but transforming them in new and unexpected ways and, from their initially small beginnings, rapidly spreading their influence throughout the land.

These transformations were observed by the kings and their retainers and the possibilities that they presented were not lost upon them. Bede in his letter to Bishop Ecgberht claimed that some laymen were posing as abbots in order to obtain grants of land under the terms that pertained to churches. It has been debated whether he is correct in seeing these establishments as entirely fraudulent. An alternative interpretation is that these were 'genuine' monasteries which merely observed somewhat less rigorous standards than a hardliner like Bede would have desired. It is the case, however, that by the middle of the eighth century the southern English kingdoms had begun to see the granting of 'land-books', the documents which guaranteed indivisible and inalienable tenure (somewhat like late medieval and early modern tailzies or entails) to lay men, although it would take some centuries for this to become a common form of tenure. Unfortunately, documentation of the sort which records these grants does not survive from northern England and Scotland so we are unable to ascertain whether similar developments in secular land holding were developing, but it is a possibility we must bear in mind when considering the various transformations which took place in the course of the period covered by this book.

COMMERCE AND THE WIDER WORLD

It has been noted that the major church-settlements had a need to engage in international trade and there is also some evidence that kings did so. There is, however, little evidence for a professional mercantile class in northern Britain in this period. In the south and east of the island a small number of *emporia* have been noted both in the archaeological and the textual record. The most northerly of these certainly noted was at York where a colony of Frisian traders, from the coastal islands of the Low Countries and northwest Germany, was established outside the walls of the old Roman fortress which defined the boundaries of the premier episcopal church-settlement in Northumbria. *Emporia* such as these, which existed at other coastal sites such as Ipswich, London, Sarre (in Kent) and Southampton seem to have developed out of the desire of English kings to monopolise the control of foreign trade. Frisians and others visiting Britain to trade were compelled to confine their activities to designated sites monitored by royal servants where they and their customers could be taxed. There is no sound evidence for any such sites north of York, although Dunbar, in Bernicia has recently begun to turn up some archaeological material that would not go unremarked on an *emporium*, although the context and quantity is not yet sufficient to claim it as such.

It is most likely that, on the east coast at least, churches and laymen maintained their own ships which will have visited *emporia* at places like York and engaged with foreign merchants or intermediaries at such places. Before the ninth century the widespread use of money seems to have been confined to the *emporia* and their hinterlands and the most northerly mint seems to have been at York. A single Frisian coin was recently recovered from excavations at the Pictish monastery at Portmahomack (Easter Ross), and although it bears witness to the fact that the Pictish Church was connected to the wider world of commerce its solitary state suggests that those connections were not direct.[51] At the beginning of the century Scotland's main trading links with the Continent seem to have come up the west coast from the Irish Sea and ultimately western France and the Mediterranean. These trade routes seem to have declined in importance in the eighth century, partly as a result of the growing importance of the Frisian network in the North Sea and partly, perhaps, due to Islamic expansion into the western

[51] M. O. H. Carver, 'An Iona of the east: The early-medieval monastery at Portmahomack, Tarbat Ness', *Medieval Archaeology* 48 (2004), 1–30.

Mediterranean.[52] The expansion of the Caliphate had finally been halted at Poitiers in 732. By the end of the eighth century it seems that the entire Insular World had become largely dependent upon southern and eastern England for its contacts with the Continent, a situation which doubtless contributed in part to the eventual dominance of that region.[53]

Scotland, then, was a land in which no money was minted and in which whatever coin travelled north was largely valued as bullion. Among the English most silver found its way into coinage, among the Picts into jewellery. The vast majority of the silver which found its way into Pictish jewellery probably came to Pictavia in the form of English and Frisian coin. Equally, Scotland was a land with no towns for even if Dunbar proves to have been an *emporium* it will have been a very small one and the urban status of even the largest is in considerable doubt.

SCOTLAND AT THE END OF THE EIGHTH CENTURY

The purpose of this introductory chapter has been to give a sense of the world as it was at the time our narrative begins. It has been necessarily vague and generalised in parts both on account of the paucity of the source material and also because at this stage the intention has been simply to set the stage and establish a broad understanding of the social context from which our characters, events and processes will emerge. The similarities between the kingdoms and communities have been played up and the differences played down yet it remains the case that these societies shared far more than held them apart, particularly at the level of the educated ecclesiastical elite who were responsible for providing us with our textual sources. Their presumptions and prejudices cannot fail to form and inform our own. Furthermore, events at the close of the eighth century were to cast their shared Christian heritage even more sharply into focus when all the Insular kingdoms came suddenly and unexpectedly under the onslaught of pagan warriors whose presumptions and prejudices were entirely alien.

[52] See A. Lane, 'Trade, gifts and cultural exchange in Dark-Age western Scotland', in B. E. Crawford (ed.), *Scotland in Dark Age Europe* (St Andrews, 1994), 103–15, and E. Campbell, 'Trade in the Dark Age west: A Peripheral Activity?', in B. E. Crawford (ed.), *Scotland in Dark Age Europe* (St Andrews, 1996), 79–92.
[53] Something else to blame upon Islam?

PART ONE

Events (789–1070)

CHAPTER I

The Coming of the Vikings

KINGS AND KINGDOMS IN 793

The Viking onslaught on Britain appears to have begun in AD 793. Relations between the kingdoms of northern Britain seem to have been relatively stable and secure at this time though internal instability, or at least disputes over succession, were rife. In Pictavia, the deaths of the great Onuist son of Wrguist (†761) and his brother Bridei (†763) and their immediate successor Ciniod son of Wrad (†775) and his brother Elphin (†780), were followed by a period of instability in which four kings (three apparently from Onuist's family) ruled in quick succession. From 789, however, Pictavia gained another strong ruler, Constantín son of Wrguist, who was to reign until his death in 820. The instability in Pictavia seems to have allowed Dál Riata to reassert its independence, first under Aed Find son of Eochaid (†778) and his brother Fergus (†781) and subsequently under Donncoirce (†792). Donncoirce seems to have been succeeded by Conall son of Tadg (†807), who had apparently challenged Constantín's succession to the kingship of Fortriu in 789.[1]

The ancestry of all these kings is somewhat obscure. It is unclear if the kings of this revived Dál Riata were descended from either

---

[1] *AU* 789.11 reads: 'A battle among the Picts in which Conall son of Tadg was defeated and escaped and Constantín was the victor'. The version of the Pictish king-list which is written in Pictish orthography names Constantín's immediate predecessor as Canaul son of either 'Tang' or 'Targ'. This might be a corruption of the Gaelic Conall son of Tadg but equally a scribe somewhere in the chain of transmission of the chronicle reference may have amended this unparalleled pair of names for the name of a roughly contemporary character with a similar name. Unfortunately, the version of the Pictish king list in Gaelic orthography that might have served as a 'control' omits this reign altogether.

Cenél nGabráin or Cenél Loairn, since a pedigree survives only for Aed Find, who was claimed as an ancestor by later Scottish kings, and this has clearly been fabricated or corrupted.[2]

In Northumbria the relatively prosperous reign of Ælfwold son of Oswulf (779–88) ended with his assassination on the orders of his 'patrician' Sicga.[3] Ælfwold was succeeded by his nephew Osred (788–90) son of King Alhred (765–74) who had been driven into exile in Pictavia. Osred himself did not last long on the throne. He was forcibly tonsured but then fled to the Isle of Man (at that time a British kingdom). In his place the same Æðelred who had expelled his father returned to the throne after sixteen years in exile. This Æðelred, of whom the chronicler clearly did not approve, drowned the young sons of King Ælfwold (791). The following year Osred returned from the Isle of Man, having secretly negotiated with nobles within the kingdom. He was betrayed, however, and executed on King Æðelred's orders. Æðelred then further secured his position by marrying Ælfflæd the daughter of Offa king of Mercia, the most powerful of the English kings at that time. The chronicler describes Ælfflæd as *regina*, 'queen', at the time of her marriage, which suggests that she may have been the widow of one of Æðelred's predecessors.

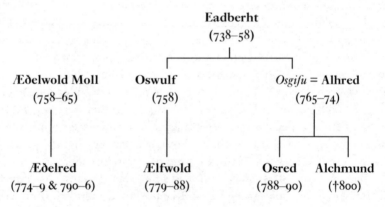

Table 1.1 Some Northumbrian kings of the later eighth century

---

[2] D. Broun, '*Alba*: Pictish homeland or Irish offshoot?', in P. O'Neill, ed., *Exile and Homecoming: Papers from the Fifth Australian Conference of Celtic Studies* (Sydney, 2005), 234–75 at 263–6.
[3] The title of *patricius*, 'patrician', emerges in late eighth-century annals preserved in the *Historia Regum Anglorum* and seems to be applied to a single senior layman, perhaps, it has been speculated, similar to the Frankish Mayor of the Palace. If so it would seem to be an office unparalleled in the other Insular kingdoms.

ADVENTUS NORTHMANNORUM: RAIDERS OR INVADERS?

This then was the world upon which the Vikings burst in 793. Constantín son of Wrguist was king of Fortriu, Conall son of Tadg king of Dál Riata, and Æðelred son of Æðelwold king of Northumbria. The dating of the earliest Scandinavian attacks on Scotland is somewhat controversial. Because the far north, Shetland, Orkney, the northern Hebrides and the northeast of the mainland are barely noted at all in our surviving chronicles it is sometimes argued that Scandinavian attacks and even settlement may have begun there earlier than 793. Indeed, the relative proximity of these regions to Norway would seem to make this very likely. Shetland in particular is almost as close to the Norwegian Westland as it is to the Scottish mainland and there is a small amount of archaeological evidence suggesting contact between Shetland and Norway from before the Viking Age. This said, the shock with which the events of 793 and 794 are recorded in the Northumbrian and Irish chronicles suggests that they were not simply the next phase of a gradual wave of advance, as indeed does the general absence of evidence for Scandinavian settlement in much of eastern Scotland. So while Shetland might perhaps have fallen under Norse control before this date, and some probing contacts into northern Pictish territory may have taken place, it seems, on balance, unlikely, though not impossible, that a conquest or severe ravaging of an important territory, such as Orkney, would have gone unnoticed.

The first recorded attack was on Northumbria in 793. It is perhaps best known from the letters sent to England by the Northumbrian scholar Alcuin (Ealhwine), formerly head of the episcopal school at York, but now attached to the court of the Frankish king Charlemagne. He wrote:

> Lo, it is nearly three hundred and fifty years that we and our fathers have inhabited this most lovely land, and never before has such terror appeared in Britain as we have now suffered from a pagan people, nor was it thought that such an inroad from the sea could be made. Behold the Church of St Cuthbert splattered with blood of the priests of God, despoiled of all its ornaments; a place more venerable than all in Britain given as prey to pagan peoples.

The attack is best described, however, in the account preserved in *Historia Regum Anglorum*:

> [793] In the fourth year of King Æðelred, dreadful prodigies terrified the wretched nation of the English. For horrible

lightening and dragons in the air and fiery flashes were often seen to gleam and fly to and fro; and these signs signified a great famine and the fearful and indescribable slaughter of many men which followed. In this year also Sicga dux, who killed King Ælfwold, perished by his own hand, and his body was conveyed to the island of Lindisfarne on 23rd April.

In the same year the pagans from the North-eastern regions came with a naval force to Britain like stinging hornets and spread on all sides like dire wolves robbed, tore and slaughtered not only beasts of burden, sheep and oxen but even priests and deacons and companies of monks and nuns. And they came to the Church of Lindisfarne, laid everything waste with grievous plundering, trampled the holy places with polluted steps, dug up the altars and seized all the treasures of holy church. They killed some of the brothers, took some away with them in fetters, many they drove out, naked and loaded with insults, some they drowned in the sea.

[794] The aforesaid pagans, ravaging the harbour of king Ecgfrith, plundered the monastery at the mouth of the River Don. But St Cuthbert did not allow them to go away unpunished; for their chief was, in fact, slain by the English, a cruel death, and after a short space of time the violence of a storm battered, destroyed and broke into pieces their ships and the sea overwhelmed many of them. Some were cast on the shore and soon killed without mercy. And these things befell them rightly, for they had gravely injured those who had not injured them.

The accounts of this attack are frequently described by modern historians as 'the raid on Lindisfarne', and have been fitted into a paradigm in which the earliest Viking attacks on Britain and Ireland were 'hit and run' raids aimed principally at undefended church-settlements which, as we have seen, were the richest sites in Britain and probably the only places where a guaranteed haul of portable non-perishable wealth could be found. According to this paradigm the Scandinavians only began to feel confident enough to mount major assaults on the Insular kingdoms from the second quarter of the ninth century. The account in *Historia Regum Anglorum*, however, a contemporary annal probably written at York, makes it clear that this was a major attack which ranged widely over the Northumbrian countryside plundering numerous settlements, secular and ecclesiastical. It is also clear from this account that the Northmen over-wintered in Northumbria and eventually encountered an English army which defeated them in the field, killing their leader. This does not look very much like a hit and run raid but more like a full scale invasion attempt.

In the same year that the Northumbrians defeated their assailants the *Annals of Ulster* note the 'devastation of all the islands of Britain by heathens'.[4] In the light of the hit and run paradigm, this notice has been interpreted as a very generalised account of small-scale raids all over Britain. Such generalised notices, however, are not common in the Irish chronicles and the entry may be compared with one found in *Chronicum Scotorum* under the year 941 when a fleet was led by one of the Irish kings to the 'islands of Alba'. This latter entry undoubtedly refers to the Hebrides and the use of *Alba* rather than *Britannia* here reflects the growing tendency in the chronicles, from around 900, to use Irish rather than Latin as the main language of record. It seems likely that the islands of Alba/Britain[5]

An imaginary raid on Skye?[6]

An entry in the *Annals of Ulster* for 795 has been taken as evidence for an attack on Skye, and thus of the earliest viking raid on Scotland. The entry reads, 'The burning of Rechru by heathens, and *scri* was broken and destroyed.' Rechru was the name of two islands with church-settlements off the coast of Ireland, now Rathlinn (County Antrim) and Lambay (County Dublin), and this is the account of the first Scandinavian attack on Ireland. Modern editors of the *Annals of Ulster* had emended the nonsense word *scri* to *Sci*, a plausible spelling of the island name Skye. In an article published in 2000, however, Clare Downham pointed out that a more reasonable emendation of *scri* was to read the Old Irish word *scrín*, 'shrine', as having originally been written *scrī* with the line over the 'i' representing a final 'n', an abbreviation widely used throughout the middle ages. If Downham is correct then it is likely that the original entry referred to the breaking of the reliquary on Rechru rather than an attack on another island, and should be translated 'The burning of Rechru by the heathens and the shrine was broken and destroyed.'

In support of this interpretation is the fact that Skye seems to have lain beyond the range of interest of the Irish chroniclers and was only mentioned three times (in 668, 701 and 710) in the period when one of the source chronicles was kept on Iona (up until c. 740), and never after that.

---

[4] *AU* 794.7.

[5] The changing meaning of the name Alba will be discussed at length in a later chapter.

[6] C. Downham, 'An imaginary Viking-raid on Skye in 795?', *Scottish Gaelic Studies* 20 (2000), 192–6. *AU* 795.3.

was the term used in Ireland specifically for the Hebrides (which makes very good sense from the perspective of our chroniclers based in the northern half of Ireland). In this light, this entry may be recording another large-scale attack, this time aimed at the island portions of Dál Riata.

Another notice in the Irish chronicle record for this period also seems to tell against the hit and run model of early Viking activity. In 798 'the heathens burned Inis Patraic [County Dublin], and took cattle tribute from the territories [*borime na crich do breith*] and made great incursions in both Ireland and Britain'.[7] The organising of a tribute of cattle would presumably have taken some time and would probably only have made some sense if the heathens had established a reasonably permanent base on Irish soil.

So who were these Northmen and what were they doing? A clue as to their place of origin comes from a southern English source, the *Anglo-Saxon Chronicle*. This chronicle was put together in its core form in the 890s but, for most of the ninth century and perhaps for some time before, it was largely dependent upon contemporary annals. As with the 'Chronicle of Ireland', versions of the chronicle put together in the 890s were distributed to different centres for continuation, probably in the early tenth century, and some of these continuations also had extra material added to the earlier sections, presumably on the basis of earlier historical writings or traditions available in each locality. The *Anglo-Saxon Chronicle* records, *inter alia*, the reign of Beorhtric (or Brihtric), king of Wessex from 786 to 802. Under the year 789 the chronicle records:

> In this year King Beorhtric married Offa's daughter Eadburh and in his days there came for the first time three ships of the Northmen (from Hörðaland) and then the reeve rode to them and wished to force them to the king's residence, for he did not know who they were; and they slew him. Those were the first ships of *Denisc* men which came to the land of the English.[8]

Despite the claim in the chronicle that these were the first *Denisc* men to come to the land of the English this attack probably followed that of 793–4 in Northumbria. The core text of the chronicle is very much

---

[7] *AU* 798.2. The significance of this entry was brought home to me by Dr Colmán Etchingham.

[8] D. Whitelock, *English Historical Documents*, 180. The information that the men came from Hörðaland is found in manuscripts D, E and F. The additional information in these manuscripts is mostly derived from Northumbria. The *Annals of St Neots* version locates the incident at Portland in Dorset.

centred on Wessex and records very few events from the North, indeed it
does not even have an account of the attack on Northumbria, though
news of this clearly reached Alcuin in the Frankish kingdom. The location of the first attack on southern England in Dorset, some way to the
west, suggests that these Northmen may have been associated with
the group who took cattle tribute from Ireland in 798. The identification
of their homeland as Hörðaland, essentially the central portion of the
Norwegian Westland including the modern city of Bergen and
Hardangerfjord, the nearest part of Norway to Shetland, allows us to construct a plausible narrative of the events of the 790s. The Hörðar crossed
to Britain via Shetland and after an initial attack, via the east coast on
Northumbria, fell back, regrouped and attempted the western passage.
Here they ravaged the Hebrides and, possibly establishing a base there,
explored the potential of the Irish east midlands in an initial attack that
took in Lambay in 795. They either remained in Ireland, relatively inac-
tive, for the next three years or else they returned, either from Hörðaland
or from a base somewhere in Scotland, to extort the cattle tribute in and
send out expeditions from the Dublin area in 798. The attack on Dorset
was probably one of the secondary raids from the Irish base. The use of
the term *Denisc*, 'Danish', for the Hörðar in the *Anglo-Saxon Chronicle*
should not worry us too much. As late as the twelfth and thirteenth centuries Icelanders, for the most part themselves descendants of migrants
from the Norwegian Westland, referred to their language as the 'Danish'
tongue, and on one level 'Dane' seems to have been synonymous with
'Scandinavian'.

The important, but at present unanswerable, question for Scottish
history is whether these Hörðar, out of sight of our chroniclers, had
established a permanent base somewhere in northern Scotland or
whether they were returning to Norway in between the recorded episodes
of activity. If they had established a Scottish base should we imagine it as
a pirate base, perhaps a good harbour with a minimal hinterland, or
should we imagine it to be a territorial land grab? Had they taken over the
governance of Shetland, Orkney or some other part of the far north?

HÖRÐAR AT HOME: NORWAY IN THE VIKING AGE

To understand the context of the incursion of the Hörðar into the Insular
world we must consider conditions in Scandinavia in the late eighth
century. Scandinavia had lain entirely outwith the Roman Empire,
although items of material culture from the Empire had reached the

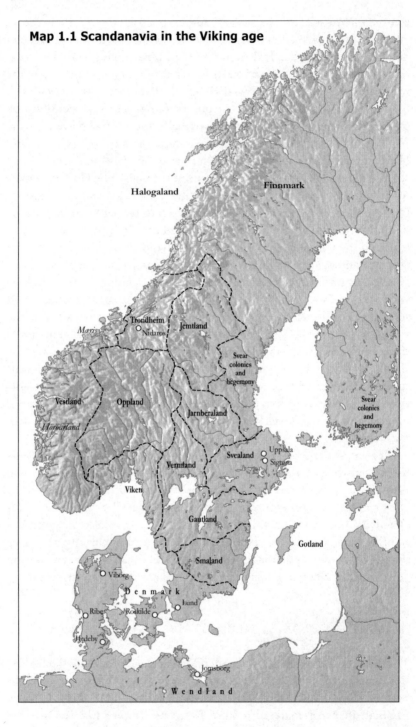

Map 1.1 Scandanavia in the Viking age

North, either as diplomatic gifts, items of trade or as plunder, or all three. During the migration period (c. 350–550) some Scandinavians, peoples and individuals, had taken part in the invasions that accompanied the collapse of the empire; indeed, some of the ancestors of the English had come from Scandinavia. It is also likely that before this some Scandinavians may have served in the Roman army as mercenaries, although the evidence for this is less clear. Broadly speaking Scandinavia is divided into a number of geographical zones: one of these, known as South Scandinavia in the academic literature, comprises the Jutland peninsula, which extends north from the frontiers of Old Saxony (the homeland of the Saxons), the Danish islands, to the east of Jutland, and the provinces of Halland, Skåne and Blekinge, located in the south of modern Sweden. South Scandinavia is flat and low-lying and contains the best agricultural land in Scandinavia. By the end of the eighth century this whole territory was inhabited by a people who were recognised by themselves and others as Danes. At the time of the Hörðar attacks on Britain and Ireland the Danes seem to have been ruled by a single powerful king named Guðfrið who was capable of facing down the might of the Frankish kingdom under Charlemagne. The Danish kingdom, however, was very fragile and although it had probably existed as a unified polity on and off since late Roman times, it was frequently divided between rival kings. In many ways it resembled Ireland or Anglo-Saxon England in so much as a strong sense of national unity existed and aspirations to national kingship were expressed, but actual functional unity and the development of even the most basic institutions of a state eluded the Danes as much as they did the Irish and the English. In other ways it was entirely unlike Ireland and England for there was little or no Christianity and consequently no literacy other than runic inscriptions, and no rich church-settlements.

North of the Danish kingdom in south central Sweden lay a band of provinces inhabited by peoples who were believed to be closely related to one another: Västergötland; Östergötland; and the islands of Öland and Gotland. Whether the Gautar of Götland and the Gutar of Gotland were really branches of a single people has been doubted, but in medieval times the connection was made and both were also linked with the Goths of Late Antiquity; indeed, in Latin sources both the Gutar and Gautar are frequently called *Gothi*.[9] Västergötland lay between the vast lakes Vänern and

---

[9] The debate is largely philological. The classical Goths first appear as *Gutones* which does look like it might be related to the name used by the inhabitants of Gotland, but the similarity between the name of the Gautar and the Goths may be more superficial.

Vättern, and Östergötland between Lake Vättern and the Baltic. To the south of Östergötland, and separating it from Danish territory, lay the sparsely inhabited upland forest zone of Småland.[10] Although legendary history accorded the Gautar kings in ancient times, including Beowulf, the eponymous hero of the only surviving Anglo–Saxon epic, there is little or no evidence for kingship in these provinces in the Viking Age and they seem to have been self-governing farmer republics dominated by very fluid and unstable chieftaincies. By the end of the tenth century they were sometimes acknowledging the overlordship of the kings of the Danes or the Svear but it is not clear if this pattern was already established by the 790s.

North of Östergötland lay Svealand, 'Sweden proper', lying along the Baltic coast from Bråviken in the south to the estuary of the Dalälv in the north, and extending around the shores of the great inlet of the sea known as Lake Mälar, at the mouth of which Stockholm stands today. As far back as the time of Tacitus in the first century AD the Svear had been ruled by kings and by the end of the eighth century their kingship was focused around the pagan cult site of Uppsala. After the Danish kingdom, Svealand was the richest and most politically developed part of Scandinavia. To the north and west of Svealand lay a number of sparsely populated and heavily forested farmer republics: Värmland; Jarnberaland; Härjedalen and Jämtland in the interior; and Hälsingland and Ängermanland along the Baltic coast. These provinces may at times have recognised Swedish overlordship, but we are told in the contemporary *Sverri's saga* that when a Norwegian king visited Jarnberaland in 1178 he was the first king the locals had ever encountered and that the concept of a king's man was alien to them. There may be a little exaggeration here but perhaps not too much. In these provinces the agrarian Scandinavians cohabited with hunter gatherer Sami.

The lands that make up the modern kingdom of Norway were, it seems, in no sense united in this period. Viken, the collection of coastal provinces between, broadly speaking, the modern cities of Gothenburg, Oslo and Kristiansand seems to have been on the fringes of the Danish kingdom. The region seems to have been composed of five or six *fylki* or tribal territories, although Norwegian *fylki* were much smaller than the big Swedish provinces.[11] From east to west these were: Alfheim; Østfold;

---

[10] Småland means 'little lands' and reflects the dispersed character of the settlement and the lack of a provincial level of political activity.

[11] Translating *fylki* is fraught with the same pitfalls as translating the Old Irish *túath*. While both words originally indicated 'people', in a fairly general sense, they have come to be associated with territorial polities. English terms such as 'tribe', 'petty kingdom', and 'shire' have been used but have rarely satisfied all scholars working in the field. Where possible it is probably best to leave them untranslated.

Vingulmörk; Vestfold; Grœnland; and Egðer. A ninth-century Frankish annal records resistance to Danish rule in Vestfold being led by *principes*, and this has encouraged modern scholars to think that these *fylki* were also 'farmer republics' dominated by oligarchies of chiefs, however, in the twelfth and thirteenth centuries Icelandic and Norwegian writers seem to have believed that each *fylki* had had its own king, much as the law-codes would have us believe Irish *túatha* had. The extremely rich burials recovered at places like Borre, Gokstad and Oseberg might give some support to this hypothesis. Immediately to the north of Viken lay Oppland, the Norwegian interior. Østerdalen, the eastern portion of this territory, roughly coextensive with modern Hedmark, seems to have been very similar to the adjacent provinces to the east, Värmland and Jarnberaland. The western portion, between Lake Mjøsa and the mountains seems to have been divided into many small territories some of which were believed to have had independent petty kings as late as the eleventh century, but in some of which, such as Gudbrandsdal, Valdres and Telemark, no such tradition survives.

North of Gudbrandsdal the passes over Dovrefjel led one into Trondheim.[12] This was the territory of the Trønder who dwelt in the valleys and peninsulas around Trondheimsfjord. By the twelfth century the Trønder were divided into eight *fylki* and had a general assembly, *althing*, which met at Frosta on a peninsula in the centre of the fjord, as well as local assemblies in each of the *fylki*. It is usually assumed that this arrangement was quite ancient. The inner part of Trondheim, furthest from the fjord mouth, played an important role in the trade which lay behind the wealth of the Svear for it was here that the overland route from Svealand through Hälsingland and Jämtland crossed the Kjolen mountains. From Inner Trondheim it then crossed to the open sea, not through the fjord mouth but via the *fylki* of Namdal to the north. This route can be plotted by the distribution of Arabic silver coins, for the key to Svear wealth was their ability to supply the Caliphate, based in Iraq since the mid-eighth century, with furs, walrus ivory and other Arctic wares that were being collected by the northernmost of all the Northmen. North of Namdal lay Hálogaland, the 'Land of High Fire', under the aurora borealis. This region, which was probably only being colonised by Scandinavians in the eighth century, was inhospitable and for the most

---

[12] The name Trondheim is now applied to the city, founded in 995, called Nidaros in the middle ages. Trondheim, 'Home of the Trønder', was originally the provincial name. The province is now known as Trønderlag, 'Trønder Law' (*cf.* the English Danelaw).

part north of the Arctic Circle. The Háleygir made a nod towards agricultural subsistence in scattered settlements in sheltered coves or islands
but their main support lay in their ability to extort Arctic produce from
the Sami. There was no tradition of kingship amongst the Háleygir,
although they possessed an *althing* on the Lofoten islands and archaeologists have recently discovered massive buildings at Borg in Lofoten that
appear to be the centre of some sort of chieftaincy.

South of Hálogaland, between Namdal and Staðir (now Stadlandet),
lay the region of Mæri comprising three *fylki*: North Mæri; Romsdal; and
South Mæri. This region lay between Trondheim and the open sea. By
the twelfth century it had declined in importance and effectively been
partitioned between Trondelag and the Westland region of the
Gulatingslag, but during the early part of the Viking Age it seems to have
been an important region in its own right and it was to play a significant
role in the relations between Norway and Scotland. We shall be explor-
ing this in due course.

Beyond Staðir, which was regarded as the turning point of the
Norwegian coast where the predominantly west-northwest facing Mæri
and Hálogaland met the predominantly west-southwest facing coastline,
we enter the Westland proper comprising five *fylki*: Fjordane; Sogn;
Hörðaland; Rogaland; and Jæren. Beyond Jæren lay Egðerness at which
point the coast turned into Viken where the Danish kings prowled. By the
end of the twelfth century all of these Westland *fylki*, together with South
Mæri and Romsdal, lay within the jurisdiction of the *althing*, or national
assembly, on the island of Gula just south of the mouth of Sognefjord,
but at an earlier phase the Gulatingslag seems to have been confined to
Fjordane, Sogn and Hörðaland. It was from this region that the earliest
Viking attacks on Britain and Ireland were directed.

CAUSES OF THE VIKING AGE

This tour of Scandinavia c. 800 may have seemed a little excessive within
the context of a book about Scotland but it is necessary if we are to understand the Scandinavian invasions. The alternative, and not entirely unjus-
tifiable position, would be that taken by Alcuin and some other
ecclesiastical writers, who presumed that the great wealth amassed by the
churches in the course of the eighth century had angered God and that
the Northmen had been sent by him as a punishment. This view is not
without its merits, as we shall see, but it is unlikely to satisfy most people
interested in history in the twenty-first century. Instead, explanations for

the beginnings of the Viking Age have been sought in what are sometimes called World Systems theory, the sub-discipline within history that seeks to explain change on the basis of interconnected economic factors across the globe. This kind of analysis has been applied quite convincingly to the Viking Age by the Danish archaeologist Klavs Randsborg who sought the origins of Danish attacks on the Frankish kingdom and on England in Tajikistan.

The Scandinavian region, from southern Jutland to Lofoten was unified by language (a cluster of north Germanic dialects which, while sharing a good deal in common with north German, Frisian and Anglo-Saxon dialects, had also developed some shared distinctive features of their own), by similar pagan cults and by other aspects of legal, social and material culture. The various provinces, however, also differed with regard to topography, agricultural potential and proximity to trade routes. In the course of the eighth century a very extensive triangular trading system had grown up. Svear had penetrated the Russian river system and established trading links that led directly or through inter-mediaries to the Islamic Caliphate which had (c. 750) moved its centre from Syria and the eastern Mediterranean to Iraq. The Iraqis were prin-cipally interested in furs and other natural products that were scarce in the Middle East but relatively common in Scandinavia. They in their turn provided silver, in the form of coins, which was very much in demand in Scandinavia because it could be exchanged for consumer goods such as wine and weapons, which could be purchased in the Frankish and English *emporia* either directly or through Frisian interme-diaries. Thus, furs from the Swedish hinterland went to Iraq, and silver returned which then passed through the southern portion of the Danish kingdom on its way to the North Sea *emporia*. The powerful Danish king Guðfrið actually compelled the merchants who controlled the western end of the Baltic leg of this trade route to move their *emporium* from Reric (near Lübeck), in the territory of the Slavic-speaking Abodrites (Old English *Afdræde*), to a new settlement just within the frontiers of his own kingdom at Haithebu (Danish Hedeby). He already controlled the north-ernmost of the North Sea *emporia* at Ribe (from where combs found their way to Dunbar). In Lake Mälar the Svear possessed their own *emporium* on the island of Birka, which the ninth-century missionary Rimbert described as a 'town of the Goths in the kingdom of the Svear'. This probably indicates that the Gotlanders played a similar role in the Baltic to that played by the Frisians in the North Sea.

The development of this triangular trade network was probably the driving force behind Scandinavian penetration of Hálogaland and the settlement of Jämtland which was believed to have taken place from Inner Trondheim (Hälsingland was said to have been settled as a sort of over-spill region for the Jämtar). The route from Birka to Hálogaland has been mapped out by archaeologists plotting the finds of Arabic silver from across Scandinavia. -The development of the inland route through Namdal, Inner Trondheim and Jämtland effectively bypassed the Norwegian Westland. Some of the Hálogaland trade certainly found its way down the coast, and the mountains of the interior probably supplied small amounts of furs, but this route, from Hálogaland to Egðerness, the original Norway (either Nórvegr, 'fjord-way', or Norðvegr, 'north-way', scholars cannot agree which), led directly to the Danish *emporia*, where it was the Islamic silver rather than the furs themselves which had the highest premium.

Randsborg's argument is that the Danish attacks on the Frankish kingdom, which were initially aimed, it seemed, on the Frisian *emporia*, occurred at periods when the flow of silver from the Caliphate was inter-rupted, especially towards the middle of the ninth century when Badakshan (now in Tajikistan), the region where most of the silver mines were located, fell out of the control of the Caliphs. The Danes, he argued, were dependent upon imports from the West and if they could not afford to purchase them then they were forced to steal them. The control that Danish kings and chieftains had over exotic foreign goods was one of the main factors that enabled them to exert control over their countrymen. The phases of silver shortage which Randsborg charted correlated very well with Danish attacks on the Frankish and southern English kingdoms.[13]

It seems, however, to be completely at odds with the recorded attacks by Norwegian Westlanders on Scotland and Ireland.[14] The explanation for this seems to be that the triangular trade effectively sidelined the Westland and so it was precisely during the periods when those engaged in the trade were doing well that they felt themselves under pressure. A need among Westland chieftains to provide their followers and clients with the same access to foreign luxuries drove them overseas and encouraged them to exploit the Shetland 'corridor' with which they had probably long been familiar but for which they had previously had little use. The attacks on northern Britain and Ireland in the 790s were thus driven by a need to keep up with the Joneses (or perhaps the Johanssons, in this case).

[13] K. Randsborg, *The Viking Age in Denmark* (London, 1980).
[14] I owe this observation to Dr John Moreland.

THE HÖRÐAR IN SCOTLAND

The two richest and most populous regions in the Westland were Hörðaland and Mæri and so it is perhaps not surprising that it would be the Hörðar and Mærir who would play the leading parts in the expeditions to the west. The question which set us off on that digression into Scandinavian proto-history was whether or not it was likely that the Hörðar had, when they appear attacking Northumbria, Dál Riata and Ireland in our sources, already established themselves in the far north of Scotland. It may be that the understanding that we have now gained into their motivation might help us find an answer to that question.

What Scandinavian chieftains required to satisfy their clients and retinues was a supply of mass-produced goods such as weapons, armour, tableware and exotic textiles along with wine. These were usually purchased via the Danish *emporia*, having come ultimately from the Rhineland or southern England. None of these things were mass produced in Ireland or northern Britain so what the Hörðar hoped to get from these areas must have been something which they could have exchanged in the Danish *emporia*. Although major church-settlements would have been able to provide some church plate and other finery it is unlikely that the quantities were quite sufficient to justify the risks involved in such long distance overseas expeditions. What the Hörðar were after was almost certainly a commodity which was discussed in the Introduction: slaves. Unlike the Insular world, or Scandinavia itself, the Frankish kingdoms, the Byzantine Empire and the Caliphate did practice large-scale gang slavery and were constantly crying out for new supplies. The trade in prisoners of war from the pagan East into the Frankish world is responsible for the word 'Slav' entering western languages with the meaning 'slave'. The Danish *emporia* provided ideal markets from which slaves could be sent on either west towards the Rhine mouth or east across the Baltic to Byzantium and the Caliphate.

While slaves could be gathered from any populated district, slaving would have been more cost effective in populous regions and the larger church-settlements may still have been attractive targets if they were generally surrounded by larger and less militarised populations.[15] The opportunities to gather inanimate wealth from the churches themselves

---

[15] The dependants of church-settlements are likely to have been poorer since the mechanisms alleviating the partition of their patrimonies will have been fewer than under secular lords. Smaller tenancies would have led to an increased proportion of the population being married couples, thus an exponential growth in population would have occurred.

may have been something of an added bonus. It may also be the case that the gathering together of church dependants on Sundays and other holy days provided an ideal opportunity for slavers to maximise the efficiency of their collection. Bearing these factors in mind it would seem that while the Northern and Western Isles may have provided temporary bases for slave-raiding the targets may have specifically been the richer lands dominated by older and larger church-settlements. This would explain the early targeting of eastern Northumbria and the relatively rapid move on to the Irish east midlands. But what of eastern Pictavia?

On the basis of surviving sculptural remains it seems likely that Pictavia was well endowed with wealthy church-settlements, from Portmahomack in Ross to St Andrews in Fife via coastal or near coastal sites such as Rosemarkie (probably the episcopal see for Fortriu), Kineddar, Inchbrayock, St Vigeans and Abernethy. No raids on these sites are recounted in the chronicles, but the very fact that we are largely reliant upon the sculptural remains rather than chronicle references for the identification of these sites should alert us to the fact that the Pictish Church, by and large, did not feature in either the Irish or the Northumbrian chronicles. The obituary of a bishop of Fortriu is noted in the *Annals of Ulster* in 725 but then not again until 865 and then only, one suspects, because he held the abbacy of Dunkeld, the leading Columban house of the day, in plurality.[16] Only one obituary is recorded for a head of the house at Rígmonaid (St Andrews), in 747, and one cannot help but wonder if the individual concerned is noteworthy for other reasons, as an alumnus of Iona or Armagh perhaps.[17] None of the other Pictish churches listed above warrants a single mention in the chronicles. Thus, attacks by the Hörðar upon Pictish church-settlements in the 790s cannot be ruled out, but the surprise with which the attack on Northumbria was noted strongly suggests that if they occurred they did so almost simultaneously with the attacks further south.

One alternative scenario is worth considering. The major Danish interventions in the Frankish kingdoms in the early ninth century were frequently carried out in support of one faction or another in the internecine struggles that sprang up following the death of Charlemagne (†814). In 841 Charlemagne's grandson Lothar actually granted the island of Walcheren in the mouth of the Scheldt to an exiled Danish prince named Harald in return for his military aid. In the light of such political manoeuvrings it is not entirely implausible that the attacks on

---

[16] *AU* 725.7 and 865.6.
[17] I owe this suggestion to Professor John Koch.

Northumbria and Dál Riata might in part have been directed by Constantín of Fortriu or even that he may have handed over some marginal part of his territory (perhaps Orkney or Shetland) to an exiled Hörðr in return for a non-aggression pact or mutual aggression against third parties. The Hörðar appeared in Northumbria immediately following the killing of Osred, whose father Alhred had gone into exile in Pictavia, and in Dál Riata shortly after the death of Donncoirce (†792) whose successor, Conall son of Tadg, had opposed Constantín's succession in Fortriu in 789.

THE DYNASTY OF WRGUIST (789–839)

Whether or not he was implicated in the incursions of the Hörðar, or was a fellow sufferer at their hands, Constantín son of Wrguist remained the strongest and most secure king in northern Britain. Following the traumatic events of 793–4, Northumbria continued much as before with intrigue at court but external stability and, if the distribution of coinage across the kingdom from York to Whithorn is anything to go by, with increasing economic strength. Unfortunately, the Northumbrian chronicle embedded within the *Historia Regum Anglorum* comes to an end in 802. This has led people to claim that the see at Whithorn came to an end shortly thereafter because the last known bishop was Badwulf, whose consecration was recorded in this chronicle under the year 790, but this is simply a problem caused by the chronicle coming to an end. There is some evidence that Badwulf had at least one mid-ninth-century successor, Heaðored.

After the Irish expedition of 798 there is no sign of the Northmen again until 802 when the *Annals of Ulster* tell us, simply, that 'Iona was burned by the heathens'.[18] They appeared again in 806 when they slew sixty-eight of the *familia* of Iona, presumably, though not certainly, on Iona.[19] It should be stressed that these two attacks on Iona are the only Scandinavian attacks recorded in Britain and Ireland since 798. In 807, however, the heathens burned the monastic island of Inishmurray, near Sligo in the northwest of Ireland, and attacked the church-settlement at Roscommon. The fact that Roscommon lies some thirty-five miles from the coast should alert us to the facts that: (a) the Northmen were capable of carrying out attacks well inland; and (b) our chroniclers, themselves

[18] *AU* 802.9.
[19] *AU* 806.8.

occupants of wealthy church-settlements, cared little for the fate of other kinds of settlements. While it is conceivable that Iona or Inishmurray could be hit by raids from the sea without warning, any attack on Roscommon must have led the heathens across dozens of miles of settled country occupied by lay-folk and clerics alike. Just as Alcuin was able to comment on a wide-ranging assault on Northumbria lasting several months as if it were merely the sack of St Cuthbert's church on Lindisfarne, so our Irish chronicler recounts the sack of Roscommon as if, like Iona and Inishmurray, it were an isolated island and not in the very heart of the kingdom of Connacht. This is a salutary warning of how mis-leading our sources can be. Had the Northmen really been absent since 798 or had they simply confined their attention to laymen and -women? The Irish historian Colmán Etchingham has compared the geographical distribution of recorded Viking raids in the ninth-century annals with the notices of the obituaries of church hierarchs, bishops, abbots and the like. The maps he produced indicate that in both cases the region in which the 'Chronicle of Ireland' was kept, the northeast midlands, probably some-where in counties Dublin, Meath or Louth, was much better represented, and the further from this region one looks the more important a church had to be to have either its burning by heathens or the death of its head noticed.[20] Indeed, the west coast of Ireland almost never features in the chronicle record and so could, in theory, like the north of Scotland, have been a centre of Scandinavian activity from an early period. The most economical reading of the record, however, would be to suggest that the same heathens who attacked the *familia* of Iona in 806 then sailed into Sligo bay, sacked Inishmurray and, after making landfall somewhere in County Sligo, crossed overland to Roscommon. The first mention of con-flict between the heathens and the secular powers in the *Annals of Ulster* appears under the year 811 when we are told simply of 'a slaughter of the heathens by the Ulaid'.[21] The Ulaid, the real Ulstermen, controlled a ter-ritory broadly coextensive with modern County Down, and were thus quite close to the home of the chronicler (Ulaid territory extended into the north of Louth where he may have been based). If we are not to allow ourselves to be too worried by the silence of the chronicle noted above then we can hypothesise that this battle, where Ireland comes close to Scotland, may, like the events of 806 and 807, indicate that the heathens

[20] Colmán Etchingham, *Viking Raids on Irish Church Settlements in the Ninth Century* (Maynooth, 1996). The argument is slightly circular since the location of the chronicle keepers has only been determined on the basis of their geographical bias but the general point holds true.
[21] *AU* 811.6.

were operating either from or via the Western Isles. The events of the following year might lead us to revise this judgement, however, for three battles were fought against heathens on the west coast of Ireland, two in west Connacht and one in County Kerry, a victory for Cobthach son of Mael Duin, the king of Loch Lein.[22] Given the usual obscurity of these regions the fact that these events are recorded at all might hint at a Scandinavian base in this area and that events in the west of Ireland were independent of those in the northeast and the west of Scotland. The more one thinks about how the process of chronicling actually worked the less certain one becomes about what was actually happening.

The attacks on Iona are usually associated with a project begun in 807 and completed in 814, the building of a new *ciuitas*, or major church-settlement, at Kells by the abbot Cellach of Iona.[23] This has been widely interpreted as a reflection of a growing disquiet on Iona in the context of repeated attacks by heathens. The plan may have been to move the relics of St Columba and the headship of the *familia* from Iona to Kells, more safely located in the interior of Ireland. There is no record during this period of conflict between the kings of Dál Riata and the heathens. In 807 regime change had been effected when Conall son of Aedán slew Conall son of Tadg and took the kingship.[24] The chronicler notes this as occurring in Kintyre. Whether this simply notes the location of the killing or hints at the restricted jurisdiction of the kings (the islands, perhaps, having fallen to the heathen) is not clear. Conall son of Aedán was accorded a reign of only four years by our surviving sources so he was probably dead or expelled by 811, although no notice is taken of this event by the chronicles.

The most likely explanation of subsequent events in Dál Riata is that put forward by Dauvit Broun in 1998.[25] It must be understood that our sources for understanding the history of Dál Riata at this period are extraordinarily poor. The killing of Conall son of Tadg by Conall son of Aedán in Kintyre is the last explicit reference to the secular history of the kingdom in any contemporary source. Were we reliant upon the Irish chronicles alone we would be happy to end the history of Dál Riata at this point. The other information we have all comes from much later sources, principally various king-lists. The king-lists of the Picts and Dál Riata have been mentioned from

[22] *AU* 812.8 and 812.11.
[23] *AU* 807.4 and 814.9.
[24] *AU* 807.3.
[25] D. Broun, 'Pictish Kings 761–839: Integration with Dál Riata or separate development', in S. M. Foster, ed., *The St Andrews Sarcophagus and its International Connections* (Dublin, 1998), 71–83.

time to time up to this point without much explanation as up to the end of the eighth century they are relatively unproblematic sources which correspond very closely to the obituaries of kings found in the Irish chronicles. Something needs to be said now about their nature and how they come down to us. The kingdom of Alba, or Scotland as we may call it, had by the end of the eleventh century been in existence for at least two hundred years. It had produced a catalogue of the regnal succession of its kings going back to about AD 900.[26] At some point, probably in the eleventh century, attempts had been made to extend the history of the kingdom much further back in time by appending to the early portions of the regnal list further regnal lists of either the Pictish kings or the kings of Dál Riata in an effort to present Alba as the same kingdom, existing continuously, as one of these two. Exactly who did this or where (was it the product of deliberate propaganda or antiquarian zeal and what governed the choice of Fortriu or Dál Riata as the ancestral kingdom?) is unclear and will be discussed in detail later in this volume. What is more important is the nature of the material which was available to them. A list of Pictish kings down to about 842 or 843 still survives appended to some versions of the Scottish king-list and this list has the names written in a form of British Celtic orthography and was, therefore, actually compiled before Gaelic became the dominant language of the kingdom. Indeed, it was probably compiled in the reign of the last king listed, Bridei. The authenticity of the list of kings of Dál Riata is less clearcut. Indeed, there is a great deal of confusion. This confusion can best be summed up by quoting Marjorie Anderson whose thorough survey of the king-lists remains the standard work. She summarises the prototype of the extant Dál Riatan lists as follows:

> it has been very carelessly transmitted. Two batches of names in the eighth century have been transposed, nos. 24–26 being put before nos. 20–23, so that Alpín (no. 23) came to stand at the end. Either because this Alpín was then equated, by accident or consciously, with Alpín (no. 34) the father of Kenneth, or for some other reason, all the remaining nine kings before Kenneth, covering about sixty years, were dropped. Two kings called Eogan were apparently inserted (nos. 18a and 24a in my table); if their patronymics are to be trusted they were members of the house of Lorn. Later three seventh-century kings were lost (nos. 11, 12, 14), . . .[27]

---

[26] The exact starting point of the kingdom and the relationship of this to the regnal lists will be discussed in depth a little later.

[27] M. O. Anderson, *Kings and Kingship in Early Scotland* (Edinburgh, 1973), 46–7.

She goes on at some length but this extract should give the reader a sense of the problem. The phrase 'a dog's breakfast' springs to mind.

For these reasons, by the early ninth century there is little real connection between what can be gleaned from the chronicle record and the king-list. This has led scholars to place more reliance on two other works from the late eleventh and early twelfth century, respectively. These are the poem known as *Duan Albanach* ('Scottish Poem'), which appears to have been composed in the reign of Mael Coluim son of Donnchad (1058–93) but which survives only in manuscripts from the seventeenth century or later, and an expanded version of a text known as the 'Synchronisms of Irish Kings' dating from 1119 or shortly after.[28] This latter text was an attempt to produce parallel lists of the claimants to the kingship of Ireland alongside the major provincial kings. The kings of Alba seem to have been regarded as provincial kings of the Irish under this schema! Many of the details in the 'Synchronisms' can be checked against the chronicle record and, although they are broadly accurate, errors do occur.[29] A further problem is that only the 'Synchronisms' name the fathers of kings and only *Duan Albanach* gives the reign lengths. It should also be noted that these sources simply regard their Scottish kings as kings of Alba and do not distinguish between Dál Riata and the later kingdom of Scotland. Putting the two sources together one comes up with the following king-list for the period with which we are concerned:

Domnall son of Constantín	24 years
Conall	2 years
Conall	4 years
Constantín son of Fergus	9 years
Oengus son of Fergus	9 years
Aed son of Boanta	4 years
Eoganán son of Oengus	13 years

The accumulation of the reign lengths gives a total of sixty-five years. Eoganán's death in battle is noted in 839 so we can work backwards thus:

Eoganán	826–39
Áed	822–6
Oengus	813–22

[28] Broun, 'Pictish kings', 76.
[29] Anderson, *Kings and Kingship*, 44.

Constantín   804–13
Conall   800–4
Conall   798–800
Domnall   774–98

These reign lengths and dates clearly bear no relation to those in the *Annals of Ulster* which note the deaths of Áed Find in 778, his brother Fergus in 781, Donncoirce in 792 (all within the supposed reign of Domnall), and the killing of Conall son of Tadg in 807 (in the middle of Constantín's supposed reign). A telling inconsistency is that the *Annals of Ulster* note the death of Aed son of Boanta alongside Eoganán in the battle of 839.[30]

It has not escaped the notice of historians that three of the kings in this list also appear in the Pictish king-list, which is almost a contemporary document at this point. These are Constantín, Oengus and Eoganán, who appear in the Pictish list as Constantín and Onuist, sons of Wrguist, and Wen son of Onuist.

The British dialects spoken in Fortriu were familiar enough to the Gaelic-speaking chroniclers on Iona, and perhaps in Ireland as well, that they were able for the most part to recognise the common Celtic names which both languages had inherited and adapted, and in texts emanating from Gaelic-speaking milieux Pictish names were regularly, and generally, Gaelicised. Thus, Onuist son of Wrguist appears in the Iona chronicle as Oengus son of Fergus, both sets of names deriving from a common Celtic *Oinogustos son of *Uerogustos (or possibly *Uirogustos).[31] That the chroniclers were able to do this should not surprise us since modern English language historians have tended to do the same with European names and write and speak of Peter the Great and Catherine the Great of Russia, rather than Pyotr and Katarina, and of French kings called Henry and John, rather than Henri and Jean. This means that it is actually impossible to tell, on the evidence of texts produced in a Gaelic-speaking milieu, such as the Irish chronicles, or subsequent Scottish pedigrees and king-lists, whether a given individual was actually Pictish or Gaelic although there are some names, such as Bridei (Pictish) and Eochaid

---

[30] *AU* 839.9.

[31] The Insular Celtic dialects underwent a series of transformations between about AD 350 and AD 650 which included, *inter alia*, the loss of final syllables and unstressed vowels (e.g. Oinogustos). Some of these changes, such as those just noted, were shared by all the Insular Celtic dialects and some, such as the spirantisation or lenition of certain consonants, were peculiar to individual dialects or clusters of dialects.

(Gaelic), which do not seem to have had cognate forms in use across the frontier.[32]

Returning to the problems of succession in Dál Riata, the modern scholarship presents a morass of attempts to square the conflicting evidence. The most frequent solution offered is that Wrguist, father of Constantín and Onuist, was the same person as the Fergus son of Eochaid who died as king of Dál Riata in 781, and that the dynasty ruling Fortriu in this period was actually of Gaelic origin.[33] Given the orthographic practices noted above this is, of course, theoretically possible but it does nothing to solve the chronological difficulties with the later regnal material. Broun has offered an alternative and, to my mind, far more convincing explanation of our sources. This involves combining the obituaries found in the annals with the reign lengths given for the rulers in our list who were not, demonstrably, kings of Fortriu. This gives us the following data:

King	Reign length	Obit.
Fergus		†781
Donncoirce		†792
Domnall son of Constantín	24 years	
Conall son of Tadg	2 years	†807 reigned 805–7?
Conall son of Aedán	4 years	reigned 807–11?
Aed son of Boanta	4 years	†839 reigned 835–9?

This list leaves us with a problem between Donncoirce's death and Conall son of Tadg's accession. The thirteen-year period is far too short to fit in Domnall's twenty-four years. Broun noted, however, that the gap that now existed between the end of Conall son of Aedán's reign, 811, and the beginning of Aed son of Boanta's, 835, was exactly twenty-four years. Most historians have considered it likely that Domnall son of Constantín

---

[32] Pictish Bridei (or Bredei) is regularly Gaelicised as Brude, but no individuals bearing this name are known from a Gaelic milieu until we begin to get ample sources from eastern Scotland in the thirteenth century. No British form of Eochaid survives but one might have expected something like *Ebid or *Ebdei in Pictish orthography.

[33] For the most articulate examples of this see: M. Miller, 'The last century of Pictish succession', *Scottish Studies* 23 (1979), 39–67; M. O. Anderson, 'Dalriada and the creation of the kingdom of the Scots', in D. Whitelock, R. McKitterick and D. N. Dumville, eds, *Ireland in Early Medieval Europe: Studies in Memory of Kathleen Hughes* (Cambridge, 1982), 106–32, J. Bannerman, 'The Scottish takeover of Pictland and the relics of Columba', *Innes Review* 48 (1997), 27–44, and B. T. Hudson, *Kings of Celtic Scotland* (Westport, 1994) 26–33.

was the son of Constantín son of Wrguist (Constantín had never previously appeared as a name among either the Picts or the Gaels in either Ireland or Scotland), and if this were so it would seem more likely that his reign as king of Dál Riata would have overlapped with the latter part of his father's reign rather than the former. Broun's solution was that after the unchronicled death or expulsion of Conall son of Aedán in 811 Constantín reasserted Verturian hegemony over Dál Riata and placed his own son in as *sub-regulus* or tributary king. The gap between the death of Donncoirce and the start of Conall son of Tadg's reign may have been the result of a scribal error, Conall's reign length being mis-copied, but since it coincides in part with the attack of the Hörðar on Dál Riata and their possible use of the region as a base for further attacks on Ireland, it may coincide with the period of their occupation. Indeed, the appearance of the Northmen along the west coast of Ireland in 807 may have been as a result of the abandonment of their occupation of Dál Riata. Thus, we may now produce a king-list for Dál Riata which looks something like this:

Fergus son of Eochaid	778–81
Donncoirce	781–92
Hörðar occupation	c. 793–806
Conall son of Tadg	805–7
Conall son of Aedán	807–11
Domnall son of Constantín	811–35
Aed son of Boanta	835–9

The appearance of the Pictish kings in the 'Synchronisms' and in *Duan Albanach*, may simply have resulted from the fact that by the eleventh century rulers of both Pictavia and Dál Riata were being described, anachronistically, as kings of Alba in Gaelic literary texts.

Professor Thomas Clancy has also drawn attention to another piece of evidence that might support the interpretation of events outlined above. In 825 a further Scandinavian attack on Iona had resulted in the martyrdom of one Blathmac son of Flann who had refused to reveal the hiding place of the shrine of Columba to the raiders. In the Frankish kingdom news of this atrocity inspired Walahfrid Strabo, a leading scholar of the day, to compose a poem on Blathmac's martyrdom. In this poem, Clancy points out, Iona is described as an island of the Picts.[34] That Iona was in some sense under Constantín's control may also be hinted at by the claim,

---

[34] T. O. Clancy, 'Iona in the kingdom of the Picts: a note', *Innes Review* 55 (2004), 73–6.

A royal monument at Dupplin

By the end of his reign, Constantín son of Wrguist, seems to have placed his son Domnall into the kingship of Dál Riata. His overlordship may have extended from Islay in the south to Orkney in the north. A material monument to his greatness may survive in the Dupplin Cross.[35] Now displayed in Dunning kirk, this free-standing high cross, unique in form in Scotland, owing more to models on Iona than elsewhere, originally seems to have stood on the northern edge of the lands of Forteviot in Strathearn (its position seems to have been mirrored by a less well preserved cross on the Invermay estate). It depicts a mounted warrior, perhaps a king, and ranks of foot soldiers bearing spears. Its side panels also contain depictions of David, the biblical king, playing his harp and wrestling with wild beasts. A panel on the western face of the cross bears a now only partially legible inscription that reads 'Custantin filius Fircus', which seems to be an attempt to render the Gaelic form of the king's name by a non-Gaelic-speaker.

added to a version of the king-list in the reign of Alexander II (1214–49), that Dunkeld was founded by Constantín. Although we cannot know how old this tradition was he would seem an unusual patron to foist upon the Columban cult at a later date. Dunkeld was to become the chief church of Columba in the kingdom of Alba and it is possible that since Pictish overlordship over Dál Riata seems to have been established in 811, while the building of the new *ciuitas* at Kells was in progress (807–14), this reflects a desire by Constantín to keep the relics of Columba in Scotland. Columba was, after all, the apostle of Fortriu, and it is likely that he, and Iona, occupied a special place in the Pictish *mentalité*.

Constantín son of Wrguist died after more than thirty years as king of Fortriu in 820. He was succeeded by his brother Onuist, who bore the same name and patronymic as the great eighth-century king. Onuist ruled for fourteen years but we know nothing of the events of his reign. The same version of the king-list which named Constantín as founder of Dunkeld names Onuist as the founder of Rígmonaid (St Andrews), but since sculptural fragments and the obituary of an Abbot Tuathalán in the *Annals of Ulster* under the year 747 make it clear that the church-settlement was in

[35] K. Forsyth, 'The inscription on the Dupplin Cross', in C. Bourke, ed., *From the Isles of the North. Early Medieval Art in Ireland and Britain* (Belfast, 1995), 237–44, L. Alcock and E. A. Alcock, 'The context of the Dupplin Cross: a reconsideration', *Proceedings of the Society of Antiquaries of Scotland* 126 (1996), 455–7.

place by the middle of the eighth century most scholars believe this to be an error for the earlier Onuist. It is not impossible, however, that he may have been involved in some new work at Rígmonaid (Kells after all had not been new when Abbot Cellach began his new *ciuitas* there in 807). He may even have been responsible for the establishment of the cult of St Andrew at the site.[36] It was in his time that Blathmac was killed on Iona, but this is the only Scandinavian activity recorded in Scotland in his reign and may have been overspill from the frenetic warfare between the heathens and the Ulaid between 823 and 825.[37]

On his death in 834, Onuist was followed in the kingship by his nephew Drest son of Constantín who seems to have shared the kingship (whether amicably or not is not clear) with one Talorcan son of Wthoil. Neither of these kings is mentioned in the chronicle record but the reign lengths accorded them and the obituaries accorded to Onuist and his son Wen (the Eoganán of the Scottish lists) allow us to calculate that they reigned until 836 or early 837. Wen's reign was equally short but it ended in shocking violence. The *Annals of Ulster* read:

> 839.9 The heathens won a battle over the men of Fortriu and Wen son of Onuist and Bran son of Onuist and Aed son of Boanta and others almost innumerable fell there.

The fury of the Northmen had finally, and unambiguously, fallen upon the Picts. Aed's presence at the battle suggests that, although we cannot connect him to the house of Wrguist, Dál Riata was still under Pictish dominion. The fact that the kings of Fortriu and Dál Riata, and almost innumerable others, were slain suggests that this was not a fortuitous raid by the heathens but that it was the culmination of a campaign which had been sufficiently prolonged to allow Wen to gather his forces. This battle may be one of the most decisive and important battles in British history but we know nothing of its details and even its location, although it is tempting to suppose that it took place in the heart of Fortriu on the shores of the Moray Firth.

The house of Wrguist had dominated Pictavia for at least fifty years. For much of that time it had probably also dominated the Britons of Clydesdale and the Gaels of Dál Riata. Three of its kings, Constantín,

---

[36] Tuathalán, whom we know of only from the Irish chronicler, bears a name which in British would be Tudwal. A St Tudwal was widely culted in the British-speaking world, though little is known of him: his feast is celebrated variously upon the 1 December or the 30 November. The latter date is, of course, the Feast of St Andrew.

[37] *AU* 823.8, 824.2, 825.9, 825.10 and 825.11.

Onuist and Wen had their names recorded in the *Liber Vitae* of the *familia* of Cuthbert, then kept at Lindisfarne and now at Durham, the list of men and women for whose salvation St Cuthbert's monks would pray.[38] The Cuthbertine *familia* held the churches at Edinburgh and Abercorn on the Forth, close to, if not in, Pictish territory and good relations with the house of Wrguist were clearly worth maintaining. It may also be the case that most of the finest works of Pictish sculpture were also produced under the patronage of the house of Wrguist. But now, fighting against assailants of unknown origin, they had been wiped out and their empire began to crumble.

---

[38] A. Hamilton Thompson, ed., *Liber Vitae Ecclesiae Dunelmensis: A Collotype Facsimile of the Original Manuscript*, Records of the Surtees Society 136 (1923). The fact that the linguistically neutral Northumbrian clergy at Lindisfarne chose to pray for these kings using the British rather than the Gaelic form of their names is further evidence, were it needed, that this family was indeed Pictish.

CHAPTER 2

The *Scaldingi* and the Transformation of Northumbria

In order to understand events in Pictavia and Dál Riata following the deaths of King Wen and King Aed in the battle against the heathens in 839 we must first examine how interaction with the Scandinavians affected their southern neighbour, Northumbria. Events in this vast kingdom, which stretched from Ayrshire to Yorkshire, are hard to follow after 802 when, as already noted, the set of contemporary annals preserved in *Historia Regum Anglorum* comes to a close. That the keeping of these annals had not been abandoned is demonstrated by the fact that the 'Northern Recension' of the *Anglo-Saxon Chronicle*, based on a version of the core text sent to York in the mid- to late tenth century and subsequently maintained there, contains a selection of these annals and later ones, almost certainly from the same chronicle, translated into English. Following the attack of the Hörðar in 793–4, Eardwulf, who had miraculously survived an execution attempt on him by King Æðelred in 791, became king in 796 and, although he faced opposition and was even temporarily ousted, he was, perhaps, able to pass the kingship directly to his son Eanred, who then enjoyed a reign of about thirty years.

KINGS AND COINS IN NINTH–CENTURY NORTHUMBRIA

Unfortunately our precise chronology for this period is very confused. Roger of Wendover, a thirteenth-century chronicler who had access to a set of northern annals similar or, indeed, identical to those used by Symeon of Durham in the early twelfth century, used them very sparingly and seems to have misplaced them within an absolute chronology (this suggests that the original annals were perhaps not equipped with incarnation dates). One specific example of the problems caused by this is that Roger seems to have presumed that Eardwulf's expulsion from the kingdom in 808 marked the end of his reign, whereas we know from contemporary Frankish annals that he was returned to the kingship in 810 with backing from Charlemagne. Thus, Roger begins the reign of Eanred, Eardwulf's son, with the expulsion of the usurper Ælfwold in 810 when, in fact, his father was restored at this point. Studies of the quantity of Eardwulf's coinage, together with the context of its recovery (and in particular what other coins have been found with his) suggest that he enjoyed quite a lengthy reign after his return, perhaps as much as twenty years. The same methodology would put his son Eanred reigning into the early 850s. The discrepancy between the later chroniclers and the numismatic analysis can be tabulated thus:

King	Chronicle date	Numismatic estimate
Eardwulf (restored)	808–10?	c. 810–30
Eanred	810–40	c. 830–54
Æðelred (first reign)	c. 840–5	c. 854–8
Rædwulf	844	c. 858
Æðelred (restored)	844–8	c. 858–62
Osberht	c. 848–67	c. 862–7
Ælle	862–7	c. 867

Such a radical reassessment of dates on the basis of what are, ultimately, guesstimates must be treated with caution, but it should be noted that these numismatists are used to working with very analogous data sets and the Northumbrian material simply does not fit into the established pattern. It may be that other factors affected coin production and preservation and we should probably keep both sets of dates in mind when examining other evidence.[1]

No Viking attacks are recorded on Northumbria for the entire period of Eardwulf and Eanred's reigns, but this may simply reflect the poverty of the chronicle record.[2] The west coast of the kingdom from the Mersey to Cunninghame was a blind spot for our surviving chroniclers, even at the best of times, with only the occasional notice of the consecration of

---

[1] P. Grierson and M. Blackburn, *Medieval European Coinage: 1, The Early Middle Ages (5th–10th centuries)* (Cambridge, 1986), 298–303.
[2] The one exception is the sacking of the churches of Hartness and Tynemouth which Roger of Wendover records under the year 800. As we have seen, however, Roger's absolute dates are insecure and this may simply be part of the Hörðar attack of the 790s.

a bishop of Whithorn making it into the record.[3] It is hard to imagine that Galloway and Ayrshire received no attention from the Northmen who were in conflict with the Ulaid in the mid-820s, but there is no positive evidence for this. None the less, the recovery of Northumbrian *stycces*, the relatively low bullion coins which were issued in this period (the only coinage regularly in use in Scotland before the twelfth century), from across the kingdom, including Galloway, suggest that both the economy and royal control held out into the middle of the century. What is particularly striking is that the coins found at Whithorn carry on to the very end of the sequence and, although only one *stycce* of Osberht has been recovered, a considerable number survive from the period of Æðelred's restoration. Since Northumbrian coinage ceased after 867, the end of Osberht's reign, and did not recommence until the early years of the tenth century, it was perhaps unwise for the excavators at Whithorn to place too much reliance upon the end of the coin sequence for the dating of the end of their Northumbrian phase (that is, c. 730–845) and they seem, in any case, unaware of the potential which the coins provide for correcting Roger of Wendover's regnal dates. The final coin from the site, of Osberht, almost certainly dates to the 860s, and the relatively large number from Æðelred's restoration may not be much earlier.[4]

The problem with the security of the regnal dating creates a difficulty with the first notice of heathen activity which we get from our sources. Roger of Wendover notes the brief usurpation of Rædwulf stating that he fought a battle against the heathens, in which he was slain, at the unidentified place *Alutthèlia*. Roger dates this episode to 844 but, if the numismatists are correct, it may have been in the later 850s. There is also some evidence that during the 840s and 850s Northumbria was under attack from the Picts and that the church-settlement at Melrose and the royal villa (and possible *emporium*) at Dunbar found themselves targets, but we shall examine the evidence for this in more detail in Chapter 3.

---

[3] And this probably because the archbishop of York was involved.

[4] P. Hill, *Whithorn and St Ninian: The Excavation of a Monastic Town, 1984–91* (Stroud, 1997). The *stycces* are discussed at 332–45. To some extent these issues are confused by the decision to create a major period gap between the burning of the church (at the end of the excavator's Period II) and its rebuilding shortly thereafter (Period III, phase I). Period III, phase I, might have been better designated as the final phase of Period II, since Period III, phase II, is initiated with the demolition of the church and its replacement with an entirely innovative set of structures.

THE COMING OF THE *SCALDINGI*

In 865 a large force of Danes landed in East Anglia and over-wintered there. In the spring, the East Anglian king, Edmund, gave them horses and they travelled into Northumbria. On 1 November 866 they captured and sacked York and then moved on to the Tyne. The Northumbrians, under King Osberht, and a rival named Ælle, united to retake York, but on 21 March 867 the Danes returned and stormed the city killing both Osberht and Ælle.

The force of Danes responsible for inflicting this disaster upon the Northumbrians were a group which has become known in English historiography as the 'Great Army', after its designation in the *Anglo-Saxon Chronicle* as *mycel here*. The men of the *mycel here* are usually identified by the *Chronicle* as *Dene* ('Danes'), *hæðnas* ('heathens') or simple the *here* (the 'army'). Their point of Continental origin is less clear. It is now generally agreed that they arrived in Britain directly from Ireland where Ivarr, the senior partner by 865, had been active for at least a decade. The Great Army are explicitly identified as the 'Black Gentiles' by the *Annales Cambriae* in its account of their capture of York in 867 and this group arrived in Ireland in 851.[5] Their 'blackness' served to distinguish them from the men of 'Laithlind' who had maintained a presence in Ireland for some years previous to this and who seem to have come from the north, down the west coast of Scotland.[6] It seems likely that the Black Gentiles approached Ireland around the southern end of Britain and they may have been a portion of the Danish force described as assaulting Frisia in the *Annals of St Bertin* under the year 850, and perhaps even the same portion of that fleet, comprising 350 ships, which entered the Thames early in 851, sacking Canterbury and London and defeating Beorhtwulf of Mercia in pitched battle before being defeated in turn by the West Saxons Æðelwulf and Æðelbald.[7] The suspicion that the great army was in origin a portion of the force that Rorik led to Frisia in 850 receives some support from *Historia de Sancto Cuthberto* which twice, in chapters 10 and 14, refers

---

[5] *AC* 867 and *AU* 851.3.

[6] The location of Laithlind has been the cause of much debate among scholars and no consensus has been arrived at. It is mentioned at *AU* 848.5 and 853.2. It has been hypothesised to be either a district of Norway, a pirate base in Ireland, a pirate base in Scotland or a district in Scotland. There is no doubt, however, that the men of Laithlind were ultimately of Scandinavian origin.

[7] *ASC* 851.

to Ubba, an associate, and (according to Geoffrey Gaimar) brother, of Ivarr, as *dux* of the Frisians.[8]

> [§10] For Ubba *dux* of the Frisians, with a great army of Danes, came into the kingdom and on Palm Sunday approached the city.

> [§14] Then the army which Ubba *dux* of the Frisians and Healfdene King of the Danes had led into England divided into three parts; one rebuilt the city of York, cultivated the surrounding land and stayed there.

Belgian Vikings?

It is possible that we should imagine Ubba as coming directly from Frisia to join his 'Irish' kinsmen in England. The term *Scaldingi*, used in several places in the *Historia* as the descriptor for what the *Chronicle* calls *mycel here*, 'the Great Army', seems to mean 'people from the River Scheldt'. This river is called *Scald* in Old English and Old East Flemish, and *Scaldis* in Latin, and may indicate that, within Frisia, Ubba came specifically from the island of Walcheren which lies in the mouth of the Scheldt. Walcheren was occupied by Danes for much of the ninth century, following the Frankish King Lothar's grant of the island to the exiled Danish Prince Harald in 841. Lothar's intention was that Harald would act as a poacher come gamekeeper and defend the coast against other Scandinavian raiders. If this identification of the Great Army is correct then it suggests that the core of the 'Black Gentile' force had left the Scheldt fourteen years before arriving in England and there is little evidence that they would make any attempt to settle down for a further decade. If they were indeed part of Harald's settlement on the Scheldt then they had left Denmark nearly a quarter of a century before arriving in England. Many of them had presumably been born in Frisia. If this is the case then these 'Danes' had been cohabiting with Christians speaking a West Germanic dialect almost identical to Old English for a very long time. This may explain, in part, their skill at playing the system. The settlement on Walcheren survived, in one form or another, until about 915.

---

[8] *Historia de Sancto Cuthberto* is a tenth- or eleventh-century text written in either Chester-le-Street or Durham. Geoffrey Gaimar translated a no longer extant version of the *Anglo-Saxon Chronicle* into French verse in the early twelfth century.

The policy of Ivarr, who seems to have led the force from at least 856 following the death of their leader Horm in a failed invasion of Anglesey,[9] seems to have been not to seize territory but to exist parasitically upon the backs of established kingdoms in the Insular world. He led his army backwards and forwards across Britain and Ireland, extracting tribute, and when necessary, fighting and defeating local kings. It may be that this mode of existence, of supporting a large army on the basis of tribute or protection extorted from neighbouring rulers, reflects the *modus operandi* established by the rulers of Walcheren with regard to Frisia and the surrounding lands in the 840s. At his death, in 873, the Irish chronicles described him as king of the heathens of all Ireland and Britain.[10] Apart from a parenthetic statement in the post-Conquest MS F, Ivarr is only named once in the *Anglo-Saxon Chronicle* and this reference is indirect, noticing the death in Devonshire of a man described as the brother of Ivarr and Healfdene.[11] At first sight this seems somewhat enigmatic but closer examination suggests that, at this period, Danish leaders are usually named in the *Anglo-Saxon Chronicle* only when it records their defeats and Ivarr did not lose battles.[12] Æðelweard's Latin chronicle of the later tenth century, however, concurs with the Irish record in ascribing leadership of the Great Army to Ivarr.

The killing of the Northumbrian kings Osberht and Ælle by the *Scaldingi* in 867 did not lead to the establishment of a Danish kingdom but to the appointment of an English king called Ecgbert to rule over the Northumbrians under loose *Scalding* overlordship. The received wisdom is that the appointment of Ecgbert heralded the partition of Northumbria into an English kingdom, roughly corresponding to ancient Bernicia, and a 'Viking kingdom of York', roughly corresponding to ancient Deira. Contemporary sources, however, do not make this distinction. This interpretation of events would seem to go back only as far as the early twelfth century and to have been the work of Symeon of Durham. In his *Libellus de Exordio*, a History of the Church of Durham, written at some point

---

[9] *AC* 853 [*recte* 855?] and *AU* 856.6.

[10] *AU* 873.3

[11] *ASC* 878. Gaimar names this brother as Ubba, but whether this is inference or was in the version of the *Chronicle* that he had before him is unclear.

[12] It is perhaps of interest that the first three Scandinavian leaders to be named in the *Annals of Ulster* were also only named at their deaths at the hands of the Irish: Saxolb (837.9); Tuirgéis (845.9); and Tomrair (848.5). The first 'live' Northman to be named is Stain (852.3). For the Irish chroniclers the appearance of rival groups of Northmen in the 850s created the need for their individuality to be acknowledged. After this their leaders are frequently named.

between 1104 and 1115, and probably before 1107, Symeon concluded his account of the killing of the Northumbrian kings Osberht and Ælle by the Vikings in 867 by adding the information:

> When these had been killed (as has been described), the Danes installed Ecgbert as king over the Northumbrians who had survived, but only over those who dwelt in the district north of the River Tyne, and then, under their dominion, did he rule.

A similar passage is found in the second set of annals in *Historia Regum Anglorum* where it forms an addition to a passage lifted, ultimately, from Asser's *Life of King Alfred* (transmitted via John of Worcester's *Chronicle*):

> After these events, the aforesaid pagans, under their dominion, made Ecgberht king. Ecgberht reigned, after this, over the Northumbrians beyond the Tyne, for six years.

This addition to Asser's account and the passage in *Libellus de Exordio* bear a close relationship with part of the thirteenth-century chronicler Roger of Wendover's account of these events. The relationship between the three texts is not altogether clear though. Roger, Symeon and one of the compilers of *Historia Regum Anglorum* clearly had access to material deriving from an annalistic chronicle recording events in ninth-century Northumbria. It is quite likely, though by no means certain, that the compiler of this phase of *Historia Regum Anglorum* was actually Symeon, although writing nearly twenty years after his work on *Libellus de Exordio*, and modern scholars are undecided as to the nature of the common source that Symeon and Roger may have shared or the degree to which differences are the result of their editorial choices or differences in their exemplars. Roger's version of the relevant passage is as follows:

> Then, since the kings of the Northumbrians had been killed, a certain Ecgbert, of English race, acquired the kingdom under the Danish power and ruled it for six years.

Roger's version clearly does not contain the limitation of Ecgbert's power beyond the Tyne, but is this because Symeon added this phrase for his own reasons or is it because Roger left it out? A possible solution to this conundrum is contained in the sequel to these events recorded once again in the same three sources and in John of Worcester's *Chronicle*. The account in *Libellus de Exordio* reads:

Meanwhile the Northumbrians expelled their king Ecgbert and archbishop Wulfhere from the province.

While John of Worcester, followed by *Historia Regum Anglorum*, reads:

The Northumbrians expelled their king Ecgbert and their archbishop Wulfhere.

What seems clear from this account of the end of Ecgbert's reign is that the rebellion that ousted him also ousted the archbishop of York. Since the northern boundary of the diocese of York lay on the Tees, more than fifty kilometres south of the Tyne, it seems unlikely that Ecgbert's dominion was restricted to the region to its north. The Northumbrian people in 873 were reacting against the same duumvirate which had dominated their politics since the 730s when the brothers Ecgbert and Eadbert held the archiepiscopal and royal offices in tandem. It should also be noted that none of our sources for this period, those just discussed and the *Anglo-Saxon Chronicle*, claim that the Danish army even stayed in Northumbria after the elevation of Ecgbert. They had passed on to the south of England to make a nuisance of themselves in Mercia and East Anglia.

Symeon of Durham[13]

Symeon of Durham has been one of the most influential writers of Northumbrian history in the early middle ages. Studies of his hand-writing suggest that he was taught to write in Normandy or an adjacent province in northern France and he was probably from this region. He probably came to Durham as a monk in the company of William of St Calais, the reforming bishop, in 1091. He was certainly in post before the death of Mael Coluim III in 1093 and was present, alongside the future Alexander I, at the translation of St Cuthbert's relics in 1104. Numerous manuscripts survive in Symeon's hand and he copied both important legal contemporary documents as well as historical and hagiographical texts. The latest texts in his hand are charters of Bishop Ranulf Flambard dating from 1128. As well as working as a scribe, or copyist, Symeon increasingly seems to have become interested in

---

[13] David Rollason's edition of *Libellus de Exordio* contains a fuller account of Symeon's career and works. The identification of Symeon of Durham with the scribe of the prayer to Columba was suggested to me by Kenneth Veitch. The prayer is translated in Thomas Clancy's *Triumph Tree*.

Symeon of Durham (*continued*)

contributing to historical works, initially simply modifying or glossing existing texts he eventually graduated to writing his own full length version of the history of the Church of St Cuthbert, *Libellus de Exordio atque Procursu istius hoc est Dunhelmensis Ecclesie*, which seems to have been completed by 1115. The fullest version of the composite *Historia Regum Anglorum* seems also to have reached its final form at Symeon's hand in 1129, although an autograph manuscript does not survive. Symeon's views have heavily coloured modern understandings of Northumbrian history.

A scribe called Symeon also made a copy of Adomnán's *Life of St Columba* at the behest of Alexander I of Scotland (1107–24) and his wife Sybilla (†1122) to which he appended a prayer to St Columba asking for blessings for Alexander, his queen, the 'Island of Bishops' (perhaps Lindisfarne or Durham itself), himself, and William the illuminator (in Symeon's time there was both an archdeacon of monks and another monk of this name at Durham).

As the most influential Northumbrian historian since Bede, Symeon had the means to alter history; as author of *Libellus de Exordio* and the editor of *Historia Regum Anglorum* he had the opportunity, but did he have a motive? I believe a case can be made that he did. In 1095, a decade or so before Symeon wrote *Libellus de Exordio*, Robert Mowbray had been deprived of the earldom of Northumberland and the far north of England was taken directly into royal control. One Robert Picot was appointed sheriff of Northumberland. Ultimately the sheriffdom of Northumberland was confined to the lands north of the Tyne and shrieval authority between the Tyne and the Tees was left in the hands of the bishop of Durham.

As a result of these turbulent times County Durham today sports brown signs declaring it 'The Land of the Prince Bishops', yet it is far from clear that the idea enshrined in this appellation, the idea of a circumscribed contiguous block in which the episcopacy exercised secular power, was something to which the *familia* of St Cuthbert had aspired before the time of Symeon. The main pre-Conquest statement of the aspirations of the *familia*, *Historia de Sancto Cuthberto*, put together at some point between the mid-tenth and the mid-eleventh centuries, indicates that their Church had interests stretching the length of the former dioceses of Lindisfarne and Hexham (the joint heir of which it claimed to be) from the Forth to the Tees with a few estates to the south of this in the diocese of York. *Historia de Sancto Cuthberto* does indeed claim secular jurisdiction for the bishops in a number of vast tracts, but these are scattered across the diocese. Similarly this pre-Conquest text does not seem to have seen the secular power in Northumbria as divided.

Expelled by their own people, King Ecgbert and Archbishop Wulfhere went into exile and the following year, 873, on Ecgbert's death, Wulfhere returned and Ricsige was elected king of Northumbria. He ruled for three years. Ecgbert's death, however, coincided with that of Ivarr, and the policy of the *Scaldingi* began to change. The following winter the army moved, as it had done every winter, on this occasion from Torksey in Lindsey, up the River Trent to Repton, site of a royal church-settlement and mausoleum of the Mercians. At this point they expelled King Burgred, who abdicated to go on pilgrimage to Rome, and set up Ceolwulf in his stead as king of Mercia. From Repton, however, things began to change. The army, which was now headed by four kings, Healfdene, Guthrum, Oscytel and Anwend (presumably close kinsmen), divided.

Healfdene took his men into Northumbria, which he used as a base for attacks on the Britons of the Clyde and the Picts. In 876 we are told that Healfdene shared out, or divided up, the lands of the Northumbrians and that they either ploughed or harried (the difference is but a single character in Old English: *ergende* or *hergende*) and supported themselves. This event is usually taken as the beginning of proper settlement, and indeed Asser's version of this event is perhaps more explicit and perhaps more telling since it identifies Healfdene as king of at least a part of the Northumbrians rather than simply one of the kings with the *here* or the *Dene*. It should be noted, however, that at this point Asser is following the *Anglo-Saxon Chronicle* closely and his reading of that text is simply that, a reading. A salutary warning can be found almost immediately following this passage. Asser's text of the *Chronicle* seems to have been missing the entry for the year 877 and as a result of this he has the Danish attack on Chippenham being directed from Exeter, where the southern portion of the army spent the winter of 876, rather than from Mercia, to which kingdom, the extant copies of the *Chronicle* tell us, they had relocated the previous year. Asser himself, writing in the 890s, had not even been living in England in the 870s (he was from Dyfed in southwest Wales). Healfdene's sharing out of Northumbria does, however, seem to have coincided with the death of King Ricsige, who one chronicler tells us died of a broken heart, but Ricsige was succeeded by another Englishman, Ecgbert. Since our sources are unanimous in stating that Healfdene entered Northumbria at the mouth of the Tyne and used it as a base for harrying the Picts and Strathclyders it would seem very strange

if his kingdom were limited to Yorkshire and Ricsige and Ecgbert ruled
an independent territory between his base on the Tyne and his victims on
the Forth. Asser presumably knew that Healfdene was a king and also
knew of the native Northumbrian kings and had difficulty squaring this
with his own world view.[14]

In the event, in 878 Healfdene was driven away from Northumbria by
his own army (apparently for smelling badly, if we are to believe the
Historia de Sancto Cuthberto) and the army was left without a royal
leader.[15] The following year Ecgbert also died, and after a brief interregnum an Anglo-Danish kingdom was created with the election of the
Danish prince Guðfrið son of Harðacnut at the unidentified site of
Oswigesdun. Following Healfdene's expulsion the Danish army had been
left without a candidate to replace him, presumably because they put
great store in genuine royal blood. The head of the *familia* of St Cuthbert,
Eadred of Carlisle, however, located Guðfrið (apparently miraculously),
who had been sold into slavery to an English widow, at Whittingham on
the River Aln, halfway between the Tyne and the Tweed, redeemed him
and presented him to the Danish army. Guðfrið had converted to
Christianity while in captivity and this factor, together with the advocacy
of the Church of St Cuthbert, created the opportunity for establishing
the first Anglo-Danish kingdom in which a single king was recognised by
both the army of the *Scaldingi* and by the Northumbrians.[16] This Anglo-
Danish kingdom of Northumbria seems to have been created as a result
of fortuitous simultaneous interregna in both the *here* and the English
kingdom. The Northumbrian king-list preserved in the text known as *De
Primo Saxonum Adventu* gives the second Ecgbert, who succeeded Ricsige
in 876, a two-year reign, and although *Historia Regum Anglorum* claims
that he continued to rule north of the Tyne while Guðfrið ruled at York,
this is clearly a twelfth-century addition to a passage drawn from
Symeon's *Libellus de Exordio*, which makes no such claim. Once again its
aim seems to have been to legitimise the comital power claimed by
bishops of Durham in the Anglo-Norman period and to deny claims for
jurisdiction in the region between the Tyne and the Tees made by earls
or sheriffs of Northumbria as then constituted. There are clear indications that Guðfrið's jurisdiction stretched as far as Lindisfarne. What

---

[14] By the 890s, when Asser was writing, a Danish ruler had indeed become king of the
Northumbrians.
[15] *Historia de Sancto Cuthberto* §§ 12 and 13.
[16] Guðfrið is described as a boy so, bearing in mind that the *Scaldingi* had been in
Britain for about fifteen years at this point, he may have had an English mother.

was perhaps most significant in determining Guðfrið's ability to unite the *Scaldingi* and the Northumbrians was the fact that, while in captivity, he had become a Christian. When he died, nearly twenty years later in 894 or 895, he was buried in the cathedral church at York.

NORTHUMBRIA AFTER 867, PROBLEMS AND PROBABILITIES

Between the first assault by the *Scaldingi* in 867 and the death of Guðfrið in 894 or 895 Northumbria was ruled by four kings:

Ecgbert	867–73
Ricsige	873–6
Ecgbert II	876–8
Guðfrið	878/80–894/5

Although the chronicle record for the accession of these kings is somewhat more reliable than that for their predecessors, we know little more about them than their reign length. The three native kings are not even supplied with the usual patronymics. Our understanding of the reigns of these kings is also hampered by the fact that no royal coinage was produced in Northumbria during their reigns. Earlier in this chapter we saw coinage being used in a rather unorthodox fashion as a corrective on potentially defective chronicles. Numismatics, however, are more normally employed by historians in twofold fashion. First, the quantity and regularity of modification of coinage bear witness to the degree of monetarisation which a given economy is experiencing along with the degree of central control of the money supply. Second, the distribution of coinage recovered bears some witness to the political extent of the economy of the kingdom. Thus, in our case the regularity of coinage being recovered from the episcopal site at Whithorn right up until the second reign of King Æðelred, and the presence there of at least one coin from the reign of his successor Osberht, one of the kings killed in 867, bears witness to the continued integration of Whithorn into the Northumbrian kingdom right up to the time of the *Scalding* intervention. Between this date and the appearance of the coins of Guðfrið's successors, Sigfrið, Cnut and Healfdene, which can only be dated as a sequence occurring sometime between 894 and 910, the character of the site at Whithorn changed radically, suggesting a major disjuncture, probably to be associated with the abandonment of the episcopal see. Unfortunately, without coinage in the vital period we cannot say for sure whether this abandonment was closer to 870 or to 910.

The abandonment of Whithorn as an episcopal see, not to be revived before the twelfth century, may not have simply reflected heathen military action or occupation. It will be recalled that at the beginning of our period there were three Bernician sees: Lindisfarne; Hexham; and Whithorn. By the end of the ninth century there was only one, and this not located at any of these places but instead at Chester-le-Street. Unfortunately for us, our understanding of how this came about is obscured by the fact that the documentation produced by this see in the tenth, eleventh and twelfth centuries strove to emphasise the continuity of the see with that of Lindisfarne, the cradle of Bernician Christianity and, in some sense, the premier see under the old dispensation. As with other aspects of the history of Northumbria in this period historians have been very much at the mercy of the twelfth-century writer Symeon of Durham both through his own *Libellus de Exordio* and through his work as editor of *Historia Regum Anglorum*. The one substantial earlier text, *Historia de Sancto Cuthberto*, surviving as a mid-eleventh-century recension of a mid-tenth-century composition, does provide a corrective view, and this has been highlighted by its most recent editor, Ted Johnson South.[17] Johnson South draws attention to §9 of *Historia de Sancto Cuthberto* which claims that:

> . . . Bishop Ecgred [c. 830–45], transported a certain church, originally built by St Aidan in the time of king Oswald, from the isle of Lindisfarne to Norham [-on-Tweed] and there rebuilt it, and translated to that place the body of St Cuthbert and that of King Ceolwulf and gave the villa itself to the holy confessor [Cuthbert] with two other villas, Jedburgh and Old Jedburgh and whatever pertains to them, from Dunion Hill as far as Jedmouth, and from there to Wilton, and from there beyond the hill towards the south.

Johnson South points out that this passage almost certainly relates the translation of the episcopal see from Lindisfarne to Norham as St Cuthbert's body was probably the principal relic of the see, Aidan's original wooden church being another. We might recall the plans made to remove Columba's relics to Kells, discussed in the previous chapter. Symeon of Durham, however, in his work, mentions only the translation

---

[17] T. Johnson South, ed., *Historia de Sancto Cuthberto: a History of Saint Cuthbert and a Record of his Patrimony* (Woodbridge, 2002). Henceforth *HSC*.

of King Ceolwulf's body and makes no reference Lindisfarne losing either the relics or the see as early as Ecgred's time.[18] The southern boundary of the diocese of Lindisfarne ran up the Aln and then along the line of the Cheviots; and the diocese comprised, broadly speaking, the northernmost quarter of Northumberland, Roxburghshire, Berwickshire and East and Mid-Lothian. Chester-le-Street, however, to which the see was transferred at some point in Guðfrið's reign, lies, within the bounds of the diocese of Hexham, which extended south from Lindisfarne's southern boundary to the Tees and probably extended west of the Pennines, its southern boundary being preserved in the old county boundary between Westmorland and Cumberland.[19] Clearly by the time St Cuthbert's body arrived at Chester-le-Street these two sees had been combined.

There is a possible hint that this combination of the Bernician diocese may have occurred earlier and may have included Whithorn as well as Hexham and Lindisfarne/Norham. We have already noted that the head of the *familia* of St Cuthbert at the time of Guðfrið's election to the kingship was Eadred, abbot of Carlisle.[20] We are told later in *Historia de Sancto Cuthberto* that Eadred, together with Bishop Eardwulf, had tried to flee with St Cuthbert's body to Ireland but that a miraculous storm had prevented them from going, much to the relief of all the saint's 'people' who had accompanied them to the mouth of the Derwent, near modern Workington.[21] The leading role played by an abbot of Carlisle in these stories is curious. It should be recalled, however, that Carlisle was the only proper Romano-British city in Bernicia and also that such cities were deemed appropriate places for episcopal sees. -It may be that at some point after Ecgred's transfer of the northernmost see to Norham a further consolidation occurred and a single Bernician see was created at Carlisle, which, with its Roman past and monuments and its defensible potential, would have seemed an appropriate setting. Carlisle's location some thirty-five miles west of Hexham might suggest that the diocese of Whithorn was also included in this schema.[22] The events of 867 might have provided the impetus for such a consolidation of sees, but we cannot

---

[18] *HSC* 96–101.

[19] Charles Phythian-Adams, in his *Land of the Cumbrians* (Aldershot, 1996), envisages a southwestern extension of the see of Lindisfarne which encircles Hexham to the west and southwest. I find the map that this produces incredible.

[20] *HSC* §13.

[21] *HSC* §20.

[22] We know from the life of St Cuthbert that there was already a major church-settlement patronised by royalty at Carlisle by 685.

be certain of this, and unrecorded heathen attacks or indeed the Pictish attacks on the diocese of Lindisfarne in the 850s might provide alternative contexts. One clue exists that such a consolidation may have happened by 854. Under this year Part I of the *Historia Regum Anglorum* records:

> In the sixth year after the birth of king Alfred, in the reign of King Osbert over the Northumbrians, Wulfhere received the *pallium*, and was confirmed in the archbishopric of York, and Eardwulf received the bishopric of Lindisfarne; to which pertained: *Lugobalia*, that is *Luel* (now called Carlisle) and Norham, that anciently was called Ubbanford, and also all of those churches between the river called Tweed and the southern Tyne, and beyond the desert to the West, pertained at this time to the aforesaid church, and these estates, *Carnam* and *Culterham* and the two Jedworths and the south-side of Teviot which bishop Ecgred donated; and Melrose and *Tigbrethingham* and Abercorn, to the western extent, Edinburgh and Pefferham and Aldham, and Tyninghame and Coldingham and Tillmouth and Norham, as said above . . .[23]

That this list begins with Carlisle, followed by Norham, is very suggestive. That it is genuinely old is suggested by the fact that *Lugubalia* has been glossed twice, first with *Luel* (in use in the ninth century) and then with Carlisle (first noted in the eleventh). The fact that all the lands between the Tweed and the southern Tyne are included, as well as those beyond the 'desert to the West' (the Pennines?) shows that this list postdates the merger of Lindisfarne and Hexham. That the list begins and ends with Norham may suggest that when its prototype was drawn up Norham was the seat of the bishop, but the appearance of the rather sententious *Lugubalia* at the head of the list may indicate that Carlisle had usurped this position.

Following the attempted escape to Ireland, Eadred and Eardwulf took the saint's relics to Crayke, not far from York and, after a few months there, negotiated the establishment of a new see at Chester-le-Street with Guðfrið. *Historia de Sancto Cuthberto* claims that the period of wandering without a fixed see lasted seven years and implies that the establishment of the see at Chester-le-Street occurred in Guðfrið's first year as king. The

---

[23] The text has been most recently printed by T. Johnson South in *Historia De Sancto Cuthberto* (Woodbridge, 2002).

year of his election is generally given as 883 in the later sources (perhaps, as Johnson South suggests, on the basis of the seven-year period of wandering and the notion, first expressed in the twelfth century, that Healfdene's expedition to the Tyne precipitated the wandering), but his reign length is regularly given as fourteen years and we know that he died in 894 or 895, so it was probably 880 or 881. If this was the case then a seven-year period would begin in 873, the year that the Northumbrians expelled Ecgbert I and Archbishop Wulfhere. The upheaval associated with these events may also have provided a context for the establishment of a see at Carlisle. Alternatively, the linkage between the election of Guðfrið and the translation of the see may be spurious. All we can really say is that the see was established at Chester-le-Street during Guðfrið's reign (c. 880–95).

What is perhaps more interesting for understanding what was happening to Northumbria in this period is the question of why, c. 880, Abbot Eadred and Bishop Eardwulf would abandon the Carlisle area, first attempting to flee overseas and then taking refuge near York. Was this because of problems in Bernicia as a whole or was it due to more specific stresses in the Solway region? It would be tempting to read into these events the collapse of Northumbrian control or at least English rule in the Solway region, but evidence of one sort or another weighs against this being the period in which this happened. Bishop Eardwulf of Chester-le-Street, we are told, died at about the same time as Alfred the Great (†899) and his successor Cutheard accepted the see in the time of Alfred's son Edward. We should be wary of taking such crude synchronisms as indicators of precise dates and, indeed, they may only have been computed after the Community of St Cuthbert fell under West Saxon rule in the mid-tenth century. Symeon in his *Libellus de Exordio* says that Cutheard succeeded in the nineteenth year after the move to Chester-le-Street and that he died in the fifteenth year of his episcopate. As we have seen the establishment of the see at Chester-le-Street was located in Guðfrið's reign and that this was probably c. 880–95. Thus, Cutheard's first year will have fallen in the range 898–912 and his death in the range 912–26.[24]

It is to Cutheard's episcopate that three episodes are noted in *Historia de Sancto Cuthberto* which may relate to the falling away of the west from the Northumbrian kingdom. In the first of these we are told that Tilred

[24] One apparently unselfconscious synchronism in the *Libellus* dates Edward the Elder's death to the seventh year of Cutheard's successor Tilred. If this were correct it would put Cutheard's episcopate in the range c. 904–18. Using this chronology then the seven-year wandering would begin at the end of the reign of Ecgbert II, the last Anglo-Saxon king.

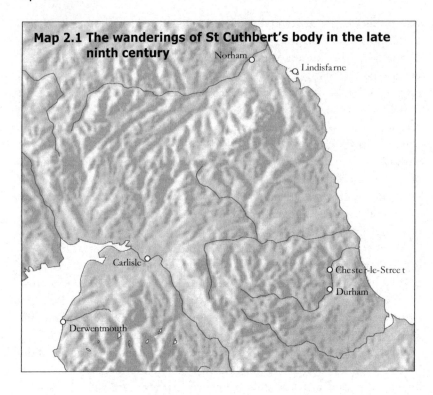

Map 2.1 The wanderings of St Cuthbert's body in the late ninth century

abbot of Heversham (just north of Lancaster) purchased the estate at *Iodene* (probably Castle Eden in Country Durham) and gave it to St Cuthbert so that he could be admitted into the *Familia* and be made abbot of Norham.[25] It is possible that this is an account of ecclesiastical pluralism, and that Tilred was simultaneously abbot of Heversham and Norham, but it is equally possibly that he had abandoned Heversham. In the following chapter we are told that Alfred, son of Beorhtwulf, 'fleeing pirates, came over the mountains to the west and sought the mercy of St Cuthbert and Bishop Cutheard so that they might present him with some lands.'[26] The lands then listed amount, by Johnson South's calculation, to some 6,900 hectares, a considerable estate. This account is pretty unambiguous in its broad meaning, but exactly where across the mountains is intended is less clear: Lancashire, western Cumberland, the Solway plain or Dumfries and Galloway could all fit the description 'over the mountains to the west'. Confirmation that some land west of the

---

[25] *HSC* §21.
[26] *HSC* §22.

mountains was still in English hands in Bishop Cutheard's time can be found in the account in chapter 24 of Eadred son of Ricsige (perhaps a son of the king who reigned in the 870s?), who having crossed west over the mountains to slay the *princeps* Eardwulf and elope with his wife, fled to the *familia* of Cuthbert and Bishop Cutheard for sanctuary and land. The implication is that Eadred was from the east but that he had English enemies in the west who could have pursued him back east had he not had Cuthbert's protection. These accounts indicate that until at least the first decade of the tenth century Northumbrian society remained intact in at least some part of the kingdom west of the Pennines. In Whithorn and its neighbourhood the ecclesiastical sculpture, mostly in the form of high crosses and including some pieces with Old English runic inscriptions, also seems to have continued to the very end of the ninth century if not a little beyond. Of course, it is possible that far-flung regions such as Galloway and Ayrshire might have retained their Northumbrian character but failed to recognise the Anglo–Danish kings, but there is nothing in the evidence that makes this scenario more likely than the alternative.

One major transformation was beginning to take place, however. At some point, probably under either Healfdene or Guðfrið, the army that the *Scaldingi* had brought with them began to settle down. The evidence for this is largely in the form of place-names, personal names and later dialect, all of which indicate a massive settlement of Old Norse speakers in parts of Northumbria – at this stage probably mostly within Yorkshire, although not evenly distributed through the country. Philologists and historians argue endlessly about how large or small a number of settlers would have been necessary to effect the changes which are apparent in the evidence, and precise figures are probably irretrievable: suffice to say, quite a large number of Danes must have been involved in the late ninth-century settlement. Archaeologists have expressed anxiety that the amount of Danish material culture retrieved from Yorkshire in this period is relatively small, but we should remember that most of the men in the Great Army had probably left Denmark twenty-five years or more before they began to settle in the late 870s or 880s.[27] Their Danish clothes and equipment would have worn out and been replaced several times before they finally settled down. These issues of language shift and demography will be looked at in more detail in a later chapter. We need note only that linguistically, at least, Yorkshire, and to some extent

---

[27] Remember that the original settlement at Walcheren, in Friesland occurred in 841, the expedition to Ireland in 851 and the combined operation from Ireland and Friesland to England in 865.

Lancashire, began to have more in common with areas of the English north midlands, where Danes also settled in great numbers, than with northern Northumbria.

NORTHUMBRIA C. 900

By 900 Northumbria had suffered an enormous trauma of invasion and transformation but, so far as we can see, the integrity of the kingdom had held out. Pictish attacks in the northeast had not led to boundary changes and while the far northwest, broadly Ayrshire, is a complete blank, the Whithorn area seems to have remained within the kingdom, and under a new Anglo-Danish *Scalding* dynasty coin production, which had ceased for a quarter of a century, was beginning to return. Both the archbishops of York and the bishops of the newly re-unified diocese of Bernicia had established good relations with the *Scaldingi*, and the Church was able to assert its rights to old lands and to acquire new. At the dawn of the tenth century there is just the hint that something unsettling was happening on the western fringes of the kingdom, but by and large, after a sticky patch in the late 860s and 870s, things seemed to be getting back to normal.

Last Days of the Pictish Kingdom (839–89)

We left Pictavia in 839 contemplating the defeat of the men of Fortriu and the killing by the heathens of Wen son of Onuist, king of Fortriu, his brother Bran and Áed son of Boanta, king of Dál Riata. The following sixty years would see the disappearance of the Picts from the historical record but how and why they disappeared is far from clear. This chapter must thus begin with a brief discussion of the source material for this key period in early Scottish history. This is not easy territory but it is unavoidable if the reader is to grasp the nature of the problems we face in constructing a coherent narrative.

The sources of Scottish History for the late ninth and early tenth centuries

Until very recently the basic narrative for this period has been derived from John of Fordun's *Chronica Gentis Scottorum* written in the 1380s. Fordun probably had access to fewer contemporary or near contemporary sources than the modern scholar and he made up for the shortcomings of his sources with imagination and legendary writings from the recent past. What follows will attempt to abandon Fordun as a guide before we even start. This may mean that the reader will miss some familiar legends, but legends they are and they have no place here.

Thankfully, for most of this period we still have the Irish chronicles, the *Annals of Ulster* (*AU*) and *Chronicum Scotorum* (*CS*), both based on the 'Chronicle of Ireland' which at this point is a contemporary source, being written in the Irish east midlands. Where *AU* and *CS* agree the entries were certainly in the 'Chronicle of Ireland'; where they contain unique entries later interpolation or corruption (that is, accidental mistakes) are

---

The sources of Scottish History for the late ninth and early tenth centuries (*continued*)

possible but not certain. The *Anglo-Saxon Chronicle* is also a contemporary source for this period but it contains very few entries of significance for Scottish history, and much the same can be said of the Welsh *Annales Cambriae*.

The fullest source for Scottish affairs for this period, however, is a particularly troublesome text sometimes called simply the 'Scottish Chronicle' or the 'Older Scottish Chronicle' and more recently, following the coinage of Professor David Dumville, the *Chronicle of the Kings of Alba* (*CKA*). Unfortunately, although this text covers the period from the mid-ninth to the late tenth centuries and probably contains some information drawn from contemporary or near contemporary sources, it has come down to us through a complex history of transmission and revision. Some scholars see fit to treat it as a more or less contemporary source of equal value to the Irish chronicles, while others recognise severe limitations on its reliability. Much of the present chapter will be concerned with comparing and contrasting *CKA* with the truly contemporary chronicles and examining clues within its own form and language to decide what we can accept and what we can not.

AN INTRODUCTION TO THE 'CHRONICLE OF THE KINGS OF ALBA'

The text known as the *Chronicle of the Kings of Alba* or the 'Older Scottish Chronicle' has come down to us in a single medieval manuscript. This manuscript was written in about 1360, probably at the Carmelite priory at York, at the behest of one Robert of Poppleton, a brother of that house who would, in 1364, become prior of the Carmelite house at Hulne, near Alnwick, in Northumberland.[1] The manuscript is now preserved in the Bibliothèque Nationale in Paris.[2] The Poppleton manuscript (as it is known) contains no original compositions but instead is a compilation of historical and geographical treatises, some by well known authors such as Orosius or Gerald of Wales. The whole manuscript contains

---

[1] The manuscript contains a papal decretal issued in August 1357 which provides a *terminus post quem* for its production.

[2] Paris, Bibliothèque Nationale, Ms Latin 4126.

296 folios.[3] Seven short texts relating to early Scottish history are found together running from folio 26 verso to folio 32 recto. These comprise:

(1) *De Situ Albaniae*: a rather abstract description of Albania or Scotia, by which is meant explicitly the mainland north of the Forth.

(2) A text entitled *Cronica de origine antiquorum Pictorum* which is largely extracted from the seventh-century work of the Spanish scholar Isidore of Seville, with some additions from a twelfth-century recension of *Historia Brittonum*.

(3) A list of Pictish kings (the so-called 'A' version) comprising a pseudo-historical prologue and early section in Gaelic orthography followed by the bulk of the list in British orthography ending with one 'Bred'. This king-list is extremely closely related to those found in the Irish manuscripts Bodleian Laud 610; Dublin, Trinity College 1336; and Dublin, Royal Irish Academy Stowe D ii 1. In all three cases it seems that the king-list was originally appended to a version of *Lebor Bretnach*, the Gaelic translation and adaptation of *Historia Brittonum*. In all these Irish manuscripts the king-list continues beyond 'Bred' and through 'Cinaed filius Alpin' to 'Maelcoluim mac Dondchatha' (†1093).[4]

(4) The text we are concerned with here, being a chronicle covering the reigns of kings of Pictavia from 'Kinadius filius Alpini' to 'Doniualdus filius Constantini', and of Albania from 'Constantinus filius Edii' to 'Cinadius filius Maelcolaim'.

(5) *Cronica regum Scottorum, ccc.xiiii. annorum*, a king-list apparently compiled in the reign of King William (1165–1214): his reign length is left blank and it starts with 'Fergus filius Eric [*sic.*]', the legendary founder of Dál Riata, Fergus mac Erc.

(6) A pedigree for King William, tracing his descent back through earlier kings of Alba and Dál Riata to legendary Irish figures and eventually to 'Adam, son of the Living God.'

(7) An account of the founding of the church at 'Rigmund', that is, Rígmonaid/St Andrews, which it ascribes to 'Ungus filius Hurguist',

---

[3] It is traditional in manuscript studies to write and speak of folios rather than pages. Each folio comprises both the right-hand facing page, the *recto*, and its reverse, the *verso*. Thus, typically, the first side encountered when opening a codex, or volume, would be 1 recto, the next side 1 verso, the next 2 recto and so on.

[4] For the suggestion that *Lebor Bretnach*, including the king-list, was produced in eastern Scotland in Mael Coluim's reign see T. O. Clancy, 'Scotland, the "Nennian" recension of *Historia Brittonum* and *Lebor Bretnach*', in S. Taylor, ed., *Kings, Clerics and Chronicles in Scotland, 500–1297* (Dublin, 2000), 87–107.

a Pictish king. Another version of this text survives which makes it clear that it was written in St Andrews c. 1100.[5]

A diplomatic edition of the Scottish pieces in the Poppleton manuscript has been published (without translation) by Marjorie Anderson in her *Kings and Kingship in Early Scotland* and she has described them at length in an earlier article for the *Scottish Historical Review*.[6] Items (5) and (6) were clearly composed during the reign of King William and item (1), *De Situ Albaniae*, cites as its authority Bishop Andrew of Caithness, who witnesses royal charters from 1147 and who died in 1184, and is thus of about the same date. Item (2) appears to cite a version of *Historia Brittonum* that came into existence in William's reign (though not necessarily in Scotland). While item (7) probably originally dates to c. 1100 it may well have found itself deployed during William's reign when the *ecclesia Scoticana* was struggling to have its independence from the province of York recognised by the papacy. Item (1) appears to cite items (4), (5) and (6) and may have used information drawn from item (3). The inference has to be made that all seven pieces were brought together during the reign of William, probably in his later years, and probably by the author of *De Situ Albaniae*. Minor scribal errors suggest that at least one copying of the collection lies between the Wilhelmite compilation and the production of the Poppleton manuscript.

Item (4), our chronicle, has been edited with a translation under the name 'The Scottish Chronicle' by Benjamin Hudson.[7] It has also been discussed at length by a number of scholars.[8] None of the titles accorded it by modern scholars are particularly helpful: 'The Scottish Chronicle' is far too vague and yet Dumville and Broun's preferred *Chronicle of the Kings of Alba* (*CKA*) skirts over the fact that half the kings whose reigns

[5] D. Broun, 'The Church of St Andrews and its foundation legend in the early twelfth century: recovering the full text of version A of the foundation legend', in S. Taylor, ed., *Kings, Clerics and Chronicles in Scotland, 500–1297* (Dublin, 2000), 108–14, and 'The Church and the origins of Scottish independence in the twelfth century', *Record of the Scottish Church History Society* 31 (2001), 1–35 at 31–4.

[6] M. O. Anderson, *Kings and Kingship in Early Scotland* (Edinburgh, 1973), 235–60, and 'Scottish Materials in the Paris Manuscript, Bib. Nat., Latin 4126', *Scottish Historical Review* 28 (1949), 31–42.

[7] B. T. Hudson, 'The Scottish chronicle', *Scottish Historical Review* 77 (1998), 129–61.

[8] E.g., M. Miller, 'The last century of Pictish succession', *Scottish Studies* 23 (1979), 39–67; E. J. Cowan, 'The Scottish chronicle in the Poppleton manuscript', *The Innes Review* 32 (1981), 3–21; D. Broun, 'The birth of Scottish history', *Scottish Historical Review* 76 (1997), 4–22; D. N. Dumville, 'The Chronicle of the Kings of Alba', in S. Taylor, ed., *Kings, Clerics and Chronicle in Scotland, 500–1297* (Dublin, 2000), 73–86.

are covered are described as ruling over 'Pictavia' and it is only from the time of the seventh king onwards that 'Albania', for which Latin construction 'Alba' is the vernacular Gaelic form, appears in the text. What all the kings do appear to have in common is descent from one Alpín and this should perhaps be reflected in the nomenclature, though I hesitate to introduce a new term into such a confused mêlée.[9] Our main problem with using this text, however, lies not in our indecision about how to label it but in our inability to determine its fundamental nature.

CKA (if I must!) is not an annalistic chronicle after the fashion of the Irish or Northumbrian chronicles, or the *Anglo-Saxon Chronicle*, but is, instead, structured around a regnal list. Accounts of the reigns of twelve kings are presented in sequence and the opening sentence of each account, saving the last, gives us the number of years the king is said to have reigned. The account of the final reign begins with the same formula but leaves a space where the number of years (in Roman numerals) should be added. This has led most commentators to presume that the king-list was abandoned during the reign of this king 'Cinadius filius Maelcolaim'. It seems odd that such a simple *lacuna* was not filled during one of the several copyings of the text but this seems, none the less, to be the best explanation. No absolute dates whatsoever are found in the chronicle, but events are sometimes dated to the precise year within a reign or to a precise interval since the preceding event mentioned. Calendar dates must thus be supplied when events within the chronicle are noted elsewhere and by calculating the intervals. Such a methodology, however, demonstrates that not all the intervals or reign lengths noted can be accurate. In some cases this may be due to simple copyists' errors, in others to more complex problems. Some events are simply dated to a period within the reign of a given king but without a specific year being noted. As soon as we recognise that the basic chronological structure was a regnal list then we should immediately become aware of the fact that all the material other than the king's names, patronymics (where supplied) and reign lengths are secondary and are not the result of contemporary annalistic recording. It may be that some of this material was derived by the author of the text from an annalistic chronicle, but if so it has been spliced together with the king-list and we cannot be certain that it has been entered in the correct place.

Further evidence suggests that the splicing of the king-list and the other material was not necessarily the product of a single phase of

[9] It is perhaps worth noting that in the one place in the chronicle where it fundamentally disagrees with the other surviving king-lists it supplies a king descended from Alpín in place of the one king found elsewhere who was not.

composition. Although *CKA* is, as it stands, a Latin text, it, in common with many documents from the Gaelic-speaking world, contains a liberal mixing of Gaelic forms and even short phrases in Gaelic. This has led some earlier scholars, notably the great W. F. Skene, to suppose that the text was originally written in Gaelic and then translated. This is unlikely to have been the case, but it may be that its source material included some texts which mixed their language. An example of such a mixed text from the *Annals of Ulster* should serve to give a flavour of this:

> *AU* 864.4   Muiredach *m. Neill,* **abbas** *Lughmaidh ala n-aile cell* **moritur**.
>
> Muiredach *son of Niall,* **abbot** *of Lugbad* and *other churches,* **dies**.

In this example bold indicates Latin and italics indicate Gaelic. Note that, as well as the words 'mac' and 'other churches' being in Gaelic, a Gaelic genitive is also used for Niall and Lugbad. This is particularly striking in the case of Lugbad which is governed by the Latin *abbas* and might have been rendered with a Latin genitive such as 'Lugbadi'. In the case of *CKA* the degree of mixing of forms varies considerably in different parts of the text. In the tenth reign the name of the king and his rival are fully translated into Latin, Dub, 'black', being rendered *Niger* and Cúlen, 'little dog', being rendered *Caniculus*. In the account of the next reign, however, the successful rival, Cúlen, is accorded his real name. Surely these two accounts cannot be by the same hand? Professor Dumville has also noted the inconsistency with which the name represented by Domnall in early Gaelic and Donald in modern Scots and English appears. It is found in the expected early medieval Gaelic form at the end of the seventh reign and in the eighth and tenth reigns, but in forms that are more redolent of twelfth- and thirteenth-century texts in the accounts of the second, sixth and early seventh reigns. Is this the result of inconsistent modernisation by a twelfth- or thirteenth-century copyist, or does it bear witness to a late origin of the text in its present form?[10] A book of this sort is not the place to deconstruct a complicated text of this kind at length, but the reader should be warned of its complexities and be prepared to encounter some of them over the course of this chapter and those which follow.

[10] Dumville, 'Chronicle of the Kings of Alba', at 83–4. Is it worth noting that, by and large, the later forms appear in the Pictavia section and the earlier forms in the Albania section?

To summarise the nature of *CKA* as a whole: it comprises a king-list covering twelve reigns; this king-list may have originally ended with reign nine before being continued one reign at a time; to this king-list has been added information. Some of this information appears to be derived from chronicles very similar to surviving Irish chronicles, while other information appears to be more discursive or subjective in nature. Since we can be fairly certain that the text had reached its present form (barring minor scribal errors and emendations) by c. 1200 the question we must ask of every detail preserved in *CKA* is: does it derive from a tenth-century construction of the king-list-based chronicle or is it more likely to reflect a folkloric or literary addition of the eleventh or twelfth centuries? Now we have got that straight we can return to the narrative.

CINAED SON OF ALPÍN OR CINIOD SON OF ELPHIN?

After the disastrous defeat at the hands of the Northmen in 839 the next mention of the Picts in the Irish chronicle record is the notice of the death of Cinaed son of Alpín, *rex Pictorum*, under the year 858.[11] If we were entirely dependent upon the chronicle record we would imagine that this Cinaed was the successor to Wen son of Onuist, but the Pictish king-list preserved in the Poppleton manuscript follows Wen with Wrad son of Bargoit, who is given a reign length of three years (839–41?) and then Bred, with no patronymic, who is given a reign length of only one year (842?). In the Poppleton manuscript this Bred ends the list, but in the closely related king-lists preserved in manuscripts of *Lebor Bretnach* Bred is indeed followed by Cinaed son of Alpín who is accorded a reign length of sixteen years. Working back from the death date of 858 found in the *Annals of Ulster*, this gives us a starting point for Cinaed's reign in 842, so our chronology seems sound.

Our problems begin when we turn to *CKA*. Cinaed's reign is the first reign recorded in this chronicle and the account of it reads as follows:

Kinadius, then, the son of Alpin, first of the Scots, ruled this Pictavia happily for xvi years. Pictavia, moreover, was named from the Picts, whom, as we have said *Cinadius* destroyed. For God condescended as reward for their wickedness, to make them alien from, and dead to, their heritage; they who not only spurned the

[11] *AU* 858.2.

Lord's mass and precept but also did not wish to be equal to others in the law of justice. He, indeed, two years before he came to Pictavia, assumed the kingship of Dál Riata. In the seventh year of his reign he transported the relics of Saint Columba to the church he had built, and he invaded, six times, 'Saxony' and burned Dunbar and overthrew Melrose. Also the Britons burned Dunblane and the *Danari* wasted Pictavia to Clunie and Dunkeld. He died eventually from a tumour before the ides of February, on a Tuesday, in the palace of Forteviot.[12]

This appears to be a full and detailed account, but when was it written: a hundred years after Cinaed's death; when the king-list was put together; or in King William's reign, more than 300 years after his death? There are a number of things one might note. First, there is the word *Danari* used for the attackers who waste Pictavia to Clunie and Dunkeld. This word is a Latin plural formed from the Gaelic word *Danair*, itself based upon Old Norse *Danir*. It first appears in the Irish chronicles only in the 980s, and there it seems to denote actual royal Danish forces, in contrast to other groups of Vikings. In Cinaed's reign the Northmen most active on the Insular world were most likely to have been either from the Norwegian Westland or to have been *Scaldingi*. In English language sources *Dene* seems to have been used as a generic for all Northmen, but had English usage been the source of this terminology in *CKA* then we might have expected Latin *Dani*. Second there is the phrase 'whom, as we have said, Cinadius destroyed', relating to the Picts. This does not appear to be strictly true. We have not been told this before. This is after all the beginning of the account of his reign; it follows immediately on from his reign length (the first statement in all the reigns). Clearly any prior account of Cinaed's destruction of the Picts was not part of this chronicle, so the passage to which it alludes must also be a later gloss. It seems likely that either our compiler of c. 1200 found *CKA* in company with an account of the destruction of the Picts which he chose not to include in his compilation, or that he did include such an account which a subsequent copyist omitted. It seems likely that the section:

[Pictavia, moreover, was named from the Picts, whom, as we have said *Cinadius* destroyed. For God condescended as reward for their wickedness, to make them alien from, and dead to, their

---

[12] Following Hudson's translation with some modifications.

heritage; they who not only spurned the Lord's mass and precept
but also did not wish to be equal to others in the law of justice.]

originated as a parenthetic statement by a copyist compiling a history of
the Scots who found that his 'Chronicle of the Kings of Albania' (which
he knew as an alternative name for Scotia) actually started with an
account of kings of Pictavia. To an historian of the twelfth century the
fact that the Picts had disappeared at all would be evidence enough of
God's displeasure with them. Divine providence was the dominant historical theory of the day. The subsequent information looks much more
like the original contents of the chronicle:

1. *Kinadius*, then, the son of Alpin, first of the Scots, ruled this
   Pictavia happily for xvi years.
2. He, indeed, two years before he came to Pictavia, assumed the
   kingship of Dál Riata.
3. In the seventh year of his reign he transported the relics of
   Saint Columba to the church he had built, and
4. He invaded, six times, 'Saxony' and burned Dunbar and
   overthrew Melrose. Also
5. The Britons burned Dunblane and
6. The *Danari* wasted Pictavia to Clunie and Dunkeld.
7. He died eventually from a tumour before the ides of February,
   on a Tuesday, in the palace of Forteviot.

The fact that the information regarding Cinaed's kingship in Dál Riata
came *after* the initial statement of his reign length in Pictavia underlines
the fact that the core text here was a Pictavian regnal list which simply
adds the information on Cinaed's past incidentally. Clearly, had an
account of campaigns conquering Pictland preceded this, then we would
already have been told that Cinaed had been king of Dál Riata. One also
has to wonder that his reign in Pictavia should be described as *feliciter*
(happy) had it begun with an act of genocide and conquest. Also, could a
newly arrived occupying power have expended so much energy on wars
against the Northumbrians? The statement that he was king of Dál Riata
seems likely to be original – not simply from the way the text is phrased,
but because this name for the Gaelic kingdom in Scotland was not well
remembered in later years and does not appear in other texts from a
twelfth- or thirteenth-century milieu.

If Cinaed's reign ended with his death in 858 and had lasted for sixteen
years then his assumption of the kingship of Pictavia would have taken

place in about 842 (*CKA* never notes fractions of years, so one cannot be precise). If Cinaed did indeed rule in Dál Riata for about two years before this then that interval might take us back to 839 and he may have succeeded directly following the death of Áed son of Boanta. Áed, of course, had died fighting alongside Wen son of Onuist, king of Fortriu, and his own predecessor had been Domnall son of Constantín, a Pictish prince, who had ruled under his father and uncle since 811. It is thus perfectly plausible that Cinaed had continued the tradition of the previous three decades and ruled Dál Riata under Pictish suzerainty. Is it possible that Cinaed was a Pict?

As has been noted, pedigrees of later Scottish kings tracing their descent back through Cinaed and earlier kings of Dál Riata to legendary figures in Ireland, and eventually to Adam, 'son of the Living God' do exist. Like the king-list for Dál Riata, however, these pedigrees run into trouble between the mid-eighth and the mid-ninth centuries. They seem, for a start, several generations too short, and they appear to get some characters in the wrong order. Pedigrees for several leading kindreds in Dál Riata survive from the early eighth century and it seems that these formed the basis for the reconstruction of Cinaed's pedigree. Guessing how to fill the gap between Cinaed's father Alpín and the latest names in the genuine pedigrees seems to have caused major problems for the scholars who undertook this task, probably in the late tenth century.[13] As for Cinaed's name, Cinaed son of Alpín, it appears only in Gaelic form but this is because the version of the Pictish king-list in which the names are written in British orthography stops with Bred. Had a Pict written Cinaed's name he would undoubtedly have written 'Ciniod son of Elphin'. Both the names Ciniod and Elphin had featured as the names of Pictish kings in the eighth century, indeed as brothers who ruled from 763 to 780, and although Alpín was current as a name in Dál Riata it does not seem to have been used in Ireland and may have been a British name borrowed by the ruling houses of Dál Riata through intermarriage.[14] By the ninth century Cinaed had also become quite a common name in Ireland but it does not seem to have had an earlier history there and may

[13] For the genuine pedigrees see D. N. Dumville, '*Cethri Primchenéla Dáil Riata*', *Scottish Gaelic Studies* 20 (2000), 170–91. For the problems caused by the splicing of the Albanian and the Dál Riatan pedigrees see now D. Broun, '*Alba*: Pictish homeland or Irish offshoot?', in P. O'Neill, ed., *Exile and Homecoming: papers from the fifth Australian conference of Celtic Studies, University of Sydney, July 2004* (Sydney, 2005), 234–75.
[14] The name Elphin may ultimately have either been a borrowing of the Anglo-Saxon name Ælfwini or a form based upon the name of the British proto-martyr known to us as St Alban.

also have been a British name borrowed into Irish.[15] All this means that neither Cinaed's name nor that of his father is diagnostically either Gaelic or Pictish. He might as easily have been Ciniod son of Elphin as Cinaed son of Alpín. Of course, our chronicle does describe him in its opening sentence, as *primus Scotorum*, but this is just the kind of phrase that it is impossible to date. Is it a gloss dating to the same period as the splicing of Cinaed's pedigree, or to the twelfth-century editing, or is it original to the chronicle, that is to say still about a hundred years after Cinaed's time?

There is some evidence that the beginning of Cinaed's rule in Pictavia may have been disputed. Although the best witnesses to the Pictish king-list have Cinaed preceded immediately by Bred, whom they say ruled for one year, another set of lists, transliterated into Gaelic orthography and quite badly mangled in transmission, list four other kings as well as supplying a patronymic for Bred.[16] It is easiest to understand this if we compare the two lists:

Wen f. Onuist	iii	Eoganan f. Hungus	iii
Wrad f. Bargoit	iii	Ferat f. Barot	iii
Bred	i	Brude f. Ferat	i month
Cinaed f. Alpín	xvi	Kyneth f. Ferat	i
		Brude f. Fochel	ii
		Drust f. Ferat	iii

The fact that Brude son of Ferat, who seems to correspond to Bred, is followed immediately by a Kyneth, which must represent an original Cinaed/Ciniod, does not inspire confidence, but if we take the list at face value it would seem to indicate that three sons of Wrad son of Bargoit (a.k.a. Ferat f. Barot) competed for the kingship along with another Bridei (who may have been the brother of the Talorgan son of Wthoil who shared the kingship with Drest son of Constantín between c. 834 and 836).[17] A further suggestion that we should take these

---

[15] The earliest recorded Pictish bearer of this name was Ciniod son of Lutrin whose death is noted at *AU* 631.1, the earliest Irish bearer seems to have been Cinaed son of Irgalach, king of southern Brega, whose killing appears at *AU* 728.1.

[16] This is the group of lists which Marjorie Anderson labelled 'Q' and Molly Miller, *Series Brevior*, the 'shorter list'. They are discussed in full in Anderson's *Kings and Kingship*.

[17] That Wthoil is the British form of Gaelic Fochel, or rather vice versa, depends upon the normal development of original /w/ to /f/ in Gaelic together with a presumption of the common scribal error of confusing 't' with 'c'. This latter phenomena was particularly common when later scribes tried to read early Insular handwriting.

additional kings seriously is perhaps offered when we notice that their accumulated reign lengths total six years and that *CKA* ascribes the first event in Cinaed's reign to his seventh year. If the chronicle were, either in its first recension or as a result of subsequent editing, attempting to gloss over troubles in Cinaed's early years this might be the result that would ensue. Of the family of Wrad there is only one trace outwith the king-lists and this is in the longer version of the St Andrews foundation legend written in the mid-twelfth century at the time of the foundation of the Augustinian priory there. The author of this text seems to have copied out the colophon from his exemplar. This colophon claimed to have been written in the royal villa of King Wrad at Meigle (Perthshire). Meigle now contains one of the largest of all the collections of Pictish ecclesiastical sculpture and was almost certainly an important church-settlement. One can only suppose, if the colophon is to be believed, that either King Wrad had a royal hall within the ecclesiastical complex, which would not be unusual for the ninth century, or that the sculpture post-dates Wrad's time. In the later Middle Ages much of the land around Meigle belonged to the bishops of Dunkeld and it is to Dunkeld that we now turn.

THE TRANSLATION OF THE RELICS OF COLUMBA

We saw in an earlier chapter how the Columban *familia* based on Iona responded to the attacks of the heathens by building a new *ciuitas* at Kells, on the border between the two great Irish kingdoms of Mide and Brega, between the years 807 and 814. After this date, however, the relics of Columba must have remained at Iona for they were still there when Blathmac was martyred in 825. It is possible that the plans to move Columba's relics to Ireland were forestalled by the Pictish occupation of Dál Riata under Constantín son of Wrguist and his son Domnall, which seems to have begun in 811. Doubtless the men of Fortriu, who saw Columba as their apostle and who must have made frequent pilgrimages to his shrine, were loathe to see his relics taken overseas. We have also seen that in the later middle ages there was a tradition alive that Constantín had founded Dunkeld, a house that was to become the chief Columban church in Scotland.

CKA claims that in his seventh year Cinaed 'conveyed the relics of Columba to the church that he had built'. Cinaed's seventh year as king of Pictavia would seem to be c. 849 and under this year the *Annals of Ulster* record that 'Indrechtach, abbot of Iona, came to Ireland with the relics of Colum Cille'.[18] The simplest reading of these two records together would be that Cinaed had built a church in Ireland to which Indrechtach was conveying the relics. This, however, seems unlikely and is not the view taken by most historians.[19] The prevailing view among Scottish historians has been that in 849 the relics of Columba were divided between Kells and Dunkeld. This may have happened but there is little hard evidence for this and the clear division between the communities seems to have occurred at a slightly later date. It is likely, however, given the general scope of interest shown by *CKA*, that Cinaed's church was in southern Pictavia and it may well have been at Dunkeld. In 865, some sixteen years later, the death is recorded of Tuathal son of Artgus, *primepscop* of Fortriu and abbot of Dunkeld.[20] This is the earliest notice of Dunkeld in a contemporary source and yet it was clearly already an important place if its abbot had been elected 'chief-bishop' of Fortriu (and it is more likely that an abbot should be elected to the episcopate than that a bishop should become an abbot). The obituary of only one other bishop of Fortriu, Brecc, has survived, and that from 725,[21] so the Irish chronicler's interest in Tuathal son of Artgus may reflect the fact that he was a senior member of the Columban *familia*, most of whom were drawn from the northern Cenél Conaill dynasty of Donegal. The death notice in the same year, however, of Cellach son of Ailill, abbot of Kildare and Iona, prevents us from assuming that the community of Iona had been transferred wholesale to Dunkeld.[22]

The period of Cinaed's reign does seem to have coincided with a major new offensive from the Northmen. Under the year 847 the Frankish chronicler, Prudentius of Troyes, whose chronicle makes up the early part of the text known as the *Annals of St Bertin*, recorded:

---

[18] *AU* 849.7.

[19] It might also be noted that in 849 the king in whose territory Kells lay was actually named Cinaed. He was Cinaed son of Conaing son of Flann, styled king of Ciannacht in the chronicles but in fact the senior member of the dynasty of northern Brega. He was, however, a bad lot and was judicially drowned by the kings of Tara and of southern Brega in 851. See *AU* 850.3 and 851.2.

[20] *AU* 865.6.

[21] *AU* 725.7.

[22] *AU* 865.2. Máire Herbert, in her *Iona, Kells and Derry: the History and Hagiography of the Monastic familia of Columba* (Oxford, 1988), 73, n. 24, urges caution in accepting that the Cille Daro of this entry is the famous Kildare in Leinster. This seems unnecessary and perhaps reflects the difficulty in explaining pluralism between two *familiae* which did not have a history of close co-operation. Cille Daro is the normal spelling for Kildare in ninth-century annals.

the Northmen also got control of the islands all around Ireland and stayed there without encountering any resistance from anyone.[23]

This account almost certainly refers to the southern Hebrides, the island portion of Dál Riata, for nothing similar is noted in the Irish chronicles. Under the year 849 the *Annals of Ulster* record:

A naval expedition of six score ships of the household of the king of the *Gaill* came to exact obedience from the *Gaill* who were in Ireland before them, and afterwards they caused confusion in the whole country.[24]

These events may reflect the conquest of the island portion of Dál Riata by the Northmen and the effective end of the kingdom. That the islands of Dál Riata suffered a more traumatic fate than the mainland portions is indicated by the preservation of the names of two of the four leading kindreds of the kingdom, Cenél Comgaill and Cenél Loairn, in the districts of Cowal and Lorn, while the names of the remaining kindreds, Cenél nGabráin (based in Kintyre and Arran) and Cenél nOengusa (based on Islay) have disappeared from Argyll without trace. If this interpretation is correct then these events may also have some bearing on the transfer of Columban relics away from Iona, whether to Kells or to Dunkeld.

What all this does seem to indicate is that in Cinaed's time a major Columban cult centre was established south of the Mounth. Bede, in his account of St Columba had clearly stated that he was considered to be the apostle of the northern Picts (and the Old English translation of Bede explicitly names the men of Fortriu), and indicates that south of the Mounth the Picts claimed to have been converted to Christianity by a British bishop named Nynia.[25] The establishment of a Columban house at Dunkeld and the election of its abbot to the premier position in the Pictish Church could be seen as a direct assault on the ecclesiastical traditions deriving their legitimacy from Nynia. Columba had been the premier saint of both Dál Riata and Fortriu but not, apparently, of the

---

[23] J. L. Nelson, ed., *The Annals of St-Bertin* (Manchester, 1991), 65.

[24] *AU* 849.6. The words *Gall* (singular) and *Gaill* (plural) are used frequently from about this time to refer to the Northmen and the Danes. In origin the word is borrowed from Latin *Gallus*, 'a Gaul', and indicated a person from the Continent of Europe. It is usually translated 'foreigner' but this is not a good translation, for Picts, Britons and Saxons are never designated *Gaill*. In this book it will be left untranslated.

[25] See *Historia Ecclesiastica* III.iv. for Columba's role as apostle of the Picts.

southern Picts. If Wrad and his dynasty had drawn their support from the Tay basin (and we have only the one allusion to Wrad's royal villa at Meigle upon which to base this supposition) then Cinaed's victory may have been one in which Dál Riata and Fortriu were allied against the people of the Tay basin. Columba, to whom such a victory would have been ascribed, may well have shared in its fruits.

CINAED'S WARS

Following its account of Cinaed's transfer of the relics of Columba to the church he had built, *CKA* relates the military activity associated with Cinaed's reign. First, we are told that he invaded 'Saxony', that is Northumbria, six times. Presumably this reflects six expeditions south of the Forth in the course of his reign, probably each in a separate year. This immediately alerts us to the fact that the source for this information is not an annalistic chronicle, which would have listed each expedition and any notable facts about it separately and probably interspersed with his other deeds – indeed it reads more like a line from a praise poem or an elegy. If this were the case then it would allow us to say that in 858 or thereabouts Cinaed was believed to have crossed the Forth six times and burned Melrose and Dunbar, but what we cannot tell is whether this was a sustained campaign, a six years' war, or whether these raids (and they can have been no more than that for they led to no territorial acquisition) were dispersed across the whole of his time as king. Unfortunately, as we saw in the previous chapter, this is one of the least well documented periods of Northumbrian history, so we cannot see Cinaed's raids from the other side. The following item in *CKA* allows us to speculate that Cinaed would have crossed the Forth from Fife for we are told that in his reign the Britons burned Dunblane, suggesting that the upper Forth probably marched with British territory.

This reference to the Britons burning Dunblane is of interest for two reasons. First, it is the first notice of independent north British activity since at least 760, and perhaps since 756.[26] It seems quite likely that they had reasserted their independence from the Picts following the debacle of 839, and this attack on Dunblane may even show them taking the war into Pictish territory. The second reason why the reference to the

[26] *Annales Cambriae s.a.* 760 record the death of Dyfnwal son of Teudebur, who appears in the pedigree of the kings of the Britons. *HRA* 756 records a successful joint expedition by the Northumbrians and Picts against Dumbarton.

burning of Dunblane is of interest concerns its patron saint Bláán (modern Scots 'Blane'). Bláán appears to have been a Briton, broadly contemporary with Columba, and was said to have dwelt at Kingarth on Bute. Kingarth was certainly an important church in Dál Riata, probably the head church of Cenél Comgaill, and perhaps home to the bishops of Dál Riata in the middle decades of the seventh century. By the later middle ages Dunblane (earlier *Dol Bláin, 'meadow of Blane') had become the centre of Blane's cult. The fact that the site already had the saint's name by the mid-ninth century, if we are to take *CKA* as a more or less contemporary witness at this point, suggests, perhaps, that his relics, like Columba's, had already been translated from the west coast. Just as Columba's relics were moved to Dunkeld, and Cuthbert's, after some wandering, to Chester-le-Street, so Bláán's may have moved inland to escape the fury of the heathens.

By the middle of the ninth century such moves were no longer sufficient to guarantee security from the Northmen. The final notice of warfare in Cinaed's reign tells how the *Danair* wasted Pictavia as far as Clunie and Dunkeld. We have already seen how the use of *Danair* is unlikely to come from a ninth-century annal, but it may simply be a modernisation, and by the later tenth, eleventh or twelfth centuries an obscure (and more specific?) term may have been replaced with something less ambiguous. What this notice does indicate, however, is the geographical interest of the chronicler. Both Clunie, later a major royal site, and Dunkeld, a major church-settlement, lie in Stormont where the Tay flows out of the Highlands. 'Pictavia as far as Clunie and Dunkeld' probably means the lower and middle Tay. There is no direct mention of any events north of the Mounth or west of Druim Alban. The question we are left with is: does this reflect the myopia of our chronicler or the extent of Cinaed's power? It is particularly noteworthy that *CKA* appears to record no events on the west coast.

The final notice of Cinaed's death at Forteviot probably belongs to the original king-list that lay at the core of *CKA* and thus reflects the opinion of a mid-tenth-century writer, probably at Dunkeld (the settlement most frequently mentioned in *CKA*).[27] This is close enough in time and space, and uncontroversial enough in content, that it can probably be trusted.

---

[27] For Dunkeld as the place of authorship of *CKA* see D. Broun, 'Dunkeld and the origin of Scottish identity', *The Innes Review* 48 (1997), 112–24. Of particular relevance is the notice in reign seven of the Northmen plundering 'Dunkeld and all Albania', which suggests a specific interest, if nothing else, in Dunkeld.

DOMNALL SON OF ALPÍN (858–62)

The king-lists and chronicles all agree that Cinaed was succeeded as king of the Picts by his brother Domnall. The same arguments apply to Domnall's name as they do to Cinaed's regarding what language it was coined in. It might have been either British or Gaelic, although it has come down to us only in Gaelic form. The *Annals of Ulster* note only his death:

> *AU* 862.1 Domnall son of Alpín, king of the Picts, died.

CKA's entry is short but of interest:

> *Duuenaldus*, his brother, held the kingdom *iiii* years. In his time the rights and laws [*iura et leges*] of the kingdom, of Áed son of Eochaid, were made by the Gaels [*Goedeli*] with their king at Forteviot. He died in the palace at *Cinnbelathoir* on the ides of April.

This is a far shorter account than that covering the reign of Cinaed and, of course, Domnall ruled only for a quarter of the time that his brother did. Presumably he had grown old in waiting. The spelling of his name is one of the later forms that Dumville noted, but it is hard to see how it can be an interpolation rather than simply a modernisation here. The only alternative explanation would be that the whole chronicle dates to the twelfth century and that it is the older forms that are affected. Domnall's reign length matches the interval between Cinaed's death and his own in *AU*, which is reassuring. The place of his death has generally been identified with the *Bellathor* mentioned, along with *Rigmonath*, as urbes[28] in *Scotia* in the late-tenth-century Life of Cathróe of Metz, a continental abbot who had been born and brought up in Scotland in the early tenth century.[29] *Rigmonath* is evidently Rígmonaid (St Andrews), which frequently appears prefixed with either *ceann* (literally 'head' or 'end') in earlier texts, or *cille* (a 'church') in later ones, so *urbs* in this context almost

---

[28] *Urbes* is the plural of Latin *urbs*, in classical Latin a city but in the context of tenth-century Scotland, which had no towns or cities, probably either a hilltop citadel or a major church-settlement.

[29] D. N. Dumville, 'St Cathróe of Metz and the hagiography of exoticism', in J. Carey, M. Herbert and P. Ó Riain (eds), *Studies in Irish Hagiography: Saints and Scholars* (Dublin, 2001), 172–88 at 175. A complete translation of the life of Cathróe has yet to be published.

certainly means 'major church-settlement'. The versions of the Scottish
king-list which have had places of death added to them in the twelfth
century place Domnall's death at Rathinveramon (the former Roman fort
at the point at which the Almond flows into the Tay[30]) near Scone, and so
it is possible that Bellathor is the original name for the church-settlement
at Scone.[31] 'Scone' itself, as a name, almost certainly refers to the mound
used in later Scottish royal inauguration ceremonies and it may be that
an informal use, 'the Mound', gradually replaced an earlier name.

Forteviot: a Pictish palace[32]

The *Chronicle of the Kings of Alba* describes Forteviot as a *palacio*, a
'palace', and identifies it as the place where Cinaed son of Alpín died
and where his brother Domnall met 'the Gaels and their king'. This
village in lower Strathearn, in Perthshire, is thus one of the few sites in
the heartland of the southern Picts the identity of which is known.
Today Forteviot is the site of a model village built by the first Baron
Forteviot, a Perth whisky magnate, in the early years of the twentieth
century. It is a sleepy village with no pub or shop and even the church
is of recent construction. The village sits on a low terrace above the
flood plain of the Earn. One of the tributaries of that river, the Water
of May, cuts along the western side of the village and it is this feature
which seems to be responsible for the disappearance of the medieval
remains for the burn has progressively cut away its eastern bank over
the centuries. A new parish kirk was consecrated in 1241 suggesting
that the old kirk, mentioned in twelfth-century documents, may already
have been undermined by that date.

　　None the less, Forteviot can tell us something about Pictish royal
settlements. Besides a few small fragments, a single arch from the old
kirk survives bearing figurative sculpture dating from about the ninth
century. This suggests that there was a significant stone building, probably of an ecclesiastical nature, on the site in the days of Alpín's sons.
This arch is now on display in the Museum of Scotland in Edinburgh.
The modern kirk at Forteviot still retains an early medieval bronze-cast
hand-bell of a sort produced in Ireland and Scotland between the
eighth and tenth centuries. It is thought that this is also a relic of the

---

[30] Or just possibly the fort at Cramond near Edinburgh, though this probably lay
outwith Pictavia in this period.
[31] For the various texts see Anderson, *Kings and Kingship*.
[32] N. Aitchison, *Forteviot: a Pictish and Scottish Royal Centre* (Stroud, 2006).

Pictish period foundation. It is also noteworthy that the terrace around the modern village was extensively used for ritual monuments in earlier prehistoric times and, although most of these monuments survive only as crop marks today, they probably stood in relief as grass grown humps and bumps in the Pictish period. This hypothesis is supported by the fact that archaeological investigation has shown that Pictish period burials were placed within some of these monuments.

In contrast to many sites associated with late pre-Viking Age royalty, such as Dunadd, Dumbarton or Dunnottar, Forteviot is a low-land site and apparently unfortified. It may also have been principally an ecclesiastical site with which kings wished to associate themselves.

Both Domnall's reign length and his place of death are likely to have been in the original regnal list. This leaves only one piece of independent information in *CKA*:

> In his time the rights and laws [*iura et leges*] of the kingdom, of Áed son of Eochaid, were made by the Gaels [*Goedeli*] with their king at Forteviot.

This is the only place in *CKA* where the word *Goedel* appears. The spelling looks to be the authentic product of an early medieval writer who was literate in Gaelic. The word is very rare and rarely spelled accurately in Scottish sources of the twelfth or thirteenth century. Scottish histor-ians working on the presumption that Cinaed had led a Scottish conquest of the Picts have always assumed that the king of the Gaels in this passage was Domnall himself, but if that was what the writer intended then the wording is very peculiar: 'in his time . . . the Gaels and their king' [*In huius tempore . . . Goedeli cum rege suo*]. The text seems to imply that the king of the Gaels was someone other than Domnall. This would not be remarkable. Although we have seen that Cinaed may well have been king of Dál Riata as well as king of the Picts there is no reason to assume that Domnall would have succeeded to both kingships. In the early middle ages kingship could pass to sons, brothers or cousins of previous kings; indeed, descent from a previous king rather than one's immediate prede-cessor was the defining requirement. In addition to royal descent, per-sonal ability and one's social network (including maternal kin, in-laws and clientage) counted for a great deal. Indeed, these factors governed which of many royal princes actually succeeded. The event being com-memorated in this passage may have been that of oaths taken to preserve good relations between Dál Riata and Pictavia. The Áed son of Eochaid referred to was probably that Áed Find, son of Eochaid (†778), who seems to have been instrumental in liberating Dál Riata from the Verturian hegemony in the 760s. We know little of the details of that period, simply a reference to conflict between Áed and Ciniod son of Wrad, king of Fortriu in 768 and the notice of Áed's death as king of Dál Riata ten years later,[33] but it may be that the price paid for the revival of Dál Riatan kingship was the continuation of limited subjection to Pictavia: devolution rather than full independence. The event at Forteviot in Domnall's reign may have been a rearticulation of this kind of relationship. What remains unclear, however, is the extent and location of any Dál Riatan polity in this period, given the possibility that much of the kingdom's traditional heartland was under Scandinavian rule.

CONSTANTÍN SON OF CINAED (862–76)

Domnall's successor was his nephew, Cinaed's son Constantín. That Cinaed's son bore the name of the great Pictish king Constantín son of Wrguist has been taken by many historians as a suggestion that this dynasty claimed descent, perhaps in the female line, from the house of Wrguist. This may have been the case but it is equally possible that Cinaed had chosen this name for his son simply to create an association of this sort and to bolster his legitimacy as king of the Picts. A great deal more is known of Constantín's reign than of that of his uncle or indeed of his father. This is largely because important Scandinavian leaders, of interest to English and Irish chroniclers, began to engage with the Picts. Let us begin with the account of his reign in *CKA*, and then attempt to synchronise it with the other sources:

> *Constantínus* son of Cinaed reigned *xvi* years. In his first year
> Maelsechnaill king of the Irish died and Áed son of Niall held the
> kingdom, and after two years Amlaíb, with his heathens, wasted all
> Pictavia and occupied it from the first of January to the Feast of
> Saint Patrick. In the third year, yet, Amlaíb, drawing tribute,[34] was
> killed by Constantín. After a short while, in his fourteenth year a
> battle was fought at *Dolaír* between the *Danair* and the *Scotti* and

[33] *AU* 768.7 and 778.7.
[34] The word that I have translated 'tribute' actually reads *centum*, 'a hundred', but 'drawing a hundred' makes no sense whatsoever and Anderson's suggestion that this should read *censum*, 'tribute', must be correct.

the *Scotti* are slain at *Achcochlam*. The *Normanni* spent a whole
year in Pictavia.

The reign length of sixteen years does not match with the fourteen-
year interval between Domnall's death and Constantín's, but xvi for xiv,
or even xiiii, would be a very easy slip for a scribe to make while copying
the text. Maelsechnaill's death is indeed recorded at *AU* 862.5,
Constantín's first year, and Áed son of Niall was his successor. It might
be worth noting that *rex Hiberniensium*, 'king of the Irish', was not a style
that appeared in Irish chronicles, where *rex Hiberniae* or *rí hErenn*, 'king
of Ireland', would be more usual. The invasion of Amlaíb is recorded in
the Irish chronicles:

> *AU* 866.1 Amlaíb and Auisle went to Fortriu with the Gaill of
> Ireland and Britain, plundered the entire Pictish nation
> [*Cruithentúath*] and took hostages from them.

There is a chronological problem here, in as much as 866 was not the third
year of Constantín's reign. Since *CKA* tells us that Amlaíb occupied
Pictavia from 1 January it is possible that his arrival in Fortriu occurred
in 865, but this still leaves us at least a year out. It has been suggested that
an intervening piece of information, dated to 864 (or 863?), has been
omitted without the dependent chronological marker being revised.[35]
   Amlaíb was an important Scandinavian leader who first appears in the
record in 853 when the *Annals of Ulster* record:

> *AU* 853.2 Amlaíb, son of the king of Laithlind, came to Ireland
> and the Gaill of Ireland submitted to him, and he took tribute
> from the Irish.

The men of Laithlind had been in Ireland since at least the 840s,
allthough the location of Laithlind itself is unknown. In the late 840s they
suffered setbacks at the hands of Maelsechnaill, and then in 851 a new
group of Scandinavians, the 'Black Heathens', probably to be identified
with the *Scaldingi*, arrived and set upon them.[36] Amlaíb's arrival seems to

---

[35] M. Miller, 'Amlaíb Trahens Centum', *Scottish Gaelic Studies* 19 (1999), 241–5.
[36] *AU* 851.3. The designation of the *Scaldingi* as Black Heathens, or Black Gaill, and
the men of Laithlind as White Gaill seems simply to be a method for distinguish two
groups, as we might say 'Heathens A' and 'Heathens B'. In time 'Black Gaill' appears to
have come to mean 'Anglo-Danish' and 'White Gaill' 'Hiberno-Norse', but these are
later developments.

have led to a reconciliation between the two groups and their co-operative exploitation of the native peoples followed. From 857, at least, Amlaíb seems also have been working in close collaboration with Ímar, whom we have already encountered as the *Scalding* leader Ivarr.[37] At times these two Northmen collaborated with native Irish kings. In 863, for example, they had plundered Brega in alliance with Lorcán, king of Mide.[38] In the following year, however, Amlaíb drowned Lorcán's successor Conchobar.[39] The Auisle who accompanied Amlaíb to Fortriu seems to have been his brother and co-king, who he was, eventually, to slay.[40] Amlaíb and Auisle, it would seem, over-wintered in Pictavia, and the taking of hostages mentioned in the *Annals of Ulster* was probably intended to afford them some sense of security so they did not need to be on a full alert throughout their sojourn. The hostages, if this were the case, would probably have been returned on St Patrick's Day when the brothers left the country.

If the above interpretation were correct, then what follows in *CKA* would seem to require that something has certainly been missed out:

> In the third year, yet, Amlaíb, drawing tribute, was killed by Constantín. After a short while, in his fourteenth year a battle was fought at *Dolaír* between the *Danair* and the *Scotti* and the *Scotti* are slain at/to *Achcochlam*.

It is hard to see how an event within three years of 17 March 866 could be described as shortly before Constantín's fourteenth year (875–6). Alfred Smyth has suggested a plausible solution. He noted that the first notice of Amlaíb being active in Ireland after his departure for Fortriu occurred in *AU* 869.6:

> Armagh was plundered by Amlaíb and burned with its oratories. A thousand [people] were carried off or killed and great rapine also committed.

---

[37] *AU* 857.1. The names Amlaíb and Ímar are the standard Gaelic renderings of the Norse names which we tend to spell in their later medieval Icelandic forms Ólafr and Ivarr. In the ninth century these names may actually have been pronounced more like Áleifr and Ingwarr. In all but initial position the letter 'm' in early Gaelic has a tendency to be pronounced more like a nasalised /v/ (or sometimes /w/) and thus the Gaelic spellings do approximate the Norse pronunciations.

[38] *AU* 863.4.

[39] *AU* 864.2.

[40] *AU* 867.6. By the eleventh century an Irish saga had developed about this kin-slaying; see J. Radnor, ed., *The Fragmentary Annals of Ireland* (Dublin, 1978), 127.

Smyth noted that it was a great coincidence that Amlaíb was said to leave
Scotland on St Patrick's Day and to turn up next at St Patrick's chief
shrine at Armagh. The number of slaves taken and the number of casualties also suggested to Smyth that the attack on Armagh coincided with
a major festival, perhaps St Patrick's own feast. He suggested that the
phrase 'in the third year' had originally appeared twice in the text and that
a scribe had either suffered 'eye-skip' and only copied it once or assumed
that this was a mistake. He therefore read:

> after two years Amlaíb, with his heathens, wasted all Pictavia and
> occupied it from the first of January to the Feast of Saint Patrick,
> in the third year.

The sequence as Smyth read it was that Amlaíb sailed to Fortriu in 866,
ravaged all Pictavia, and then settled down on 1 January 867, having taken
hostages, until 869 when he left in time to arrive at Armagh for the Feast
of Patrick.[41] The failure of the chronicler of *CKA* to name specific places
in his account may mean that Amlaíb was based in Fortriu, where the
Irish chronicler tells us he had gone, north of the Mounth. This would
then mean that the phrase which I translated 'in the third year, yet', *tercio
iterum anno*, actually means 'after another three years', placing the killing
of Amlaíb by Constantín between 17 March 871 and 17 March 872. This
would fit with Amlaíb's final appearances in the Irish chronicles:

> *AU* 870.6 The siege of Dumbarton by the Northmen, that is
> Amlaíb and Ímar, the two kings of the Northmen, laid siege to the
> fortress and, at the end of four months, they destroyed and
> plundered it.
>
> *AU* 871.2 Amlaíb and Ímar returned to Dublin from Britain with
> two hundred ships, bringing away with them in captivity to
> Ireland a great prey of English, and Britons and Picts.

These events are clearly of importance in themselves to Scottish history.
Dumbarton would not be mentioned again in any source until it emerged
as a royal castle in the thirteenth century. Doubtless during the siege
of Dumbarton Rock the Northmen provisioned themselves by ravaging
widely in the neighbouring country and the 'great prey' of slaves from the
different peoples of the central belt were presumably gathered up as part

---

[41] A. P. Smyth, *Scandinavian Kings in the British Isles* (Oxford, 1977), 143–9.

of this foraging process. The motivation for this attack on Dumbarton is uncertain. It may simply have been perceived as a rich target, as Armagh had been in 869, or perhaps the resurgent British kings were proving a threat to shipping in the outer Clyde.[42] It is even possible that Dumbarton, at the mouth of the River Leven, was considered as a possible north British *longphort* or pirate base, similar to those that were growing up at places like Dublin, Waterford and Limerick. In recent years some historians have become very attached to the idea that the Forth Clyde isthmus provided a vital route-way connecting 'Viking Dublin' to 'Viking York', but this is, frankly, absurd. There is no easy portage or water-way connecting the Forth and the Clyde, the two rivers are not that close, and the tributaries which do come closer are far too shallow and full of rapids.[43] Besides this, the easiest route from Dublin to York would have been the direct east–west route that cuts through the Pennines at the Aire Gap (near modern Skipton), all of which was inside the kingdom of Northumbria, which for most of this period was under Scandinavian control.

When Ímar died in 873 he is styled king of the Northmen of all Ireland and Britain, even though in previous annalistic references, where he appears with Amlaíb, he always comes second. This strongly suggests that Amlaíb was dead by then, supporting Smyth's solution to the chronological problems. One interesting sideline on the Dumbarton expedition which concerns our narrative appears in *AU* 872.5:

> Artgal, king of the Britons of Strathclyde, was slain at the
> instigation of Constantín Cinaed's son.

This is actually the earliest reference to Strathclyde, and presumably reflects the political reconfiguration of the northern Britons following the destruction of Dumbarton. Presumably what we are being told is that Constantín had Artgal assassinated in an event that echoes one of the previous year:

> *AU* 871.1 Cathalán son of Indrechtach, one of two kings of the
> Ulaid, was deceitfully killed at the instigation of Áed.

---

[42] Attacks on this area by Somerled, leading a force drawn from Dublin and the Isles, in 1164 and by Norwegian royal fleets in the 1230s and 1260s were motivated by the threat posed by Scottish forces to the outer Clyde region. These expeditions seem the best parallels to the events of 870–1.

[43] Once again we can turn to the twelfth and thirteenth centuries, when ships were much the same size and design as in the ninth and tenth centuries, and point to the lack of evidence that this route was ever used.

'Instigation', in both cases, translates the Latin word *consilio*. Áed, in the latter case, is presumably Áed son of Niall, the king of Tara and aspiring king of Ireland. Whether this was a period in which the cloak and dagger came to the fore or whether we are simply reading the words of a chronicler who is not afraid to call a spade a spade and to speak ill of the great it is impossible to tell. Constantín's motivation in having Artgal slain may have been to promote his brother-in-law. As we shall see, one of his sisters was married to Rhun, who was a king of the Britons. A pedigree for a Rhun son of Artgal, which traces his descent from earlier kings of Dumbarton, was preserved in tenth-century Wales and he is usually presumed to be Constantín's brother-in-law. If the Artgal slain was his father it may reflect anxiety on his part, or that of Constantín, that the old king was keen to promote the succession of other children, perhaps by a different mother. It is very likely that Rhun succeeded to the kingship of Strathclyde in 872.

The end of Constantín's reign followed hot upon the heels of his triumph over Amlaíb:

> After a short while, in his fourteenth year a battle was fought at *Dolaír*, between the *Danair* and the *Scotti*, and the *Scotti* were slain at/to *Achcochlam*. The *Normanni* spent a whole year in Pictavia.[44]

Constantín's fourteenth year was his last year, 875–6, and the attack by the *Danair* appears in the *Annals of Ulster* at *AU* 875.3:

> The Picts encounter the Dubgaill [Black Gaill] and a great slaughter of the Picts resulted.

As we have seen the Dubgaill seem to have been the *Scaldingi*, and this event would appear to relate to the account in the *Anglo-Saxon Chronicle s.a.* 875:

> Healfdene went with part of the army into Northumbria and set up winter quarters by the River Tyne, and the army conquered the land and they often ravaged among the Picts and the Strathclyde Britons.

Dolaír is almost certainly Dollar in Clackmannanshire, lying in the extreme south of Pictavia close to the borders of both Strathclyde and

---

[44] *Paulo post ab eo bello ín xiii. Eius facto in Dolaír inter Danarios et Scottos occisi sunt Scoti co Achcochlam.*

Northumbria, a likely spot for conflict between the Picts and a fleet cruising the Forth. It is interesting to note that the contemporary *Anglo-Saxon Chronicle* and the *Annals of Ulster* both refer to Constantín's forces as Picts while *CKA* describes them as *Scotti*, the first use of the term in *CKA* since the allusion to Cinaed as *primus Scottorum*. Just as the term *Danair* looks like a form that could not have come into use before the late tenth century, we might suggest the same for *Scotti*. The phrase 'between the *Danair* and the *Scotti*' may have originated as a parenthetic gloss, explaining a more laconic statement at a relatively late stage in the chronicle's composition. Bearing this in mind, we should look again at the peculiar clause 'and the *Scotti* were slain at/to *Achcochlam*'. If the word *Scotti* is not likely to be original then we may wonder if this phrase is quite corrupt indeed. *Achcochlam* is usually thought to be a slightly garbled form of *Athfothla*, 'Atholl', with a Latin dative ending stuck on it. Whoever introduced all the *Scotti* into this passage seems to have thought that this phrase was part of the account of the battle at Dollar, but the idea that the rout led all the way from the Forth to Atholl seems unlikely. It is more probably a sequel and may be the otherwise missing notice of Constantín's death. The original king-list may have read:

> *Constantinus filius Cinadi regnavit annos xiv et occisus est co Athfothlam.*

> Constantín son of Cinaed reigned fourteen years and was killed in Atholl.

Once all the other material had been inserted between his reign length and his death notice the *occisus est* lost contact with its subject (*Constantinus*) and some poor copyist, perhaps as late as the twelfth century, found that the closest subject available was the *Scotti* in the gloss on the battle and so 'corrected' the grammar from *occisus est* to *occisi sunt*. Thus textually, if not actually, Constantín became lost among the other casualties of his war against Healfdene. The twelfth-century king-lists attribute Constantín's death to Norwegians and locate it at an unidentified place called Inverdufat (or similar). If he was killed in Atholl we should probably be looking for the mouth of a stream running into the Tay or the Tummel.

It is possible that *AU* tells us something else about Healfdene's expedition to Pictavia:

> *AU* 875.4 Oistín, son of Amlaíb king of the Northmen, was slain through treachery by Alband.

'Alband' is likely to be a Gaelic attempt at representing the name 'Healfdene' (Old Norse 'Halfdan', 'Oistín' represents Old Norse 'Eysteinn'). If this is the case then what we have here is Ímar's brother killing Amlaíb's son, presumably when under truce. As we saw earlier the death of Ímar led to the collapse of solidarity among the various Scandinavian factions active in the Insular world. Although some historians have presumed that this act of treachery happened in Dublin, largely on the basis of late saga material that was probably dependent on the same Irish chronicle sources we have before us here, other evidence relating to Healfdene's movements would make Pictavia or Northumbria a more likely venue. We know that he was back in Northumbria in 876 and *CKA* tells us that the *Normanni* (a more acceptable ninth-century name than *Danair*) were in Pictavia for a whole year following the battle of Dollar. It leaves no time for Healfdene to get to Dublin. It is even possible that Oistín was ruling in some part of Scotland, perhaps Fortriu, where his father seems to have based himself in the 860s.

One other event that occurred during Constantín's reign may be of significance for Scottish history. Under the year 871, the same year in which Amlaíb and Ímar returned to Ireland from the siege of Dumbarton, the *Annals of Ulster* record:

> The storming of Dunseverick, which had never been achieved before: the Gaill were at it with Cenél nEógain.[45]

Dunseverick was, and is, a promontory fort in County Antrim, not far from the Giant's Causeway. It was the chief royal site of Dál Riata in Ireland and lies within sight of Islay and Kintyre. It is usually claimed that the Irish and Scottish parts of Dál Riata had gone their separate ways back in the seventh century, but the evidence for this is not good and recent work indicates that this argument may be based upon a misunderstanding.[46] Earlier in the present volume it was suggested that Onuist son of Wrguist's conquest of Dál Riata in the 730s and 740s might have provided a context for such a split, but it has to be admitted that the desire to identify a division within Dál Riata may owe as much to the recent nationalistic concerns of Scottish historians, faintly embarrassed by their Irish heritage, as to any contemporary evidence. No medieval source uses

---

[45] *AU* 871.3.
[46] D. N. Dumville, 'Ireland and north Britain in the earlier Middle Ages: contexts for *Míniugud Senchusa Fer nAlban*', in C. Ó Baoill and N. R. McGuire, eds, *Rannsachadh na Gàidhlig 2000* (Aberdeen, 2002), 185–212.

any terms that could legitimately be translated 'Irish Dál Riata' or 'Scottish Dál Riata'. To the authors of our sources there was simply Dál Riata. That said, it may be that the assault on Dunseverick has meaning for Scottish history. The Gaill involved may have been of the party of Amlaíb and Ímar, although other Scandinavian groups may still have been active in Ireland in this period, but the identity of Cenél nEógain is absolutely clear.

Cenél nEógain, the kindred of Eógan, were one of the major segments of the Uí Néill kindred which had dominated the northern half of Ireland since at least the middle of the sixth century and which aspired to the kingship of all Ireland. The Uí Néill had split into two main settlement groups, one based in the Irish midlands controlling the three territories of Mide, Brega and Tethba (which in turn were sometimes sub-divided), and one based in County Donegal in the northwest. The northern Uí Néill were themselves divided into two segments, Cenél nEógain and Cenél Conaill, and these two groups recognised an over-kingship that took its name from the royal site of Ailech a mile or two west of the modern city of Derry.[47] In the earliest period both *cenéla* competed for the kingship of Ailech but from 734 it became the preserve of Cenél nEógain, and Cenél Conaill, while continuing to rule parts of Donegal under their overlordship, gained most of their prestige by supplying the senior members of the Columban ecclesiastical *familia*, for it was claimed that Columba himself had been of their kindred. By the middle of the ninth century Cenél nEógain had expanded westwards into Tyrone (Gaelic *Tír Eógain*, the 'Land of Eógan'), and had also become the chief patrons of Armagh where their kings maintained a house, much as King Wrad may have maintained one in the church-settlement at Meigle. The Cenél nEógain kings of Ailech had also, since the mid–eighth century, alternated with their distant kinsmen the Clann Cholmáin kings of Mide in holding the kingship of Tara, the notional over-kingship of the island of Ireland.

In 871 the Cenél nEógain king was Áed Findlaith, son of Niall, who since 862 had also been king of Tara. The storming of Dunseverick seems to have been part of the *Drang nach Osten* which had characterised Cenél nEógain policy since the kindred first emerged in the sixth century. In the same year Áed had arranged for the assassination of Cathalán son of

---

[47] Traditionally Ailech has been identified with the ancient fort on Grianan Hill, but Brian Lacey has recently argued persuasively (in an as yet unpublished paper) that the site of the later medieval O'Docherty's Tower, in the nearby townland of Elagh Beg (which preserves the name Ailech) is the more likely location.

Indrechtach, co-king of the Ulaid.[48] The question that concerns us is the identity of the defenders of Dunseverick. If the chronicler is to be believed that Dunseverick had never been taken before (or at least not for a long time) then we might be inclined to think that it was still in the hands of Dál Riata. As we saw earlier, after the death of Cinaed son of Alpín, Dál Riata seems to have gone its own way but much of it may have been under Scandinavian occupation. Did Gaelic kings still rule in Kintyre and if so were they the defenders of Dunseverick? Is this the point at which Dál Riata ceased to rule over territory in Ireland? Or, alternatively, had the kingdom already fragmented and was Áed simply mopping up 'local militia'? Perhaps of relevance to this question is the evidence provided by Áed son of Niall's third and final marriage. On succession to the kingship of Tara in 862, Áed had set aside his first wife, a princess of the Ulaid, and had married the widow of his predecessor, the Clann Cholmáin king Maelsechnaill, Lann, sister of the king of Osraige (around modern Kilkenny). At some point after this marriage Áed took as his final wife Mael Muire, daughter of Cinaed son of Alpín.[49] This marriage must have happened during Constantín's reign and it is notable as the only recorded marriage between an Irish king and a Pictish princess in the historical period. This marriage produced a son, Niall Glundub, who was briefly to be king of Tara between 916 and 919. Royal marriages, until very recently, were acts of state. Áed's first marriage reflects the same *Ostpolitik* that took him to Armagh and Dunseverick. His second marriage was clearly linked to his need to secure his succession to the kingship of Tara. Lann, as queen of Tara, would have had in her household officers whose experience would prove useful to Áed in effecting a smooth assumption of kingship. What did he have to gain from Mael Muire? A vital question to which we do not know the answer is whether she had already been married, in other words was her value, like that of Áed's first wife, in the ties she created with her natal kin, or, like Lann, was it her marital links that gave her value? If the former were the case it might suggest that, despite the silence of *CKA* on the matter, Constantín did have an interest in the west coast of Scotland. Perhaps his own assassination of Artgal of Strathclyde, reflects interests in that direction. Alternatively, Mael Muire may have been previously married to someone else (a king of Dál Riata?), whose heritage tempted the aggressive and ambitious Áed son of Niall. Because of the taciturn nature of our sources this appears to be very much a side show, but it may be that the storming

---

[48] *AU* 871.1.
[49] Lann died, *in penitencia*, presumably as a nun, in 890. *AU* 890.5.

of Dunseverick and the marriage of Mael Muire daughter of Cinaed hint at great events occurring just out of sight.

ÁED SON OF CINAED (876–8)

Constantín's successor was his brother Áed, who may have taken the kingship only after an interregnum coinciding with the occupation of Pictavia by the Northmen. Of his reign *CKA* has only this to say:

> Edus held the same for one year. The shortness of his reign has bequeathed nothing memorable to history. He was slain in the *ciuitas* of *Nrurim*.

The *Annals of Ulster* add only:

> *AU* 878.2 Áed son of Cinaed, king of the Picts, was killed by his own companions.

The word translated companions here, *socii*, literally 'friends', probably means in this case members of his own household. The killing of a lord by his own retainers was regarded as a heinous crime, but it was not unprecedented. The identity of *ciuitas Nrurim* has excited much speculation but none of it very fruitful. The twelfth-century king-lists say that he was killed in battle in Strathallan by Giric son of Dúngal (of whom more anon). The value of this is uncertain, but as far as we know there was only ever one *ciuitas* in Strathallan, if *ciuitas* here means major church-settlement, and that is Dunblane. Clearly even the most careless scribe could not produce *Nrurim* from *Dol Blááin*, but if Blane's relics had only been transferred to Strathallan in the recent past it is possible that an older name for the church there survived (one might compare 'St Asaph's', the English language name for Llanelwy, the episcopal centre of northeast Wales, or indeed St Andrews for Rígmonaid).

There is an interesting note in one of the surviving manuscripts of the *Annals of Ulster*. Here a couple of Gaelic quatrains have been added in a fifteenth-century hand to the entry for 878, immediately following 878.3, the notice of the death of Gairbíth king of Conaille. The language of the quatrains seems to be nearly contemporary with the death. They read:

> Rhodri of Manu, splendid here,
> Áed from the lands of Kintyre,

Donnchad, lustrous stuff of sovereignty,
Gairbíth, diadem of smooth Macha.

Whenever I bring it to mind
It inflames the limits of my heart,
Cold slabs over the temples,
Barrfinn of Bile is distraught.

Rhodri, Áed and Gairbíth have all had their obituaries noticed in the preceding annal. Each is connected here with a place: Rhodri with the Isle of Man; Áed with Kintyre; and Gairbíth with Emain Macha, the legendary royal centre of the Ulaid just outside Armagh. Gairbíth was king of the Conaille of County Louth who were claimed to be an offshoot of the Ulaid, although neither they nor any other Ulaid rulers had had jurisdiction at Emain Macha for generations. Similarly, Rhodri son of Merfyn was king of Gwynedd in North Wales but his father is said to have originally come from the Isle of Man. If a pattern is emerging here, then it is one in which the poet associates the dead kings with a lost ancestral homeland and not with the kingdom they had ruled at their deaths, perhaps to emphasise the transience of earthly power. The second quatrain seems to identify the poet in some way with 'Barrfinn of Bile', almost certainly Bishop Finnbarr of Moville (Mag Bile), County Down, who may have been the teacher of St Columba in the sixth century.[50] Such an identification may suggest that the poem was composed at Moville, which actually lies fairly centrally in relation to the places mentioned. If this is a genuine ninth-century lament it may bear witness to two facts about Áed. His kindred were no longer ruling in Kintyre but it was believed that they had done so in the past.

EOCHAID AND GIRIC (878–89)

In the Irish chronicle tradition Áed is the last *rex Pictorum*, 'king of the Picts', to be named as such. In the *Anglo-Saxon Chronicle* the last mention of the Picts is the account of Healfdene's expedition against Constantín in 875. From Áed's death until 900, we are entirely dependent upon *CKA*

---

[50] The name Finnbarr derives from an earlier Uindobarros. Barrfinn is constructed by simply reversing the order of the two elements. The same name can also appear as Finian, Uinniau, Finnio, etc. See P. Ó Riain, 'St Finnbarr: a study in a cult', *Journal of the Cork Historical and Archaeological Society* 82 (1977), 63–82.

and much later sources. For the next reign *CKA* supplies the following account:

> *Eochodius*, then, son of Rhun king of the Britons, grandson of
> Cinaed by a daughter, reigned *xi* years; but *Ciricius* son others say
> [*Ciricium filium alii dicunt*] reigned then because he became the
> *alumnus* and *ordinator* of Eochaid. In his second year Áed son of
> Niall died and in his ix year on the very day of *Ciricius* there was
> an eclipse of the sun. Eochaid with his *alumnus* was expelled then
> from the kingdom.

Clearly this is not entirely a contemporary account. If we cut back to the basic king-list material, that is the identity, reign length and ending of the reign of the king we should be left with:

> *Eochodius autem (filius Run regis Britannorum) nepos Cinadei ex
> filia regnauit annis xi. Eochodius expulsus est de regno.*

> Eochodius, then (son of Rhun king of the Britons) grandson of
> Cinaed by a daughter, reigned xi years. Eochaid was expelled from
> the kingdom.

The additional material falls into two categories. These are two events dated by regnal years and one explanatory intervention in which a scribe seems to be self-consciously contradicting his exemplar. The two entries that are dated by regnal years are relatively straightforward. The first records the death of the Irish king, Áed son of Niall, which it dates to Eochaid's second year. He died in 879 and so the dating could well be correct, Eochaid's second year being 879 to 880. The second event is an eclipse on 'the day of Ciric'. This is dated to his ninth year, which should be 886 to 887. In fact, in the manuscript the scribe originally wrote 'xi' but crossed out the 'i' and added another one before the 'x'.[51] If it had been allowed to stand uncorrected it would have given 888 to 889. It may be that this correction was due to momentary confusion on the part of the scribe of the Poppleton manuscript. Having just copied out the account of Constantín's reign which contained a number of instances of sequential dating, notably 'three years again', rather than regnal dates (for example, 'in his third year'), the scribe may have miscorrected xi to ix because he thought that he was being told that the eclipse happened nine

---

[51] Anderson, *Kings and Kingship*, 251, n. 135.

years after Áed son of Niall's death. Áed's death occurred in Eochaid's second year and so the sum of the two intervals should equal the reign length; thus ii plus ix equals xi. Since the event was intended by the author of the text, as opposed to the scribe, to herald the end of the reign, the eleventh must have been the intended regnal year. Unfortunately, although this makes sense of the internal logic of the text it falls foul of astronomy. The eclipse alluded to must have been that on 16 June 885.[52] The 16 June is indeed the feast day of one of several saints named Cyriacius. This would suggest either that the reign was only seven or eight years long, rather than eleven, or that the eclipse did not actually happen in the last year of the reign. Since an eleven-year reign is required to fill the gap between the next reign and the previous, based on *CKA* reign lengths and the obits in *AU*, then it is easier to believe that the eclipse simply occurred within the reign. One could easily forgive the compiler of the chronicle, working some sixty or seventy years later, for allowing himself (or for basing his account on authorities which had allowed themselves) to increase the dramatic tension in the narrative by placing the eclipse at the moment of the expulsion.

Curiously, none of the later king-lists, indeed no other texts at all, mentions Eochaid. In his place Giric, supplied with a father, Dúngal, who must be the 'Ciricius filius' of *CKA*, rules after Áed son of Cinaed, usually for eleven or twelve years. It seems likely that the intervention concerning Ciricius was added by a copyist who knew his king-list and was puzzled that his exemplar gave a different story. This probably happened after the original composition of the king-list which lies behind *CKA*, that is to say after the mid-tenth century. If Ciricius entered the text only at this point one wonders if the account of the eclipse might also have done so. This conflicting evidence regarding Eochaid and Giric is unparalleled elsewhere in our material and the mystery is increased by the fact that the Irish chronicles give an obituary for neither Eochaid nor Giric. As noted in the introductory discussion on the *Chronicle of the Kings of Alba* the real core to the chronicle seems to be a chronicle of the dynasty of Alpín. Eochaid may have been of particular importance to the original complier if his message was the manifest destiny of the House of Alpín. He could not admit a king who was not an Alpínid in some sense even when it meant accepting a ruler whose descent was only through the female line. Ultimately this reign must remain a puzzle, although chronologically it seems to stand at a key point in the transformation of Pictavia into Albania.

---

[52]   *AU* 885.5.

The puzzle becomes more intriguing if we allow ourselves to notice a couple of very late allusions to Giric's reign. In a thirteenth-century addition to some versions of the Scottish king-list we come across a note that Giric 'conquered all of Ireland and the greater part of England (*Anglia*), and that he first gave liberty to the Scottish Church, which, up to that time, had laboured under the customs and mores of the Picts'.[53] The second document is, in its extant form, very late. The Dunkeld Litany was a liturgical text rescued from Dunkeld at the time of the reformation and taken to Ratisbon (Regensburg) in Germany. The litany is essentially the text of a prayer for the souls of the saints and others that seems to have been used in Dunkeld. Some elements of it must belong to the sixteenth century so it is not a genuinely ancient document, but many of the saints are obscure characters from Scotland's early history so it looks as if the litany has an ancient core but was updated and revised on several occasions. Towards the end of the litany God is implored to 'protect and defend our king Girich and his army from all the intents of his enemies and concede to him victory and long life'. This appears to be a contemporary prayer for a living king. If it is genuinely so then this is our only absolutely contemporary account of this reign. But can we trust it?[54]

The plot thickens. The author of the original king-list lying behind *CKA* seems not to have heard of Giric or to have deliberately suppressed knowledge of him. Instead he tells us that Eochaid grandson of Cinaed by his daughter ruled in this period. Later writers, including at least one of the 'editors' of *CKA*, all attribute this reign to Giric, and it is quite clear that the note in the thirteenth-century king-list bears witness to a tradition that made him a very important king indeed.[55] If the Dunkeld Litany's prayer for a living Giric is genuine then it bears witness to the fact that he was indeed king and not simply the *alumnus* and *ordinator* ('foster-father', or 'foster-son', and 'governor' or 'king-maker') of Eochaid. If we wished to try to construct a narrative of this period without excluding any of the evidence it might go something like this: 'Giric, a *socius*, of Áed son of Cinaed, slew his lord, and placed his own foster-son, the dead king's nephew, on the throne. This regime change led to some sort of reform of the Church which, either at the time or later,

[53] Anderson, *Kings and Kingship*, 274.
[54] A. P. Forbes, *Kalendars of Scottish Saints* (Edinburgh, 1872) at lxiii.
[55] The king-lists also state that he died at Dundurn. Dundurn is an early medieval citadel constructed on a rock in upper Strathearn, close to Loch Earn. Since the name 'Earn' derives from Gaelic *Eriu* (genitive *Erenn*), and is identical with the name of Ireland in Gaelic, it may be that it was a conquest in the Loch Earn/Strathearn area that was transformed into a conquest of Ireland.

was seen as somehow anti-Pictish. Towards the end of the period he took the kingship into his own hands.' But this does not quite work. *CKA* says that Giric and Eochaid were expelled together. How then could Giric have been king as the Dunkeld Litany claims? Could Eochaid have been king of Strathclyde and Giric some kind of sub-king? Perhaps they simply reigned in different kingdoms. We shall return to these problems in a later chapter.

CHAPTER 4

The Grandsons of Cinaed and the Grandsons of Ímar

RETURN OF THE ALPÍNIDS

With a neatness unusual in history, the year 900 sees a new kingdom appear in the pages of the Irish chronicles. Both the *Annals of Ulster* and *Chronicum Scottorum* record:

> Domnall son of Constantín, king of Alba, dies.[1]

Alba was the Irish name for the island of Britain and had consistently been used in the chronicles in that sense up to this point.[2] Was this Domnall son of Constantín king of the whole island? This seems unlikely since he is not noticed at all in English or Welsh records. He is, however, one of the kings whose reign is recorded in the text some modern historians have chosen to label *The Chronicle of the Kings of Alba* (*CKA*). In that text the expulsion of King Eochaid, the uterine grandson of Cinaed son of Alpín, is immediately followed by an account of Domnall.

> *Doniualdus* son of Constantín held the kingdom xi years. The Northmen then wasted Pictavia. In his reign occurred a battle [at?] *inuisibsolian*, between the *Danair* and the *Scotti*. The *Scotti* had the victory. [At] Dunnottar he was slain by the heathens.

Domnall's eleven years, counted back from his obit in 900, take us to 889 and thus confirm the reign length assigned to Eochaid, the previous

---

[1] *AU* 900.6. *CS* 900.
[2] D. N. Dumville, 'Ireland and Britain in *Táin Bó Fráich*', *Études Celtiques* 32 (1996), 175–87. This article is much more wide-ranging than the title would suggest.

king in the list, who lacks an obit in the chronicles. The account of the wasting of Pictavia is the final reference to Pictavia in *CKA*. The peculiar *inuisibsolian* is taken to be in part, or in whole, a place name. Marjorie Anderson suggested that the first part should read *innisib* the dative plural of Gaelic *innis*, 'island'.[3] Thus, we should perhaps read this as 'a battle on the isles of Solian'. Benjamin Hudson has suggested that this might mean the islands off the coast of mid-Argyll including Seil, Luing and Scarba.[4] As noted in Chapter 4, the terms *Danair* and *Scotti* look slightly anachronistic and may have been added as a gloss to clarify the meaning of the passage. The same would then apply to the notice of the 'Scottish' victory. It is noticeable that neither the wasting of Pictavia nor the battle is ascribed to a specific year. The phrase 'in his reign' (*in huius regno*) is reminiscent of the 'in his time' (*in huius tempore*) in the account of the making of the laws of Áed son of Eochaid by the Gaels and their king, in the reign of Domnall son of Alpín. This may indicate that the two notices belong to the same phase of editing. Since we have seen that 'Northmen' is a more common way of describing the Scandinavians in the ninth century, and since it appears here with the final notice of Pictavia, we can probably identify three, or possibly four, phases of composition:

1. Doniualdus son of Constantín held the kingdom xi years, he was slain by the heathens at Dunnottar.
2. The Northmen then wasted Pictavia.
3a. In his reign occurred a battle [at?] *inuisibsolian*.
3b. between the *Danair* and the *Scotti*. The *Scotti* had the victory.

The pedigrees, backed up by some degree of common sense, tell us that Domnall was the son of Constantín son of Cinaed, who had been slain in 876. His taking of the kingship in 889 would seem to mark a restoration of the dynasty that had been interrupted by the killing of his uncle Áed in 878, yet on one level it marks a new beginning.

On the death of his father Domnall may have been too young to be considered for the kingship, for rule by minors was rarely, if ever, acceptable in this age. It may also have been the case that he and his cousin, Constantín son of Áed, were in danger from the usurper, whether this was Eochaid or Giric, and may have fled or been taken out of the country. It is interesting to note that in 878, the year of the usurpation, the Irish chronicles record:

---

[3] Anderson, *Kings and Kingship*, 251, n. 137.
[4] Hudson, 'The Scottish Chronicle', 155, n. 29.

> The shrine of Columba and his other relics arrived in Ireland, having been taken in flight to escape the Gaill.[5]

If the relics of Columba were still on Iona at this stage, this action might have been instigated by otherwise unattested activity in the Hebrides, but if they were, in fact, in Dunkeld an alternative interpretation might be put forward. *CKA*'s account of the reign of Constantín son of Cinaed (862–76) ended with the statement that the Northmen occupied Pictavia for a year after his death, and the same text ascribes a reign of only one year to Áed son of Cinaed, even though he was slain in the second year after his brother. It is possible that the Alpínid regime truly collapsed on Constantín's death and that Áed's brief reign and violent death represent an abortive attempt at restoration. Further evidence for this appears in the earliest versions of the king-list in which the notice of Constantín's reign is preceded by an 'and'. This suggests that at one time the list ended with Constantín.[6] A passage in one version of *Lebor Bretnach*, the Gaelic adaptation of *Historia Brittonum*, states that there were seventy kings of the Picts from the legendary Cathluan to 'Constantín, who was the last'. The king-list demonstrates this Constantín to be Constantín son of Cinaed. All this would seem to indicate that there was at least one point of view, current by the mid-eleventh century if not before, that the killing of Constantín by Healfdene's *Scaldingi* in 876 marked the end of the Pictish kingdom. It was certainly the last event to be recorded in the *Anglo-Saxon Chronicle* in which the Picts are mentioned.

The relics of Columba, then, may have been taken from Dunkeld in 876, and after wandering around Scotland for more than a year, much as Cuthbert's relics were wandering around Northumbria at almost the same time, they were finally taken to Ireland. It is tempting to think that the young princes, Domnall son of Constantín and Constantín son of Áed, sons of the last two Pictish kings, went with them. Their aunt Mael Muire was at that time married to Áed, king of Tara, the most powerful king in Ireland and, although he was to die the following year, she went on to marry his successor Flann Sinna, king of Mide, who would reign until 916. The court of the kings of Tara may have seemed the most hopeful place of succour for the exiled Pictish princes. A diplomatic failure to recognise the usurper in Pictavia on the part of their Irish kinsmen may also go some way to explaining the absence of any obituary for either Eochaid or Giric in the 'Chronicle of Ireland'.

---

[5] *AU* 878.9.
[6] Anderson, *Kings and Kingship*, 78–9.

Whether a bid for the kingship by Domnall led to the expulsion of his predecessors in the kingship, or whether they were expelled by the great men of the realm who then sent for him, we shall probably never know. In the reign of David (1124–53) the places of the kings' deaths were added to the king-list, and here we find that Giric was said to have died at Dundurn, presumably the rocky citadel at the head of Strathearn in Perthshire. Perhaps this was the location of a confrontation between Giric and Domnall but we should be cautious about building too much on this. Although Domnall restored his dynasty he seems to have faced renewed conflict with the Northmen. Whether these were the Anglo-Danish kings in York, one of whom, Guðfrið (c. 880–95), is said to have won a battle against a Scottish king in eleventh-century sources,[7] or whether they were Northmen based elsewhere in Scotland is unclear. Indeed, they may even have been refugees from the *longphort* at Dublin for we are told that the force there had a falling out in 893, one group following Sitriuc (ON Sigtryggr) son of Ímar and the other Jarl Sichfrith (ON Sigurðr). If Hudson's identification of 'Innse Solian' is correct then it is important evidence for Domnall's interest in Argyll. His death at the hands of the heathens at Dunnottar in the Mearns suggests that, like the other kings whose reigns were recorded in *CKA*, his main interests lay in the east midlands, between the Forth and the Mounth.

Alba: what's in a name?

The appearance of the name Alba as a label for a specific kingdom rather than as a general Gaelic term for the island of Britain must require some explanation. The sources are not explicit about this and modern scholars have come up with various suggestions as to how this happened.

One possibility is that it represents a Gaelocentric perspective, just as English use of 'America' to denote the United States, the most significant English-speaking part of the Americas, appears to deny the undeniable Americanness of Canadians and Latin Americans. Irish writers may have thought the only people in Britain (that is, Alba) worth noticing were those who spoke their own language.

Alternatively, it has been suggested that the Alpínids adopted an ethnically neutral geographical term in order not to be made to chose between their Gaelic and their Pictish heritage. Something similar was

[7] T. Johnson South, ed., *Historia de Sancto Cuthberto* (Woodbridge, 2002), text at 68–71 and editor's discussion at 116–17.

Alba: what's in a name? (*continued*)

happening in Ireland at the time where kings of Tara, the high kings, were increasingly being described as 'kings of Ireland'.

Alba, may, however, have long denoted a more specific region. Within Dál Riata it is likely that the natives distinguished between the part that lay in Ériu, Ireland, and the part that lay in Alba, Britain.

Dauvit Broun, however, has drawn attention to the fact that the Pictish king-list drawn up in the time of Constantín son of Cinaed appears to describe Pictavia as Alba. Later Welsh sources regularly describe Scotland as *Prydyn*, apparently a northern dialect variant of *Prydain*, 'Britain', and this may represent the Pictish British name for their own country. Or it may simply translate Alba.

CONSTANTÍN SON OF ÁED

Domnall's successor was his cousin, another Constantín, the son of Áed son of Cinaed. His death is recorded in the *Annals of Ulster* under the year 952.[8] The account of his reign in *CKA* is as follows:

> *Constantínus* son of Ed held the kingdom for xl years in whose third year the Northmen plundered Dunkeld and all Albania. In the following year the Northmen were slain in *Strath Erenn*. And in the vi year king Constantín and bishop Cellach pledged to keep the laws and disciplines of the faith and the rights of the Church and the Gospels *pariter cum Scottis* on the Hill of Belief next to the royal *ciuitas* of Scone. From that day the hill earned its name, that is the Hill of Belief. And in his eighth year was slain the most excellent king and archbishop of the Irish, by the Leinstermen, that is Cormac son of Cuilennán. And there died in his time Dyfnwal, king of the Britons, and Domnall, king of Ailech, and Flann son of Maelsechnaill, and Niall son of Áed who reigned three years after Flann. And the battle of *Tinemore* happened in his xviii year between Constantín and Ragnall and the *Scotti* had the victory. And the battle of *Dún Brunde* in his xxxiiii year in which was slain the son of Constantín and after one year he died. Dubucan son of Indrechtach, *mormair* of Oengus, Æðelstan son of Edward, king of the Saxons, and Eochaid son of Alpín died.

[8] *AU* 952.1.

And in his old age and decrepitude he took the staff and served the Lord and he handed the kingdom to Mael son of Domnall.

Cross-referencing *CKA*'s account with the *Annals of Ulster*, produces the following:

1. *Constantínus* son of Ed held the kingdom for xl years and in his old age and decrepitude he took the staff and served the Lord and he handed the kingdom to Mael son of Domnall.

2. In his third year the Northmen plundered Dunkeld and all Albania.

3. In the following year the Northmen were slain in *Strath Erenn*.

    3. *AU* 904.4 Ímar grandson of Ímar, was slain by the men of Fortriu, and there was a great slaughter about him.

4. and in the vi year king Constantín and Bishop Cellach pledged to keep the laws and disciplines of the faith and the rights of the Church and the Gospels *pariter cum Scottis* on the Hill of Belief next to the royal *ciuitas* of Scone. From that day the hill earned its name, that is the Hill of Belief.

5. and in his eighth year was slain the most excellent king and archbishop of the Irish, by the Leinstermen, that is Cormac son of Cuilenan.

    5. *AU* 908.3 A battle between the men of Munster . . . and the Laigin . . . and Cormac son of Cuilennán was slain there.

6. and there died in his time Dyfnwal, king of the Britons,

7. and Domnall, king of Ailech,

    7. *AU* 915.2 †Domnall king of Ailech.

8. and Flann son of Maelsechnaill,

    8. *AU* 916.1 † Flann king of Tara.

9. and Niall son of Áed who reigned three years after Flann.

9. *AU* 919.3 †Niall son of Áed.

10. and the battle of *Tinemore* happened in his xviii year between Constantín and Ragnall and the *Scotti* had the victory.

10. *AU* 918.4 Ragnall fought the men of Alba 'on the banks of the Tyne in North Saxony'.

11. and the battle of *Dún Brunde* in his xxxiiii year in which was slain the son of Constantín

11. *AU* 937.6 A great and lamentable battle fought between the Gaill and the Saxons.

12. and after one year he died.

13. Dubucan son of Indrechtach, mormair of Oengus,

14. Æðelstan son of Edward, king of the Saxons

14. *AU* 939.6 †Æðelstan, king of the Saxons.

15. and Eochaid son of Alpín died.

Constantín's reign has increasingly come to be seen as one of the most significant in the history of Scotland. Not only was it very long, at least forty years, but it was also the period during which conflict and diplomatic relations between a kingdom recognisably ancestral to Scotland and one recognisably ancestral to England first occurred. Although Constantín is said, in *CKA*, to have reigned for forty years there is some conflict between our sources. Constantín's obituary appears in the *Annals of Ulster* under the year 952,[9] and *CKA* itself says that he died in the tenth year of his successor Mael Coluim son of Domnall. This would make Mael Coluim's first year 942/943. Our ability to correlate some of the events dated to specific years of Constantín's reign in *CKA* to events which the Irish chronicles give absolute dates (see above) allows us to see that, whoever inserted most of these entries, counted the beginning of Constantín's reign from AD 900, the year of the death of his cousin Domnall. Thus, the defeat of the Northmen in *Strath Erenn* in his fourth year coincides with the killing of Ímar grandson of Ímar by the men of Fortriu in 904 and the death of Cormac son of Cuilennán in his eighth year happened in 908. If this correlation were correct then his final year, and Mael Coluim's first, should have been 940/941. One of the correlations, however, does not fit this pattern. The battle of Dún Brunde is

---

[9] *AU* 952.1.

dated by *CKA* to Constantín's thirty-fourth year. It actually happened in 937. If this correlation were correct then it would put Constantín's first year in c. 903, making his fortieth year 942/943, as the information relating to Mael Coluim's reign would suggest.

Two solutions to this problem present themselves. One is to presume that the killing of Domnall by the pagans in 900 was followed by an effective three-year occupation of the kingdom before Constantín, in his turn, defeated them. At the time the original regnal list was drawn up this may have been recognised, but the editor who added the notices of events dated to specific regnal years did not know or realise this and simply presumed that Constantín succeeded on Domnall's death. The second possibility is that the battle of Dún Brunde, in which Constantín confronted Æðelstan of Wessex, has at some stage been confused with the events of 934 in which these two kings, as we shall see, also came into conflict.

ÍMAR GRANDSON OF ÍMAR

The period immediately following Domnall son of Constantín's death is further complicated by a unique entry in *Chronicum Scottorum* under the year 904:

> Ead, king of Cruithentúath, fell by the two grandsons of Ímar,
> and by Catol, along with five hundred [others].

This entry has caused historians a great deal of anxiety. The term Cruithentúath is Gaelic for 'Pictish Nation', but its use is confined almost exclusively to literary texts (poems and sagas), and it is, I believe, unparalleled in the chronicles. Alan Anderson speculated that this 'Ead' was either a predecessor of Constantín, or a regional sub-king or a garbled form of an English king's name.[10] The latter seems unlikely given the notice of Cruithentúath. The further possibility remains that it could be a garbled account of Constantín's victory over the Norse and the 'Ead' stands for his patronymic, the original perhaps reading 'Constantín son of Áed, king of Cruithentúath, felled two grandsons of Ímar, and Catol along with five hundred others', but this would require quite a severe emendation. To some extent the occasional enigmatic annal of this sort serves to remind us how few notices of events survive and from what a

[10] A. O. Anderson, *Early Sources of Scottish History* (Edinburgh, 1922, and Stamford, 1990), 398, n. 8.

restricted area of Scotland. This might be a garbled account of some happening recorded elsewhere, but it might be the sole surviving record of an
altogether different event. The literary form Cruithentúath and the
unparalleled names 'Ead' and 'Catol' must, however, make us suspicious
that this annal has crept into the chronicle from elsewhere.

If we accept the dominant chronology of the *Chronicle of the Kings of
Alba* then the first event of Constantín's reign of which we are told is the
plundering of Dunkeld and all Albania in his third year. The use of the
phrase 'Dunkeld and all Albania' is the best evidence that this strand of
the chronicle, at least, was put together either in Dunkeld or in a house
closely associated with it.[11] In the following year we are told that the
Northmen were slain in 'Strath Erenn'. This battle has been identified,
probably correctly, with that recorded in the *Annals of Ulster*:

> *AU* 904.4 Ímar grandson of Ímar, was slain by the men of Fortriu,
> and there was a great slaughter about him.

On the basis of this correlation W. F. Skene, in the nineteenth century,
suggested that Strathearn must lie in Fortriu.[12] This was an unnecessary
presumption. 'Strath Erenn' is probably an early form of the name
Strathearn, but it is equally the early form of the name that would become
Strathdearn, in the north, since the Findhorn was also originally the Earn
(note the farm of Invererne, just north of Forres).[13] Even if Strathearn in
Perthshire were intended, as may be marginally more likely given the geographical bias of the chronicle, then it is not a given that the men of
Fortriu were necessarily fighting on their home territory. Other evidence,
in fact, suggests that Fortriu lay north of the Mounth.[14] Perhaps, more
interestingly, this is the last appearance of the name Fortriu in a chronicle source.

Chronicum Scotorum's enigmatic annal refers to the 'two grandsons of
Ímar' and the *Annals of Ulster*'s to Ímar grandson of Ímar. The assumption has always been that these men were grandsons of that Ivarr who had
led the *Scaldingi* between 856 and his death in 873. The death of Ímar

---

[11] D. Broun, 'Dunkeld and the origin of Scottish identity', *Innes Review* 48 (1997),
112–24 at 120. See also B. T. Hudson, 'Kings and Church in early Scotland', *Scottish
Historical Review* 73 (1994), 145–70, at 154–5.
[12] W. F. Skene, *Celtic Scotland* (Edinburgh, 1876–80), iii. 43, n. 4.
[13] W. J. Watson, *Scottish Place-Name Papers* (Edinburgh, 2002), 137–54. The name
'Findhorn' derives from the Gaelic for 'White Earn'.
[14] A. Woolf, 'Dún Nechtain, fortriu and the geography of the Picts', *Scottish Historical
Review* 85 (2006), 182–201.

grandson of Ímar did not mark the end of this family for at least three more grandsons of Ivarr will come to play their part in our story and they will, together, found a dynasty that would play an important role in Insular history for some time to come. No source, however, makes it clear precisely how they were descended from Ivarr, whether they were all brothers or whether they claimed descent through their mother or their father.[15]

It is widely speculated that the appearance of the grandsons of Ímar in Albania in 903 to 904 was connected with the expulsion of the Northmen from Dublin in 902. This event was recorded in the *Annals of Ulster*:

> *AU* 902.2 The heathens were driven from Ireland, that is from the
> *longphort* at Dublin, by Mael Finnia son of Flannacán, with the
> men of Brega, and by Cerball son of Muiricán, with the
> Leinstermen; and they abandoned a good number of their ships
> and escaped half dead after they had been wounded and broken.

After this the Irish chronicles make no mention of Scandinavian activity in Ireland until 914.[16] The heathen refugees from Ireland seem to have settled along the eastern shores of the Irish sea. The only contemporary annalistic account of this appears in the Welsh *Annales Cambriae* which state under the year 902:

> Igmunt came into Anglesey and held Maes Osmeliaun.[17]

A sequel to this account is preserved in a short saga about 'Hingamund' (both Igmunt and 'Hingamund' seem to represent Old Norse Ingimundr), which survives in the so-called *Fragmentary Annals of Ireland*, preserved only in a seventeenth-century copy but probably dating from the mid-eleventh century.[18] This story tells how Ingimundr was driven out of Anglesey by the local Welsh ruler and how he then settled near Chester,

---

[15] Three sons of Ímar were known to the Irish chronicles: Bárid, killed in 881; Sichfrith, killed in 888; and Sitriuc, killed in 896, all by fellow Northmen. The first grandson of Ímar to be noted was Amlaíb, slain by the Ulaid and the Conaille of County Louth in 896.

[16] *AU* 914.5. It should be noted, however, that archaeologists have, to date, failed to find evidence of a phase of abandonment at Dublin. This may mean that a small presence was maintained, perhaps under local Irish rule.

[17] D. N. Dumville, ed. & tr., *Annales Cambriae, AD 682–954: texts A–C in Parallel* (Cambridge, 2002), 14.

[18] J. N. Radner ed., *Fragmentary Annals of Ireland* (Dublin, 1978), 167–73.

with the permission of the king and queen of Mercia (Æðelred, 879–911, and his wife Æðelflæd, who survived him until 918). After a while Ingimundr grew dissatisfied and persuaded other 'Norwegians' and 'Danes' who were settled nearby to rise up against their hosts and to seize Chester. The saga recounts their attempts to take the ancient Roman fortress which ultimately proved unsuccessful. Ingimundr finds no place in English sources, but the *Anglo-Saxon Chronicle* notes the 'restoration' of Chester under the year 907. This might represent a response to Scandinavian settlement in the region or it may have provoked the oath-breaking which the *Fragmentary Annals* ascribe to Ingimundr and his fellows. It also seems likely that the major invasion of western Mercia from Northumbria in 910 included forces from this area.[19]

Unfortunately, as noted in a previous chapter, the western coast of Northumbria from the Mersey to Ayrshire is a 'chronicle blind-spot' in the early middle ages and almost no events occurring there are recorded. There is some evidence, however, that the settlement from Ireland in this period was not simply confined to the immediate hinterland of Chester. *Historia de Sancto Cuthberto*, probably originally composed in the 940s but surviving only in a mid-eleventh century edition, tells us that Abbot Tilred of Heversham (Westmorland) came to St Cuthbert's land and purchased the abbacy of Norham on Tweed during the episcopate of Cutheard (c. 904–18), perhaps as a refugee, and, more explicitly, that one Alfred son of Brihtwulf, 'fleeing from pirates, came over the mountains in the west and sought the mercy of St Cuthbert and bishop Cutheard so that they might present him with some lands.'[20] Bishop Cutheard's episcopate clearly included the period immediately following the expulsion of the heathens from Dublin and the restoration of Chester. Place-names and personal names recorded from the later middle ages make it quite clear that there was a major Scandinavian influx into this area at some point and that that influx included a substantial admixture of people with some kind of Gaelic background. The linguistic evidence would seem to cover the whole coastline from the Wirral, in Cheshire, northwards into Dumfries and Galloway.[21] The absence of chronicle evidence, however,

---

[19] *ASC* 910. F. T. Wainwright's classic account of 'Ingimund's invasion', *English Historical Review* 247 (1948), 145–67, has been twice reprinted in F. T. Wainwright and H. P. R. Finberg, eds, *Scandinavian England* (Chichester, 1975), 131–62 and more recently in P. Cavill, S. Harding and J. Jesch, eds, *Wirral and its Viking Heritage* (Nottingham, 2000), 43–59.

[20] *HSC* §§ 21 and 22, respectively.

[21] For the place-name evidence see various papers in the volumes cited in the penultimate note.

makes it impossible to say that all of this region became 'Hiberno–Norse' in character in the years 902–7, but it seems likely that the process which led to these changes was initiated in this period. Such a date range would also seem to fit with a distinctive change in the character of the buildings excavated at Whithorn, which from the early years of the tenth century began to resemble the architectural styles found at Dublin. Unfortunately, modern national agendas have largely prevented the evidence from southwest Scotland being considered alongside that from northwest England and so this large and important cultural zone has tended to be viewed as marginal in both countries. It seems very likely that the Isle of Man also lay within this zone and may even have been its political centre.

This digression into the Irish Sea zone has been necessary both to set the scene for later developments in Constantín's reign and to discuss the identity of his enemies at home in the first years of his reign. It has often been assumed that Ímar grandson of Ímar was one of the refugees from Dublin and that his appearance in Albania in 903 and 904 followed on from his flight from that place. One wonders, however, if that is a necessary conclusion. Western Northumbria and North Wales must have provided ample opportunities for the refugees, and the Tay basin, which seems to be the core area of Albania in this period, is some way away. We should also recall that Domnall son of Constantín had been slain at Dunnottar in 900 by heathens who had been wasting Pictavia during his reign. On balance it seems more likely that Ímar grandson of Ímar was the leader of this force which had been active in the kingdom since at least 900 and possibly for some years before. Once more we need to recall that we have no idea what the political configuration north of the Mounth was in this period.

Interestingly the *Fragmentary Annals*'s account of Ingimundr makes a brief mention of 'young Ímar' in Alba. It says that some years before the battle around Chester:

On another occasion, when king Ímar was a young lad, and he came to plunder Alba with three large troops, the men of Alba, lay and clergy alike, fasted and prayed to God and Colum Cille [Columba] until morning, and beseeched the Lord, and gave profuse alms of food and clothing to the churches and to the poor, and received the Body of the Lord [the Eucharist] from the hands of their priests, and promised to do every good thing as their clergy would best urge them, and that their battle standard in the van of every battle would be the crozier of Colum Cille – and it is on that account that it is called *Cathbuaid* [battle triumph] from them onwards; and the name is fitting, for they have often won victory in battle with it, as they did at that time, relying upon Colum Cille.[22]

This account almost certainly refers to the battle of 904, although the author seems to have misunderstood his source slightly when he refers to the event as occurring when King Ímar was a young lad. It seems more likely that Ímar grandson of Ímar was distinguished from his grandfather in the writer's sources by being called 'Ímar the younger' or some similar description. This account emphasises the centrality of the Columban cult in the kingdom at this time.

SCONE (905–6)

Two years after his defeat of the Northmen, so the *Chronicle of the Kings of Alba* tells us, Constantín was involved in an extraordinary ceremony at Scone. This is described as follows:

> And in the vi year king Constantín and bishop Cellach pledged to keep the laws and disciplines of the faith and the rights of the Church and the Gospels *pariter cum Scottis* on the Hill of Belief next to the royal *ciuitas* of Scone. From that day the hill earned its name, that is the Hill of Belief.

Unfortunately the precise meaning of the Latin text, and in particular the phrase which I have left untranslated, is unclear. This is the first mention of Scone in any historical source and the 'Hill of Belief' is presumably the low mound which can still be seen today and which may have been used in royal inaugurations later in the medieval period. The description of Scone as a royal *ciuitas* probably indicates that there was a major church-settlement at the site along with a royal hall, as we have speculated may have been the case at Meigle in the days of King Wrad and as was certainly the case at places like Dunfermline and St Andrews in the early twelfth century.

Cellach is one of four bishops named in *CKA* and these same four appear as the first four in a list of bishops of St Andrews preserved

[22] Radner, *Fragmentary Annals*, 171.

in the fifteenth-century chronicles of Andrew of Wyntoun and Walter Bower.[23] In *CKA* no see, or bishop's seat, is mentioned and this might reflect the fact that the territorial term 'bishop of Alba' may have been prevalent when the chronicle was first drawn up. Whether these bishops of Alba all had their see at St Andrews, as was later the case, is open to debate. Indeed, these early bishops may not have had a fixed see. Walter Bower mentions that there were three bishops at Abernethy (Perthshire) before the location of the see at St Andrews.[24] What is not clear is whether his source intended three additional bishops, whose names have not been preserved, or whether the first three bishops in this list were thought to have had their see at Abernethy. The two fifteenth-century chroniclers also claim that Bishop Cellach was appointed during the reign of Giric.

The nature of the oath-swearing is somewhat unclear. Are the bishop and the king swearing together, and addressing the public, or are they, effectively, making some kind of agreement between themselves, more like a treaty. In some ways one might be tempted to see this as the first royal inauguration at Scone, with Bishop Cellach presiding, but the fact that it was held in Constantín's sixth year would seem to make this unlikely. This would make sense only if one took the view that an interregnum existed between Domnall and Constantín during which Ímar effectively ruled the Tay basin (900–4). Even in this case, however, the ceremony at Scone took place something like two years after Constantín had vanquished Ímar, so it seems unlikely that this could provide a full explanation. Taken at face value the oath is basically an undertaking, presumably by Constantín, to uphold Church laws and rights. The problematic phrase, *pariter cum Scottis*, however, is open to a number of interpretations. In 1922 Anderson translated the phrase 'in conformity with [the customs] of the Scots', drawing attention to Skene's presumption that it was effectively a Gaelicisation of the Pictish Church.[25] Hudson, in his recent translation, took a similar view and rendered it 'in the like manner with the Scots'. Thomas Clancy, following a similar line, interprets the events at Scone as 'the establishment of parity between the practices of the Irish church and the Scottish church', and in particular goes on to emphasise the role of bishops which he seems to be

[23] D. E. R. Watt, *Series Episcoporum Ecclesiae Catholicae Occidentalis ab initio usque ad annum MCXCVIII, Series VI, Britannia, Scotia et Hibernia, Scandinavia*, vol. 1 *Ecclesia Scoticana* (Stuttgart, 1991), 75–9.

[24] Watt, *Series Episcoporum*, 39.

[25] A. O. Anderson, *Early Sources of Scottish History* (*ESSH*), 445.

suggesting might be new in this period.[26] Thomas Charles-Edwards, however, suggests that *pariter cum Scottis* means 'along with the Gaels', and implies a wider participation in the oath taking: 'King Constantín and bishop Cellach, along with the Gaels, swore . . .'.[27] A suggestion I have made when presenting this material to students, has been that it was the nature of the ceremony that was 'Scottish' and that we should read the passage thus:

> And in the sixth year King Constantín and Bishop Cellach
> vowed – on the Hill of Belief near the royal *ciuitas* of Scone, after
> the fashion of the Gaels – to keep the laws and disciplines of the
> faith and also the rights of the churches and the gospels; from this
> day the hill has received its name, that is, the Hill of Belief.

Thus, the term *Scotti* refers either to the wider group of people involved in the ceremony, the national origin of the Church customs being promoted, or the national origin of the nature of the ceremony. Any one of these interpretations, or none of them, could be correct.

The events at Scone in Constantín's sixth year are reminiscent of a meeting held at Kingston-upon-Thames, in the south of England in 838, nearly seventy years earlier. This meeting was described as a *uenerabile concilium* and was held between Ceolnoth, archbishop of Canterbury, and the West Saxon King Ecgbert and his son, heir designate and sub-king of Kent, Æðelwulf. The Kingston meeting seems to have marked the recognition by Archbishop Ceolnoth that secular over-lordship in the extreme southeast of England, principally the ancient kingdoms of Kent and Essex, had passed from the Mercians of the English Midlands to the West Saxons of southwest England. Ecgbert and his son Æðelwulf guaranteed to stand surety for the freedom of elections to the headship of ecclesiastical houses and to prevent any other secular lord, lay or clerical, from intervening in the due process laid down by canon law. Ceolnoth in his turn recognised these kings as the final arbiters in such decisions. Essentially the Church had switched its patronage, or perhaps its

---

[26] T. O. Clancy, 'Iona, Scotland and the Céli Dé', in B. E. Crawford, ed., *Scotland in Dark Age Britain* (St Andrews, 1996), 111–30 at 122.

[27] T. M. Charles-Edwards, *The Early Medieval Gaelic Lawyer* (Cambridge, 1999), 60–1. A similar view was taken by Marjorie Anderson who translated the phrase 'and the Scots likewise', in 'Dalriada and the creation of the kingdom of the Scots', in D. Whitelock, R. McKitterick and D. Dumville, eds, *Ireland in Early Medieval Europe: Studies in Memory of Kathleen Hughes* (Cambridge, 1982), 106–32 at 127.

clientage, from one dynasty to another.[28] This had not been an instant or an easy decision for the archbishops to make. Ecgbert had defeated the Mercians in battle in 825 and sent his son Æðelwulf into Kent to expel the native King Baldred and install himself as his father's sub-king. Wulfred, who had been archbishop at the time, had resisted reaching an accommodation with the West Saxons. As late as 836 Ceolnoth, who had succeeded in 833, had still seemed to favour Mercian supremacy, which had, after all, been in place for 150 years. The 'venerable council' of Kingston in 838 marked the end of a thirteen-year period during which the Kentish Church had failed to come to terms with regime change.

It may be that the meeting at Scone in 905 or 906 represented a similar contract between Church and dynasty, particularly if Cellach had indeed been a friend of Giric and if the hints found in documents (such as the thirteenth-century king-list and the Dunkeld Litany) of a close link between the Church and Giric, have any basis in genuine ninth-century history. The parallels between Kingston and Scone go somewhat further than the nature of a social contract between Church and dynasty. Kingston, like Scone, would go on to become the royal inauguration site. The first royal inauguration at Kingston that we know of was that of Edward the Elder, on 8 June 900, who may well have been anointed as 'king of the Anglo-Saxons', a title his father, Ælfred, had taken part way through his reign to signify that his authority beyond the ancestral kingdom of Wessex was something more than that of *primus inter pares*. English kings continued to be inaugurated at Kingston until the Danish conqueror Cnut in 1016 who, through an act of coronation in St Paul's Cathedral, London, sought to signal the part God had played in the ousting of the West Saxon dynasty. The English royal inauguration stone is still kept at Kingston.[29] Scone and Kingston are also both at the tidal reach of the great national rivers, the Tay and the Thames, respectively. Can this really be coincidence?

To summarise, then: it seems likely that the meeting at Scone in 905 or 906 between King Constantín and Bishop Cellach, marked the end of a period perhaps beginning with the kingship of Domnall in 889 in which internal divisions within the kingdom and warfare with the heathens had created conditions in which the bishop of Alba was not at one with the returning Alpínid dynasty. The Council of Scone may have resolved

[28] N. Brooks, *The Early History of the Church of Canterbury* (Leicester, 1984), 197–201 and 323–5.

[29] S. Keynes, 'Kingston-upon-Thames', in M. Lapidge *et al.*, eds, *The Blackwell Encyclopaedia of Anglo-Saxon England* (Oxford, 1999), at 272.

many of these issues. The turn of the ninth and tenth centuries marks a period when a wave of reform was spreading through the western Church and it may well be that Cellach had been in direct contact with Canterbury and had been inspired by the example of Ceolnoth in 838, or perhaps Constantín was inspired by that of Edward in 900 to seek a new social contract between king and Church that would set the kingdom on a firm footing for the new century.

RAGNALL GRANDSON OF ÍMAR

While the bishop of Alba and his king set about reconstructing the kingdom of Albania following the depredations of Ímar grandson of Ímar, another grandson of Ímar, Ragnall, was biding his time out of sight of our chroniclers. When he finally chose to show himself he sent shock waves through the entire Insular world. The first years of the tenth century must have seemed a dire time for the Scandinavian colonies in Britain and Ireland. The expulsion or pacification of all the Northmen in Ireland in 902 may have led to colonisation along the western littoral of Northumbria but this had not, for all Ingimund's efforts, led to a serious threat against the native kingdoms of the region. Mercia, despite having a disabled king, had resisted them under its queen, and the men of Gwynedd, in North Wales, seem to have managed to expel the settlers there. In East Anglia 902 had seen the death of its last recorded *Scalding* king, Eohric.

In Northumbria proper, Guðfrið's relatively stable reign had come to an end with his death and subsequent burial in York Minster. He seems to have been followed by two kings with relatively short reign lengths, Sigurðr and Cnut, who are known only from numismatic evidence. It is curious, not to say perverse, that only a single coin, and that doubtfully, can be ascribed to Guðfrið who is said to have ruled for fifteen stable years, when his short-lived successors are known only from coins. Some have identified Sigurðr with the jarl of that name who left Dublin in 893, but this identification cannot be accepted with any certainty (particularly in light of the fact that the jarl's title seems to have been reserved for those not of royal birth). The reigns of Sigurðr and Cnut, which may have over-lapped, appear to have extended into the early tenth century, for a hoard from Cuerdale in Lancashire, which seems to have been deposited in, or shortly after, 905, contains many of their coins. This understanding of Northumbrian succession is somewhat confounded by the apparent claim of the *Anglo-Saxon Chronicle* that in 899, or shortly thereafter, the senior

West Saxon ætheling (royal prince), Æðelwold, excluded from the kingship by his cousin Edward (they were both grandsons of that Æðelwulf
who had taken part in the Council of Kingston, their fathers following
one another in the kingship[30]), 'went to the *here* in Northumbria and they
accepted him as king and gave allegiance to him'.[31] The following year he
brought a fleet to Essex, where the population accepted him as king and
then persuaded Eohric of East Anglia to join him in an attack on Edward's
lands. He and Eohric were both slain at the battle of the Holme, in East
Anglia in 902. Fitting Æðelwold into the Northumbrian kingship is problematic. Sigurðr and Cnut's coinage seems to run across Æðelwold's
floruit and there is only one single coin surviving that might bear his
name. An alternative explanation of his career might be that it was his
claim to the West Saxon kingship that was accepted by these people and
that they gave him their allegiance in the tradition in which his uncle
Ælfred had received the submission of Mercian, East Anglian, Welsh
and, perhaps, Northumbrian kings.

Whatever the sequence of Northumbrian kingship was in the years
around 900, by 910, when the Northumbrians invaded western Mercia,
two kings appear to have been present. One of these, Healfdene, may have
been the same man who issued coins in the northeast midlands (probably
from Lincoln) at about this time. Whether the coin distribution reflects
his political authority or whether he simply did not issue coins in his own
name north of the Humber, where the archbishops seem to have been
issuing coins in this period, is unclear. The other king, Eowils (ON
Auðgisl, Gaelic Auisle), is otherwise unknown. After raiding deep into
the Severn basin they were intercepted at Wednesfield near Tettenhall,
not far from modern Wolverhampton, by a joint West Saxon and Mercian
army and wiped out, both kings being killed. The location of their campaign and the large number of *hölðar* (non-royal chieftains) present may
suggest that the Hiberno–Norse settlers from the west coast were also
engaged in this venture.

The deaths of Healfdene and Eowils seem to have signalled the end of
the Anglo-Danish *Scalding* dynasty that had taken root in England in the
870s. The next Northumbrian king we hear about is the native Eadwulf
who died in 913.[32] He seems to have been succeeded by his son Ealdred.
It is in his time that we first hear of Ragnall grandson of Ímar, whose role
would be to revive Scandinavian fortunes in Northumbria.

---

[30]   Æðelwold was the son of Æðelred (865–71), and Edward of Ælfred (871–99).

[31]   *ASC* 900.

[32]   *AU* 913.1.

Following the expulsion of the Dubliners in 902 the Irish chronicles notice few events concerning the Northmen for a decade. Then from 913 they start to indicate an awareness of events in the Irish Sea. The first notice is an almost unique record of Irish activity outwith Ireland:

> *AU* 913.5 The heathens inflicted a battle-rout upon the crew of a
> new fleet of the Ulaid, on the 'Saxon shore' and many fell,
> including Camuscach son of Mael Mochergi, king of Lecale.

An expedition by the Ulaid, in particular the king of Lecale, the area around Downpatrick, to the 'Saxon shore' was probably directed at Galloway. No account survives of heathen raids on the Ulaid that might have provoked this expedition, so it may be that the Irish were attempting to take advantage of the collapse of western Northumbria. The Rhinns of Galloway, at least, might easily be regarded as the back yard of the Ulaid. Alternatively, we know that Whithorn had a reputation for piety and education in Ireland, particularly within the lands of the Ulaid, so Camuscach may have been leading a 'humanitarian' expedition to relieve the site from the pagans, or at least to rescue any relics that remained there. One wonders what the long-term consequences might have been had the Ulaid managed to establish their hegemony in Wigtownshire.

The following year internal conflict is noted among the Northmen in the Irish Sea:

> *AU* 914.4 A naval battle off the Isle of Man between Bárid son of
> Oitir and Ragnall grandson of Ímar, in which Bárid and nearly all
> of his army were destroyed.[33]

Neither of these leaders had been mentioned before in our sources, although a *jarl* named Ohtere (the Old English spelling of 'Oitir') was cited by the *Anglo-Saxon Chronicle* among the dead at Wednesfield in 910. The information we are given is not enough to explain the context of the conflict. Were the two leaders both members of the Scandinavian oligarchy that had been settled in the region for a decade? Was one of them the effective ruler of the region and the other an intruder attempting to muscle in on his patch? If so which was which? We can really only speculate, but if Ragnall was the successor to the leadership of that Ímar

---

[33] The names here are Gaelic renderings of the Old Norse names which are usually normalised as Barðr, Ottar, Rögnvaldr and Ivarr.

grandson of Ímar who had died in Albania in 904, and if Bárid was the son of the Earl Othere who had fallen at Wednesfield, then this battle off Man may have been between Northmen driven out of Scotland by Constantín seeking new hunting grounds in the Irish Sea, and the Hiberno-Norse settlers who had recently colonised the region. The Isle of Man itself, as has been noted, may well have been the base from which the beachheads in Galloway, Cumberland and Lancashire were controlled. It had been in British hands, possibly even ruled by the same dynasty as Gwynedd, in the mid-ninth century, but had probably fallen to the *Scaldingi* by 877 and was certainly occupied by Scandinavians by 900.[34]

In the same year that Ragnall asserted himself in the Irish Sea (914), the heathens returned to Ireland, landing, with 'a great new fleet' at Loch Dá Cháech (Waterford harbour).[35] These men had come from Brittany via South Wales where they had been worsted by Edward of Wessex acting as an effective overlord. At Loch Dá Cháech they set up a base from which they ravaged the church-settlements of Munster, not, seemingly, attempting to establish political control over the region. Over the next few years their numbers swelled and they proved a serious threat to the stability of southern Ireland. In 917, however, came new developments. Ragnall appeared on the scene accompanied by his brother Sihtric, each commanding a formidable fleet. Sihtric's fleet landed at a place called Cenn Fuait (identity unknown) on the coast of Leinster, while Ragnall moved against the heathen base at Loch Dá Cháech. At the same time the Munstermen inflicted a defeat on the heathens and the survivors seem to have submitted to Ragnall's leadership. Clearly large forces were involved for the sequel represented an almost unparalleled display of military unity among the Irish. Niall son of Áed, king of Tara, led an army from the northern half of Ireland to the aid of the Munstermen, at the same time urging the Leinstermen to attack Sihtric. Inconclusive fighting in Munster ended with Niall besieging Ragnall for twenty days, but in Leinster Sihtric defeated the army of the province killing the king of Leinster and two of his leading sub-kings.[36] The *Annals of Ulster* conclude the account of the year's campaigning with the terse but ominous statement:

AU 917.4 Sihtric grandson of Ímar entered Dublin.

---

[34] *AU* 877.3.
[35] *AU* 914.5.
[36] *AU* 917.2 and 917.3.

The following year Sihtric remained in Ireland, engaged in inconclusive warfare with Niall, his only success being the submission of Mael Mithig of Knowth, king of northern Brega.[37] Ragnall, however, had other plans:

> *AU* 918.4 The Gaill of Loch Dá Cháech, i.e. Ragnall, king of the Dark Gaill, and the two earls Oitir and Gragabai, forsook Ireland and proceeded afterwards against the men of Alba. The men of Alba, moreover, moved against them and they met on the banks of the Tyne in northern 'Saxony'. The heathens formed themselves into four battalions: a battalion with Gothfrith grandson of Ímar, a battalion with the two earls, and a battalion with the 'young lords' [Gaelic *óctigerna*]. There was also a battalion in ambush with Ragnall which the men of Alba did not see. The men of Alba routed the three battalions which they saw, and made a very great slaughter of the heathens, including Oitir and Gragabai. Ragnall, however, then attacked in the rear of the men of Alba, and made a slaughter of them, although they did not lose a king or mormaer. Nightfall caused the battle to be broken off.

This battle is clearly the same as that described in *CKA*:

> And the battle of *Tinemore* happened in his xviii year between Constantín and Ragnall and the *Scotti* had the victory.

The long account in the *AU* makes it clear that, as in many battles, both sides had some claim to victory. The battle is also described in *Historia de Sancto Cuthberto*. This text had already given some hints regarding the original Hiberno-Norse settlement of western Northumbria after 902. One account we have noted described how Elfred son of Brihtwulf fled over the mountains in the west from pirates and was given lands by Bishop Cutheard of St Cuthbert in return for services. This account continues:

> These he performed faithfully until king Rægnald came with a great multitude of ships and occupied the territory of Ealdred son of Eadwulf, who was a friend of King Edward, just as his father Eadwulf had been a favourite of King Alfred. Ealdred, having

[37] Mael Mithig was married to Lígach, the daughter of Mael Sechnaill of Mide and Mael Muire daughter of Cinaed son of Alpín.

been driven off, went therefore to Scotia, seeking aid from king
Constantín, and brought him into battle against Rægnald at
Corbridge. In this battle, I know not what sin being the cause, the
pagan king vanquished Constantín, routed the Scots, put Elfred
the faithful man of St Cuthbert to flight and killed all the English
nobles save Ealdred and his brother Uhtred.[38]

'Rægnald' is the English spelling of the name which the Gaelic writers
spelled 'Ragnall' (ON Rögnvaldr), and Corbridge stands on the banks of
the Tyne. Clearly all three sources recount the same battle. Surprisingly
not all historians have thought so. The problem has been caused by the
vexed issue of the date of Cutheard's episcopate. Following Symeon of
Durham's dating of the establishment of the see of St Cuthbert at
Chester-le-Street to 883, historians have calculated Cutheard's episcopate to have lain in the period between 901 and 915. Chapter 23 of
Historia de Sancto Cuthberto deals with the aftermath of the battle just
described and clearly portrays Cutheard as still alive. Thus, it has been
argued that this battle, for all its similarities to those described in the
Annals of Ulster and the *Chronicle of the Kings of Alba*, must in fact be a
different battle.[39] Symeon's chronology, however, is based on the assumption that the 'seven years wandering' which *Historia de Sancto Cuthberto*
tells us preceded the establishment of the see at Chester-le-Street was initiated by Healfdene's invasion of Northumbria in 875. This date then
became the fixed point for attaching absolute dates to his history of the
see:

Healfdene's invasion:	875
Seven years' wandering:	875–83
Eighteen years at Chester prior to Cutheard's election:	883–901
Fourteen-year episcopate of Cutheard:	901–15
Thirteen-year episcopate of Tilred:	915–28

Nothing in the earlier sources equates the period of wandering with
Healfdene's invasion, however, and as we have seen above, other factors
may have been involved. One synchronism that Symeon preserves in
chapter 17 of his *Libellus* is not predicated upon this equation and presumably comes from an independent source. Here he states that Edward
the Elder of Wessex died in Bishop Tilred's seventh year. Edward's death

---

[38] *HSC* § 22.
[39] The arguments are most clearly laid out by F. T. Wainwright in his 'The battles at
Corbridge', *Saga-Book of the Viking Society* 13 (1950), 156–73. Reprinted in
Wainwright and Finberg, eds, *Scandinavian England*, 163–80.

is securely dated to 924 and so this synchronism provides us with an alternative set of absolute dates for the see of Chester-le-Street:

Seven years' wandering:	878–86[40]
Eighteen years at Chester prior to Cutheard's election:	886–904
Fourteen-year episcopate of Cutheard:	904–18
First seven years of the episcopate of Tilred:	918–24

This alternative chronology has Cutheard dying in the same year as the battle record in the *AU* and *CKA*. However, further grist to the mill of those historians who have supported the idea of two battles at Corbridge is the fact that *Historia de Sancto Cuthberto* gives two accounts of the battle, in chapters 22 and 24. The reason for this is not, however, that there were two battles but because *Historia de Sancto Cuthberto* is largely structured around the history of specific estates donated to St Cuthbert. Many of the chapters take the form of brief histories of the leasing and depredation of an individual landholding or group of estates donated in a single act. Chapter 22 tells of the lands leased to Elfred son of Brihtwulf and chapter 24 of those leased to Eadred son of Ricsige. Both estates were confiscated by Ragnall after he had won the battle, thus the battle is mentioned in the account of both estates. Rather than there being two battles there was a single battle which played a part in two separate stories.

There was just one battle of Corbridge, in 918, in which Ealdred son of Eadwulf, English ruler of Northumbria, attempted with help from Constantín son of Áed, king of Alba, to return to the kingdom from which he had been expelled by Ragnall grandson of Ímar. Intervention, although not ultimately successful, as far south as Corbridge marks a new departure for the Alpínid kings, and initiates a period when Northumbria would be the battleground for regional hegemony in Britain.

The immediate result of the battle was that Ragnall, who had presumably dominated the western regions of Northumbria since at least 914, became undisputed ruler in the east also. At some point in 918, perhaps while Ealdred was persuading Constantín to come south with an army, the inhabitants of York put themselves under the protection of Æðelflæd, queen of Mercia, but she was dead by the middle of June and shortly afterwards Ragnall stormed the city.[41] At the same time Edward of Wessex, Æðelflæd's brother, annexed Mercia, taking his niece, the sole surviving member of the Mercian royal family, into custody.

---

[40] 878, the first year of the seven-year wandering by this calculation, was the last year of the reign of Ecgbert II the last English king of Northumbria.
[41] *ASC* 918 and *HRA* I. 919.

THE MAKING OF ENGLAND

The conquest of Northumbria by Ragnall grandson of Ímar and the annexation of Mercia by Edward of Wessex radically changed the political map of Britain. Northumbria was once more united but now by a dynasty that also controlled the Isle of Man and the Scandinavian ports in Ireland, while most of southern England, the richest part of the island, was in the hands of a single king ruling directly and not through autonomous sub-kings. Immediately following his annexation of Mercia Edward received the submission of the three leading kings in Wales, the brothers Hywel and Clydog, sons of Cadell, and their cousin Idwal son of Anarawd.[42] From English Mercia he moved eastwards into Danish held territory and captured and refortified Nottingham. After this 'all the people of Mercia, both Danish and English', submitted to him.[43]

Ragnall's arrival had introduced a new dynamic into the political alignments of eastern England. For forty years Danes and English had cohabited and viewed each other with suspicion. During this time, however, there had been much intermarriage and the Danes seem, for the most part, to have accepted some form of Christianity. Ragnall's people, however, were not Christian and what intermarriage there had been among their parents' generation had been largely between people of Norwegian extraction and the Celtic inhabitants of these islands. Thus, the Anglo–Danish population of those parts of Northumbria, East Anglia and the English east midlands which had been settled by Scandinavians in the 870s and 880s found themselves culturally torn between the Scandinavian affinities they shared with the followers of the grandsons of Ímar and the Christian English affinities they shared with their English neighbours and the southern kingdom of Edward. This dilemma of cultural identity would plague them for the better part of two generations to come. For the time being the Anglo–Danish populations, deprived of their own *Scalding* dynasty, found themselves torn between loyalty to a dynasty claiming descent from their national founder, Ivarr, but showing little evidence of common cultural experience, or the culturally less alien southron dynasty descended from their great national enemy Ælfred of Wessex.

By the end of 918 the frontier between Ragnall's *imperium* and Edward's was established along the old pre-Viking Age Mercian Northumbrian

---

[42] *ASC* 918. The exact division of territories between these three grandsons of Rhodri Mawr is not known.

[43] *ASC* 918. The East Angles had submitted to him and accepted his kingship in the previous year.

boundaries. The following year Edward constructed fortresses at Thelwall and Manchester on the Mersey ('Mersey' means 'boundary river'). In 920 he built a second fortress at Nottingham, on the other side of the River Trent from the first, and also a new fortress at Bakewell, blocking off the approach over the moors from the southern portion of Northumbria around modern Sheffield. The sequel to this operation is told in the 'A' text of the *Anglo-Saxon Chronicle*, the version which comes closest to being an official organ of the West Saxon dynasty:

> And then the king of the *Scottas* and all the people of the *Scottas* and Rægnald, and the sons of Eadwulf, and all who live in Northumbria, both English and Danish and Northmen and others, and also the king of the Strathclyde Welsh and all the Strathclyde Welsh, chose him [Edward] as father and lord.

Among other things this is the first contemporary English use of the term *Scottas* to describe the inhabitants of the Alpínid kingdom. It is also the earliest recorded diplomatic exchange between a kingdom that can legitimately be regarded as ancestral to Scotland and one that can be legitimately regarded as ancestral to England. The traditional view, going back at least as far as the twelfth century, has been that this marks the beginning of southern English hegemony over the whole island of Britain, the first step on the road to Bannockburn, or perhaps to the Union of 1707. By the middle of the twentieth century, however, historians were beginning to doubt whether Edward, who had only really advanced north of the Thames after 911, could possibly have had realistic ambitions of dominating Constantín and the, unnamed, king of the Strathclyde Welsh, whose territories lay beyond the potentially hostile and clearly militarily very efficient and ruthless Ragnall. F. T. Wainwright argued that, in the light of Scandinavian encroachments in the Irish Sea region in the recent past, this treaty of 920 was an anti-Viking alliance, but it is hard to see how Ragnall, the chief pagan and chief Northman of his age, could then have been involved.[44]

Bearing in mind that our sole source for this event is presenting a West Saxon perspective on the proceedings, but at the same time recognising that Edward was almost certainly the most powerful ruler on the island, having effective overlordship of all the kingdoms south of the Mersey, on the west, and probably south of the Humber, or at least the Welland, on

---

[44] F. T. Wainwright, 'The submission to Edward the Elder', *History* 37 (1952), 114–30, reprinted in Wainwright and Finberg, eds, *Scandinavian England*, 325–44.

the east, we must assess the situation with subtlety. Michael Davidson has pointed out that neither Rægnald nor the sons of Eadwulf are accorded the royal titles which the kings of the *Scottas* and the Strathclyde Welsh are allowed. He points to the fact that from the time that Edward's father Ælfred adopted the style 'King of the Anglo-Saxons', neither the chronicle, nor the scribes who drew up royal charters, had accorded any other *English* ruler the royal title.[45] This is particularly clear-cut in the case of Æðelred of Mercia who appears in a surviving Mercian king-list, and who the contemporary and well connected Bishop Asser described as having submitted to Ælfred under the same terms as Anarawd of Gwynedd, but who is consistently termed *ealdorman*, *hlaford*, *dux* or *dominus* rather than 'king' in West Saxon documents.[46] The implication of the absence of royal titles for Rægnald and the sons of Eadwulf would seem to be that Edward was in some way claiming a level of overlordship that he was not claiming over Constantín and the king of Strathclyde. In reality Edward's main anxiety may have been the possibility that Rægnald would threaten his newly acquired superiority in the Anglo-Danish areas of eastern England. Rægnald's greatest fear may have been that the allies of 918, Constantín and the sons of Eadwulf, would attempt once more to oust him from Northumbria. The deal that Edward brokered after constructing his fortress at Bakewell in 920 may have been that he would recognise Rægnald's rule in Northumbria in exchange for assurances that the Northmen would not attempt to 'liberate' the Danes of eastern Mercia and East Anglia, and that, further, Edward would require that the northern kings did not attempt to oust Rægnald. In this sense they may have accepted his arbitration and in some sense his lordship. In reality they were simply given to understand that Edward would assist Rægnald against attack from the north if he, in his turn, respected the boundary on the Mersey and the Humber. What is not clear is what was left for the sons of Eadwulf. Were they to remain exiles at Constantín's court or were they allowed some lordship in the north of Northumbria north of the Tyne, as the twelfth-century Durham writers claimed, or perhaps north of the Tweed under Constantín's protective wing?

[45] M. R. Davidson, 'The (non-)submission of the northern kings in 920', in
N. J. Higham and D. H. Hill, eds, *Edward the Elder, 899–924* (London, 2001), 200–11.
[46] For the Mercian king-list, and Æðelred generally, see S. Keynes, 'King Alfred and the Mercians', in M. Blackburn and D. Dumville, eds, *Kings, Currencies and Alliances: History and Coinage of Southern England in the Ninth Century* (Woodbridge, 1998), 1–46 at 19. For Asser see S. Keynes and M. Lapidge, eds & tr., *Alfred the Great: Asser's Life and other Contemporary Sources* (Harmondsworth, 1983), at 96.

The following year Ragnall grandson of Ímar died. He may have been sick for some time for he seems to have arranged for his brother Sihtric to vacate Dublin and join him in Northumbria in 920.[47] The *Annals of Ulster* describe Ragnall in his obituary as 'King of the Fair Gaill and the Dark Gaill',[48] and by this date these terms seem to have taken meanings approximating to the modern terms 'Hiberno-Norse' and 'Anglo-Danish', respectively. He had effectively ruled Northumbria, the Isle of Man and the Scandinavian ports in Ireland. What we do not know is whether he retained any control of territories within the boundaries of modern Scotland but beyond the boundaries of early medieval Northumbria. Was he king of the Isles? Did he control Orkney and Shetland? Were there, at this date, major Scandinavian colonies on the northern mainland? Because these areas lay outwith the range of our chroniclers in this period these questions are difficult to answer and impossible to deal with within a narrative of this sort. A later chapter will look at the complex evidence for the history of Scandinavian settlement and rule on this 'dark side' of Scotland.

In the event Sihtric, who had reconquered Dublin in 917, and, while Ragnall was capturing York in 919, had slain in battle Niall son of Áed, king of Tara, took over as king of Northumbria and sent, in his place, to Dublin another grandson of Ímar, Gothfrith, who was probably, but not certainly, his brother. Gothfrith inaugurated his rule in Ireland with an attack on Armagh, the chief church of the Irish, but his attack was of a kind not noted before for:

> he spared the prayer-houses with their complements of Céli Dé
> and sick from destruction, and also the cells, save for a few
> buildings which caught fire by accident.[49]

Had Gothfrith's sojourn in Northumbria, where Guðfrið's regime had laid the foundations for collaboration between Church and Northman, softened him? Was this the beginning of a new phase in Gaelic Norse relations?

On 17 July 924 Edward died at Farndon in Cheshire. It seemed for a moment as if his empire would break up, for the Mercians elected his eldest, but less well connected, son Æðelstan as king while the West Saxons elected Ælfweard, a son by his second marriage to a member of

[47]　*AU* 920.5.
[48]　*AU* 921.4.
[49]　*AU* 921.8.

the West Saxon nobility. Ælfweard, however, survived his father by only weeks[50] and, although there are hints that the West Saxons took some persuasion to accept Æðelstan he was eventually inaugurated into the kingship at Kingston-upon-Thames on 4 September 925.[51] Within five months he had entered into a relationship with Sihtric:

> In this year King Æðelstan and Sihtric, king of the
> Northumbrians, met together at Tamworth on 30th January and
> Æðelstan gave him his sister in marriage.[52]

There are a number of noteworthy points to be taken from this short notice. First, Tamworth was an ancient royal centre of the Mercians and lay securely inside Æðelstan's kingdom. The fact that the meeting took place there, and not at a border, suggests that Sihtric was in some sense recognising Æðelstan's superiority. None the less, it is noteworthy that the chronicler does not mention submission, that Sihtric is accorded the royal title, and that Æðelstan gave his sister to the Northumbrian. At first sight this looks very different from the earlier account of Edward's dealing with Sihtric's brother. We must be cautious, however. This account appears only in the D text of the Chronicle, which includes additions to the common stock made in York. It may well be that this entry derives from a Northumbrian chronicle which would have been less inclined to pander to West Saxon pretensions. This would almost certainly explain why Sihtric is accorded the royal title when Rægnald was not. It would be interesting to know whether the reference to the marriage alliance was dependent upon this different perspective. Æðelstan had a great many sisters but all the others, that we know of, were married to continental husbands. Indeed, although Æðelstan's aunt, Æðelflæd had been married to the Mercian king, probably in the early 880s, no subsequent West Saxon princess is known to have been married to an Insular ruler. The implication is that bride exchange occurred between equals or that bride-giving could be part of an act of submission. The fact that we are reliant upon a Northumbrian source for our knowledge that a West Saxon princess was given to a Northumbrian king in marriage raises

---

[50] He is accorded a four-week reign in the regnal list preserved in *Textus Roffensis*, see D. N. Dumville, 'The West Saxon genealogical regnal list: manuscripts and text', *Anglia* 104 (1986), 1–32.

[51] It is principally the delay between Ælfweard's death on 2 August 924 and the inauguration, over a year later, that suggests some negotiation was necessary to bring the West Saxons on board.

[52] *ASC* (D), 926.

questions about royal marriages elsewhere in the Insular world. It is always assumed that the West Saxon dynasty did not give brides to the Scots or the Welsh, but this might simply be an accident of the paucity of chronicles surviving from the Celtic-speaking regions. If bride-giving was seen as an act which humbled the kin group of the bride it may well be that any record of such acts in relation to those they came to regard as their sub-kings was glossed over by the house-chroniclers of the West Saxon dynasty.[53]

Caution must be exercised, however, before jumping to conclusions. Another possible explanation is at hand. While the 'A' text of the *Anglo-Saxon Chronicle* generally functions as the mouthpiece of the regime it was, in fact, for this period the copy of the chronicle maintained at Winchester, the traditional burial ground of the West Saxon dynasty. Winchester appears to have been the centre of resistance to Æðelstan's succession, and even after his succession the chronicler there seems to have grudgingly recorded very few of his deeds. Indeed, for much of his reign the 'A' text is almost a local chronicle recording only the doings of the church of Winchester itself. The blow by blow account of Edward's years and those of his father Ælfred is simply not provided for Æðelstan.

One thirteenth-century chronicler, Roger of Wendover, claims that Sihtric cast off his bride without consummating the marriage, but Roger may have been motivated by the identification of the young woman concerned with St Edith of Polesworth (in Staffordshire, near Tamworth). The identification itself may well be correct, but the cults that grew up around female saints almost always required them to have retained their virginity and repudiation by an apostate husband was a common hagiographical trope. One of Æðelstan's half sisters was certainly called Eadgyth (the Old English form of Edith), but she was already married to Otto I of Germany at this point. William of Malmesbury writing c. 1120, however, does not name Sihtric's bride but describes her as Æðelstan's only full sister, so she may have been called Eadgyth as well.[54] Repudiation of his bride by Sihtric would almost certainly have led to

---

[53] See S. Sharp, 'The West Saxon tradition of dynastic marriage with special reference to the family of Edward the Elder', in Higham and Hill, eds, *Edward the Elder*, 79–88.

[54] R. A. B. Mynors, R. M. Thomson and M. Winterbottom (eds & tr.), *William of Malmesbury: Gesta Regum Anglorum* (Oxford, 1998), vol. I, 199. Against William's assertion that Sihtric married Æðelstan's full sister is the problem of chronology. Æðelstan was born in the mid-890s and it is generally thought that his mother was repudiated fairly early in Edward's reign. Since girls usually entered their first marriages in their early to mid-teens this creates a slightly awkward though not insurmountable chronological schema.

warfare with her brother. That such warfare did not take place probably suggests that the bride was not repudiated.

Sihtric, however, died the following year, 927, and although Gothfrith led a fleet from Dublin and Anagassan (County Louth) across to Northumbria, he was home within six months having been driven out by Æðelstan. Doubtless Æðelstan had hoped that Sihtric would have begotten an heir upon his sister but this does not seem to have been the case. Sihtric had at least one and probably two sons both of whom were politically active by the end of the 930s so they are unlikely to have been Æðelstan's nephews. Æðelstan's Northumbrian expedition of 927 is described thus by the northern, 'D', text of the *Anglo-Saxon Chronicle*:

> In this year fiery lights appeared in the northern quarter of the sky, and Sihtric died, and King Æðelstan succeeded to the kingdom of the Northumbrians; and he brought under his rule all the kings who were in this island; first Hywel, king of the West Welsh, and Constantín king of the *Scottas* and Owain king of the people of Gwent, and Ealdred, son of Eadwulf, from Bamburgh. And they established peace with pledges and oaths in the place which is called Eamont, on 12 July, and renounced all idolatry, and afterwards departed in peace.

William of Malmesbury has a more colourful account of this expedition. In his version 'Anlaf', Sihtric's son, fled to Ireland and Gothfrith to 'Scotia'. Threats bring Constantín and Owain king of the Cumbrians (that is, Strathclyde) to meet Æðelstan at Dacre. Gothfrith, who was to attend this meeting, slips away with another Northman, Thurfrith, and they besiege York. Æðelstan turns on them and they flee but Thurfrith drowns and Gothfrith is captured and eventually allowed to return home under oath. Æðelstan then dismantles the fortress at York and loots the city before returning south. It is unclear how much of this story is legend, how much based on early written sources and how much is owed to William's imagination.

Most historians have accepted William's identification of Owain as king of the Cumbrians, rather than of Gwent, although both identifications are possible. An Owain son of Dyfnwal seems to have been active as king of Strathclyde in the 930s and from 931 a king of Gwent and Glywysing, in southeast Wales, named Morgan son of Owain, attested Æðelstan's charters; he died in 974. Possibly both were included in the original record and copyists presumed the duplication was in error and took their choice as to which to keep in. William's identification of the meeting place as Dacre rather than Eamont is slightly more problematic. Eamont is now a river name but it is likely that the river name is a back-formation from the place name Eamont Bridge. Eamont actually derives from Old English *éamotum* [at the] 'river junction'. Eamont Bridge stands at the point where the River Lowther and River 'Eamont' almost join before bowing apart again, for about a mile, and then finally joining just above the old Roman fort at *Brocavum*, where the Roman road from York to Carlisle crosses the now conjoined river. It is just possible that Dacre, which is an ancient Celtic river name, was the old name of the Eamont, but it should also be noted that an early church-settlement, dating back to the seventh century at least, was located at Dacre and it may have played some part in the proceedings. The water meadow, now Carleton Hall Park, which lies within the bow of the two rivers would seem an ideal location for a boundary meeting, being neither on one side nor the other. That there was a boundary there is suggested by the fact that in later days this was the frontier between Westmorland and Cumberland.[55]

THE PROBLEM OF STRATHCLYDE OR CUMBRIA

It was noted in the previous chapter that, after the sack of Dumbarton by Amlaíb and Ímar in 870, that centre of British power is not mentioned again. Instead we begin to get notices of Strathclyde and 'Strathclyde Welsh' in both Irish and English sources. It is widely believed that Dumbarton had been abandoned and that the new centre of the British kingdom was higher up the Clyde. The later ninth century sees the begin-ning of a sequence of monumental sculpture at Govan on the Clyde that is second only to Iona in early medieval Scotland. The sculpture here dates broadly from the mid-ninth to the mid-eleventh centuries, although no texts mention Govan by name until the mid-twelfth century, when the church there was presented to Glasgow Cathedral. None the less histori-ans and archaeologists are inclined to see in Govan the premier ecclesias-tical site of the new Strathclyde.[56] By the central middle ages the church

---

[55] Two prehistoric henge monuments lie adjacent to Eamont Bridge, the Mayburgh and King Arthur's Table. Either or both of these might also have provided venues for some part of the ceremonies at this meeting.

[56] See, for example the essays collected in A. Ritchie, ed., *Govan and its Early Medieval Sculpture* (Stroud, 1994), S. T. Driscoll, 'Church archaeology in Glasgow and the kingdom of Strathclyde', *Innes Review* 49 (1998), 95–114, and S. T. Driscoll, *Govan, from Cradle to Grave* (Govan, 2004). This last item is one of a series of annual lectures,

there was dedicated to a St Constantine, though whether this was the first
Christian Roman Emperor or some later Insular saint is unknown. There
is also a significant amount of material surviving from the twelfth and
thirteenth centuries that suggests that the kingdom had, at some point
between the later ninth and the mid-eleventh centuries, expanded south
of the mountains to encompass the Solway plain. Unfortunately, no
sources tell us when such an expansion took place, when it was reversed,
or indeed when this kingdom finally came to an end.

Further confusion has been caused by the use of the two terms
'Strathclyde' and 'Cumbria'. Led by modern political geography a
number of scholars have sought to define two kingdoms, Strathclyde
within modern Scotland and Cumbria within modern England. The evidence for this is not good, however, and does not stand up to investigation.[57] The *Anglo-Saxon Chronicle* uses the term 'Strathclyde' on two
occasions, which we have already encountered. These are the account of
Healfdene's ravaging of the Picts and the Strathclyde Welsh in 875 and the
submission to Edward of Wessex in 920. Subsequently the Chronicle uses
the term 'Cumberland' twice, in 945 and 1000, and Symeon of Durham,
writing of events in the 930s, which we shall shortly come to, uses the term
'Cumbrians', as do the northern annals dealing with this period in the
Historia Regum Anglorum. By the end of the eleventh century it is clear
that the term Cumberland had become attached to the district around
Carlisle, north of Westmorland and Allerdale.[58] The change in terminology in the English sources probably reflects the incorporation of
Northumbria into the English kingdom. The use of the very specific term
'Strathclyde' probably came to the West Saxon writers of the period 875
to 920 from Welsh informants for whom the location rather than the ethnicity of these Britons was their defining feature.[59] 'Cumbrian' on the
other hand, was probably the normal term used by the Northumbrians for
Britons, and for them it meant principally the northern Britons with
whom they had a land border and, perhaps, the inhabitants of British communities surviving within Northumbria.[60] The name itself, Old English

published by the Friends of Govan Old Kirk, celebrating the site many of which deal
with the early medieval period.

[57] P. A. Wilson, 'On the use of the terms "Strathclyde" and "Cumbria"', *Transactions of
the Cumberland and Westmorland Antiquarian and Archaeological Society* 66 (1966), 57–92.

[58] But possibly still including some parts of what is now eastern Dumfriesshire.

[59] A. Woolf, 'Reporting Scotland in the *Anglo-Saxon Chronicle*', in A. Jorgensen, ed.,
Studies in the Anglo-Saxon Chronicle (Woodbridge, forthcoming).

[60] These might be the 'others' living in Northumbria along with 'English', 'Danes' and
'Norwegians' in *ASC*'s account of the submission of the Northumbrians to Edward in 920.

Cumer or *Cumber* (pl. *Cumera*), derives from one of the Britons' own names for themselves which gives the modern Welsh *Cymru*, Wales, and *Cymry*, the Welsh. For the Northumbrians the 'Cumbrians' were synonymous with the Strathclyders, for they had minimal contact with any other Britons, though had a Northumbrian encountered someone from Wales they may well have recognised him as a Cumbrian. Part of the argument put forward by those moderns who seek to separate the two kingdoms is that in modern times the name Cumberland is confined to England. This is largely because 'Cumberland' is an English word. The Scots and, indeed, the Picts will have had their own names for the people of Strathclyde. The fact that Dumbarton, called *Al Clud* ('Rock of the Clyde') by the Britons themselves, was called *Dún Breatann* in Gaelic, the fort of the Britons, indicates that they, like the Northumbrians, simply referred to this isolated northern kingdom by the ethnic name of its inhabitants. Other Britons were far away and of little concern.

The question of the date and context of the Strathclyde expansion into the Solway region is vexed. This area was quite central to the kingdom of Northumbria, presumably part of the diocese of Hexham, at the beginning of our period. Much of the area was clearly occupied by the Hiberno-Norse at some point in the tenth century. The question is both one of absolute date and of relative date. When did the Britons take Carlisle and from whom did they take it? The Northumbrians had called Carlisle simply *Luel* and the prefixing of the British *Caer* on to this to produce *Caerluel*, whence Carlisle, is part of the evidence for this British reoccupation, as are the dedications in the area to a number of saints connected with Clydesdale, including Constantine, Kentigern and Patrick. Placename scholars have found it impossible to agree on the layering of English, Danish, Hiberno-Norse and British names in the region and it may be that, rather than thinking in terms of waves of language replacement, as we might in other parts of the British Isles, we should imagine a situation more like that found in the Balkans until very recently, with the whole province a patchwork of communities speaking different languages.

Suffice to say Æðelstan's decision to meet the northern kings at Eamont suggests that by July 927 this area had been established as a border between Northumbria and Cumbria. Whether this border was new, a result of Cumbrian exploitation of Sihtric's death, or whether it had been there for a decade or two is hard to say.[61] By this date, however,

---

[61] One possibility is that the apparent move of the relics of St Cuthbert from the Carlisle area to Crayke in Yorkshire in 886 represents flight from the Cumbrians, but this may be a little early.

we might guess that Cumbria comprised most or part of Lanarkshire, Dunbartonshire, Renfrewshire, Stirlingshire, Peebleshire, West and Mid-Lothian, eastern Dumfriesshire and Cumberland.

Two myths also need to be dispelled concerning Strathclyde in this period. First, a chronicle entry included in Alan Anderson's *Early Sources of Scottish History* and thus still widely used by Scottish historians, which reads:

> The men of Strathclyde, those that refused to unite with the English, had to depart from their country and go into Gwynedd. Anaraut gave them permission to settle in the country that had been taken from him by the English (namely Maelawr and the Vale of the Clwyd and Rhyfoniawg and Tegeingl), if they could drive away the English; and that they did energetically. But the English came against Anaraut a second time because of that; and the battle of Cymryd was there, and the Cymry routed the Saxons and drove them from that country completely. Thus Gwynedd was freed from the English, through the might of the men of the north.[62]

This entry purports to come from a version of the Welsh chronicle which goes by the title *Brut y Tywysogyon*, under the year 890. *Brut y Tywysogyon* is the name given to a chronicle surviving in three slightly different versions. The core of each is a translation into Welsh of a Latin chronicle originally compiled in the late thirteenth century, probably at the Cistercian monastery of Strata Florida in Ceredigion. Although this Latin compilation does not survive, for its early sections it was, dependent upon the annalistic chronicle know as *Annales Cambriae*, which survives in three manuscripts.[63] The entry reproduced by Anderson, and copied above, however, does not derive from a surviving copy of *Brut y Tywysogyon* but from a forgery perpetrated in 1801 by Edward Williams, otherwise known as Iolo Morgannwg, a well known Welsh antiquary, romantic poet and forger. Iolo, in typical fashion, pretended to have found an additional manuscript of the *Brut* but Welsh scholars have long recognised this as a forgery.[64] The style of the entry above is completely out of

---

[62] A. O. Anderson, *ESSH*, vol. 1, 368.

[63] For a comparative edition of the relevant section of *Annales Cambriae* see D. N. Dumville, ed. & tr., *Annales Cambriae, AD 682–954: Texts A–C in Parallel* (Cambridge, 2002).

[64] For a full discussion of these texts see the introduction to T. Jones, ed. & tr., *Brut y Tywysogyon or the Chronicle of the Princes: Peniarth MS. 20* (Cardiff, 1952).

character with the terse ninth-century records of events and clearly bears no relationship to the *Annales Cambriae*, from which the vast majority of the early medieval entries in the *Brut* derive. Iolo, however, was not entirely responsible for this story. Although his presentation of it was fraudulent, the story itself is derived from David Powel's corrected and augmented edition of Humphrey Lloyd's English translation and expansion of a chronicle similar to, but probably not identical with, surviving versions of *Brut y Tywysogyon*.[65] Lloyd's original translation survives in manuscript copies made for the famous sixteenth-century wizard John Dee and these make it apparent that his contribution went far beyond mere translation. In short this work has much the same value for early Welsh history as Bellenden's translation of Hector Boece's *History* has for the early history of Scotland. The story can be associated with a very brief entry in the *Annales Cambriae* for 881 which appears to recount a victory of Anarawd of Gwynedd over the English.[66] The contribution of men of Strathclyde who did not wish to be 'joined with the English' (a dilemma it is hard to imagine can have really faced Britons in late ninth-century Scotland), if it has any early value, probably arises from a confusion between the Clyde and the Clwyd (*Clut* and *Clwyt* in Middle Welsh), for at this time north east Wales, the vale of the Clwyd, had been under English rule for perhaps half a century. This confusion is unlikely to have arisen in the medium of Welsh and may, perhaps, have arisen in the rewriting of the translation. It is certainly the case that neither Iolo's version nor Lloyd's have the character, or value, of genuine early medieval texts. It is much to be regretted that Scottish historians have failed to note this fraud which has been known in its homeland for a century.

The second myth that requires dispelling can be dealt with more swiftly. John of Fordun, writing in the fourteenth century, claimed that the kingship of Cumbria in the tenth and eleventh centuries was an appanage for the heir to the kingship of the Scots, much as the English king's heir bore the title 'Prince of Wales' and the French king's 'Dauphin of Vienne'. This kind of arrangement is very much a late medieval one for which no clear parallels could be found this early, and the idea was

---

[65] D. Powel, *The history of Cambria, now called Wales: A part of the most famous Yland of Brytaine, written in the Brytish language above two hundred years past: translated into English by H. Lloyd Gentleman: Corrected, augmented and continued out of Records and best approued Authors by David Powel Doctor in Diuinitie* (London, 1584, reprinted 1697 and 1774).

[66] *AC* 881 'The Battle of Conwy: the avenging of Rhodri by God.' See Dumville, *Annales Cambriae*.

probably put into Fordun's mind by the example of David I who held the principality of Cumbria before becoming king of Scots in 1124. At the time David became prince of the Cumbrians, however, he was probably not expected to be his brother Alexander's heir to the Scottish kingship. The primary sources provide us with no shortage of genuine kings of the Cumbrians in this period, but one text has appeared to lend some credibility to the idea that the Cumbrian royal family might have been a cadet branch of the Alpínid dynasty. This text is our old friend the *Chronicle of the Kings of Alba*. The section on Constantín son of Áed's reign contains, as we have seen, a number of obits for contemporary rulers presented as list. The middle portion of this list, in the original Latin, reads:

> *Doneualdus rex Britanniorum et Dunenaldus filius Ede elig₇ et Flann filius Maelsethnaill.*

In the past the small symbol that resembles, and has been represented here by, a subscript seven, ₇, has been taken as a mark indicating that an abbreviation has been made in the text and readers have consequently expanded *elig₇* to *eligitur*, 'was elected'. This would give the meaning 'Dyfnwal king of the Britons died and Domnall son of Áed was elected [to succeed him]'. Historians have presumed that this Domnall might be an otherwise unattested brother of the Alpínid king Constantín son of Áed. In 1988, however, Benjamin Hudson published a short but important article pointing out that this is not the abbreviation mark used for *-itur* elsewhere and that several other 'g's in the same text have this seven-like mark where no expansion would make sense. Hudson also drew attention to the *punctus*, or stop mark, which follows this word. He then demonstrated that *Elig* is an acceptable genitive spelling of the Irish place name Ailech, the royal centre for the Cenél nEógan kings of the north. Since a Domnall son of Áed, king of Ailech, did indeed die in 915, the year before Flann son of Maelsechnaill, whose obit immediately follows, Hudson argues, it is certainly his death that is noted here. Hudson's argument seems to have received universal acceptance. There is no evidence that Constantín had a brother named Domnall and no evidence that any Alpínid prince became king of the Cumbrians.[67]

After these cautionary words concerning Strathclyde, the Cumbrian kingdom, we may proceed with our narrative.

[67] B. T. Hudson, '*Elech* and the Scots in Strathclyde', *Scottish Gaelic Studies* 15 (1988), 145–9.

THE ROAD TO BRUNANBURH

Following the meeting at Eamont in 927 the status quo seems to have been preserved for nearly seven years. How Northumbria was ruled in this period is unclear. It is generally assumed that it was taken directly into Æðelstan's hands, but the evidence for such direct rule is slight. No identifiable northerners regularly attest his charters and none appear to have been issued north of Mercia, nor did he mint coins in Northumbria. It seems plausible that Ealdred son of Eadwulf ruled in this region with the same ambiguous status that Æðelred of Mercia had enjoyed in the period 886–911.[68] What we do know is that from 928 the scribe who drew up Æðelstan's charters, who appears to have been the first dedicated royal chancery scribe in Britain, began to style his master not 'king of the Anglo-Saxons', as his father and grandfather had been called, but 'king of the English'. This same scribe noted also the presence of Welsh kings at some of Æðelstan's courts given the title *sub-regulus*, 'under-kinglet'. The appearance of the Welsh kings only in Æðelstan's charters and in a handful of charters from the late 940s and 950s has caused much debate about whether the Welsh were only securely under English domination in these periods or whether it tells us more about the style or spin of the chancery scribes at the time. The appearance of the British kings in Æðelstan's charters, between 928 and 935, should probably be considered alongside another feature they present. As well as styling Æðelstan 'king of the English', he is described as ruler of 'all *Albion*', and in one charter, from 934, he is described as 'elevated by the right hand of the Almighty, which is Christ, to the throne of the whole kingdom of Britain'.[69] On his coins Æðelstan appears crowned, the first English king to do so, surrounded by the legend *rex totius Brittaniae* – 'king of all Britain'. Clearly King Æðelstan was a man who had pretensions.

In 934 Æðelstan turned his attentions once more to the North. *Historia de Sancto Cuthberto* records that he led:

a great army from the southern part to the northern region, taking it to Scotia.[70]

---

[68] One might also compare the powerful Æðelstan 'Half-king' who ruled the former *Scalding* kingdom of the East Angles under King Æðelstan and his successors. See C. R. Hart, 'Athelstan "Half-king" and his family', *Anglo-Saxon England* 2 (1973), 115–44.

[69] This charter is translated by Dorothy Whitelock as no. 104 of *English Historical Documents*, vol. 1.

[70] *HSC* § 26. Symeon of Durham, in his account of this expedition in the *Libellus* (ii.18), described the king's companions as 'the whole army of Britain'.

Map 4.1 Southumbria

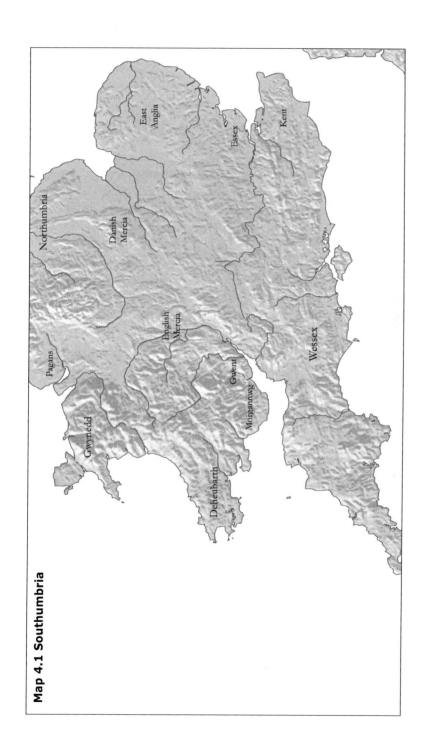

We can, in part, trace this army as it moved north, for the king issued
several charters which survive from places where he paused en route.
The army was gathered at Winchester by 28 May and had reached
Nottingham by 7 June. Among those who travelled into the north with
Æðelstan were three Welsh kings, Hywel, Morgan and Idwal (presumably accompanied by their military followings), eighteen bishops (including the two English metropolitans), and thirteen *duces* or local rulers, six
of whom bore Danish names. At Nottingham, just south of the
Northumbrian frontier, he issued a charter granting the large territory of
Amounderness (the hinterland of Blackpool, in central Lancashire),
about the size of East Lothian, to the Church of York, possibly as a bribe
to win Archbishop Wulfstan of York's support. Æðelstan states that he
had bought Amounderness, in the heart of the Hiberno-Norse colonial
territories, 'with no little money of my own', presumably from the *jarl* or
hold who had previously held it.[71] Shortly after this he stopped at
Chester-le-Street where the *Historia de Sancto Cuthberto* preserved a
portion of a charter issued to St Cuthbert:

> In the name of the Lord Jesus Christ. I, King Æðelstan, give to
> St Cuthbert this gospel book, two chasubles, and one alb, and one
> stole with maniple and one belt, and three altar-coverings, and
> one silver chalice, and two patens, one finished with gold, the
> other of Greek workmanship, and one silver thurible, and one
> cross skilfully finished with gold and ivory, and one royal
> headdress woven with gold, and two tablets crafted of silver and
> gold, and two silver candelabra finished with gold, and one
> missal, and two gospel books ornamented with gold and silver,
> and one Life of St Cuthbert written in verse and prose, and seven
> palls, and three curtains, and three tapestries, and two silver cups
> with covers, and four large bells, and three horns crafted of gold
> and silver, and two banners, and one lancc, and two golden
> armlets, and my beloved villa of South Wearmouth with its
> dependencies, that is Weston, Offerton, Silksworth, the two
> Ryhopes, Burdon, Seaham, Seaton, Dalton-le-Dale, Dawdon,
> and Cold Hesledon. -All these I give under witness of God and
> St Cuthbert, so that if anyone steals anything there, let him be
> damned on the Day of Judgement with the traitor Judas and be

[71] Buying land back from the pagans was not unprecedented in tenth-century England.
The Amounderness grant is printed in translation by Whitelock as n. 104 of *English
Historical Documents*.

thrust 'into everlasting fire which was prepared for the devil and his angels'.[72]

Some of these treasures survive to this day, such as the first Gospel Book mentioned which is kept in the British Library, and the prose and verse Life of St Cuthbert, which now belongs to Corpus Christi College, Cambridge. Some of the textiles removed from St Cuthbert's tomb in modern times, and now on display in the Durham Cathedral treasury, may also have been among these gifts. After Chester-le-Street the story is taken up by the *Anglo-Saxon Chronicle*:

> 934. In this year King Æðelstan went into *Scotland* with both a land force and a naval force and ravaged much of it.[73]

The northern annals preserved in *Historia Regum Anglorum* give more details:

> 934. King Æðelstan, going towards *Scotia* with a great army, came to the tomb of St Cuthbert, commended himself and his expedition to his protection, and conferred on him many and diverse gifts befitting a king, as well as estates, and consigned to the torments of eternal fire anyone who should take any of these from him. He then subdued his enemies, laid waste Scotia as far as Dunottar and the mountains of Fortriu with a land force, and ravaged with a naval force as far as Caithness.[74]

Why had Æðelstan chosen to march north now? The explanation probably lies in three deaths which are recorded, one in 933 and two in 934. The first was the drowning, apparently in the English Channel, of Æðelstan's half-brother Eadwine. The *Anglo-Saxon Chronicle* records this event in a matter-of-fact fashion but the northern annals state:

> 933. King Æðelstan ordered his brother Eadwine to be drowned at sea.[75]

---

[72] *HSC* § 26. The final phrase is from *Matthew* 25:41.

[73] This is the earliest surviving instance of the use of the term 'Scotland' to describe a part of Britain. In the ninth century there are several instances of 'Scotland' being used for Ireland.

[74] Translated in Whitelock, *EHD*, n. 3. This is the first use of the name 'Caithness' on record.

[75] *EHD*, n. 3.

Map 4.2 Æðelstan's campaign of 934

A longer account of the *æðeling* Eadwine's death appears in the *Acts of the Abbots of St Bertin's*, a monastery in Flanders, written by a member of the house, Folcwine, about a generation after the events with which we are concerned. He wrote:

> In the Year of the Incarnate Word 933, when the same *King* Eadwine, driven by some disturbance in his kingdom, embarked on a ship, wishing to cross to this side of the sea, a storm arose and the ship was wrecked and he was overwhelmed in the midst of the waves. And when his body was washed ashore, Count Æðelwulf [of Flanders], since he was his kinsman, received it with honour and bore it to the monastery of St Bertin for burial.

Whether or not we chose to believe the conspiracy theory presented by the northern annalist, it is worth noting that the monks of St Bertin, who possessed Eadwine's body, and who doubtless prayed for his soul on a regular basis, believed that he had himself been a king. No English record supports this claim but he was the full brother of that Ælfweard who had briefly preceded Æðelstan in the kingship of Wessex and whom the Church of Winchester, the West Saxons' principal see, had apparently supported. Possibly tension had been bubbling up between the half brothers and 933 had seen an abortive coup on Eadwine's part. If this was the case, then the outing, and subsequent purging, of dissidents within the West Saxon court may well have left Æðelstan holding a stronger hand by 934.

The second death was that of Gothfrith, grandson of Ímar, the king of the Gaill.[76] Although expelled from eastern Northumbria in 927 he had still dominated Dublin, and probably the Isle of Man and much of the coastline of Galloway and northwest England. The opportunity Æðelstan was presented with to purchase Amounderness may have been connected with power-play among Gothfrith's potential successors: a hopeful contender needing Æðelstan's silver to win friends and influence people. With the Northmen of the Irish Sea world preoccupied with their own succession crisis, they could probably be relied on to keep away from the kingdom of the English.

The third death which may have convenienced or provoked the king is slightly less secure. It is recorded only in the *Annals of Clonmacnoise*. This chronicle appears to be a reliable member of the family of Irish chronicles that includes our friends the *Annals of Ulster* and *Chronicum Scotorum*, but

[76] *AU* 934.1.

it survives only in a translation into English of 1627. The translator has been very faithful to his original and was not an embellisher, but he did have a bad habit of modernising and anglicising personal names. So, for example, 'Gothfrith' becomes 'Geoffrey', and in his account of Æðelstan's invasion of Scotland *Dunfoither* (Dunnottar) becomes 'Edenburrogh', doubtless because he did not recognise *Dunfoither* but knew Edinburgh (*Dún Etin*) to be the obvious target for any English invasion of Scotland in his own day. In the same year as Æðelstan's invasion he records:

> Adulf mᶜEtulfe king of the North Saxons died.[77]

This is clearly the obit of a king of Northumbria, for whom the term 'king of the North Saxons' was commonly used in the Irish chronicles. The problem is that the king's name and that of his father appear to be versions of the same name, Eadwulf, and the bestowing of the names of living parents on children was very rare, if it occurred at all in this period.[78] In the *Annals of Ulster*'s obit for Eadwulf of Northumbria in 913 his name is spelled 'Etulbb'.[79] This 934 obit appears to be of a son of his and it is very tempting to see it as the only surviving notice of the death of that Ealdred who had succeeded his father in 913, been defeated by Ragnall in 918 and met with Edward of Wessex in 920 and Edward's son Æðelstan in 927. If this were the case then Scottish intervention in Northumbria on Ealdred's death may have been the *casus belli* in 934. We should, however, also note the witness of the twelfth-century historian William of Malmesbury. William, unfortunately, appears to have conflated the 927 meeting at Eamont with the expedition of 934, which makes his text very difficult to use at this point. He does say, however, that Æðelstan subdued Northumbria 'after having driven out a certain Aldulf who was in revolt'.[80] This might also be a mistake for Ealdred, but it might describe someone entirely different. If this Aldulf (representing

---

[77] D. Murphy, ed., *The Annals of Clonmacnoise* (Dublin 1896 and Felinfach 1993), *s.a.* 928 (= 934).

[78] This is one of the major cultural changes of the Anglo–Norman era in Britain. Both the Anglo-Saxons and the Celtic-speaking peoples steered clear of naming sons for living fathers, but among the French of the eleventh century and later it was almost the rule. In Scotland this is perhaps most notable in the Brus family who received Annandale from David I, whose heads, a succession of fathers to sons, are all called Robert for two hundred years. On the other hand, if an early medieval man bears the same name as his father it almost certainly indicates that he was born after his father's death.

[79] We might have expected only a single 'b' here which would have given the phonetic value /v/.

[80] *Gesta Regum*, ii. 131.

earlier Ealdwulf) is the Adulf of our Irish source then we might imagine that Ealdred remained loyal to Æðelstan, his death passing unnoticed, but that he was succeeded by a brother Ealdwulf, otherwise unnoticed, who did not renew the submission to the southern overlord. Whichever detailed explanation is correct the basic point holds: a Northumbrian king died in this year and Constantín and Æðelstan probably fell out either because they backed alternative competitors to the succession, or because Æðelstan now wished to do away with an autonomous sub-king altogether, driving Ealdred's heir into the arms of Constantín.

Æðelstan's land army penetrated Constantín's kingdom as far as Dunnottar and the mountains of Fortriu (*Wertermorum* in the original), probably a lose term for the Mounth. His fleet is said to have ravaged as far as Caithness. It would be interesting to know what route the army took. Was it transported across the Forth by ship from Lothian to Fife, or did it travel via the Fords of Frew (a few miles upstream of Stirling), and then up Strath Allan and into Strathearn. If the advance was entirely unsupported by ships it would probably have had to progress through the interior coming close to places like Scone and Dunkeld. This would have been very risky though. It seems more likely that the fleet closely supported the army, ferrying it across the Forth and the Tay, and that the expedition to Caithness took place during a protracted siege at Dunnottar. It would have been almost impossible to support such a large army entirely from what could be foraged in and around Dunnottar and Fetteresso so Æðelstan probably sat it out at Dunnottar with the western English, while the eastern English, including the Anglo-Danish forces who had probably supplied the fleet, harried northwards around the coast, and the Welsh, under King Hywel, more familiar with this kind of highland-fringe landscape, may have been engaged in foraging raids into the interior of Angus and the Mearns, bringing back cattle, cheese and women for Æðelstan's soldiers. That the fleet ravaged as far as Caithness raises the intriguing question as to whether this province lay within Constantín's kingdom. Were this a disciplined modern campaign we might be justified in presuming that it did, and was thus a legitimate military target. In this period, however, we are dealing with warriors who received no pay but who performed military service as a kind of tax, a universal obligation. The only return they could hope for was plunder. In 1000, sent to support a land expedition against Strathclyde, the English fleet diverted to the Isle of Man and raided there rather than support the land army.[81] The pickings were richer and the journey not so dangerous. Presumably some *dux* or *duces*, notionally in charge, got shouted

[81] *ASC* 1000.

at when they returned home, but, in reality, they will have had little control over the fleet. The ships would each be provided by a local district, or rich church, whose freemen would make up the crew.[82] One can easily imagine that on rounding Kinnaird Head and seeing land across the Moray Firth curiosity may have driven the more adventurous captains to Caithness. It may also have been caution which prevented them sailing right up into the Beauly Firth where they might have been boxed in by naval levies from Moray and Ross. Unfortunately, we have absolutely no idea to what extent the various provinces north of the Mounth would have identified with Constantín's cause.

Although the chronicles do not tell us the outcome of this expedition in detail we can infer it from Æðelstan's charters.[83] By 12 September 934, the king was back in the south of England at Buckingham. The charter he issued from here, granting a small estate in Wiltshire to one of his household retainers, was attested by 'Constantín *subregulus* with many others'. Constantín had clearly been brought south with the army. His position at the head of the witness list and the title accorded him, *subregulus*, clearly indicates that he was no disgraced prisoner. He had been forced to submit to the *rex et rector totius Brittaniae* but he had retained his own high status. We next see Æðelstan at Frome, in Somerset, on 16 December, where he may have been preparing to spend Christmas or at the nearby palace at Cheddar. The only *subregulus* present was Hywel; Constantín had presumably returned home. Had Æðelstan detained Constantín too long, especially following such a humiliating defeat, it is likely that an alternative king would have been elected by the Scots, although it is quite possible that many of the leading men of the kingdom had been forced to give hostages at Dunnottar, not simply for Constantín's security but to secure the English rearguard from being attacked during its withdrawal. Constantín was no longer a young man. His father had been killed in 878 so he must have been at least fifty-six and was probably somewhat older.[84] There must have been several young men among the

---

[82]   For a detailed discussion of the Anglo-Saxon fleet see C. Warren Hollister, *Anglo-Saxon Military Institutions on the Eve of the Norman Conquest* (Oxford, 1962 and 1998), ch. 5, 103–26. For a clear and illustrated explanation of the workings of the levy see D. Hill, *An Atlas of Anglo-Saxon England* (Oxford, 1981), 92–3.

[83]   An essential tool for the kind of analysis of attendance at the English court which follows is S. Keynes, *An Atlas of Attestations in Anglo-Saxon Charters, c. 670–1066* (Cambridge, 1998).

[84]   To be fifty-six he would have had to have been born in the year following the death of his father. It is quite likely, given his name, that he was born during the life time of his uncle and namesake, that is in or before 875. This would probably put him in his sixties by 934.

Alpínids, and perhaps others, who would have been ready to step into his shoes.

The trip to Buckingham was not the end of Constantín's submission to Æðelstan, however. The following year, the exact date is unknown, the English king seems to have held a great plenary court at Cirencester, an ancient Roman city on the border between Wessex and Mercia. Here he was attended by no fewer than five kings. First in order of precedence was Constantín, and he was followed, for the first time (on record) by Owain of Strathclyde; only then came Hywel, who usually topped any list to which his name was appended, and then Idwal and Morgan. It is likely that the Roman setting – the amphitheatre at Cirencester was still standing in the early middle ages – was deliberately chosen for a show of pomp and power by the 'king and governor of the whole island of Britain'. We cannot doubt that a major part of the proceedings was a public act of submission by the *subreguli* each adorned in appropriate national costume and perhaps handing over symbolic gifts conforming to southern English stereotypes of their various regions.[85] The English nobility and diplomatic guests from the Frankish kingdoms and perhaps further afield would have looked on. Æðelstan's sisters had been married to the heirs of Charlemagne and he too aspired to an imperial title.

Whether Constantín and Owain enjoyed their day out in the Cotswolds as much as their host must have done is hard to calculate. The food was almost certainly very good and they would undoubtedly have returned home laden with gifts. They must also have been quite pleased to have taken precedence over Hywel. This was recognition that Constantín was in the number two position and also an indication that Æðelstan, unlike John of Fordun and many modern historians, did not regard Owain as simply an insignificant appendage of Constantín.[86] There would also have been the assurance from the English king that he would support them against their enemies, foreign or domestic. Some *subreguli*, and Hywel is a classic example, could make much of their position.[87] This said, there must have been some at home, those not invited to

[85] While it is easy to imagine Constantín leading a Highland cow and clutching a tin of shortbread, these were probably not the kinds of stereotypes current in the tenth century. More likely he would have been expected to present a trained eagle, the horn of a wild ox or something of that sort.

[86] And I think it goes without saying that Æðelstan probably had a better grasp of the political situation in early tenth-century Britain than the rest of us.

[87] For a very realistic assessment of Hywel's relations with his English contemporaries see D. P. Kirby, 'Hywel Dda: Anglophile?', *Welsh History Review* 8 (1976–7), 1–13. Many of Kirby's observations might as easily be applied to Constantín and Owain.

the party perhaps, or whose daughters had been raped the previous summer by English or Welsh troops, who would have seen this as a national humiliation, adding insult to injury.

It seems that benorth the Forth it was these cold counsels that prevailed. The week before Christmas only four kings came to spend the festive season with Æðelstan at Dorchester in Dorset, another Roman city with an extant amphitheatre (this one still visible today). On this occasion, however, it was Owain of Strathclyde who topped the guest list; Constantín son of Áed was nowhere to be seen. An aged king, surrounded by eager young whelps, had been forced to prove his manhood. The supposition that the establishment in Albania did not approve of recent developments is perhaps borne out by the absence of any record of the events of 934 and 935 in the *Chronicle of the Kings of Alba*. Doubtless the chronicler felt that some things were best forgotten.

BRUNANBURH

Secure in his empire of Britain, Æðelstan spent the following year intervening in the near Continent and effecting regime change in the Western Kingdom (of the Franks),[88] where his nephew Louis was placed on the throne, and in Brittany, where Alan son of Matuedoi was helped into the kingship by an English fleet. It may also have been at this time that he intervened in the young kingdom of Norway.[89] His position at home was not, however, as secure as it may have seemed to him.

Not only was Constantín licking his wounds, but across the Irish Sea the kingship of the Gaill had been secured by Gothfrith's son Amlaíb (ON Óláfr, OE Anlaf). In 935 he had sacked the chief royal centres of both northern and southern Brega, securing his dominance in the Irish east midlands.[90] The following year he sacked the richest church-settlement in Ireland, at Clonmacnoise, patronised by the kings of Mide and Connacht.[91] Having established his western front Amlaíb now turned to his British frontier. It seems likely that he controlled or at least had strong influence in Man and Galloway and perhaps some parts of the far northwest of

[88] This was the kingdom that would eventually develop into France but its extent and character was considerably different from that of the later kingdom.

[89] Norwegian tradition claims that King Hákon Haraldsson was Æðelstan's foster son and that he seized the kingship with English help. The precise date of these events, however, is unknowable.

[90] *AU* 935.4.

[91] *AU* 936.2.

England (Furness and Coupland lay closer to Man than to any other centre of power). He also had a claim to the kingship of Northumbria, which was probably under direct West Saxon control for the first time following the expedition of 934. What happened next is recorded in a wide variety of sources.

The *Chronicle of the Kings of Alba* gives a very brief account:

And the battle of *Dún Brunde* in his xxxiiii year in which was slain the son of Constantín.

While the *Annals of Ulster* tell us:

AU 937.6. A great, lamentable and horrible battle was cruelly fought between the Saxons and the Northmen, in which several thousands of Northmen, who are uncounted, fell, but their king, Amlaíb, escaped with a few followers. A large number of Saxons fell on the other side, but Æðelstan, king of the Saxons, enjoyed a great victory.

The *Anglo-Saxon Chronicle* at this point has a longish poem (about seventy-three lines in a modern edition) in lieu of a proper entry. The poem appears to have been composed in the reign of Æðelstan's successor, his half-brother Eadmund, since it gives him equal credit for the victory although he was probably only a teenager at the time. The poem states that Constantín, whom it refers to as 'hoary' (grey-haired), was present and concurs with *CKA* that one of his sons was slain in the battle.[92] The poem refers to the English forces as West Saxons and Mercians and to their enemies as Scots, shipmen and Northmen. It also claims that five kings were slain, but this may be poetic licence.[93] The northern annals preserved in *Historia Regum Anglorum* tell us that 'Onlaf' came with 615 ships and was supported by Constantín king of Scots and an unnamed king of the Cumbrians.

The site of the battle is unknown. *CKA* calls it *Dún Brunde*, the poem in *ASC* calls it *Brunanburh* (which has been followed by most modern scholars), while the northern annals call it *Wendun*. The *Annales Cambriae* note laconically '*bellum Brune*'. Ealdorman Æðelweard's Latin epitome of

---

[92] The *Annals of Clonmacnoise* name this son as 'Ceallagh', for 'Cellach' (this is the name from which modern 'Kelly' ultimately derives).

[93] For an edition of the poem and a lengthy commentary see A. Campbell, *The Battle of Brunanburh* (London, 1938).

Map 4.3 Suggested locations for the battle of Brunanburh, 937

ASC calls it *Brunandun*, while Symeon of Durham, who seems to have had a version of the northern annals before him, calls it *Weondune*, but adds that it is also known as *Brunnanwerc* and *Brunnanbyrig*. Clearly there are two alternative names at stake here: one with the specific element *Wen/Weon* and the other with a specific element *Brun*. Gaelic *dún* and Old English *burh/byrig* and *werc* are all words meaning 'fortification'. The terms could be used both for sites in contemporary use and for archaeological sites, such as Iron Age hill-forts. Old English *dun*, on the other hand, means 'hill' and is preserved in the modern words 'down' (as in the South Downs) and 'dune'. None of the contemporary sources gives any clue as to what region the battle was fought in and only one of the twelfth-century chroniclers gives a clue. This is John of Worcester, who states that Anlaf landed in the Humber. This is fundamentally unlikely, since he came from Dublin, and probably reflects an attempt at verisimilitude by John based on the late eleventh-century expeditions of Harald of Norway (1066) and Sven of Denmark (1069) which did indeed make landfall in the Humber.[94] As noted earlier, the obvious route between Dublin and York lay across central Lancashire and through the Aire Gap, and it is probably on the Lancashire coast that we should seek Amlaíb's landfall.

Modern historians have located the battle in a number of places ranging from Brinsworth, near Sheffield, to Bromswald in central England. A favourite location, which has much to commend it, is Bromborough in the Wirral, in precisely the kind of location where Amlaíb might have felt it secure enough to leave his ships.[95] One Scottish site has been suggested, Burnswark, an Iron Age hill-fort between Lockerbie and Ecclefechan, and this hypothesis has recently been revived.[96] It must be said, however, that the evidence is not good enough for us to securely locate the site at any of these places and most arguments rely far too heavily on very late sources based as much upon folklore as anything. The battle rapidly became very important in English historical tradition and plays a part in a number of hagiographical works. Æðelweard tells us that in his own day it was still referred to as 'the Great Battle' by the common people, and the extraordinary, if not very informative notice in the *Annals of Ulster* would seem to bear witness to a contemporary recognition of its magnitude.

[94] John of Worcester also claims that Anlaf of Dublin was Constantín's son-in-law, a statement repeated with unwarranted confidence by most modern historians.

[95] See most recently P. Cavill, S. Harding and J. Jesch, 'Revisiting *Dingesmere*', *Journal of the English Place-Names Society* 36 (2004), 25–38.

[96] K. Halloran, 'The Brunanburh campaign: a reappraisal', *Scottish Historical Review* 84 (2005), 133–48.

The Brunanburh poem

Under the year 937 the surviving manuscripts of the *Anglo-Saxon Chronicle* have, in place of the original annal, an Old English alliterative poem:

Æðelstan king, lord of nobles,
Men's ring-giver, and his brother also,
Eadmund æðeling, everlong glory,
Won in the strife, by the sword's edge,
Around Brunanburh. Cleaving the shield-wall,
Hewing the linden boards, with the hammer's children,
Edward's sons. To them it was innate,
From their breeding, that they battled often,
Against every foe, to defend their land,
Their wealth and homes. The haters were slain,
The Scots people and the ship-fleet,
Doomed to fall. The field darkened,
By men's blood, after the sun rose,
In the morning tide, that famous sphere,
Glided over the earth, God's bright candle,
The eternal Lord's, until that noble shape,
Sank at its setting. There lay many warriors,
Destroyed by spears, northern men,
Shot over their shields, and Scots also,
Weary and war sated. The West Saxons pursued,
The end-long day in choice troops,
In the footsteps of the hostile nations,
Hewing the routed, sorely in the rear,
With whetted swords. The Mercians did not refuse,
Hard hand-play, to any of the heroes,
Who, with Amlaíb, over the sea's swell,
In the ships' bosom, sought land,
Doomed to fight. Five lay,
On that battlefield, young kings,
Sent down by swords, and also seven too,
Of Amlaíb's earls, and countless soldiers,
Of the fleet and of the Scots. There were put to flight,
Northmen princes, compelled by necessity,
Towards the ships' stems, a little troop.
Pushing the ship into the swell, the king departed,

On the muddy flood, saving his skin.
So then also the wise-man, came in flight,
To his northern land, Constantín,
The hoary warrior. He had no need to rejoice,
In the congregation of men, he was deprived of his kinsmen,
Parted from friends on the battlefield,
Slain in the strife, and his son forsaken,
At the place of slaughter, wounded to destruction,
Young at the war. Not needing to boast,
The grey-haired warrior, at the clash of blades,
The old traitor, no more did Amlaíb.
With their survivors they had no need to laugh,
That their warlike deeds were better,
On the place of strife, where banners clashed,
Spears mingling, warriors met,
In conflict, since they, on the slaughter field,
Played with Edward's sons.
The Northmen departed thence, in nailed ships,
Dreary spear-leavings, on Dingesmere,
Over the deep water, seeking Dublin,
Back to Ireland, ashamed.
So then the brothers, both together,
King and æðeling, sought their home,
The West Saxon land, rejoicing in the war.
Leaving behind them, to enjoy the corpses,
That sallow coated one, the black raven,
Horny beaked, and that dun-clad,
White-tailed eagle, to savour the prey,
The greedy war-hawk, and that grey beast,
The wolf from the wold. There had not been greater slaughter,
On this island, ever yet,
Of the slaying of people before this,
By the sword's edge, as books tell us,
Or old wits, since, from the east, hither
Angles and Saxons came up,
Over the broad ocean, seeking Britain,
Bold battle-smiths, defeating the Romans,
Nobles eager for glory, got a country.

[my translation]

AFTER THE STORM

Despite the heavy casualties sustained on both sides in the battle it seems that none of the principals were slain and there was no major change in the political map of Britain. The charter recording the meeting at Dorchester, just before Christmas 935, was the last of Æðelstan's charters to be attested by *subreguli* and to include bombastic styles, and some historians have seen this as evidence that his power was waning. More likely, however, it marks the death or promotion of the clerk responsible for drafting these charters. After all, the character of the charters changes well before Brunanburh and during the period when Æðelstan was flexing his muscle on the Continent. Partly because the poem on the battle appears to have overwritten the account of his last years in the chronicle, little is known of Æðelstan's last years. The next entry, following the poem on *Brunanburh*, records his death on the 27 October 939, at Gloucester, just over two years after the battle. He was forty-three years old. The *Annals of Ulster* also record his death:

> *AU* 939.6. Æðelstan, king of the Saxons, pillar of dignity of the western world, died an untroubled death.

All that he had achieved crumbled with his death. The northern, 'D', text of the *Anglo-Saxon Chronicle* follows the notice of his death with the ominous statement:

> In this year the Northumbrians were false to their pledges and chose Anlaf as their king.

Not only was Amlaíb elected king by the Northumbrians, but he also stormed Tamworth and subdued the eastern, Anglo-Danish, portion of Mercia, including Leicester, Lincoln, Nottingham, Stamford and Derby. He was not to enjoy his victory for long, for turning north he ravaged Lindisfarne and then moved on to Tyninghame in East Lothian where, in 941, he sacked the major church-settlement which housed the shrine of St Balthere (†756, known now as St Baldred). Days later he was dead, struck down, the northern annals claim, by the power of St Balthere.[97] He was succeeded as king of Northumbria by his cousin, another Amlaíb, the son of that Sihtric who had died in 927. Æðelstan's successor, his brother Eadmund, probably still under twenty, could only look on.

[97] *HRA* I.941.

North of the Forth, in Albania, little of note is recorded. *CKA* notes the death of Dubucan son of Indrechtach, mormaer of Oengus, the first notice of a named *mormaer*, the office later styled 'earl' in Scots, and the first notice of the province of Angus. It is doubtful whether either the office or the province was new at this point; rather, the nature of the source material feeding into *CKA* has changed, and from now on the deaths of several mormaers and bishops are noted, whereas before only the obits of kings appeared. Two other deaths are noted in *CKA* in the final years of Constantín's reign. One is that of Æðelstan, styled simply 'king of the Saxons', and the other of an otherwise unknown, and untitled, Eochaid son of Alpín. We have no idea who this man was but his presence here is faintly reassuring. The names Eochaid and Alpín both feature higher up the pedigrees of the kings of Alba and are suspiciously absent from the tenth-century king-lists. The obit of this individual suggests that the names were still current among the high born of the kingdom and that it is simply chance that no princes bearing them came into the kingship. It should be remembered that most of these kings probably had several sons, but generally we are told only of those who succeeded.[98]

Constantín's long reign probably came to an end in 943. He had reigned long enough to see his oppressor's empire turn to dust and this must have been satisfying. He was now in his late sixties or seventies, and although he was to live a further nine years he entered religion and the kingdom passed to Mael Coluim, the son of his predecessor Domnall son of Constantín son of Cinaed. Whether Mael Coluim, who can have been no spring chicken himself, had to persuade the old man to retire or not we do not know. Later versions of the king-list say that Constantín spent his retirement at St Andrews, and even that he became abbot of the Céli Dé there for the last five years of his life.

This chapter has largely focused on the reign of Constantín son of Áed but the attentive reader will have noted that by far the greater part of the discussion has concerned his relations with his southern neighbours: with the fate of Northumbria and the ambitions of the West Saxon dynasty and the grandsons of Ímar. Constantín must have had diplomatic relations with his northern and western neighbours, and more complex relations with the Cumbrians of Strathclyde than have been noted here. He must surely have fought wars in the north and west. Unfortunately, our surviving sources are extraordinarily silent on these matters. Even our one Scottish source from this period, *CKA*, confines its attentions to

[98] The Cellach son of Constantín who was slain at Brunanburh is an exception.

the area south of the Mounth. Up to this point no place north of the Mounth has been mentioned at all in *CKA*, Dunnottar, in Kincardineshire, being the most northerly. Why is this? Did the kingdom of Albania not stretch north of the Mounth? But even if this were the case we should expect some mention of events and places there, as we have for places in Northumbria. If our chronicle was maintained at Dunkeld, as Broun has argued, do we hear of only those wars and battles in which the relics of Columba were carried before the Albanian army?[99] Were other churches responsible for protecting the north of the kingdom? We shall return to these questions in a later chapter.

[99] For the use of Columba's relics in this way see S. Airlie, 'The View from Maastricht', in B. E. Crawford, ed., *Scotland in Dark Age Europe* (St Andrews, 1994), 33–46.

CHAPTER 5

The Later Tenth Century:
A Turmoil of Warring Princes

MAEL COLUIM SON OF DOMNALL (943–54)

On the retirement of the aged Constantín son of Áed into religious life in around 943, the kingship of Alba passed to Mael Coluim, the son of his cousin Domnall who had died in 900. Mael Coluim was probably born during his father's reign (889–900) and is the first individual known to have borne his name, which means 'devotee of Columba', underlining once more the importance of the relationship between the Alpínid dynasty and the cult of St Columba. His succession raises certain questions: was he Constantín's designated successor and, if not, did he represent a particular faction or region within the kingdom? Constantín had had at least two sons: Cellach, who had been slain at Brunanburh; and Ildulb, who was probably still a teenager at the time of his father's retirement (see below). That Constantín had further sons seems likely given the proclivities of Gaelic kings and the length of his active career, but none are known. It may be that Cellach had been his father's preferred choice as successor but that his death encouraged Mael Coluim to have the old man set aside before Ildulb reached maturity. It would be interesting to know if Mael Coluim had been kept at court throughout his predecessor's reign, whether he had ruled some province under Constantín, or if he had even been in exile. The *Chronicle of the Kings of Alba* has this to say of him:

> Mael Coluim son of Domnall reigned xi. years. With his army he crossed into *Moreb* and slew Cellach. In the vii year of his reign he plundered the English as far as the river *Thesis* and carried off many people and many droves of cattle, which raid the *Scotti* call the raid of [the] *Albidosi* that is *nainndisi*. Others, however, say that

Constantín made this raid, asking of the king, that is Mael Coluim, that the kingship be given him for the space of a week to visit the English. In fact it was not so, Mael Coluim made the raid but Constantín who incited him, as stated. Constantín died in his x. year wearing the crown of penitence and in happy old age. And the men of the Mearns slew Mael Coluim in Fetteresso, that is in *Claideom*.

Once again we are looking at a multi-layered text. The original king list presumably read:

Mael Coluim son of Domnall reigned xi. years and the men of the Mearns slew [him] in Fetteresso.

The remaining account contains a number of interesting features. The reference to *Moreb* is the first reference to Moray in any text, and the spelling here suggests that this is a British name related to Middle Welsh *moreb*, and Cornish *morab* (surviving as 'murriph' in Cornish English), meaning 'low lying land near to the sea', a perfect description of lowland Morayshire around Elgin and Forres. The Cellach whom Mael Coluim slew in Moray is otherwise unknown. He is usually presumed to be a local ruler there, though whether he was a subject or kinsman of the Alpínids, or the representative of another polity altogether is unclear.

The long and complicated account of the raid in Mael Coluim's seventh year is particularly noteworthy. The notion that Constantín asked for the kingship back for a week to visit the English seems to have been drawn straight from folklore. The use of the term 'English' (*Anglos*) twice in this section is suspicious since elsewhere in the chronicle, and in the Irish chronicles of the time, the term 'Saxon' is consistently used for the Southrons. The river *Thesis*, to which the raid extended, is probably the Tees, separating County Durham from Yorkshire, and the theft of people taken into slavery and livestock is usual. It may even have been the principal motivation for the raid.

There is no agreement among scholars as to the meaning of the words *Albidosi* and *nainndisi*. Hudson, in his edition of the text, has suggested that the first word (which appears as *albidosorum*, a genitive plural in the Latin) should be read as *albi dorsorum*, 'of the white ridges', and refers to the colour of the cattle stolen.[1] This interpretation has not met with

---

[1] B. T. Hudson, 'The Scottish Chronicle', *Scottish Historical Review* 77 (1998), 129–61 at 158. Alan Anderson, in *ESSH*, also emended to *albi dorsorum* but did not explain the meaning.

widespread acceptance. More recently scholars have been inclined to see in it the stem *albid*, an early spelling of the British word which in modern Welsh is spelled *elfydd* (the two would be pronounced very similarly with British intervocalic 'b' and Welsh 'f' both representing /v/, and the 'd' and 'dd' both representing /ð/). *Elfydd* now simply means 'earth' or 'soil', but it is in fact the Welsh cognate of Gaelic *Alba*. Both come from a common Celtic word **Albijo* which originally meant the 'the surface of the earth'. This word survives in the personal name of the Gaulish king 'Albiorix' – 'king of the earth' – and in the Latinised *Albion* – an early name for the island of Britain. In Irish **Albijo* became first *Albu* and then *Alba* and retained its meaning as 'Britain', until, in the very period we are dealing with, it came to mean something approaching English 'Scotland'. In Welsh there is no evidence that the word survived as a proper name, although *elfydd* meaning 'soil' or 'earth' did survive.[2] In Breton, however, which like Welsh descended from early British Celtic, the word did survive as a name for Britain, into the eleventh century at least, and appears in the Latinised form *Albidia*.[3] This was probably because by that time the Bretons had come to refer to their own country in western France as *Brittania* or *Pretania* in Latin and thus needed a new name for the island of Britain. If this word is the stem of *Albidosi* then that term probably means 'people of *Albidia*'.[4] This raises a number of issues. First, it would suggest that the text which supplied the author of this passage in *CKA* was probably written, albeit in Latin, by a speaker of a British Celtic dialect rather than Gaelic. If we accept this, however, we then have to decide whether the stem was being used in its Welsh sense, simply 'the earth', or in its Breton sense as a territorial name. If the former interpretation is correct *albidosi* could mean something like 'common people', '*nativi*', 'neifs'.[5] If the latter is correct we have to decide whether *Albidia* is most likely to be a Brittonicisation of Gaelic *Alba* or, in fact, an isolated clue to the Picts' own name for their country, which may itself have

[2] D. N. Dumville, 'Ireland and Britain in *Táin Bó Fraích*', *Etudes Celtiques* 32 (1996), 175–87.

[3] *Vita Sancti Uuohednouii* §1, translated by J. T. Koch in J. T. Koch with J. Carey, eds, *The Celtic Heroic Age: Literary Sources for Ancient Celtic Europe and Early Ireland and Wales* (Aberystwyth, 2000), at 391.

[4] See D. N. Dumville, 'The Chronicle of the Kings of Alba', in S. Taylor, ed., *Kings, Clerics and Chronicles in Scotland, 500–1297* (Dublin, 2000), 85. For a dissenting voice see D. Broun, '*Alba*: Pictish homeland or Irish offshoot?', in P. O'Neill, ed., *Exile and Homecoming: papers from the Fifth Australian Conference of Celtic Studies, University of Sydney, July 2004* (Sydney, 2005), 234–75 at 258, n. 85.

[5] I owe this suggestion to Dauvit Broun.

influenced the changing meaning of Gaelic *Alba*.[6] The meaning of the
word *nainndisi* is even more obscure. Hudson suggests that it might represent *n-ann Disi*, possibly Gaelic for 'to the Tees', but most commentators have regarded it as unintelligible, presumably obscured by inaccurate
copying.

The reference in *CKA* to a particular name for this raid must be a later
gloss and the original entry probably read simply:

> In the vii year of his reign he plundered [the English] as far as the
> river *Thesis* and carried off many people and many droves of cattle.

A subsequent scribe has then added additional information which
included the curious words just discussed and also the following account
of Constantín's involvement:

> Others, however, say that Constantín made this raid, asking of the
> king, that is Mael Coluim, that the kingship be given him for the
> space of a week to visit the English.

This looks very much like a piece of literature or folklore and Hudson
is probably correct in thinking that the scribe was adding information
from a saga or a poem concerning these events. The use of the term
Anglos is evidence that this phase of the chronicle is twelfth century and
it may be that this scribe has inserted the clarificatory *Anglos* into the basic
account of the raid he copied (hence my square brackets). Having realised
that he has overstepped the mark with his use of 'late literary sources', a
temptation to which all historians of early Scotland are prone, our scribe
attempts to redeem himself by concluding:

> In fact it was not so, Mael Coluim made the raid but Constantín
> who incited him, as stated.

One cannot help wondering whether the idea that Constantín incited the
raid is the twelfth-century scribe's own attempt to salvage something
from the saga he so clearly enjoyed but fundamentally distrusted. The
degree of intervention by this later scribe also raises questions about the
detail. The identification of the prey as *Anglos* appears to be his and

---

[6] A term originally denoting the whole of Britain might, conceivably, have come to
mean only the northern part during the Roman occupation when 'Pictishness' may have
been fostered by an ideology which presented the northerners as 'Free Britons'.

although his saga source probably did tell of an attack on Northumbria we cannot be absolutely certain that his identification of this story with the raid mentioned in his exemplar is correct.[7]

Although in purely textual terms *CKA*'s account of Mael Coluim's reign is quite lengthy it should be noted that, apart from his death and the killing of Cellach, the raid in his seventh year is the only event noted. It should also be borne in mind that we cannot be certain that the killing of Cellach in Moray actually preceded the raid to the Tees since it is not dated at all and may simply have been something that was known to have happened in Mael Coluim's reign.

SOUTHERN APPROACHES

We have seen that the identification of Mael Coluim's enemies, in his raid to the Tees, as the *Anglos* was probably a gloss by a twelfth-century scribe. Unfortunately, precisely who his foes were is hard to ascertain. At the end of Constantín's reign we had seen that Northumbria, and Danish Mercia, had, despite Æðelstan's victory at Brunanburh, fallen to Amlaíb son of Gothfrith, grandson of Ímar, and that following his death, after the sacking of Tyninghame in East Lothian, his cousin Amlaíb Cúarán had taken over the kingship (941). In 942, however, Æðelstan's young half brother Eadmund, who had succeeded him, overran Mercia.[8] The entry in the *Anglo-Saxon Chronicle* for this year is a short poem:

Here King Eadmund, lord of the English,
Men's protector, overran Mercia,
(Dear deed-doer), as bounded by Dore,
Whitwell Gate, and the Humber river,
The broad brimming stream, And five burghs:
Leicester and Lincoln
Nottingham, and also Stamford and
Derby. Danes were before,

---

[7] If one wished to be really difficult, one could raise the possibility that the *Thesis* was the Spey, called *Tuesis* by the Roman geographer Ptolemy, A. L. F. Rivet and C. Smith, *The Place-Names of Roman Britain* (London, 1979), 480–1.

[8] Eadmund and his brother and successor Eadred were the sons of Edward the Elder's third wife Eadgifu of Kent. Æðelstan's regime seems to have depended upon collaboration between himself (the son of his father's first marriage) and Eadgifu, whose children were still infants at his succession, at the expense of the children of Edward's second marriage to Ælfflæd of Wiltshire.

Under the Northmen, forced into submission,
In heathen bondage,
A long time, until he afterwards freed them,
For his honour, defender of warriors,
Edward's offspring, king Eadmund.

This poem, a contemporary view, emphasises the distinction we have noted before between Christian Anglo-Danes, settled in eastern England, and heathen Hiberno-Norse from the Irish Sea province.

Following his conquest of Danish Mercia, Eadmund, in 943, came to terms with Amlaíb and 'received him from the font' in baptism. Accepting baptism at Eadmund's hands was almost certainly one act in formal rites of submission to the West Saxon king. Submission, however, was either not enough or too much. According to *Historia Regum Anglorum*, the Northumbrians immediately drove Amlaíb out of the kingdom. A little later that same year Ragnall son of Gothfrith (Rægnald son of Guðfrið), the new Northumbrian king, was also baptised by Eadmund. He, however, did not last long. In 944 *ASC* tells us that Eadmund had 'taken all Northumbria into his hands' and driven out both Amlaíb and Ragnall. Ealdorman Æðelweard, in his Latin epitome of *ASC* written some thirty years later, gives more detail ascribing the expulsion of the two kings to Archbishop Wulfstan of York and a certain *dux* of the Mercians. Æðelweard does not name this *dux* but it was almost certainly Æðelstan, known as 'Half King', ealdorman of the East Angles (932–57), who ruled most, if not all, the Anglo-Danish territories south of the Humber as if he were a *subregulus*.[9] It seems likely that Amlaíb had made a bid to regain his throne, and that civil war between the cousins had provided the opportunity for Æðelstan 'Half King' to intervene.[10]

By 945 Amlaíb had returned to Ireland where he ousted Ragnall's brother Blácaire from Dublin and entered into alliance with Congalach of Knowth, king of northern Brega and, since 944, usurper of the kingship of Tara.[11] It is not clear what Amlaíb's fate had been in the intermediate

---

[9]   C. Hart, 'Athelstan "Half King" and his family', in his *The Danelaw* (London, 1992), 569–604. Æðelstan's brothers Æðelwold and Eadric were ealdorman of Kent and Essex (940–6) and Wessex (942–9), respectively. Æðelstan was the foster-father of King Eadmund's son Edgar and may perhaps have been a kinsman of Eadmund's mother Eadgifu.

[10]   The possibility cannot be overlooked that the Scandinavian tradition, preserved mostly in Icelandic sagas, has conflated King Æðelstan and Æðelstan 'Half King'.

[11]   For an account of Amlaíb's Irish career see A. Woolf, 'Amlaíb Cuarán and the Gael, 941–81', in S. Duffy, ed., *Medieval Dublin III* (Dublin, 2002), 34–42.

year. Æðelweard's account implies, though it does not state explicitly, that the Norse kings had been captured, but it is possible that they had fled to the Cumbrians of Strathclyde, perhaps hoping to retake Northumbria from a northern base. Under the year 945 the *Annales Cambriae* state that:

> Strathclyde was wasted by the Saxons.[12]

The *Anglo-Saxon Chronicle* gives more, and intriguing, detail:

> In this year King Eadmund harried across all Cumberland and *let* it to Mael Coluim, king of the Scots, on condition that he should be his co-worker on both land and sea.[13]

Further details are given by the late, and less reliable, Roger of Wendover:

> King Eadmund, relying upon the help of 'Leolin', king of Dyfed, despoiled the whole of Cumbria of all its property, and having deprived the two sons of Dyfnwal, king of that province, of their sight, he gave the kingdom to Mael Coluim, king of the Scots, to hold of him, that he might defend the northern parts of England against raiders by land and by sea.[14]

In this passage 'Leolin', an English spelling of the Welsh name Llywelyn, probably represents a mistaken emendation of Hywel (usually spelled 'Hoel' by contemporary scribes), who was indeed king of Dyfed (and other territories) at this time.[15] If Roger's detail about the blinding of the sons is to be believed, then it is likely that they were hostages handed over to the English sometime previously and that Dyfnwal had broken pledges given to Eadmund, or perhaps his predecessor. It is most likely that he was accused of giving succour to Amlaíb.

More curious is the fate of the kingdom. The *Anglo-Saxon Chronicle* says that Eadmund *let* it to Mael Coluim. This word is the same as modern English 'let', and this phrase might mean either 'abandoned to' or 'leased to'. Later medieval historians, including Roger of Wendover,

[12] D. N. Dumville, ed., *Annales Cambriae, AD 682–954: Texts A–C in Parallel* (Cambridge, 2002), 16.

[13] *ASC* 945.

[14] D. Whitelock, ed. & tr., *English Historical Documents, vol. 1. AD 500–1042* (London, 1955), 257.

[15] Hywel, you will recall, accompanied Æðelstan on his expedition to Dunnottar in 934. Does this make him the only Welsh king to have visited Scotland twice?

saw this as more evidence that parts, or all, of Scotland were fiefs held of the English king, but this kind of language was anachronistic, and the interpretation relates to the politics of the thirteenth century. In the present context it could mean either that Eadmund 'surrendered' Cumberland to Mael Coluim or that he granted it to him. In real terms the difference might be said to depend on whether there was any formal ceremony involved or whether Eadmund simply returned from his harrying of the north with the understanding that Mael Coluim would keep the Cumbrians in line. To what extent Mael Coluim actually ruled Strathclyde is harder to say. Possibly there was a total Scottish takeover, but if so it was not permanent for further kings of the Cumbrians appear in our sources, and Dyfnwal son of Owain, presumably the Dyfnwal of 945, lived on until 975. By the time of his death the kingship of the Cumbrians had passed to Mael Coluim son of Dyfnwal, who was himself to survive until 997.[16] One feels a slight anxiety that the Cumbrian king who died in 997 has the same name as the Scots king to whom the kingdom was *let* in 945; for Mael Coluim is a Gaelic name and Dyfnwal is simply the British form of Domnall.[17] Were we reliant entirely upon a late source like Roger of Wendover we might be tempted to think that he had simply confused the two Mael Coluims, but since the *Anglo-Saxon Chronicle* is thought to be a contemporary witness at this point it is hard to see how it can have made a retrospective error, and it is unlikely that the king who died in 997 could have begun reigning as early as 945. Indeed, the most likely solution to the problem is that 'young Mael Coluim', the Briton, was the god-son of 'old Mael Coluim', the Scot, and that his naming reflects a relationship of submission between the Scottish king and Dyfnwal. It is hard to see what English Eadmund would have gained from having Dyfnwal submit to Mael Coluim rather than directly to himself, so this result probably reflects an English recognition of the limits of their power and the potential of Mael Coluim's. None of Eadmund's advisers can have wanted to fight another Brunanburh with the Scots lined up with their enemies. Withdrawal from Strathclyde, a territory so far from their West Saxon heartland that they can have had no realistic hope of controlling it, may have been a price worth paying.

The Cumbrians, for their part, may have been inclined to support Amlaíb in part because they were perhaps particularly exposed to

[16] *AU* 975.2, 997.5.
[17] Indeed, this Cumbrian king's death notice at *AU* 997.5 uses, as one would expect, the Gaelic form. The name itself was probably British in origin: the earliest Gael to possess it seems to have been the Cenél nEógain king, Domnall son of Muirchertach, who died in 566.

aggression from the pagans of the Irish Sea, and had more to gain from their friendship than most, and in part because the incorporation of Northumbria into the West Saxon *imperium*, would, presumably, have put their territories, in whole or in part, at the top of Eadmund's shopping list.

Eadmund's expedition to Cumberland in 945 was not quite as impressive as Æðelstan's expedition to Dunnottar eleven years earlier, but it almost certainly created resonances of that high point of West Saxon empire, both north and south. Eadmund was a dozen years younger than his brother had been on that occasion and much might be expected of his kingship. It was not to be. On 26 May 946, coming to the aid of his steward who had been assaulted by an outlaw named Leofa (whom twelfth-century writers claimed was trying to gate-crash a royal feast), Eadmund was mortally wounded. He was twenty-five years old. The manner of his death serves to emphasise the hands-on nature of kingship, even for the quasi-imperial West Saxons, in tenth-century Britain.

EADRED AND ERIC, A TALE OF TWO KINGS

Eadmund, whose sons were still infants, was succeeded by his surviving brother, the fifth of Edward's sons to aspire to the kingship, Eadred. One of his earliest charters, in alliterative Latin, opens:

> The grace of God conceding, in the year of our Lord's incarnation 946, after the death of King Eadmund who royally guided the government of the kingdoms of the Anglo-Saxons and Northumbrians, of the pagans and the Britons, for a space of seven years, it happened that Eadred, his uterine brother, chosen in his stead by the election of the nobles, was in the same year by the pontifical authority orthodoxly consecrated king and ruler to the sovereignty of the quadripartite rule. And he, the king, constantly presented many gifts to many, in the king's residence which is called Kingston, where also the consecration was performed.[18]

This style clearly distinguishes the kingdom of the Northumbrians from that of the Anglo-Saxons. Interestingly, it also distinguishes the 'kingdom of the pagans', which must mean the Hiberno-Norse realm on the shores of the Irish Sea, at least in its English portions and perhaps beyond the

[18] Whitelock, *English Historical Documents I*, nos 105, 508.

Solway into southwest Scotland. The Pennines, which had lain at the centre of pre-Viking Age Northumbria, were now an international border. The kingdom of the Britons, in this instance, probably refers to Wales where all the local rulers still recognised West Saxon hegemony. Eadred refers to himself as Eadmund's 'uterine brother', born of the same womb, and while this term is usually used to describe maternal half-brothers, it is here used to emphasise that the two men belonged to the same faction among Edward's children: the sons of Eadgifu.

Eadred aspired to the same *imperium* which his brothers had enjoyed and, having been inaugurated as king of the Anglo-Saxons at Kingston, the following year went north to be recognised as king by the Northumbrians at Tanshelf (near Pontefract, in the West Riding of Yorkshire). Tanshelf lay close to the southern frontier of Northumbria and it is likely that the archbishop and councillors of the Northumbrians chose to meet the king there in order to minimise the impact of his visit. Alternatively, it may reflect a lack of nerve on Eadred's part. Whichever it was, the young king clearly failed to impress the Northumbrians, for once he had returned south they elected a certain Eric as king. Eadred, understandably, was furious and in 948 led an expeditionary force into Northumbria and burned the minster at Ripon, the centre of the arch-bishop of York's richest estate. Presumably Eadred held Archbishop Wulfstan responsible for the perceived perfidy of the Northumbrians. Wulfstan, however, was not to be cowed on this occasion and, as Eadred's army headed south, a force from York fell upon its rearguard and inflicted a serious defeat upon the Anglo-Saxon forces. Eadred reacted by starting preparations for a full-scale invasion of Northumbria and the northern recension of the *Anglo-Saxon Chronicle* tells us:

> When the councillors of the Northumbrians understood that,
> they deserted Eric and paid compensation to King Eadred for
> their act.[19]

Despite their apparent reconciliation with Eadred, the Northumbrians proved themselves unable to resist a bid for their kingship mounted, late in 949, by Amlaíb Cúarán, who seems to have been ousted from Dublin by his cousin Blácaire following a military disaster inflicted upon him and his Irish ally Congalach of Knowth by Ruaidrí Ua Canannáin, king of Cenél Conaill.[20] Peter Sawyer has suggested that Amlaíb was more acceptable to

[19] *ASC* D 948.
[20] *AU* 947.1 for the defeat and 948.1 for Blácaire's return.

Eadred than Eric, and that he may have been a collaborator rather than a rival, but the case is not strong.[21]

Erik Blood-Axe?

The identity of the Eric who ruled Northumbria in the mid-tenth century has been a cause for debate. Most of the versions of the *Anglo-Saxon Chronicle* simply supply the name 'Eric', with various spellings. The 'E' text, one of the witnesses of the northern recension kept at York, gives him the patronymic 'son of Harald'. *Historia Regum Anglorum* calls him 'a certain Dane'. Modern scholarship has tended to identify Eric with Eiríkr Blóðöx, 'Erik Blood-Axe', famed in the thirteenth-century Icelandic sagas, who seems to have briefly ruled in the Norwegian Westland in the 930s. Eiríkr was said to have been expelled from Norway in the interests of his half-brother Hákon, foster-son of Æðelstan. Recently, however, Clare Downham has pointed out that no English source notes any Norwegian connection for Eric of Northumbria and that the Scandinavian sources, if they mention Eiríkr's appearance in England at all, place it more or less directly after his expulsion from Norway and during the reign of Æðelstan. The earliest Norwegian histories, which pre-date the sagas by a generation or two, place his death in Spain. Downham argues that the saga writers, unsure about the fate of Eiríkr after his expulsion from Norway, came across the enigmatic references to Eric of Northumbria in English texts and joined up the dots in a not entirely convincing fashion. The connection between the colourful Eiríkr Blóðöx and York has proved so popular, not least with the *Jórvik* interpretation centre, that Downham's case is unlikely to carry the day in the short term, yet it has much to recommend it.[22] Contrary to Downham, one must point out that her argument is at least partly an argument from silence. No Scandinavian sources survive from before the latter part of the twelfth century, and there is little evidence that Norwegian or Icelandic writings influenced English chroniclers at all, so one should expect neither an early Scandinavian account nor English knowledge of a Norwegian career for their Eric. A further complication is found in the later tenth-century life of Saint Cathróe of Metz, a Scottish churchman who ended his

[21] P. H. Sawyer, 'The last Scandinavian kings of York', *Northern History* 31 (1995) 39–44.
[22] C. Downham, 'Eric Bloodaxe – axed? The mystery of the last Scandinavian king of York', *Medieval Scandinavia* 14 (2004) 51–78. The problems of using the Icelandic sagas as historical sources will be discussed further in a later chapter.

> ### Erik Blood-Axe? (*continued*)
>
> days on the Continent. In the account of his journey southwards he encounters King Constantín of *Scotia* (c. 900–43), King Dyfnwal of the *Cumbri* (fl. 945), King Erich at York, a nobleman called Heyfrid at a place which might be Luton (Bedfordshire), and King Eadmund (939–46) at Winchester. These details would suggest a dating of Cathróe's journey sometime between 939 and 946, yet we hear nothing of Eric in Insular sources until 947 at the earliest, and for most of this period Northumbria was ruled by one or other of the two Amlaíbs.[23]

These rapid changes of regime in Northumbria in the years following Edmund's death make it difficult to ascertain who was Mael Coluim of Alba's foe in the raid mentioned in *CKA*. His seventh year was almost certainly 949–50. Amlaíb's return would seem to have occurred in the midst of this period and therefore might have been either the cause of Mael Coluim's raid, if he remained true to the pledges he had made to the West Saxons, or its result, if the raid made the Northumbrians realise that they needed a military leader on the ground. Matters are further complicated by an entry in the *Annals of Ulster* which seems to record an event not noticed by Scottish or English chroniclers:

AU 952.2 The Gaill won a battle against the men of Alba, the Britons and the Saxons.

This is almost certainly a northern British event, the Britons being the Cumbrians of Strathclyde. The northern, 'E', text of the *Anglo-Saxon Chronicle* notes for 952 that:

In this year the Northumbrians drove out King Anlaf (Amlaíb), and received Eric, Harald's son.

How are these two events related?

---

[23] D. N. Dumville, 'St Cathróe of Metz and the hagiography of exoticism', in J. Carey, M. Herbert and P. Ó Riain, *Studies in Irish Hagiography: Saints and Scholars* (Dublin, 2001), 172–88, A. Woolf, 'Erik Bloodaxe revisited', *Northern History* 34 (1998), 189–93. The life of St Cathróe also claims that Erich's wife was a kinswoman of the saint while the Scandinavian sources make her either a Norwegian of middle rank or a sister of the king of Denmark.

The defeated faction in the battle noted by the Irish chronicle were almost certainly Mael Coluim, Dyfnwal and all or some of the Northumbrians. The question is, were the victors led by Eric, Amlaíb or Amlaíb's kinsmen in Ireland? There is even the small possibility that the Gaill here are otherwise obscure Scandinavians coming directly from Scandinavia or from the invisible world of northern Scotland. In Ireland Amlaíb's rival Blácaire had been slain by Congalach and leadership of the Gaill of Dublin seems to have passed to Amlaíb's brother Gothfrith. There were also in this period a number of attacks by Gaill on targets in the north of Ireland and these may have been the work of another force, based either in the Hebrides or Galloway. If Amlaíb had been the victor of this battle it is unlikely that the sequel would have been his expulsion. Had the expulsion preceded the battle, he would surely not have stayed expelled. The most economical explanation is that Eric was the victor and that the Northumbrian councillors made a separate treaty with him, of which expelling Amlaíb was the principal requirement. The implications of this are quite significant. If Eric was able to defeat a combined force comprising, presumably, the Northumbrians, Amlaíb's 'pagans' of the west coast, the Scots and the Cumbrians of Strathclyde then he must have commanded a significant military following and was presumably calling on men from a broad territorial base and not just a few ship-loads of personal retainers. Was this an invasion from Scandinavia or from Scandinavian Scotland? The Icelandic sagas (for what they are worth) claim that Eiríkr Blóðöx spent most of his exile from Norway in Orkney. Could this have provided a base for such an expedition? That the perspective of the English chroniclers was one which emphasised internal revolution rather than invasion, suggests that the battle took place at a sufficient distance from York, perhaps somewhere between the Forth and the Tyne.

Interestingly, the 'D' text of the *Anglo-Saxon Chronicle*, an alternative witness to the northern recension, notes for the year 952 that Archbishop Wulfstan was arrested on the orders of Eadred and imprisoned at the unidentified site of *Iudanburh*. Wulfstan had been appointed archbishop in 931 and had enjoyed a relationship with successive West Saxon kings that probably reflected the attitude of the Northumbrian aristocracy as a whole, vacillating between independence and limited devolution. He was released from imprisonment before the end of 953 but seems not to have been allowed to return to Northumbria. He died on 16 December 956, coincidently at Oundle in Northamptonshire, where an earlier turbulent pontiff of York, St Wilfrid, had died in

709.[24] Had Wulfstan fled south in 952, fearing the ire of Eric, in whose eviction he had been complicit four years earlier?

Eric's second term of office in Northumbria lasted only until 954. The northern recension of *ASC* states laconically:

In this year the Northumbrians drove out Eric and Eadred succeeded to the kingdom of the Northumbrians.

Historia Regum Anglorum states, retrospectively:

Here the kings of the Northumbrians came to an end and henceforth the province was administered by earls.

As with Scotland in 1707, the final union was not affected by a Southron invasion but by a measured decision taken by the nobility of the kingdom. Eadred finally became king of the Northumbrians through their choice, not as a result of an invasion. In a section of *Historia Regum Anglorum* that was probably penned by Symeon of Durham in the early twelfth century, we are told that after his expulsion Eric was slain by Maccus son of Onlaf (Onlaf is a form of the name Óláfr/Amlaíb/Anlaf). Roger of Wendover, writing in the thirteenth century, adds that this killing took place on Stainmore, where the Roman road between York and Carlisle crosses the Pennines.[25] Who precisely Maccus was is unclear.[26] Was he the son of one of the Amlaíbs we have previously encountered?

---

[24] For an account of Wulfstan's career see S. Keynes, 'Wulfstan I', in M. Lapidge, *et al.*, eds, *The Blackwell Encyclopedia of Anglo-Saxon England* (Oxford, 1999), 492–3.

[25] Historians trying to reconcile the twelfth-century Scandinavian accounts which place Eiríkr Blódöx's death in Spain with the thirteenth-century sagas which identify him with Eric of Northumbria point to the similarity of the name Spain and the first element of Stainmore.

[26] This character is the earliest recorded bearer of the curious name Maccus which seems to be a name intimately connected with the zone of Gaelic, Norse and Anglo-Saxon fusion in Northumbria. It is preserved in the Borders place-names Longformaccus, Maxton and Maxwell (*Longphort Maccus*, *Maccuses tun* and *Maccuses wylle*, the first being formed in Gaelic and the others in English). It is not clear in what language the name itself was first coined. See D. E. Thornton, 'Hey Mac! The name *Maccus*, Tenth to Fifteenth Centuries', *Nomina* 20 (1997), 67–98. It is, however, certain that this name is not, as is often stated, a form of the later Scandinavian name Magnus.

England in the tenth century

A word should perhaps be said about the nature of West Saxon rule in England. The union that was affected by kings like Æðelstan and his brothers and nephews was more like the union that existed between Scotland and England after James VI ascended the English throne in 1603, rather than that which has pertained since the Union of the Parliaments in 1707. In the tenth century the constituent parts of England maintained their own customary laws, and their own regional aristocracies formed courts and filled the offices of government. Though East Anglia, for example, had accepted Edward the Elder as king in 917 it had done this without the local Anglo-Danish elite surrendering their rights. They simply recognised that a West Saxon, rather than a *Scalding*, held the kingship. By the middle of the century they had as their 'Half King' a man who was almost certainly from the south but there had been no wholesale ethnic cleansing or displacement of land holders. The same was true of Northumbria where the archbishop of York and 'the Northumbrians' ran the kingdom on a daily basis, regardless of whether the king was Hiberno-Norse, Danish or West Saxon. Thus, there was no need for kings to fight their way across the kingdom but merely to convince a relatively representative assembly that they should be elected king. Turning up with a large army was usually a persuasive enough tactic. This explains why regime change was so frequent and fluid in Northumbria. It actually mattered little who was king to most Northumbrians. Submission to the West Saxons probably meant that some tribute, at least, flowed out of the kingdom, so a fully independent king was probably the ideal choice because he would redistribute wealth among the Northumbrians. The worst option was probably a notionally independent king who had submitted to the West Saxons for he would have to raise enough tax both to maintain himself in an appropriately royal style and to send a sufficient tribute to his Southron overlord. It was probably for this reason that Amlaíb was expelled in 944.

THE DEATH OF MAEL COLUIM AND THE REIGN OF ILDULB

Mael Coluim son of Domnall was killed in his eleventh year as king of Alba by the men of the Mearns at Fetteresso. Why this should have happened is unknown. Our understanding of the political geography of his kingdom is so poor that we cannot tell if the Mearns (Kincardineshire) was a marginal part of the kingdom or part of its heartland. Fetteresso lies close to Dunnottar which seems to have been a royal stronghold, which would suggest the latter, but it may be that this was a fortress guarding the way north (out of the kingdom?). Possibly the maintenance of Dunnottar placed heavy burdens on the locals, who came to see the king as a tyrant. Alternatively, a relatively trivial, immediate cause may have led to the king's death, as we saw with Eadmund of England in 946. Perhaps Mael Coluim was intervening in a brawl, or had presumed too much with some local chieftain's daughter. Perhaps the killing was at the instigation of a rival, maybe even his successor.

Mael Coluim was succeeded by a son of Constantín son of Áed who bore the peculiar name of Ildulb. Although Hudson suggested that this represents a Gaelic form of the Anglo-Saxon name 'Eadwulf', borne by a king of Northumbria who had died in 913, this suggestion has not met with widespread acceptance. 'Eadwulf' appears in Irish texts as 'Etulb' or 'Etolb', and the use of 'et' to represent 'ead' is exactly what one should expect. A more widespread view is that Ildulb represents the Germanic name 'Hildulf', of which it is a perfect representation. Most commentators have presumed that the name came into the Alpínid dynasty through intermarriage with the Norse, but although the name 'Hildulfr' was known among Scandinavians it is not known to have been borne by any high-born individuals and certainly not by any of the rulers operating in the British Isles. The nearest Hildulf, in space and time, whom we can locate, was a man who struck coins for Amlaíb son of Gothfrith in Danish Mercia in the period 939–41. Amlaíb's moneyers in this region bore both Scandinavian and continental Germanic names and Hildulf could fit into either group.[27]

An alternative hypothesis suggests itself. In his account of Æðelstan's meeting with the northern kings in 927, William of Malmesbury claimed that the meeting took place at the church of Dacre and that the English king received Constantín's son from the font. The *Anglo-Saxon Chronicle*, on the other hand, locates the meeting a few miles further east at Eamont and dates it precisely to 12 July. It is unlikely that Æðelstan, coming from Wessex, and Constantín, from benorth the Forth, would have limited the 'summit' to a single day and the chronicle's date may relate to the public ceremony, the equivalent of a modern treaty-signing or photo-opportunity.

---

[27] V. Smart, 'Scandinavians, Celts, and Germans in Anglo-Saxon England: the evidence of moneyers' names', in M. A. S. Blackburn, ed., *Anglo-Saxon Monetary History* (Leicester, 1986), 171–84.

This may have happened in an outdoor venue, perhaps even at a traditional place of assembly, to be witnessed by the maximum number of people. William's record of baptism at a nearby church may reflect another part of the proceedings, possibly taking place on a different day. Bearing this in mind, it is perhaps worth noting that 11 July, the day before the formal ceremony, is the Feast of St Hildulf.

Saint Hildulf, though not well known today, was originally a Bavarian who, in the years around 700, founded the monastery of Moyen Moutier in the Vosges mountains of Lorraine. Many of the monasteries in this region had been founded by *Scoti* in the seventh century and by the eleventh, at least, Hildulf's true origins had been forgotten and he was thought to have been a *Scotus*.[28] It seems quite plausible that Æðelstan, or his clerical advisers, noted that one of the saints whose feast was being celebrated on the day of the baptism was reputed to be a 'Scot', and thought this an appropriate name to bestow on a son of the king of Scots. Æðelstan was probably not the sort of ruler to whom one would be inclined to draw his attention to his errors.

The account of Ildulb's reign in the *Chronicle of the Kings of Alba* is as follows:

> Ildulb held the kingdom viii years. In his time the *oppidum* of
> Eden was vacated and left to the Scots, as it is to this day. A fleet
> of *sumarliðar* were killed in Buchan.

This is a very short account and has, perhaps, suffered in transmission. At first glance there is no account of the death of Ildulb, or the end of his reign, but it is quite likely that here, as we have seen previously in this very mangled chronicle, the original king-list entry has been interrupted by material inserted into the middle of it. A subsequent copyist has then miscorrected the grammar. If this hypothesis is correct then the original king-list would have read:

> Ildulb held the kingdom viii years and was slain by a fleet of
> *sumarliðar* in Buchan.

The twelfth-century king-list placed Ildulb's death at 'Invercullen'. Invercullen is the medieval name for Seaton in Banffshire, sited at the mouth of the Cullen Burn, just west of the modern town of Cullen.

---

[28] Many of the Vosges monasteries were founded by Columbanus of Bangor and his disciples. Later legend made Hildulf a brother of one of these disciples.

Although this place lay within the later medieval deanery of Boyne, rather than Buchan, at least some of Boyne was in the hands of the earls of Buchan as late as the thirteenth century and medieval earldoms tended to get smaller rather than larger as the middle ages progressed. It would not be surprising if the Spey at one time formed the boundary between Moray and Buchan. The twelfth-century king-list also describes Ildulb's killers as 'Norwegians'. *CKA*'s *sumarliðar* (*somarlidiorum* in the Latin) preserves, in a remarkably transparent form, a genuine Scandinavian word meaning, literally, 'summer followers', and by implication 'summer raiders' – that is to say farmers who engaged in raiding for part of the year rather than hardened full-time ship-warriors like the *mycel here* of the *Scaldingi*. Knowledge of Scandinavian language among Gaelic chroniclers is not unprecedented, for instance the term *erell*, representing ON *jarl* (from proto-Scandinavian **erlaR*[29]), appeared as early as 848.[30] It is none the less interesting that such a specific term is used here. The term, *sumarliða*, appears once in the *Anglo-Saxon Chronicle* under the year 871. This is the first reference in any text to Buchan, a provincial name of obscure meaning. It is also only the second record in *CKA* of an event occurring north of the Mounth. Does this mean that the kingdom was expanding in this direction or was it merely the case that while the chronicle which supplied most of the information in *CKA* was narrowly interested in the Tay basin the king-list which provided its backbone was not so myopic and recorded the death of kings wherever they occurred. Against the interpretation of this passage as a record of Ildulb's death it should be noted that *Chronicum Scotorum* notes only that he died (*moritur*) and does not explicitly state that he was killed.

The interpolated passage:

> In his time the *oppidum* of Eden was vacated and left to the Scots, as it is to this day,

seems to record the Albanian takeover of Edinburgh. It is usually presumed that it was the Northumbrians who vacated the citadel, presumably a fortress on Castle Rock, and this is probably correct, although we should not discount the possibility that it had fallen into Cumbrian

---

[29] In transcribing early Scandinavian, particularly from runic inscriptions, the final consonant of the masculine nominative is regularly represented as 'R', distinguished from 'r'. This is because this consonant began life as a /z/ and gradually evolved into /r/, but it is unclear precisely when the change came. Runic inscriptions preserve the distinction between /r/ and /R/ surprisingly late.

[30] *AU* 848.5.

hands at some point. The reference, 'to this day', suggests a rather late date for the interpolation, and the spelling of *Eden*, does not look authentic. We should really expect something more like *Eten* or *Etin*, with 't' representing /d/. This could be a very simple modernisation, however, the sort of 'correction' a scribe might make without thinking. No indication is given of when in Ildulb's reign this event occurred.

The chronicle, then, gives us little indication of the events of Ildulb's reign. He reigned eight years, was probably slain in the northeast, and his reign may mark the point at which the Albanians gained their first foothold south of the Forth. If the interpretation of the account of the *Sumarliðar* in Buchan is correct then it is also the last time that *CKA* gives us the precise location of a king's death and, indeed, the chronicle changes character for its next few entries, which suggests that it may originally have concluded with the death of Ildulb. Ildulb himself is not mentioned in any English sources and only his death is noted in the Irish chronicles.[31] Dumville has noted that no father's name is supplied for Ildulb in either *CKA* or the Irish chronicles. Since a pedigree survives for his grandson, of which more anon, which makes it clear that he was the son of Constantín son of Áed, we need hardly doubt this but it may be a further clue that the character of the text is changing at this point. Dauvit Broun has suggested that the original of *CKA* was compiled in the course of Ildulb's reign and that the pre-existing king-list went only so far as Mael Coluim son of Domnall.[32] It is certainly the case that the accounts of the reigns subsequent to Ildulb's are very different but one's judgement on the account of Ildulb's reign relies, to a large extent, upon what one makes of the episode of the *sumarliðar*.

DUB SON OF MAEL COLUIM AND CUILÉN SON OF ILDULB (962–71)

With the changing character, and shortly the end, of the *Chronicle of the Kings of Alba*, we are left on less secure ground in the later tenth century (not that the ground on which we have been travelling has been particularly firm). For an account of the next few reigns we shall begin by looking at their record as it appears in the Irish chronicles and then try and match

---

[31] *CS* 960 [*recte* 962], A.Cl. 956 [*recte* 962].
[32] D. Broun, 'Dunkeld and the origin of Scottish Identity', *Innes Review* 48 (1997), 112–24.

this to *CKA* and later sources. The following obits of kings of Alba appear in the *Annals of Ulster* in the later tenth century:

> *AU* 967.1 Dub son of Mael Coluim, king of Alba, was killed by the men of Alba themselves.

> *AU* 971.1 Cuilén son of Ildulb, king of Alba was killed by the Britons in a battle rout.

> *AU* 977.4 Amlaíb son of Ildulb, king of Alba, was slain by Cinaed son of Mael Coluim.

> *AU* 995.1 Cinaed son of Mael Coluim, king of Alba, was killed through treachery.

To which can be added the *Annals of Tigernach*'s:

> *AT* 997 A battle between the Albanians in which fell Constantín son of Cuilennan and many others.

Five kings reigned in a space of thirty-five years, giving an average reign length of seven years, as opposed to the average reign length of thirteen from Cinaed son of Alpín to Ildulb. All but one of these kings appears to have been killed by his own people. To some extent such a breakdown in order was inevitable. Since 862 all the kings, with the exception of Giric (if he really was king), had been descendants of Cinaed son of Alpín. Constantín and Áed were brothers, and their sons, Domnall and the second Constantín, were first cousins. Their friends and kinsmen were mostly mutual. As the generations progressed, however, descent from Cinaed became more of an ideological tag than a real mark of kinship. The generation of the 960s, Dub and Cuilén, were third cousins with generations of input from maternal kindreds and developing social networks of clients and co-factionalists. It is likely that regional hegemonies had built up among the Alpínids and that some provinces felt more affinity to one princely line than to the other. The problem for Scottish historians is that the amount of detail we have been left with is too small to see what precisely lies behind each conflict.

The English also experienced similar tensions emerging among the descendants of Alfred the Great. We have seen how Edward the Elder's union of Mercia and Wessex was nearly split asunder on his death by the election of different sons to the kingship, Æðelstan in Mercia and Ælfweard in Wessex. Only Ælfweard's untimely death prevented either civil war or the division of the kingdom, and a decade later his brother Eadwine also seems to have died in suspicious circumstances. After the death of Eadred in 955 the kingship went to Eadmund's elder son, Eadwig, but in 957 Eadmund's second son Edgar was elected king by the Mercians and the Northumbrians, probably at the instigation of the faction headed by Æðelstan 'Half King', who had been Edgar's foster-father. Once again fratricide or the permanent splitting of the kingdom was avoided through Eadwig's early demise in 959. To some extent, England's *Vorsprung durch Technik*, that put it so far ahead of its Celtic-speaking neighbours by the end of the century, was the result of the genetic feebleness of its monarchs: Alfred died aged forty-eight; Edward was perhaps a year or two older; Ælfweard was probably about twenty-two; Æðelstan forty-three; Eadred perhaps a little over thirty; and Eadwig perhaps not even twenty.[33] Even Edgar, the survivor, only just made it past thirty; and these are just those who avoided violent death. The relative lack of internecine strife in tenth-century England was largely due to the fact that the potential rivals were dropping like flies without a finger being laid upon them. Edgar himself left sons by two wives and the elder, who succeeded him, another Edward, was murdered by the household of the mother of the younger. Untimely death stalked the house of Wessex.

It would be exceedingly enlightening if we could identify regional bases for the factions in later tenth-century Alba, but this is very difficult. Since England tended to divide along the lines of the constituent kingdoms we might imagine that Alba would do the same. In many cases such provinces retained their 'national' character, with regional assemblies, regional ecclesiastical hierarchies and regional networks of kinship and clientage. German history, between the late ninth and twelfth centuries, while dominated by a handful of ruling kindreds, tended to fission along the lines of the 'tribal duchies', such as Saxony, Bavaria, Franconia, Swabia and, less ethnically discrete, Lotharingia (the Low Countries and Alsace-Lorraine). By this period the dukes were no longer drawn from embedded local dynasties but the factions of nobles who supported them were, and princes of a dynasty from, for example, Saxony, who were planted in Bavaria, rapidly went native.

In both England and Germany the kings, while recognised as kings throughout the realm, generally confined their own itineration to

---

[33] There are, of course, other factors explaining the precocity of the southern English, such as richer agricultural potential and proximity to the Continent, but the lack of internal strife is largely due to a shortage of disgruntled æthelings who could be manipulated by factions within the kingdom.

certain core territories where they owned much land in their own right and where they had close personal links with the nobility. English kings seem never to have visited Northumbria or East Anglia, unless on a war footing, and rarely travelled far north of the Thames into Mercia. German kings, likewise, confined themselves to southern Saxony and Franconia (the area around Frankfurt-am-Main), and almost never visited Bavaria, Swabia, the Rhineland or northern Saxony.[34] In Alba we can identify three places that were certainly in the core area: Dunkeld; Scone; and Cennrígmonaid (St Andrews), and this suggests that the 'central transit zone', through which the kings regularly itinerated was the Tay basin. Possibly they travelled up and down the Tay by ship some of the time. We can speculate that places like Clunie in Stormont and Abernethy may also have been regular ports of call. We have also noted that there is little evidence for kings travelling north of the Mounth in peace time. In the portions of *CKA* we have examined so far, only Mael Coluim, 'with his army', is recorded as having visited Moray, and Buchan appears only in the context of conflict with a Scandinavian fleet. We should not necessarily infer, however, that areas which kings are not recorded as having visited in *CKA* lay outwith the kingdom, any more than East Anglia lay outwith the kingdom of the English or Bavaria the Eastern Kingdom.[35] Indeed, had these areas been regarded as alien territories, as were the lands of the Saxons and the Britons, we might have expected them to have been accorded a higher profile as locations of potential threat or opportunity. None the less, we are still left with a problem of bounding the kingdom. How far west did it stretch? The twelfth-century king-list seems to claim that all the kings before the late eleventh century, saving only Constantín son of Áed, Cuilén son of Ildulb and Cinaed son of Mael Coluim, were buried on Iona. Does this mean that Iona, and perhaps Mull, lay within the kingdom? At first sight

---

[34] See J. W. Bernhardt, *Itinerant Kingship and Royal Monasteries in Early Medieval Germany, c. 936–1075* (Cambridge, 1993). Bernhardt develops the concept of a 'central transit zone' in which most royal business was conducted: this is well illustrated in the maps between pp. 312 and 329 of his volume.

[35] 'Germany' developed out of the Germanic-speaking provinces of the Frankish kingdom and took some time in establishing a name for itself. It was variously termed 'the Eastern Kingdom', the 'Kingdom of the East Franks', and the 'Kingdom of the Franks and the Saxons', before the term *Regnum Teutonicorum* was settled upon in the mid-eleventh century. This final name was based on the erroneous supposition that the classical people, the Teutones, were in some way linked to the Middle High German adjective *tiutisch* applied to the German language. In fact, this word, whence modern *Deutsch*, simply meant 'vernacular'; as opposed to Latin, and is not related to the earlier tribal name.

the answer would appear obvious: yes. Yet in Ireland many of the kings of Connacht were buried at Clonmacnoise even though that church-settlement clearly lay within the realm of the kings of Mide, albeit near the border. Similarly the kings of Cenél nEógain began to take a strong interest in Armagh, some being buried there and others constructing a house there, although it lay on the very fringes of their hegemony and well outside their core territories. German kings of the Ottonian dynasty likewise favoured Aachen as a place of burial, because Charlemagne was buried there, even though it lay on the fringes of their kingdom and in a province rarely visited by living kings. The import-ance of cult and symbolic association may well have guided such choices. The same influences, however, may have suggested to the com-piler of the king-list that Iona was an appropriate place to claim as a royal mausoleum. North of the Mounth we can argue that Moray and Buchan may have lain in the kingdom, but how much further can we go? What of Ross and Caithness?

Bearing these questions in mind we can now turn to the final section of the *Chronicle of the Kings of Alba* and compare its witness to the infor-mation which we can glean from external sources. The concluding sec-tions of *CKA* read:

> *Niger* son of Mael Coluim reigned v years. Bishop Fothach died. [A battle] between *Niger* and *Caniculus* on *Dorsum Crup* in which *Niger* had the victory, wherein Dúnchad, abbot of Dunkeld, and Dubdon, *satrap* of Atholl were slain. *Niger* was expelled from the kingdom and *Caniculus* held it for a short time. Domnall son of Cairell died.

> Cuilén *ríg* v. years reigned. Marcan son of Breodalach was killed in the church of St Michael. Leot and Sluagadach went to Rome. Bishop Maelbrigte died, Cellach son of Ferdalach reigned. Maelbrigte son of Dubican died. Cuilén and his brother Eochaid were killed by the Britons.

> Cinaed son of Mael Coluim reigned . . . years. He plundered part of *Britannia* constantly/instantly. Cinaed's land-forces were slain in a great slaughter at *Moin Uacoruar*. The Scots ravaged *Saxony* as far as Stainmore, and to *Cluia* and to the lakes of *Derann*. Cinaed also fortified the fords of *Forthin*. After a year Cinaed went and raided *Saxony* and carried off the son of the king of the Saxons. He it is who yielded up the great *ciuitas* of Brechin to the Lord.

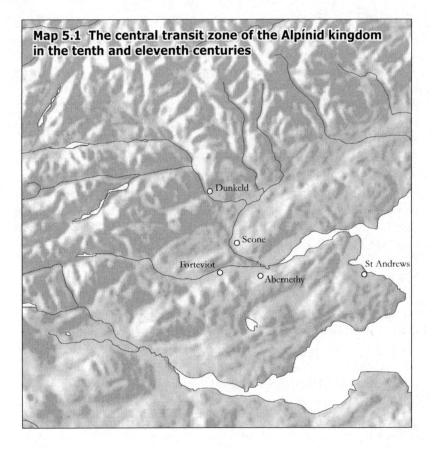

Map 5.1 The central transit zone of the Alpínid kingdom in the tenth and eleventh centuries

The first thing to note is that the names *Niger* and *Caniculus* are Latin and mean 'black' and 'little dog', respectively. Since 'black' and 'little dog' also translate the names 'Dub' and 'Cuilén', there is no problem identifying these kings with those whose deaths were recorded in *AU* in 967 and 971. What is odd is that the author of this passage should chose to play with the names in this way, and this is the clearest indication that the text here is a continuation of the original king-list and not the work of the same writer. It also seems as if the writer who then continued the account of Cuilén's reign did not necessarily recognise him as *Caniculus*. Our 'Latinate' writer has supplied the information that *Caniculus* 'held the kingdom for a short time' already. So what we see here are two separate phases of updating the chronicle.

The Bishop Fothach, whose death is noted here, would appear to be the 'Fothad son of Bran, scribe and bishop of the islands of Alba' whose obit appears in the *Annals of the Four Masters* for 963. The 'ch' at the end of the name in *CKA* is a scribal error for 'th', which like final 'd', represented /ð/ in early Gaelic. Fothad follows Cellach in the list of bishops 'of St Andrews' preserved in Walter Bower's fifteenth-century chronicle. He was said there to have been expelled by Ildulb and to have lived in exile for eight years. This would put his expulsion in Ildulb's first year and it may be a hint that the transfer of power from Mael Coluim to Ildulb was not as smooth as our sources imply, and that the new king may have purged Mael Coluim's supporters. Ildulb's expulsion of Bishop Fothad as one of the first acts of his reign leaves open the possibility that the Cellach whom Mael Coluim slew in Moray was the bishop. Chronology alone, however, makes this a slim possibility, particularly if the later tradition that Cellach was appointed by Giric is true. A record was also preserved at St Andrews in the twelfth century that Fothad had taken over the lands of St Serf in return for promising to support the community of Céli Dé on the island of Loch Leven who claimed to be the successors of St Serf. Serf's original foundation seems to have been at Culross and what we appear to have here, on a much more local scale, is yet another retreat inland by a religious community, like those which took Columba from Iona to Dunkeld and Cuthbert from Lindisfarne to Chester-le-Street. In the north something similar may have happened to the community of St Drostan at Aberdour (in Banffshire) which seems to have relocated to Old Deer (Aberdeenshire) in the tenth century.[36] This presumably happened at some point between 906 (when we know that Bishop Cellach was alive) and 955 (when Fothad was exiled). Fothad's death notice in *AFM* is the latest use of the term 'Islands of Alba' for the Hebrides (probably just the islands from Tiree south). After this they are the 'Islands of the Gaill'. Fothad's residence there, in his last years, also provides a rare glimpse of the islands and suggests that Scandinavian occupation, if such there was at this period, did not present an insurmountable impediment to structured ecclesiastical life. It seems likely that Bishop Fothad found asylum on Iona.

CKA relates only one other significant event of Dub's reign: a battle fought between Dub and Cuilén on *Dorsum Crup* in which a *satraps* of Atholl and an abbot of Dunkeld were slain. Unfortunately, it is not made clear on which side these two were fighting, although it is marginally more likely that they were fighting on the losing side, that of Cuilén. The

---

[36] This is one possible reading of the material preserved in the Gaelic notes in the Book of Deer. For these notes and a discussion of them see K. H. Jackson, *The Gaelic Notes in the Book of Deer* (Cambridge, 1972).

Latin word *dorsum*, when used to represent a place-name element by Gaelic-speakers, usually stands for Gaelic *druim* (for example, *Dorsum Britanniae* stands for Druim Alban). The final 'p' in *Crup* would have been pronounced /b/, so the name of the place where the battle was fought would probably have appeared as 'Drumcrub' had it survived. This would appear to be the same name, and perhaps the same place, as the site of the famous battle of *Mons Graupius*, between the Roman general Agricola and the Caledones in the first century AD. The most recent discussion of *Mons Graupius* has focused on the suggestion that Duncrub, near Dunning (Perthshire), which appears in a single medieval document as *Drumcroube*, may have been the site of the battle between Dub and Cuilén.[37] A further hill with the *crup* element in its name is the massif at the upper end of Badenoch, known from its twin peaks Cruban Mor and Cruban Beg. Clearly, whether we imagine this battle to have been fought upon the borders of Atholl and Badenoch or in Strathearn, effects any interpretation we may place upon it. The use of the relatively exotic term *satraps* (it appears in the Vulgate as the title for Philistine chieftains) is, like *Niger* and *Caniculus*, simply evidence that this particular writer liked to show off his Latinity. That an abbot should die in battle was not remarkable in the tenth century. Across Europe senior churchmen led the forces of their church estates into combat.

Despite the fact that Dub is said to have won the battle of *Dorsum Crup* the next thing we are told is that he was expelled from the kingdom. Bearing in mind that he reigned for four or five years, we need not suppose that there was any direct linkage between the events. The *Annals of Ulster* seem to record this battle:

> *AU* 965.4 A battle between the men of Alba themselves, where many were slain around Donnchad, i.e. the abbot of Dunkeld.

Victory may have led Dub into *hubris* and consequently he may have alienated a sufficient proportion of the nobility that they ejected him. Or it may be that the killing of an abbot of Dunkeld was viewed as an offence against St Columba for which there could be no atonement. The *Annals of Ulster* record Dub's death at the hands of the 'Men of Alba' in 967, but since *CKA* says that he was expelled we might imagine that this killing took place after his successor, Cuilén, had been inaugurated. The later

---

[37]   J. E. Fraser, *The Roman Conquest of Scotland: The Battle of Mons Graupius, AD 84* (Stroud, 2005), 72–6. Hudson, *Kings of Celtic Scotland*, 92, also favours Duncrub as the site of the battle between Dub and Cuilén.

king-lists say that he was slain at Forres, in Moray, and that his body was hidden under the bridge at Kinloss. It also says that the sun hid its rays while his body was hidden; but the only eclipse at about this time was on 20 July 966. For what it is worth, Fordun, writing in the fourteenth century, says that he was murdered in his bed rather than killed in battle.[38] It is possible that Forres was far enough from the centre of the kingdom for Dub to have been in exile there; alternatively he may, like many later pretenders to the Scots throne, have begun a rising in the north, in the hope of regaining the kingship. It is possible that the portion of *CKA* displaying the pretentious Latinity was written during this rising for it states that *Caniculus* (Cuilén) ruled a short time, and ascribed the death of an otherwise unknown individual, Domnall son of Cairell, to this period, before breaking off without mentioning Dub's death.

A new writer takes up the account of Cuilén's reign. He seems mostly to have been interested in obituaries. One curious detail at the beginning of his account has excited much speculation: he writes, 'Cuilén *rīg* v. years reigned'. The word reproduced here as *rīg* has been left as it appears in the manuscript. We should expect the line over the 'i' to signal an expansion to 'in', giving *ring*, but this makes no sense. The most oft repeated explanation is that this represents the Norse name 'Hringr', and that Cuilén had a Norse as well as a Gaelic name. There is no hint of this elsewhere and where the same writer records Cuilén's death, a line or two further on, the word is not repeated. The genitive form of the Gaelic word for king, *rí*, is *ríg*, but it is hard to see why a genitive form should be used here. The word *regnavit*, 'reigned', was abbreviated to *reg·* immediately following 'Niger son of Mael Coluim', and there preceded the tally of years, so perhaps this originated as the same indication (though it would be very odd for a subsequent copyist to fail to notice such an obvious usage and to add *regnavit* again). A number of explanations are possible and none certain, but we should be very cautious of following the crowd and presuming the rather imaginative *Hringr*.

The first death to be recorded is that of Marcan son of Breodolach who is otherwise unknown. The church of St Michael, where he was slain, might be the church of that name within the ecclesiastical complex at *Cennrígmonaid* or Kirkmichael, the mother church of Strathardle (Perthshire). Alternatively it may be at an unknown location. Marcan's obit is followed by the notice of a trip to Rome by Leot and Sluagadach, and these men were most likely clerics of the house where the chronicle

---

[38] Indeed, this is the night murder of a Scottish king at Forres which Shakespeare borrowed for his account of the killing of Duncan in Act One of *Macbeth*.

was being kept. We then move on to the death of Bishop Maelbrigde and the succession after him of Cellach son of Ferdalach. Dumville has suggested that Cellach son of Ferdalach, rather than being Maelbrigde's successor, was king of Moray.[39] This seems unnecessary and Dumville seems to have been unaware of the list of early bishops (of St Andrews/Alba?) preserved by Bower. In this list a Cellach (spelled variously) is said to have succeeded a *Malisius*. The identification of Maelbrigde with *Malisius* is problematic: one would expect the latter name to represent the Gaelic Mael Ísa ('Disciple of Jesus'), but it is possible that the Maelbrigde of *CKA* is a product of eye-skip by the copyist since another Maelbrigde appears in the next line of the manuscript. Having started with the 'Mael' the scribe may have looked up and caught sight of the 'brigde' rather than the 'isa'. Malisius is said to have reigned for eight years. If these years were counted from Fothad's death then we should expect him to have died in about 971, but he may have been appointed during the latter's exile, but after 958. Cellach was supposed to have then reigned for twenty-five years. The identity of Maelbrigde son of Dubican, the second Maelbrigde whose death is noted, is unknown, but it has been speculated that he may have been the son of the Dubucan son of Indrechtach, mormaer of Angus, whose death was noted by *CKA* in its account of the reign of Constantín son of Áed.

Of Cuilén's death *CKA* states only:

Cuilén and his brother Eochaid were killed by the Britons.

The Irish chronicles have slightly different accounts:

AU 971.1 Cuilén son of Ildulb, king of Alba, was killed by the Britons in a battle rout.

CS 969 [971] Cuilén son of Ildulb, king of Alba, was killed by the Britons in a burning house.

The king-lists, which are not contemporary accounts, add that he was slain by a son of Dyfnwal (whose name appears in several rather garbled forms which may represent British Rhydderch), on account of his daughter. The version interpolated into the *Chronicle of Melrose* claims that Cuilén had raped the British girl. Most of the king-lists locate the killing in Lothian, which was probably a debatable land in this period lying at

[39] D. N. Dumville, 'The Chronicle of the Kings of Alba', in S. Taylor, ed., *Kings, Clerics and Chronicles in Scotland, 500–1297* (Dublin, 2000), 73–86, at 82.

the bounds of Northumbria, Strathclyde and Alba.[40] If one wished to construct a narrative incorporating as much of this information as possible one might suggest that Cuilén was exercising lordship over the Britons and that, while enjoying conveth (tribute through hospitality), he overstepped the bounds of acceptable behaviour. Rhydderch, if that was his name, may well have burned his own house down over Cuilén and Eochaid's heads. Burning people in houses, with a guard mounted at the exits to finish off any escapees, is a familiar motif from Icelandic and Irish sagas, but there are enough enigmatic references of the sort we have here to suggest that it was a real phenomenon.

AMLAÍB SON OF ILDULB AND CINAED SON OF MAEL COLUIM

The conflict between the sons of Ildulb and those of Mael Coluim continued after the death of Cuilén and Eochaid. Both the *Chronicle of the Kings of Alba* and the later king-lists concur in assigning the reign of Cinaed son of Mael Coluim to the period immediately following the reign of Cuilén. The Irish chronicles, however, which probably better reflect contemporary witness, and which have a greater claim to be disinterested records, tell us of an Amlaíb son of Ildulb, king of Alba, who was slain by Cinaed in 977. What we can not tell is whether this Amlaíb was Cinaed's predecessor in the kingship, who was later airbrushed out of official histories, or whether the period 971–7 was characterised by a divided kingship, with different candidates being recognised in different parts of the kingdom.

The burning of Eochaid son of Ildulb alongside his brother in 971 answers one of our earlier questions: what did spare princes do? Eochaid had presumably remained a member of his brother's household and had accompanied him on his expedition to Lothian. This makes it quite likely that Amlaíb was also part of the regime and in a strong position to succeed. It is possible that he too had been in the burning house but had escaped death, but it seems more likely that he had remained at home,

---

[40] When it first appears on record, in the twelfth century, West Linton, in Lothian, was known as *Lyntun Ruderic*. This appears to mean 'Rhydderch's Linton'. The word order is Celtic but the core name, *Lyntun*, is English so this is probably a settlement founded by Northumbrians which came into the hands of a Strathclyder. It is tempting, if speculative, to imagine this as the site of the burning of King Cuilén. The Roman road between Biggar and Inveresk was probably the main access route between Strathclyde and Lothian.

north of the Forth, watching over the kingdom in Cuilén's absence. Cinaed, as the brother of an expelled, and perhaps murdered, rival was most likely to have been in exile. He may, however, have had friends or maternal kin within the kingdom upon whose support he could depend, and he is likely to have been considerably older and more experienced than Amlaíb.

Amlaíb's name, the Gaelic form of Óláfr, is Norse in origin, and although, by the later tenth century, Norse names were beginning to appear among Gaelic dynasties (and Gaelic names among the Insular Scandinavian families), he is among the first such cross-named individuals on record. This strongly suggests that his maternal kin may have been from a Scandinavian background and they are likely to have been a branch of the Uí Ímair dynasty that dominated the Irish Sea zone. He may well have been a grandson of Amlaíb Cúarán, or his cousin Amlaíb son of Gothfrith.

Precisely the period following Cuilén's death had seen a change in the dynamic in the Irish Sea province. Amlaíb Cúarán had recovered from his conflict with Eric in Northumbria in 952 and had finally regained his position in Dublin by 964, once again building alliances with the local Irish dynasties. In 971, however, a new force arrived on the scene. In that year, the 'B' text of *Annales Cambriae* tells us that Môn (Anglesey) was 'wasted by the son of Harald'. *Brut y Tywysogion*, a translation into Welsh of a thirteenth-century Latin chronicle which used a related but not identical text of *Annales Cambriae* for its early sections, but which also slightly embellishes its narrative, claims that the leader of this force was named 'Mark', and the target the church-settlement at Penmôn, and also states that the following year, 972, 'Gotbric son of Herald' ravaged Môn and 'through great cunning subdued the whole island'. These two brothers eventually emerge clearly as Maccus and Gothfrith, and they were to play a leading role in the region for most of the 970s and 980s. The origin of these brothers has proved a vexing problem for historians. The hunt for a suitable Harald who might have fathered them has proved problematic. Harald Blue-tooth, who was then king of the Danes (in Denmark), has been suggested. Alternatively, they may have been brothers of that Eric Harold's son who was slain in 954. Perhaps the favourite candidate, and the most likely, is Amlaíb Cúarán's brother who was slain on the Shannon in 940 while king of the *longphort* at Limerick.[41] This Harald, or 'Aralt' as the Irish chronicles call him, must have been very young so his sons may only have been in their early thirties in 971 and had perhaps only

[41] *AFM* 938.13 [*recte* 940].

recently detached themselves from some kinsman's war-band to set up on their own. Very recently Benjamin Hudson, who follows the nineteenth-century editor of the *Annals of the Four Masters* in erroneously representing the name 'Maccus' as 'Magnus' (a name which was not coined until the eleventh century), has suggested that the father of Maccus and Gothfrith was a certain Hagrold who operated out of Bayeaux in Normandy for a few years prior to 944.[42] It is hard to see how this hypothesis has much to recommend it, although Hudson is probably right to argue that we should pay more attention to the links between Normandy and the Insular world in this period. Whoever they were, the assault by the sons of Harald on Môn seems to have rung alarm bells across Britain, which suggests that they may have been active elsewhere outwith the view of our surviving chronicles.

In 973 Edgar, who had been sole king of the English since 959, held a second consecration, probably in imitation of German imperial coronations, at Bath, an ancient Roman city in southwest England, on the border of Mercia and Wessex.[43] This was followed immediately by a circumnavigation of Wales, presumably from the mouth of the Avon (near modern Bristol), by the entire English fleet, and a second quasi-imperial event at Chester, another former Roman site. Whatever the motivation for the second consecration at Bath, the circumnavigation of Wales was almost certainly a signal to Maccus and Gothfrith to stay out of Edgar's back yard. The northern recension of the *Anglo-Saxon Chronicle* describes the events of 973 as follows:

> In this year the ætheling Edgar was consecrated king at Bath on the day of Pentecost, on 11 May, in the thirteenth year after he succeeded to the kingdom, and he was but one year off thirty. And immediately after that the king took his whole naval force to Chester, and six kings came to meet him, and all gave their pledges that they would be his allies on land and sea.

Twelfth-century chroniclers up the number of kings and supply a catalogue of names, some more or less credible than others, but they were

---

[42] B. T. Hudson, *Viking Pirates and Christian Princes: Dynasty and Empire in the North Atlantic* (New York, 2005), 65–74. For a discussion of the name *Maccus* and the case for this as the correct form for our man see D. E. Thornton, 'Hey, Mac! The Name *Maccus*, Tenth to Fifteenth Centuries', *Nomina* 20 (1997), 67–98.

[43] Bath, like Charlemagne's capital at Aachen, bore the Latin name *Aquae*. This name was remembered in one of the two Anglo-Saxon names for the city *Acemannesceaster* ['Akemanchester'].

almost certainly speculating.[44] Although no king-lists survive for Wales, and even the number of kingdoms fluctuated, it is unlikely that all six could have been Welsh rulers. The meagre annalistic record suggests that Iago son of Idwal ruled in Gwynedd, Einion son of Owain[45] in Deheubarth (the southern territories ruled by the Merfynion dynasty, descendants of Rhodri Mawr), and Morgan son of (a different) Owain ruled in Morgannwg (Glamorgan). In Gwent a fourth, very small kingdom was ruled by either Nowy son of Gwriad or his son Arthfael. Although all these dynasts experienced sibling rivalry there is little evidence that any other polities of significance existed in Wales at this time. Dyfnwal of Strathclyde is likely to have seen the sons of Harald as a clear and present danger and would almost certainly have been at Chester. The list so far comprises five kings. It is, therefore, not possible that both Amlaíb and Cinaed attended. It cannot be assumed, however, the situation in Wales was such that an additional member of the Merfynion dynasty may have been able to gain English recognition of his kingship.

In the short term Edgar's intervention in the Irish Sea seems to have been effective. Maccus turned his attention to the west of Ireland, seizing that Ímar who presently controlled Limerick, from Scattery Island in the mouth of the Shannon, and his brother Gothfrith was not to return to Wales until the 980s. But Edgar's own days were numbered and, in 975, he succumbed to the frailty of his line and died leaving only under-age children as his heirs. Dyfnwal of Strathclyde seems to have taken this as the signal to resign his kingship to his son Mael Coluim and to set off on pilgrimage to Rome. These changes in the balance of power may have created the opportunity for Cinaed to move against Amlaíb and in 977 the last of the sons of Ildulb was slain.

Whether one chooses to believe that Cinaed had been ruling over some part of the kingdom since 971, or that his reign began in 977 affects the way in which one ties the account of *CKA* into absolute chronology. It is interesting that *CKA* has left the number of years Cinaed ruled blank and this has led scholars to presume that this is evidence that the final phase of compilation took place while he was still alive. This is possible but it is somewhat curious that with all the reworking and copying, between the late tenth century and the production of the Poppleton manuscript in the

---

[44]   For the most recent discussions see A. Williams, 'An outing on the Dee: King Edgar at Chester, AD 973', *Medieval Scandinavia* 14 (2004), 229–44, and D. E. Thornton, 'Edgar and the eight kings, AD 973', *Early Medieval Europe* 10 (2001), 49–80.
[45]   Einion's father actually outlived him, dying in 988, but his inactivity during his later years and the high profile of Einion, suggests that he had retired, much as Constantín son of Áed had done.

mid-fourteenth, no scribe managed to fill this gap, particularly when one considers that the Scottish collection in the Poppleton manuscript (which had probably been put together as a collection in the later twelfth century) included a king-list containing a reign length for Cinaed. An alternative explanation for the gap might be that the Poppleton scribe noticed a discrepancy between a date given in the exemplar and the king-lists and that he left a gap, intending to come back and correct it.

CKA's account of Cinaed's reign is as follows:

> Cinaed son of Mael Coluim reigned . . . years. He plundered part of *Britannia* constantly/instantly. Cinaed's 'land-forces' were slain in a great slaughter at *Moin Uacoruar*. The Scots ravaged *Saxony* as far as Stainmore, and to *Cluia* and to the lakes of *Derann*. Cinaed also fortified the fords of *Forthín*. After a year Cinaed went and raided *Saxony* and carried off the son of the king of the Saxons. He it is who yielded up the great *ciuitas* of Brechin to the Lord.

The original Latin for the word rendered here as either 'constantly' or 'instantly' is *statim*, which can bear both these meanings. It effects our understanding because it might mean either that his first act was an attack on a part of *Britannia*, or that he habitually led raids on it. *Britannia* here means 'a land of the Britons', a meaning which it bore alongside 'the island of Britain' well after our period. Brittany in France derives its usage from this meaning and Cambro-Latin texts regularly use it either for Wales or even for a part of Wales. Thus, the life of St Padarn, from around 1120, described the division of *Britannia* into three ecclesiastical provinces ruled, respectively, from Llanbadarn (near Aberystwyth), St David's (Pembrokeshire) and the Church of Saint Teilo (which may mean either Llandeilo Fawr in Carmarthenshire or Llandaff by Cardiff) – all in Deheubarth.[46] One curious feature of this is the use of the phrase 'a part of', where one might simply have expected his campaign(s) to be described as directed at *Britannia* or the 'Britons'. It may be that the subtlety is lost to us here or that he had a particular area which he was targeting; perhaps disputed lands in Lothian. The word that I have translated as 'land-forces' in the account of Cinaed's defeat (by the Britons?) has traditionally been translated as 'infantry', but the formal distinction between infantry and cavalry is probably anachronistic. All

---

[46] *Vita Sancti Paterni* §21, in A. W. Wade-Evans, ed. & tr., *Vitae Sanctorum Britanniae et Genealogiae* (Cardiff, 1944), 258–61.

who could have afforded to, would have ridden to war and the decision as to whether to fight on horseback or on foot will have been a tactical rather than a strategic one. The word, in Latin *pedestres*, can bear the meaning either of 'infantry' or a 'land force' as opposed to a naval force. I would suggest that what is being described here is a two-pronged attack across the Forth by ship and by land and that the land forces were cut down somewhere in the upper Forth basin. The first element of the name of the place where they were killed, *Moin*, means a bog or fen, and would be very appropriate for the Flanders Moss area. If the fords of *Forthín*, which Cinaed is said to have fortified, are the Fords of Frew, the lowest fording place on the Forth, then this might lend weight to this explanation.

Of particular interest is the account of Cinaed's raid into *Saxonia* as far as Stainmore, *Cluia* and the lakes of Derann. Stainmore is transparent and the lakes of Derann are almost certainly the Cumberland lakes Derwentwater and Bassenthwaite. *Cluia* is more obscure, but it could easily be a scribal error for *Cliua*, a form based on Old English *clif* which can mean not simply a 'cliff' but also a 'steep slope': indeed, this is its more common meaning in place-names.[47] Here it may mean specifically the incline of the northern face of the Lake District massif, which covers most of the territory between Stainmore and the Derwent. What is noteworthy is that these points are described as the extreme limits of a raid into *Saxonia*, rather than *Britannia*, suggesting that the Cumberland plain was in English hands at this time. This would go against the received wisdom that has tended to presume that the Cumbrians lost this territory only in the course of the eleventh century. There are no detailed accounts of the contraction and decline of Cumbria but the fact that the name 'Cumberland' became permanently fixed to this territory, and that Cumbric name forms for places like Carlisle, likewise replaced the traditional English forms, has encouraged historians to maximise the possible period of Cumbrian control. Cinaed's targeting of this region would almost certainly have required him to raid across Cumbria even if the target areas were, as we are told, in *Saxonia*. One possible way of resolving these difficulties might be to suppose that the Scottish source is being anachronistic in its terminology, and regards lands once Saxon as still in *Saxonia* even when ruled by Cumbrian kings, particularly if the bulk of the population had remained English. Alternatively, it is possible that the Solway plain had not yet become Cumbrian.

[47] D. N. Parsons, *The Vocabulary of English Place-Names* (vol. 3), *Ceafor – Cock-pit* (Nottingham, 2004), 103. An alternative explanation might be that *cluia* is a scribal error for *duia*, representing Welsh *Dwy*, the River Dee (in Kirkcudbrightshire).

Even more puzzling is the claim that on one of his raids Cinaed carried off the son of the king of the Saxons. Neither of Edgar's sons was more than about eleven or twelve in 975 and it seems unlikely that they would have been in Northumbria. Edgar's oldest grandson was probably only born in about 990. Most scholars have assumed that *CKA* is describing the son of a ruler of Northumbria. After the expulsion of Eric in 954 all of Northumbria was ruled under the English crown by a certain Oswulf, who had previously, under Eadred, appeared on charter witness-lists as high-reeve of Bamburgh (in 946, 949 and 950). Under Edgar Northumbria seems to have been split between Eadwulf, surnamed Evil-child (who attests royal charters between 968 and 970) in the north, and Oslac (from about 963 until his outlawry in 975), in Yorkshire. Oslac was replaced by Thored son of Gunner, but we hear nothing of the north until 994 when two northern earls, Waltheof and Northman (both, interestingly, Scandinavian names), appear briefly at the English court following the pirate Óláfr Tryggvason's sacking of Bamburgh and ravaging of Northumbria the previous year. The son of the 'king of the Saxons' was probably a son of Eadwulf, Northman or Waltheof.

By the beginning of the twelfth century another story was being told of Cinaed and the English. *De Primo Saxonum Adventu*, a short text produced at Durham at the very beginning of the twelfth century, states:

> These two earls [Oslac and Eadwulf] along with Ælfsige, who was
> bishop of St Cuthbert [968–90], conducted Cinaed to king Edgar.
> And when he had done homage to him, king Edgar gave him
> Lothian; and with great honour sent him back to his own.

This event, which if it happened can be dated to the period 968–75, was subsequently used to justify claims that Scottish kings held Lothian of the English crown, and the account may have been fabricated for this purpose. Given the date, however, before the killing of Amlaíb son of Ildulb, it may be that what lies behind this story is the granting of some part of Lothian to Cinaed while he was in exile as a base from which to harry Amlaíb.

The final piece of information concerning Cinaed recorded in *CKA* concerns the gift of the great *ciuitas* of Brechin to God. This is simply the story of the foundation of a major church-settlement, but its place in this chronicle has led some to suppose that the final phase of the text was com-posed at Brechin. The gift of Brechin may have been connected to Cinaed's death in 995. Although we know the details of this only from the twelfth-century king-lists and an element of folklore may have crept in, the story goes that he was slain by Finele [Fionnguala?] a daughter of

Connchar, mormaer of Angus, whose only son he had slain. Since
Brechin went on to become the chief church of Angus it is possible that
it originated as a comital centre for the region and that it came into royal
hands as a result of confiscation in the course of some dispute between
Cinaed and the comital family. Later medieval chroniclers tell bizarre
stories about the manner of Cinaed's death but the earlier king-lists say
only that he died through Finele's treachery at Fettercairn in the Mearns.
It should be remembered that Cinaed's father Mael Coluim had been
slain not far away, at Fetteresso, which may suggest that the local aristocracy were more closely tied to the family of Ildulb.

THE WESTERN SEAS IN THE TIME OF CINAED SON
OF MAEL COLUIM

We have already seen that the beginning of Cinaed's career coincided with
the appearance of a new force on the western coasts of Britain and in
Ireland in the shape of Maccus and Gothfrith, sons of Harald. The next
two decades were to see a serious reconfiguration of the political landscape in the Hebrides and the Irish Sea. Following Maccus' raid on Môn
in 971 and his brother's in 972, the Haraldsson's turned their attention
away from Wales, perhaps as a result of Edgar's show of strength and the
solidarity displayed by the other Insular kings. Their next appearance in
the record is described by the *Annals of the Four Masters* thus:

> The plundering of Scattery Island by Maccus, son of Aralt, with
> the lawmen of the Isles along with him; and Imar, lord of the Gaill
> of Limerick, was carried off from the island, and the violation of
> Seanan thereby.[48]

And in the *Annals of Innisfallen*:

> The son of Aralt made a circuit of Ireland with a great company,
> and plundered Scattery Island, and brought Ímar from it into
> captivity.[49]

Scattery Island lies at the mouth of the Shannon and was a church
complex dedicated to St Seanan which seems, by this date, to have

[48] *AFM* 972.13 [*recte* 974].
[49] *AI* 974.2.

become the main church patronised by the Gaill of Limerick. Limerick, though less well known due to the poor chronicle coverage of the west of Ireland, was a Scandinavian *longphort* which rivalled Dublin in importance. Of particular interest to Scottish historians is the allusion in *AFM*'s account to the lawmen of the Isles as Maccus' accomplices. This is the second reference in *AFM* to the lawmen of the Isles, the first being an account of a raid in 962:

> The fleet of the son of Amlaíb and of the lawmen came to Ireland, and plundered Conaille [County Louth] and Howth [County Dublin], with Ireland's Eye; and the lawmen afterwards went against the men of Munster, to avenge their brother, i.e. Oin, so that they plundered Inis-Doimle and Ui-Liathain, and robbed Lismore [not the Scottish island] and Cork, and did many other evils. They afterwards went into Ui-Liathain, where they were overtaken by Maelcluiche grandson of Maeleitinn, who made a slaughter of them, i.e. killing three hundred and sixty-five, so that none escaped but the crews of three ships.[50]

Although these are isolated incidents they give a rare glimpse of the social organisation of the Western Isles during this period. It looks very much as if the Isles were not organised into a kingdom or earldom but that, like the provinces of the Swedish interior discussed earlier, they were ruled by assemblies of freeholders who regularly elected lawmen to preside over their public affairs. The use of the plural, lawmen, suggests that each island or island group may have had its own assembly. In both the annalistic accounts it looks as if dynasts from the Irish Sea zone had persuaded the Hebrideans to join them in a raiding venture into Ireland.

The relationship between the sons of Harald and Amlaíb Cúarán is far from clear. In 975 Ferdal, the head of the Columban church-island of Rechru (now Lambay, County Dublin), which appears in the record for the first time in 150 years, was slain by heathens. It is unlikely that the perpetrators were Amlaíb's men since he seems to have become reconciled to Christianity and to have become a patron of the Columbans, so perhaps the killers of Ferdal were the sons of Harald or their allies returning from Limerick. The motive for their expedition to the Shannon is also clear. Ímar of Limerick was back on Scattery Island by 977 when he was slain there, along with his sons, by an up and coming local ruler called

---

[50] *AFM* 960.14 [*recte* 962].

Brian son of Cennétig.[51] It is most likely that Maccus had ransomed him back to his people in Limerick for cash, for the *longphuirt* were rapidly becoming the repositories of silver bullion in the western world.

THE FALL OF AMLAÍB CÚARÁN

After Maccus' kidnapping of Ímar of Limerick we hear nothing of the sons of Harald until the 980s. Whether they were building a kingdom for themselves off the radar of our chroniclers, or whether they had aligned themselves with a bigger fish and become lost temporarily in the ranks of his followers is a matter for speculation. The later 970s saw Amlaíb Cúarán, who had clearly reconciled himself to the loss of Northumbria, playing for high stakes in Ireland (the English kings may conceivably have been paying him a pension to keep him away: many English silver coins were appearing in Dublin in this period). He was engaged for most of the 960s and 970s in warfare with his erstwhile brother-in-law Domnall ua Néill, king of Ailech in the north, and of Tara from 956. In the 970s Amlaíb married another Irish princess, Gormflaith, daughter of the king of Leinster. In an ironic twist, the Irish king, Domnall, principally targeted the churches under Amlaíb's protection in the hinterland of Dublin. In 970 he sacked Louth, Dromiskin, Monasterboice and Dunleer. Warfare between Amlaíb and Domnall raged for a decade across the midlands of Ireland and every polity in the north and east of the island was sucked into the conflict.[52] In Munster, in the southwest, Brian son of Cennétig, who now had control of the fleet of Limerick, quietly took advantage of the distraction to build up a regional power base for himself.

The war ended suddenly in 980. Domnall, old and sick, retired into religion and death at Armagh. As king of Tara he was succeeded by his nephew, Amlaíb's step-son, Máel Sechnaill of Mide. In the same year, perhaps at Máel Sechnaill's inauguration, Amlaíb led a great force to Tara to confront the new king. Possibly he was making a bid for the kingship himself. The *Annals of Ulster* take up the story:

> *AU* 980.1. The Battle of Tara was won by Máel Sechnaill son of Domnall against the Gaill of Dublin and of the Isles, and a very great slaughter was inflicted upon the Gaill, and the power of the

---

[51] *AI* 977.2.
[52] See A. Woolf, 'Amlaíb Cúarán and the Gael', in S. Duffy, ed., *Medieval Dublin III* (Dublin, 2002), 34–43.

Gaill was ejected from Ireland. There fell Ragnall son of Amlaíb, the son of the king of the Gaill, and Conmael, son of a tributary king of the Gaill and many others.

The *Annals of Tigernach*, after relating a similar account of the battle, present us with its sequel:

A great hosting by Máel Sechnaill the Great, son of Domnall, king of Tara, and by Eochaid, son of Ardgal, king of the Ulaid against the Gaill of Dublin. And they besieged them for three days and three nights and rescued the hostages of Ireland, including Domnall Cloen, king of Leinster, and the guarantees of the Uí Néill besides, and they got their full demands from the Gaill, that is: two thousand head of cattle, with jewels and treasures and the exemption of the Uí Néill from tribute, from the Shannon to the Sea. It was then that Máel Sechnaill made that famous proclamation: 'Let every one of the Gaels who is within the borders of the Gaill return to his own country in peace and comfort'. That captivity was the Babylonian captivity of Ireland. It was next to the captivity of Hell.

It continues:

Amlaíb son of Sihtric, high-king of the Gaill of Dublin, went to Iona in repentance and in pilgrimage and afterwards died there.

Máel Sechnaill was in his thirty-first year, Amlaíb was probably still under sixty. Although the kingdom of the Gaill of Dublin survived and remained very significant in the politics of the region it was, henceforth, never to be the senior partner in any alliances which it made, and never to dominate either Ireland or the coastline of Britain in the way that it had. In the immediate aftermath of the battle Máel Sechnaill placed his half-brother, Glúniairn, Amlaíb's son by Dúnlaith, sister to Domnall ua Néill, on the throne of the Gaill, and reinforced his hegemony by marrying Amlaíb's wife, Gormflaith, and presumably taking her son, Sihtric, into his household.

At the battle of Tara, Amlaíb's forces had included the Islesmen, and, when he abdicated, it was to Iona that he retreated. These factors strongly hint that the Isles had in some sense recognised his kingship and, possibly, parts of the western mainland of Britain, in northwest England and Galloway had also done so. He was one of the great kings of his age and had grown up in the time of Constantín son of Áed and Æðelstan of Wessex. He had suffered disappointment and defeat time and again and yet he had always survived. In Irish tradition he was recalled both as a great king of the Gaill, and an oppression on the island, but also as a noble ancestor of many native lines, descent from whom was a cause for pride. He began his career as a pagan plunderer and ended it as a penitent on Iona. In a single life time he managed to encapsulate the entire Viking Age.

RETURN OF THE SONS OF HARALD

Amlaíb's retirement and Dublin's new status as a puppet of Máel Sechnaill created a power vacuum in the Irish Sea province. The vacancy was filled by two factions. From 982 we begin to hear of the exploits of Ímar of Waterford. He was probably connected to Amlaíb Cúarán's dynasty but he was not a son of Amlaíb. He may have been active as early as 970 when *AFM* mentions him in a list of allies of the sons of Cennétig, but this may be a mistake (in this late compilation) for Ímar of Limerick. Ímar of Waterford seems to have been attempting to take on the role which Amlaíb had played, leading Gaill resistance to Máel Sechnaill and attempting to intrude himself into Dublin. In 982 Ímar sacked Kildare and in 983 he was defeated in battle, along with his ally Domnall Cloen of Leinster, by the brothers Máel Sechnaill and Glúniairn. Ímar may also have been responsible for some of the raids in southwest England in the early 980s.[53]

The other faction to reappear were the sons of Harald and in 984 the two groups got together along with another rising star:

> A great naval expedition by the sons of Aralt to Waterford, and
> they and the son of Cennétig exchanged hostages there as a
> guarantee of both together providing a hosting to attack Dublin.
> The men of Munster assembled and proceeded to Mairg Laigen,
> and the Gaill overcame the Uí Cheinnselaig and went by sea; and
> the men of Munster, moreover, devastated Ossory in the same
> year, and its churches, and the churches of Leinster, and the
> fortifications of both were laid waste, and Gilla Pátraic, son of
> Donnchad [king of Ossory], was released.[54]

[53] *ASC* 980, 981 and 982.
[54] *AI* 984.2. Gilla Patráic's wife was a Mael Muire daughter of Harald. She may have been a sister of Gothfrith and Maccus.

Although Ímar is not mentioned here he was presumably the host at this sealing of an alliance. The planned attack on Dublin does not seem to have materialised on this occasion, but it is significant that such an alliance was considered.

Gothfrith son of Harald had appeared on the scene almost as soon as Amlaíb set sail for Iona. In 980 he materialised in his old stamping ground in North Wales ravaging Llŷn and Môn with the exiled Venedotian prince Custennin son of Iago. Custennin was slain in battle by his cousin Hywel son of Ieuaf, who had English backing, and Gothfrith responded by ravaging Cheshire.[55] We next hear of Gothfrith in 982 when he sacked St David's and ravaged Pembrokeshire. From St David's to Waterford is a relatively short crossing.

In 986 something quite unforeseen happened:

AU 986.2. The *Danair* arrived on the coast of Dál Riata, that is with three ships, and seven score of them were executed and others sold.

AU 986.3. Iona, of Colum Cille, was plundered by the *Danair* on Christmas Night, and they killed the abbot and fifteen of the elders of the monastery.

We see here for the first time in the Irish chronicles the use of the word *Danair*, literally 'Danes', and also, for the first time, since the very early ninth century, a mention of Dál Riata. Dál Riata may, and perhaps probably, means the rump territory in north Antrim, but if the Christmas atrocity on Iona was vengeance for the ill-treatment of the three ships then it might suggest that Argyll is intended. *Danair* had never previously been used for the Gaill and here must mean new invaders coming directly from Scandinavia. The following year both the Irish chronicles and the Welsh show us Gothfrith son of Harald allying himself with the Danes:

AU 987.1. The battle of Man was won by Harald's son and the Danes, and a thousand were slain in it.

AC 987 Gothfrith son of Harald with the black heathens wasted Môn and captured two thousand people. Maredudd took the survivors into Ceredigion and Dyfed.

[55] T. Jones, ed., *Brut y Tywysogyon or the Chronicle of the Princes, Red Book of Hergest Version* (Cardiff, 1955), 16–17, and *ASC* 980.

Maredudd was Maredudd son of Owain, king of Deheubarth, the leading Welsh ruler of the day. Hudson has argued that the sons of Harald were themselves the Danes described here but the term has never been used for them before 986 and it seems more reasonable to see this as a new alliance.[56] The *Danair* seem to have come from the north, from the direction of Orkney, and almost certainly had their origins in Denmark proper or southeastern Norway. The most likely candidate as the leader of these Danes is Óláfr Tryggvason who would briefly go on to be king of Norway c. 995–1000.[57] He was first named, as the leader of a fleet of ninety-three vessels at Folkestone, in the *Anglo-Saxon Chronicle* for 991, but his fleet is almost certainly that which attacked Watchet in north Devon in 988.[58] Much later Scandinavian sources insist that he came to England via Scotland and Ireland.[59] The attack on Watchet occurred in the year following the last mention of these *Danair* in the *Annals of Ulster*:

AU 987.3 A great slaughter of the Danes who plundered Iona, and three score and three hundred of them were slain.

The Welsh annals track the fleet south towards Devon:

AC 988. The heathens wasted St David's, Llanbadarn, Llantwit Major, Llancarfan and St Dogmaels.

Óláf's departure from the western sea-ways was immediately followed by a change of personnel among the remaining Gaill:

AU 989.3. Glúniairn, king of the Gaill, was killed when drunk by his own slave.

AU 989.4. Gothfrith son of Aralt, king of Innse Gall, was killed in Dál Riata.

---

[56] B. Hudson, *Viking Pirates and Christian Princes: Dynasty and Empire in the North Atlantic* (New York, 2005), 65–74.
[57] Óláf's father Tryggve was said to have been a king in the Norwegian Eastland (broadly speaking the watershed of the Glåma river, between Oslo and the modern Swedish border) in the 960s. He had probably recognised Danish hegemony.
[58] *ASC* 988 and 991.
[59] The earliest of these is probably *Historia Norwegie*, from the mid- to late twelfth century. It has been edited by I. Ekrem and L. B. Mortensen, with a translation by Peter Fisher (Copenhagen, 2003). Óláf's story is told on pp. 86–101.

Glúniairn's death might have spelled trouble for Máel Sechnaill, but luckily he had a spare son of Amlaíb Cúarán to hand; his own step-son Sihtric, perhaps still a teenager, whom he placed on the throne of Dublin. Gothfrith's obit is of interest because he is the first known individual to be styled *rí Innse Gall*, a title that would be borne by kings and lords of the Isles into the sixteenth century. The question for us at this first appearance of the title is: was the kingdom of the Isles a creation of these last few years (perhaps the autonomous lawmen we encountered earlier had been cowed or bribed into submission), or was the term simply a coinage for the old kingdom of Amlaíb Cúarán and his kinsmen, now stripped of the jewel in its crown, Dublin, which lay in the hands of Máel Sechnaill of Mide?

The years around 990 mark a real turning point in our narrative. Two major changes have taken place, one about a real transformation of the political landscape of Britain, the other about the nature of our sources. The real historical change is that which we have just explored. The dynasty descended from the grandsons of Ímar had, in the middle of the tenth century, been a major player in the Insular world, able to take on the most powerful English and Gaelic kings and to win battles and campaigns. By 990 this had changed. While men like Gothfrith son of Harald had been able to make a nuisance of themselves they were not serious competitors, and Amlaíb Cúarán was the last of his dynasty to stand in the first rank of Insular kings. From Brunanburh to Tara the Uí Ímair, the 'grandsons of Ivarr', were real contenders, but never again. The second major change relates to our sources. We have been dependent, since the mid-ninth century, upon the text known as the *Chronicle of the Kings of Alba*. For all its problems, it provides a core narrative for the emerging Scottish kingdom. That source has now come to an end and we shall henceforth be entirely dependent upon Irish and English chronicles for our contemporary witnesses.

CHAPTER 6

The Fall of the House of Alpín and the Moray Question

CONSTANTÍN SON OF CUILÉN AND CINAED SON OF DUB

After Cinaed son of Mael Coluim had been slain through treachery at Fettercairn, the kingship of Alba passed for the last time to a direct patrilineal descendant of Constantín son of Áed. This was Cuilén's son Constantín. This Constantín is the first king of Alba for whom a pedigree survives. It describes his descent as follows:

> *Constantín* [997] *son of Cuilén* [971] *son of Ildulb* [962] *son of Constantín* [952] *son of Áed* [878] *son of Cinaed* [858] *son of Alpín son of Eochaid son of Áed Find* [778] *son of Eochaid* [697] *son of Domangart* [673] *son of Domnall Brecc* [642] *son of Eochaid Buide* [629] *son of Aedán* [608] *son of Gabrán* [558] *son of Domangart* [534] *son of Fergus son of Erc* . . . and then back for about another thirty generations.[1]

Here I have added the death dates of the kings for whom annalistic obits survive. What is immediately apparent is that the gap between the death of Áed Find and that of his supposed father, Eochaid son of Domangart, is eighty-one years. This is not impossible, of course, but our evidence for Áed's active career begins only in 768 more than seventy years after the death of his supposed father. Compilers of later versions of this pedigree (for example, that appearing in the Poppleton manuscript) may have been aware of this problem for an additional Eochaid is sometimes inserted

---

[1] This pedigree is printed in full in its original form by John Bannerman in *Studies in the History of Dál Riata* (Edinburgh, 1974), 65–6.

between Eochaid son of Domangart and Áed Find. Further suspicion arises when we note that Constantín's pedigree survives in company with a group of Dál Riatan pedigrees which all end with men who died in the years around AD 700. It seems likely that, like much of the material surviving from Dál Riata, these pedigrees took shape in the time of Adomnán (Eochaid son of Domangart was one of the guarantors of *Cáin Adomnán*) and were rediscovered by historians researching Dál Riata in the later tenth century. Presumably Constantín's kindred had previously only counted their descent back to Áed Find.[2] He was known to be a son of someone called Eochaid (his patronymic is given in his obituaries in the chronicles) and this led the tenth-century antiquaries to appropriate, erroneously, a pre-existing pedigree of Eochaid son of Domangart in order to connect the kings of Alba to legendary Dál Riatan and Irish ancestors. Of course, this does not mean that the kings of Alba were not descended from earlier kings of Dál Riata. After all, Áed Find was king of Dál Riata and the interval between his death and that of Cinaed son of Alpín (eighty years) seems appropriate enough to fill the three generations the pedigree allows (though Alpín's alleged father Eochaid is not named in any contemporary sources). What it does seem to indicate, however, is that knowing about such a connection was not deemed important enough for it to have been accurately recorded. Clearly the connection with Cenél nGabráin and with their alleged Irish ancestors was something that became important to the kings of Alba only at the end of the tenth century.[3] The adoption of this pedigree marks, in some ways, the final triumph of the Gaelic, Scottish, identity of the Alpínid kingdom over its alternative Pictish roots.

This pedigree is the most interesting thing about Constantín son of Cuilén. The only annalistic notice of his reign is his obituary in *The Annals of Tigernach*:

AT 997 A battle between the Albanians in which fell Constantín son of Cuilénnan and many others.

[2] Since Cinaed son of Alpín was the common ancestor of all the kings of Alba he, rather than Áed, may have been the most ancient figure in the actually remembered pedigrees. Once a candidate for kingship had demonstrated his descent from Cinaed he need not demonstrate anything more.

[3] I am very grateful to Dauvit Broun for drawing my attention to the implications of this material in a paper given to the 'Imagining Alba' conference hosted by the Department of Celtic at the University of Aberdeen in 2004. His further thoughts on the subject have been published in '*Alba*: Pictish homeland or Irish offshoot?', in P. O'Neill, ed., *Exile and Homecoming: papers from the fifth Australian conference of Celtic Studies, University of Sydney, July 2004* (Sydney, 2005), 234–75 at 263–6.

The twelfth-century king-lists say that he was slain at Rathinveramon (probably across the Tay from Scone) by Cinaed son of Mael Coluim after a reign of eighteen months. On the face of it this looks like an error; Cinaed son of Mael Coluim had been killed in 995. The most likely solutions are that this is a mistake for Cinaed son of Dub, who actually succeeded to the kingship; that it is a mistake for Mael Coluim son of Cinaed (son of Mael Coluim), who succeeded him in 1005; or that his killer was indeed someone called, coincidentally, Cinaed son of Mael Coluim. So far as we can tell Constantín's death marks the end of the line descended from Cinaed son of Alpín's younger son, Áed. His reign and death may represent a final attempt to pursue the convention of regnal alternation between the two lines descended from Cinaed son of Alpín at a time when one branch of the family had in fact secured a monopoly of power. How such a monopoly was secured cannot be known in detail but a combination of effective social networking and land acquisition are likely to have been the main factors involved.

The same year that saw the death of King Constantín (997) saw the death of Mael Coluim son of Dyfnwal, king of the Cumbrians of Strathclyde. He appears to have been succeeded by his brother Owain. In 1000 the English king Æðelræd, Edgar's surviving son, mounted a major expedition against 'Cumberland'. His land forces ravaged 'very nearly all of it' but the naval expedition which left Chester in support of the land forces was unable to join him due to adverse weather conditions and ravaged the Isle of Man instead.[4] The failure of the fleet to join up with the land forces makes it clear that its destination was the Clyde rather than the Solway; the difficulties experienced would best be understood as occurring while trying to enter the North Channel. Æðelræd's motivation is not entirely clear. While England had enjoyed unparalleled wealth and stability for the first decade or so of his reign, from 991 his government began to pay off Scandinavian raiders, like Óláfr Tryggvason, with increasingly large amounts of silver coin. With the kingdom enjoying such a vibrant economy it was very easy for Æðelræd to give in to the temptation to throw money at a problem rather than to focus on a long-term solution but, while England could easily afford the expense, the impression given of weakness in the face of foreign aggression not only encouraged more Scandinavian adventurers to seek a place at the trough but also undermined the king's position at home. It is thus possible that his expedition into Clydesdale was simply aimed at restoring his reputation. Alternatively, the Cumbrians may have been allowing the Scandinavians to operate from bases in their waters. The career of the Danish king Sveinn Fork-beard may be of relevance here but

[4] *ASC* 1000.

unfortunately its exact chronology is unclear. Sveinn was involved in the killing of his own father in 987 but while some sources claim he succeeded to the kingship almost immediately others, notably Adam of Bremen (who knew Svein's grandson), claim that a period of exile (perhaps as long as fourteen years) ensued while Denmark was ruled by the Svear king Eiríkr the Victorious.[5] Adam claims that Sveinn was harboured by a 'Scottish' king for the latter part of this exile.[6] Sveinn was certainly in England in 994 and he attacked the Isle of Man in 996.[7] Æðelræd's expedition of 1000 was his only northern adventure and seems to have had no obvious lasting effects. For the rest of his reign he was taken up with fighting Sveinn, now certainly king of the Danes, in southern England. For a generation the northern kings would only be dealing with Northumbrian earls.

The sources are extraordinarily slim for Cinaed son of Dub's reign. We know only that after eight years as king of Alba he was slain at Monzievaird (near Crieff in upper Strathearn) in 1005. His killer was Mael Coluim son of Cinaed son of Mael Coluim, who then succeeded to the kingship. This Mael Coluim was to be the last Alpínid to rule over Alba.

The alternating kingship

From the time of the return of the Alpínid dynasty in about 889 royal succession had alternated strictly between the descendants of Cinaed son of Alpín's two sons, Constantín and Áed:

i. Domnall son of Constantín

        ii. Constantín son of Áed

iii. Mael Coluim son of Domnall

        iv. Ildulb son of Constantín

v. Dub son of Mael Coluim

        vi. Cuilén son of Ildulb

vii. Cinaed son of Mael Coluim

        viii. Constantín son of Cuilén

---

[5] Eiríkr is thought to have died in 995, so Svein's fourteen-year exile (if it is to be believed in) must include either the period during which he was outlawed by his father or some otherwise unattested interval between Eiríkr's rule and his own. He was certainly king of Denmark by 999 when he was involved in the killing of his old comrade in arms Óláfr Tryggvason.

[6] Adam of Bremen, *History of the Archbishops of Hamburg-Bremen*, tr. F. J. Tschan (New York, 1959 and 2002), 77–8. Adam was not particularly *au fait* with British affairs and his 'king of the Scots' might conceivably have been Irish, Albanian, Hiberno-Norse or Cumbrian.

[7] *ASC* 994 and *Annales Cambriae* 996.

The alternating kingship (*continued*)

As we have seen, most of the peoples of early medieval Europe followed succession practices which, while recognising that a particular lineage had the monopoly of the kingship, allowed some degree of choice to be exercised. In such systems it was usual for experienced, well connected and mature males to succeed in preference to candidates who might be considered incompetent through minority, disability, gender or simple lack of talent or charisma. Such systems regularly created situations where strings of brothers succeeded one another, as with the sons of Edward in tenth-century Wessex, or the sons of Mael Coluim III and St Margaret in twelfth-century Scotland. What is curious about succession to the kingship of Alba in the tenth century is the absolute regularity of alternation between two lines. It is hard to believe that none of these kings had suitable brothers or indeed adult sons who might have succeeded them. It seems fairly clear that some other principle underlay this alternation.

The closest parallel one can find is in the kingship of Tara, the notional high-kingship of Ireland, which between 734 and 1022 alternated strictly between two branches of the Uí Néill, Cenél nEógain and Clann Cholmáin, with only two brief periods where outsiders intruded into the kingship. This alternation in Ireland, however, worked because these two dynasties had separate territorial bases, in the north and midlands of Ireland respectively, and each king of Tara had been king of either An Foghla ('The North') or Mide ('Middle'), prior to rising to the high-kingship. Within each of these regional hegemonies a much less structured struggle for succession between qualified candidates had already taken place before the king was put in place as heir to Tara.

The regular alternation of royal succession in Alba suggests that a similar system may have been operating as that which governed succession to the kingship of Tara. In Pictish times it is clear that the kingdom had a fundamental binary division along the line of the Mounth, perhaps between Fortriu and Atholl. Following the demise of the line descended from Áed son of Cinaed in 997 a bid for the kingship by a family based in Moray. It thus seems likely that during the tenth century Áed's descendants were effectively kings in Moray and Constantín's in the south, alternating in the high kingship.

MAEL COLUIM SON OF CINAED (1005–34), LAST OF THE ALPÍNIDS

Mael Coluim's reign marks an important period in Scottish history when both Irish and English sources begin to give us a better view of what is happening inside the kingdom of Alba. There are still many questions that remain unanswered but our narrative is finally emerging from the darkness. Mael Coluim's reign overlaps with the careers of two men who had truly imperial ambitions: Brian son of Cennétig, the king of Munster, whom we have already encountered in passing towards the end of the last chapter, and who is better known to history as Brian Boru (*Borúma*); and Sveinn Fork-beard's son Cnut (Knútr), who was to rule over England, Denmark, Norway and a part of the Svear (his uterine brother Óláfr ruled the remainder). In 1005, the same year that Mael Coluim seized the kingship, Brian, who had persuaded Mael Sechnaill of Mide to hand over both the kingship of Tara and his wife Gormflaith in 1002, led his army into the far northeast of Ireland. He took hostages from the Ulaid and from the two northern Uí Neill dynasties, Cenél Conaill and Cenél nEógain and then encamped in the ancient henge monument at Emain Macha, about two kilometres from Armagh. This site was widely believed to have been the royal seat of the legendary kings of Ulster in prehistoric times and Brian was probably using it in much the same way that West Saxon kings used the ruins of Roman cities to emphasise their imperial aspirations. On this occasion Brian visited Armagh from his camp and made a gift of twenty ounces of gold to the church there. His secretary, Mael Suthain, recorded the gift in the Book of Armagh, the great gospel book, giving his master the title *Imperator Scotorum* – 'Emperor of the Gaels'! It is tempting to see Mael Coluim's rise to power as one of the series of regime changes which Brian effected at this time. The pseudo-prophetic poem known as the *Prophecy of Berchan* claims that Mael Coluim's mother was a Leinster woman, a rare piece of information about a Scottish queen, so it may be that Mael Coluim had spent some time in exile in Ireland.[8]

The *Prophecy of Berchan* also describes Mael Coluim as *biodhba Bretan, bádhudh Gall, loingseach Íle is Arann*. The first two terms mean 'enemy of Britons' and 'battler of Gaill', and are fairly self-explanatory, implying that Mael Coluim fought against both the Cumbrians and the Northmen. The term *loingseach Íle is Arann* is less clear-cut. Hudson interprets *loingseach* here to mean 'exile', which is indeed one of its meanings, and hypothesises

---

[8] B. T. Hudson, *Prophecy of Berchan: Irish and Scottish High-Kings in the Early Middle Ages* (Westport, 1996), 52–3 and 90.

that Mael Coluim was exiled to Islay and Arran (*Íle is Arann*) at some point.[9] *Loingseach* (whence the surname 'Lynch') can, however, simply mean 'voyager' or 'seaman', since *long*, its stem, is simply the word for 'ship'. In the context of this couplet, linked as it is to enmity towards the Britons and the Gaill, it seems more likely that the poet is crediting Mael Coluim with a military expedition to the Isles. No campaigns of this sort, however, are mentioned in the chronicle record.

Mael Coluim's reign also produced an interesting text that allows us to see something of how the kingdom of Alba was perceived. This is a genealogical tract closely related to the pedigree of Constantín son of Cuilén.[10] Although the core of the tract is a pedigree of Mael Coluim it also signals where his pedigree was thought to branch off from the ancestral pedigrees of other provinces of the kingdom. The core message of the tract, elucidated from other texts can be presented as in Table 6.1:

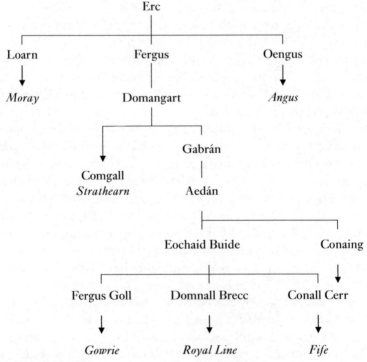

Table 6.1 The Dál Riatan origins of the men of Alba

[9] Hudson, *Prophecy*, 90 and *Celtic Kings*, 110–11.
[10] The text is translated in A. O. Anderson, ed., *Early Sources of Scottish History* I (Edinburgh, 1922 and Stamford, 1990), cliv. Its provenance in the time of Mael Coluim son of Cinaed was established by Broun in his paper 'Imagining Alba'.

The text explicitly describes Fergus Goll and Conall Cerr as the ancestors of the men of Gowrie and Fife and other texts make it clear that Strathearn was identified with the descendants of Comgall, and Moray with the descendants of Loarn. Given this information it does not require much originality to see a link between Oengus, ancestor of the Cenél nOengusa of Dál Riata, and the province of Angus in the east midlands. The tract also clearly points to the importance of the descendants of Conaing, but it is not possible to make a direct connection between this group and any Albanian province (although Atholl and the northeastern provinces are otherwise unaccounted for). Since *Ath Fothla*, as a name, goes back to Pictish times it may be that Gowrie and Atholl were originally two terms for the same area, or rather, the descendants of Fergus Goll, the *Gabranaig*, were believed to have occupied Atholl.[11] This might put the descendants of Conaing in the northeast, roughly corresponding to Mar and Buchan.

We have already seen that the connection between the royal line and the Cenél nGabráin, as laid out in the pedigrees, is unreliable and it is probably sensible to regard this whole structure from the perspective of the years around 1000. What we may be being shown here is a schematic of the degree of closeness between the kingship and the ruling kindreds of different provinces at that time. As we might have expected, the men of Fife and Gowrie, whose provinces formed the 'central transit zone' in which Dunkeld, Scone, Abernethy and Cennrígmonaid were to be found, are the closest in kinship to the royal line. Next come the descendants of Conaing (whose location is sadly uncertain) and then the men of Strathearn. The men of Angus and Moray are more distant still. How this framework relates to the question of the conquest of the Picts will be discussed in a later chapter but for our present purpose it serves to confirm that the 'central transit zone', which we identified earlier as broadly the Tay basin, was indeed recognised as the core of the kingdom and that the central provinces were Fife and Gowrie, and possibly Atholl.

The distance of Moray from the royal line in this tract is of particular interest when we note the apparent appearance of the ruling dynasty of this province in our sources in Mael Coluim's reign. The references to this dynasty in Mael Coluim's reign are as follows:

[11] This combined province might perhaps be reflected in the core territories of the later diocese of Dunkeld. Dr Steve Boardman tells me that, in the later middle ages, the term Atholl seems at times to have had a wider meaning than is generally recognised.

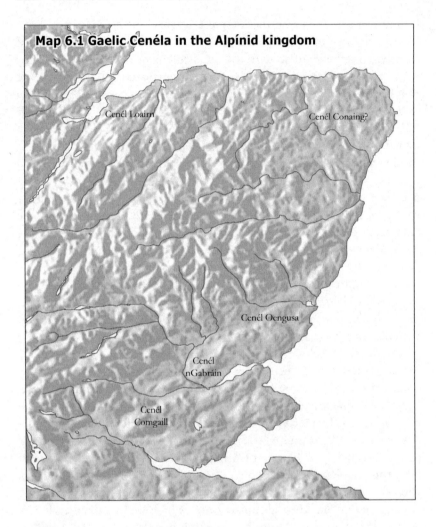

Map 6.1 Gaelic Cenéla in the Alpínid kingdom

Cenél Loairn

Cenél Conaing?

Cenél Oengusa

Cenél nGabráin

Cenél Comgaill

AU 1020.6 Findláech son of Ruaidrí, king of Alba, was killed by his own people.

AT 1020 Findláech son of Ruaidrí, mormaer of Moréb, was killed by the sons of his brother Mael Brigte.

AU 1029.7 Mael Coluim son of Mael Brigte son of Ruaidrí died.

AT 1029 Mael Coluim son of Mael Brigte son of Ruaidrí, king of Alba, died.

AU 1032 Gilla Comgáin son of Mael Brigte, mormaer of Moréb, was burned together with fifty people.

These entries pose something of a problem. Were these men kings of Alba or simply mormaers of Moréb (Moray)?

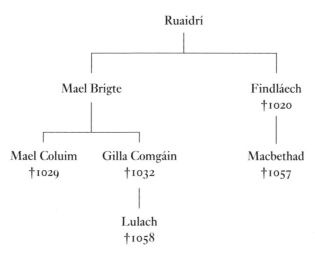

Table 6.2 The Moray dynasty

Many historians have either ignored the royal title accorded to these men and simply described them as mormaers of Moray, or they have hypothesised a separate kingdom of Moray, presuming that it had existed since the ninth century but simply lay out of sight of our chroniclers. It is noteworthy, however, that the chronicles vary the terms 'king of *Alba*' and 'mormaer of *Moréb*'. The term 'king of Moréb' does not appear in the chronicles until 1085. Both Findláech and Mael Coluim son of Mael Brigte are accorded the same title that the Alpínids had monopolised for more than a century. On the face of it this would seem to suggest that these two men contested Mael Coluim son of Cinaed's kingship. Indeed, were we dependent on the Irish chronicles alone, as we have been for so much of our story, we should be tempted to create a king-list for this period that looked something like this:

Cinaed son of Dub	997–1005
Findláech son of Ruaidrí	1005–20
Mael Coluim son of Mael Brigte	1020–9
Mael Coluim son of Cinaed	1029–34

The twelfth-century king-lists are adamant, however, that Mael Coluim son of Cinaed succeeded Cinaed son of Dub, and we should not overlook the ambiguity of the Irish chronicles. It is most likely that Cinaed's son was what the Irish would have called a 'king with opposition', that is to say that his kingship was challenged by the Moravian dynasty but initially neither side was able to get the upper hand and the kingdom was effectively divided. This crisis was finally resolved in 1040 when Macbethad, a king of the Moray dynasty, finally reunited Alba. Interestingly, a similar period of divided kingship occurred at precisely the same time in Ireland. There, after the death of Mael Sechnaill of Mide in 1022 (he had regained the kingship of Tara on the death of Brian son of Cennétig 1014), there was a period of about thirty years during which no king gained recognition as king of Ireland and where the situation was so unclear that even those retrospectively producing lists were unable to fill the lacuna for this period. The reason for these disputed kingships can be summed up in a single four-letter word: Cnut.

CNUT THE GREAT: THE MAKING OF AN EMPIRE

Scandinavia had been entirely transformed since we last visited it at the beginning of the ninth century. In Denmark Haraldr Blue-tooth, who had ruled from c. 958 to his murder in 987, had created a strong centralised kingdom with, by the 980s, something approaching a standing army. As a result of a long period of alternating conflict and collaboration with the German kings of the Ottonian dynasty he had also established Christianity in his kingdom. At Jelling in Jutland, where his parents were buried in vast pagan burial mounds, he erected a rune stone that proclaimed that he had 'united all Denmark and made it Christian'. Despite the temporary set-back and confusion following his murder, apparently instigated by his son Sveinn (who was growing tired of waiting to inherit), by 999 the kingdom was once more unified. Sveinn had married the Polish widow of Eiríkr the Victorious, king of the Svear, and secured an alliance with their son Óláfr and together these two kings had defeated the Norwegian king Óláfr Tryggvason.

Norway, which was been a patchwork of tribal chiefdoms when we last visited it, had also been transformed. In the first part of the tenth century the Norwegian Westland (the stereotypical fjord country), together with the Trondheim region, had been united under a dynasty claiming descent from one Haraldr Fine-hair (†c. 935) and based in the area around modern Stavanger. Eastern Norway and the interior continued to be ruled by various petty kings who found themselves under increasing pressure to accept either the Westlanders or Haraldr Blue-tooth as their overlord. In the late 960s the Westlanders annexed the kingdoms around Viken, the broad gulf south of Oslo. This roused the Danes into action and by the early 970s they had destroyed the Westland dynasty, killing or driving them overseas, and had taken direct control in the Viken and appointed Hákon, earl of Hlaðir (now Lade, a suburb of the city of Trondheim), as viceroy over the Westland. Hákon, who remained a pagan despite his relations with the Danes, ruled as if he were a king. After the deaths of Haraldr Blue-tooth and Eiríkr the Victorious, Óláfr Tryggvason, whose father had been a king in the Eastern dales slain by the Westlanders, returned to Norway from the British Isles where he and Sveinn Fork-beard had received a final pay off of £16,000 of silver from the English to go and not return. Óláfr had also become a Christian. Back in Norway Óláfr fought and bribed his way to power, ousting Earl Hákon (who was said to have been murdered by a slave while on the run) and overrunning Viken. The ancient dispute over domination in Viken inevitably led to Óláfr falling foul of Sveinn and, in 999, somewhere off the coast of what is now southern Sweden he was defeated and slain by Sveinn, the Svear king Óláfr and the sons of Earl Hákon. Sveinn re-established his father's hegemony over Norway and turned his attention back to England with its over-flowing coffers of silver.

Svein's initial plan seems simply to have been to extort cash from the English to fund a standing army and fleet which he could use to dominate his Scandinavian empire, but at some point his thoughts turned to conquest. This he achieved after a decade of warfare at Christmas 1013. On 3 February 1014, however, he died and was buried at York. His elder son, Haraldr, who had remained at home as regent, took over the governance of Denmark, but his younger son, by his Polish wife, Cnut, was elected king by the army in England. He was about sixteen years of age. The English king Æðelræd returned from exile in Normandy and the young Cnut retreated across the sea to Denmark, but Æðelræd's reprisals against those who had collaborated with Sveinn and Cnut were so savage that when the Dane retuned in August 1015 many of the leading men of the country went over to him. The country was divided and when Æðelræd died in April 1016 some of the English elected his son Edmund and some went over to Cnut. After a little fighting the two young men chose to divide the kingdom with Edmund getting his dynastic heartland, Wessex, south of the Thames and Cnut getting the rest. Edmund, however, succumbing to the frailty of his dynasty, died on St Andrew's Day, and Cnut assumed the kingship and sent Edmund's infant sons to his own half-brother, Óláfr in Svealand,[12] for safe keeping, while Edmund's younger brothers fled to their uncle in Normandy. In 1018 or 1019 Cnut's older brother Haraldr died and he was elected king of Denmark.[13]

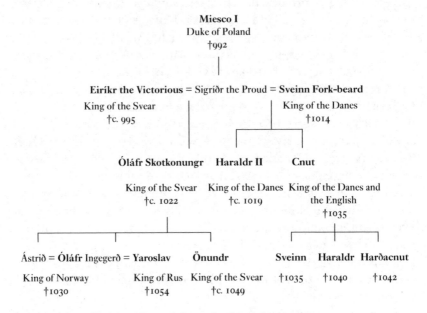

Table 6.3 Scandinavian kings of the early eleventh century

ENGLAND'S ADVERSITY, SCOTLAND'S OPPORTUNITY?

It is tempting to see the rise of Mael Coluim son of Cinaed in 1005, and perhaps even some aspects of Brian son of Cennétig's overturning of the Irish political order after 1002, as exploitation of the changing situation in England. From the time of Æðelstan in the 920s and 930s the West Saxon dynasty had, without question, been the single most powerful political force in the British Isles. Some kings were stronger than others and the extent of the lead they had over their rivals might have varied but they were always ahead of the pack. With the return of Sveinn Fork-beard to England in 1003 (and this time there was to be 'no more mister nice

---

[12] One of these infants was Edward, the future father of St Margaret.
[13] It is perhaps worth noting that Cnut had, by this date, probably spent as much of his life in England as he had in Denmark.

guy') the situation changed. King Æðelræd and his councillors were now fighting for survival in their heartland. The first English empire lay in ruins.

In the north Owain son of Dyfnwal reigned in Clydesdale and Northumbria north of the Tees was ruled by the aged Earl Waltheof. In York, southern Northumbria was ruled by Earl Ælfhelm. When Mael Coluim assumed the kingship of Alba he seems to have immediately embarked upon a campaign against the north of England. Among the Irish there had long been a tradition of the *crech ríg*, the 'king's raid', an inaugural military expedition across the border by which a new king demonstrated that he was made of the right stuff. It is probable that Mael Coluim, who had, after all, usurped his throne, felt in need of proving himself. Unfortunately for him things did not turn out as he had intended.

> *AU* 1006.5 A battle between the men of Alba and the Saxons, and it was a defeat of the Albanians and a great many of their nobles were left dead.

A northern English account, *De Obsessione Dunelmi*, goes into more detail.[14] It claims that the Northumbrian defenders were led by Uhtred, the son of Waltheof, and that he commanded the forces of both Yorkshire and the north. This account claims that Uhtred was the son-in-law of Bishop Aldhun of Durham (whither the relics of St Cuthbert had been translated in 995) and that Durham was the target of the raid. Some historians have questioned this last point as the *Annals of Ulster* do not mention a siege and the description of the attack on Durham and the fate of the Scots dead is very similar to that given by Symeon, in his *Libellus*, of a siege which took place in 1039–40.[15] Of course, it is not impossible that both attacks were aimed at Durham. In *De Obsessione* we are told that after the Scots' defeat a number of local women were paid, in cattle, to wash the heads of the prettiest Scottish dead and to braid their hair so that they might be displayed on stakes around the boundaries to the ecclesiastical precinct at Durham.

---

[14] This short, but important, text is translated in C. J. Morris, *Marriage and Murder in Eleventh-Century Northumbria: a Study of the 'De Obsessione Dunelmi'*, Borthwick Papers no. 82, (York, 1992). It is discussed at length in W. Kapelle, *The Norman Conquest of the North: the Region and its Transformation, 1000–1135* (Chapel Hill, 1979), 3–85, and R. Fletcher, *Bloodfeud: Murder and Revenge in Anglo-Saxon England* (London, 2002).

[15] Symeon of Durham, *Libellus de Exordio*, iii. 9, 169.

The Scottish attack had probably come down through Wedale (the route of the modern A7) and then along the Roman road of Dere Street (for the most part the route of the A68) which led almost directly to Durham. Wedale was to remain the main entry route for Scottish armies coming into England for centuries to come and the 'Black Priest' of Wedale, the incumbent at Stow, seems (in later times at least) to have always been a close kinsman of the earls of Fife.[16] It is a moot point, however, as to whether Wedale itself was under Scottish control at this stage. The whole question of the expansion of Scottish rule into the area between Edinburgh and Tweed is very much tied up with our reading of Mael Coluim son of Cinaed's reign. Because the main land routes into the Northumbrian heartland led south past Melrose what is now East Lothian could be effectively bypassed. Indeed, the evidence of Gaelic place-names in that county, which mostly hug the shore of the Forth in the Gullane area, together with later medieval landed interests, suggests that its links with Alba were established directly across the Forth from east Fife, rather than as part of a push eastwards along the southern shore of the firth.

We might ask at this stage what constituted Lothian. In modern parlance it comprises the whole of the southern shore of the Firth of Forth from the River Avon, with its exfluence just to the east of Grangemouth, to Cockburnspath. In earlier times, however, it seems to have been the land between Tweed and Esk (Kelso could be described as being in Lothian), comprising, roughly, Berwickshire, East Lothian and perhaps parts of Mid Lothian. Its precise western boundary is hard to define. We have seen that Edinburgh fell into Scottish hands in the reign of Ildulb (954–62) and that *Historia de Sancto Cuthberto* claimed the mouth of the Esk as the western boundary of Tyninghame's territory. It may be that the Lothian Burn, which runs from the northern end of the Pentland Hills and flows into the Firth of Forth a few hundred yards to the west of the mouth of the Esk, marks the ancient boundary. If this was the case

[16] The 'Law of Clann MacDuff', recounted by the fifteenth-century chronicler Andrew of Wyntoun, records that if a Fife man be slain his blood-price, paid by the killer, should be 24 marks for a noblemen and 12 for a commoner. The death penalty would only be pursued for the earl himself, the lord of Abernethy and the Black Priest of Wedale. It is known from other sources that the lords of Abernethy (whose late medieval status was inherited from the earlier abbots) were cadets of the comital house of Fife, and it seems clear from this provision that the incumbent of Wedale must also have been a member of the comital kindred. Andrew of Wyntoun, *Orygynale Cronykil of Scotland*, vi.19, D. Laing, ed., *Historians of Scotland*, vol. III (Edinburgh, 1872). Arkady Hodge reminds me that Gaelic for 'black' is *dubh*, the word behind the name 'MacDuff' and suggests that Wyntoun's 'Black priest' may in fact be the 'Priest of *Dubh*'.

then we might imagine that the Pentlands themselves formed the continuation of the frontier (the modern boundary between Peebles and Mid
Lothian being the ancient boundary between Cumbria and Lothian). As
suggested above, however, Scottish expansion southwards, across Mid
Lothian to Wedale may have preceded the crossing of the Esk.

St Balthere and Tyninghame

East Lothian had for centuries been dominated by the Northumbrian
church-settlement at Tyninghame, which possessed as its chief relics the
body of St Balthere (known now, erroneously, as St Baldred), who had
died in 756. This church had still been a going concern as late as 941,
when it was sacked by Amlaíb son of Gofraid, and was apparently still
important when *Historia de Sancto Cuthberto* was composed.
Unfortunately, this latter text, although originally put together in the
reign of Eadmund of Wessex as king of Northumbria (944–6), survives
only in a recension updated in Cnut's time and it is not clear whether
we should date its reference to Tyninghame as applying principally to
the 940s or to the 1020s. In any case it describes the lands pertaining
to Tyninghame as stretching between Lammermuir and the mouth of
the Esk, but, in contrast to an (apparently earlier) list of St Cuthbert's
properties found in *Historia Regum*, it does not include Edinburgh,
Abercorn or the unidentified house of *Tigbrethingham*[17] which all lay
north of the Tweed and west of the Esk. Tyninghame may have lain in
Northumbrian territory as late as the 1020s for Symeon tells the story
of a priest of Durham, Ælfred son of Westou, who at the command of
a vision set out and visited the sites of 'ancient monasteries and
churches throughout the province of the Northumbrians' and, digging
up the relics of their saints brought them to Durham. Among these relics
were those of Balthere. The other bodies he collected seem to have
come from Lindisfarne, Hexham, Tynemouth, Coldingham, Melrose and
Jarrow.[18] It is noteworthy that no relics were collected from south of
the Tees or west of the Pennines so it may be a fair assumption that

---

[17] The places named seem to be ordered geographically which would place
Tigbrethingham between Melrose and Abercorn. It is tempting to identify it with
Stow-in-Wedale, for the name 'Stow', simply means a '[Holy] place' and is probably
secondary.

[18] Symeon, *Libellus de Exordio*, iii.7. One of the bodies he collected, that of abbess
Æðelgyth, is of unknown provenance, though Rollason, *loc cit.* n. 33, suggests that she
may also have been from Coldingham.

St Balthere and Tyninghame (*continued*)

Ælfred only had access, or licence, to areas within a single political unit, the earldom of northern Northumbria. If this is the case then Tyninghame is likely to have been within the *regnum* of the earls of northern Northumbria at this point. This would seem to tie in with the claim made by *De Obsessione Dunelmi* that Lothian was conceded to the Scots in the time when Uhtred's brother Eadwulf Cuttlefish was earl (which coincided with at least the first part of Cnut's reign).

The one Scottish military victory which we know about in this period was the battle fought at Carham, probably in 1018.[19] This battle seems to have been fought by Earl Uhtred against an alliance of Mael Coluim and Owain the Bald, king of Strathclyde. The dating of the battle has caused some concern because of apparently conflicting evidence. Symeon tells us that it was fought within a month of an impressive comet making its appearance. This was almost certainly a comet which was visible in the northern hemisphere for several weeks in August 1018. He also tells us that Bishop Ealdhun of Durham died within 'a few days' of the battle whereas his account of Ealdhun's reign implies that he actually died in 1019 (although altering 'a short time', meaning 'a couple of months' to 'a few days' would be an easy slip to make). More seriously the *Anglo-Saxon Chronicle* appears to say that Earl Uhtred was killed by Cnut in 1016. This section of the Chronicle, however, recounting the Danish conquest, was written up retrospectively in the 1020s and it has been argued, quite convincingly, that the reference to Uhtred's death was a retrospective parenthetic statement. What we are actually told is that 'Uhtred submitted to Cnut and gave him hostages (but he had him killed none the less)'. This could bear a number of readings. Finally, *Annales Cambriae*, the Welsh chronicle, notes the death of an Owain son of Dyfnwal in 1015. It has usually been assumed that this man is a king of Strathclyde (the name Dyfnwal was exceedingly rare elsewhere), the brother of the Mael Coluim son of Dyfnwal who died in 997. This identification, though likely, is not certain and, in any case, there is no reason why Owain son of Dyfnwal might not have been succeeded by another Owain, perhaps the son of his elder brother.[20]

[19] The dating has caused much controversy but the most sensible discussion and conclusion remain those to be found in A. A. M. Duncan, 'The Battle of Carham, 1018', *Scottish Historical Review* 55 (1976), 20–8.

[20] See D. Broun, 'The Welsh identity of the kingdom of Strathclyde, c. 900–c. 1200', *Innes Review* 55 (2004), 111–80, at 133–5.

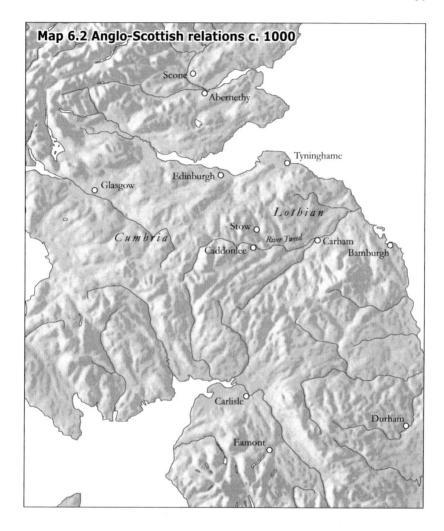

Map 6.2 Anglo-Scottish relations c. 1000

On balance the battle almost certainly occurred in 1018, or very early 1019, and the protagonists would have been Mael Coluim of Alba and Owain of Cumbria on one side, and an earl of Northumbria, probably Uhtred but just possibly his brother Eadwulf, on the other. The battle was fought at Carham-on-Tweed. This is right on the present border, more or less at the point where it turns south away from the Tweed, but, ironically, its very location makes it fairly certain that the Tweed was not the border at the time. Early medieval battles almost never happened on borders. Expeditionary forces tended to travel light and fast and there were few standing armies or border guards. If march-wards were maintained by the

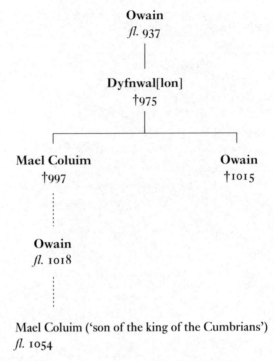

Owain
fl. 937

Dyfnwal[lon]
†975

Mael Coluim
†997

Owain
†1015

Owain
fl. 1018

Mael Coluim ('son of the king of the Cumbrians')
fl. 1054

Table 6.4 Cumbrian Kings of Strathclyde (dotted lines represent hypothetical links)

Northumbrians they would have been few in number and their job would have been to light beacons or send messengers warning of attack rather than actually confronting the attackers.[21] The defending forces would either be a relatively small posse of retainers led by the earl or one of his lieutenants, or a more general levy raised from across the country. The implication of this would be that by the time significant armed confrontation had taken place the enemy forces would almost certainly have been over the border for some time.

Mael Coluim and Owain probably met one another at or near Caddonlea (Selkirkshire), where later Scottish armies mustered. This location, where the Wedale road from Alba met the Tweeddale road from Strathclyde, lay at the northern edge of Ettrick Forest (roughly corresponding to Selkirkshire in extent) which formed a march (an underdeveloped and sparsely populated border zone) between Cumbria and Northumbria. The army would then have crossed into English territory

[21] The Borders surname Veitch derives from the Northumbrian word *wacere*, 'watcher', applied to such march-wards.

somewhere near Melrose. Such an arrangement would mean that neither Scots nor Cumbrians would be crossing each other's territory and would minimise collateral damage. At St Boswells they would have had to make the decision either to head south along Dere Street towards Durham, or to keep on heading east towards Lindisfarne and Bamburgh. From the moment of the meeting at Caddon, if not before, Northumbrian march-wards would have been aware of the expedition and sent messages to the earl. What we can not know is whether the northerners' decision to head east was governed by a pre-arranged intent or whether they were react-ing to news reaching them of Uhtred's army, presumably coming directly from his chief seat at Bamburgh. The earl's decision to meet the Scots and Cumbrians before they had the opportunity to cross or bypass Cheviot was brave but probably cost him the battle. Meeting them so close to the border almost certainly meant that he only had the opportu-nity to augment his own household troops with levies from the territories between the River Aln and Coldingham and whatever refugees from Teviotdale (modern Roxburghshire) had chosen to fly eastwards in the face of the enemy. Had the earl chosen to make a tactical retreat he could have gathered far more forces, perhaps even getting help from besouth the Tees. The cost then would have been the ravaging of a broad swathe of country and the loss of livestock and people as spoils to the northern-ers. Uhtred's failure to counter the invasion, if indeed it was he who led the Northumbrian forces, may have cost him his life. He was slain, appar-ently on Cnut's orders, by a Yorkshire *hold* named Thurbrand. Eiríkr son of Earl Hákon of Hlaðir, succeeded to the earldom of southern Northumbria while Eadwulf Cuttlefish, Uhtred's brother, was left to deal with the mess on the northern frontier.[22]

We know of two battles in the conflict between Uhtred and Mael Coluim. A victory for Uhtred in 1006 and one for Mael Coluim and his ally Owain in 1018. Historians have argued over which was the more sig-nificant but the likelihood is that these are unrepresentative glimpses of a much longer conflict which escaped the detailed gaze of our chroniclers because far more interesting things were happening in Southumbria and Ireland at the time. Interestingly, a chronicler from far away Burgundy may give us a more balanced assessment. Ralph Glaber, the chronicler in question, writing before about 1030, tells us that Cnut and Mael Coluim fought for a long time before being reconciled through the offices of Richard of Normandy and his sister Emma (who had married first

---

[22] Eiríkr was appointed earl in 1016 and seems to have had overall responsibility for the north of England.

Æðelræd and then Cnut). Ralph goes on to say that Cnut received Mael Coluim's son from the font, an act reminiscent of William of Malmesbury's account of the meeting between Æðelstan and Constantín son of Áed in 927. Duke Richard died in August 1026 so, if Ralph is to be believed, the reconciliation between Cnut and Mael Coluim must have taken place before this date. Ælfred son of Westhou's archaeological expedition to Tyninghame is said to have taken place in the time of Bishop Edmund, who succeeded Ealdhun, probably in 1019, so the window of opportunity for the settlement lies between 1019 and 1026. It seems likely that Uhtred's removal provided a perfect opportunity for a face-saving agreement between the two kings and that Cnut was happy to cede the lands north of the Tweed in return for formal submission from Mael Coluim. The lands between Cheviot and Tweed, however, remained within Northumbria until the early twelfth century.

THE MORAY QUESTION

In the early stages of this war, as we have seen, Mael Coluim was worsted by Uhtred and it may have been his defeat in 1006 which prompted Findláech of Moray (or just possibly his brother Mael Brigte) to raise the standard of opposition in the north. Mael Coluim may at this stage have seemed like a weak king and an alternative candidate may have been sought by factions within the nobility. We cannot be certain but it is likely that Findláech was the hereditary leader of the kindred that had ruled Moray under the kings of Alba. It is equally likely that he was of royal descent. It has been suggested that this claim to royal blood arose from the alleged descent from the Cenél Loairn kindred who had ruled over part, and some-times all, of Dál Riata in the seventh and eighth centuries.[23] Kindreds, however, usually lost their royal status after three or four generations without holding office. It seems far-fetched to imagine that Findláech's claim was based on such ancient history and it is worthy of note that the Moravian dynasty's kingly pretensions emerge in the first generation after the demise of the Alpínid branch descended from Áed son of Cinaed son of Alpín. Since the sons of Mael Brigte, Findláech's brother, also claimed the kingship it seems likely that a common ancestor of both Findláech and Mael Brigte, perhaps one of their parents, perhaps someone from an earlier generation, had transmitted the claim from the Alpínid dynasty. The pedigree that survives for this family does not, however, claim descent from

[23] Hudson, *Kings of Celtic Scotland*, 127–48.

Cinaed in the male line and thus it is more likely that their link to the dynasty was in the female line. Perhaps Mael Brigte and Findláech's father, Ruaidrí, had married a daughter of one of the tenth-century kings.[24]

In Pictish times the territories north and south of the Mounth had maintained distinct identities and had even, at times, had separate kings. It would probably be appropriate to think of Alba as being, like England, Germany or Norway in this period, constructed of a number of separate *regna*, each with its own laws, assemblies and aristocratic communities, and each with the right to elect a king. Historically the convention had arisen that these *regna* would share a king but such federal structures lent themselves to the creation of what German historiography has called *Gegenkönige* (translated, not entirely comfortably, as 'anti-kings'). 'Clann Ruaidrí', as we might term the Moravians, had presumably won the acceptance of the old *regnum* north of the Mounth. Indeed, if Mael Coluim's interests were increasingly focused on the lands beyond the Forth the northerners may have felt somewhat alienated from the kingship.

Whatever the legitimation that lay behind the Moravian claim it was probably triggered by the setbacks faced in Mael Coluim's early years. In the same way, the internecine struggle that had evidently broken out by 1020 (when the sons of Mael Brigte killed their uncle Findláech) may have reflected the turn in Mael Coluim's fortunes after Carham. While the kingdom is likely to have fractured along the fundamental division of the Mounth, both factions probably retained aspirations of re-unification and competed for influence in marginal areas such as the northeast.[25] Mael Coluim victorious, or perhaps already on terms with Cnut, may have wrong-footed Findláech, thus encouraging his own people to replace him with a younger more dynamic leader in the person of Mael Coluim son of Mael Brigte.

From Cnut's perspective contested supremacy within Alba, and Ireland for that matter, may have been the preferred option. As long as his Gaelic neighbours were more worried about internal competition than about asserting their autonomy he would be able to exert his own

[24] This analysis is explored further in A. Woolf, 'The "Moray Question" and the kingship of Alba in the tenth and eleventh centuries', *Scottish Historical Review* 79 (2000), 145–64.

[25] The property records in the Gospel Book from the Church of Deer in Aberdeenshire include, for example, grants by both Mael Coluim son of Cinaed and Mael Coluim son of Mael Brigte; see K. H. Jackson, *The Gaelic Notes in the Book of Deer* (Cambridge, 1972), 31. Would we be justified in inferring from the order in which these grants are listed that Mael Coluim son of Cinaed lost control of this area to the Moravians at some point before 1029?

lose hegemony without too much trouble. He may even have exerted influence to maintain the balance and prevent the emergence of an outright winner. One might compare his policy in Norway, where the Danes promoted division between the traditional provinces, playing off the earls of Hlaðir and their Trønder subjects, against the kinglets of the east and the interior. Thus, the unprecedented interregnum in Ireland and the division of the kingdom, north and south, in Alba, may have been actively promoted by Cnut. Without the clear and present danger presented by the Danish super-power Mael Coluim and Findláech might have fought to the finish very swiftly. Engaging in such damaging internal warfare, however, would almost certainly have led to the exposure of their flanks to Cnut or his henchmen.

THE EARLDOM OF ORKNEY

It is customary among Scottish historians to bring the earldom of Orkney into discussion of the conflict between the Moravians and Mael Coluim son of Cinaed. Our evidence for the earldom, however, is extremely problematic. A full length narrative account purporting to tell the history of the earldom from its alleged origins in the late ninth century, known as *Orkneyinga saga*, was composed in Iceland in the early thirteenth century (probably in the 1220s). Most of the information it contains, however, is hard to corroborate. As well as the fundamental problem of how an Icelander, writing in the 1220s, was supposed to have obtained accurate information about early Scottish history, it is demonstrably the case that many of the details of the *saga* which can be checked against contemporary sources are inaccurate and that other sections smack of folklore or confabulation. The problems of using Icelandic sagas as historical evidence for early Scottish history will be dealt with in more detail in Chapter 7, but a few points are worth making here since it is in this period that the narrative of *Orkneyinga saga* is most frequently used in conjunction with the sources regarding the kingdom of Alba.

The first contemporary reference to an earl of Orkney occurs in the account of the battle of Clontarf in the *Annals of Ulster*. This battle was fought on Good Friday 1014 on the northern shores of the Liffey just beyond Dublin. The protagonists were Brian son of Cennétig, king of Munster, and his allies on the one side and Mael Morda king of Leinster and Sihtric, son of Amlaíb Cúarán, king of Dublin, on the other. Both Brian and his enemies had called on allies and mercenaries from a wide area. Among the dead recorded on Sihtric and Mael Morda's side in the

Annals of Ulster was 'Siuchraid son of Loduir, iarla Innsi Orcc'. This was clearly the same man whom the Icelandic sources call Sigurðr Hloðvisson, earl of Orkney, whom they also claim died in this battle. Interestingly, the dead on Brian's side, listed in the *Annals of Ulster*, included 'Domnall son of Eimin son of Cainnech, mormaer of Mar in Alba'.[26] Frustratingly, Mar is in the debateable northeast so we cannot tell if Brian was aligned with Mael Coluim or Findláech.

For the period immediately following Sigurð's death we are entirely dependent upon *Orkneyinga saga* for information on Orkney, and the story it tells is very good indeed. Sigurðr, we are told, was succeeded by four sons whose relationships and quarrels are followed through until one of them, Thorfinnr (the ancestor of all subsequent earls) succeeds to the whole earldom. Thorfinnr then goes on to conquer all Scotland as far as Fife and to enforce his lordship over Ireland! None of these events is corroborated in contemporary or near contemporary sources.[27] Embedded in the saga are a number of stanzas from a poem known as *Thorfinnsdrápa* apparently composed immediately after Thorfinn's death by his court poet, Arnórr.[28] It seems that these verses provided the saga-writer with much of his material on Thorfinnr. Elsewhere Thorfinn's career seems to prefigure, remarkably, the career of a later earl, Haraldr Maddaðarson (†1206). Both Thorfinnr and Haraldr, we are told, were of Scottish royal descent on one side of their families; both were made earls of Caithness when five years old (by a Scottish king); both struggled for domination of Orkney with a kinsman named Rögnvaldr; and both were earls for seventy years. This latter fact is clearly not true for Thorfinnr, whom we know to have been succeeded by his sons by 1066 at the latest, only fifty-two years after the death of Earl Sigurðr at Clontarf. Further to this the Scottish king whom the saga says that Thorfinnr defeated before extending his conquest as far as Fife was called Karl Hundisson; not the name of any

---

[26] This is not the only notice of Albanian mormaers active in Ireland. According to the *Annals of Tigernach* three such men fought alongside Gilla Columb, king of Cenél Conaill in 976. Their names were Cellach son of Finguine, Cellach son of Bairid and Donnchad son of Morgand. We are not told which provinces or kindreds they led. Simon Taylor suggests to me that the rather curious name 'Eimin', given to the father of the mormaer of Mar at Clontarf, may represent Old Norse 'Eyvindr'.

[27] The closest thing we have to a contemporary account is Adam of Bremen's statement, written in the 1070s, that Haraldr of Norway (1047–66) conquered Orkney and brought it under Norwegian rule. Adam's source on Harald's career came from the king's close friend and frequent enemy Sveinn Estriðsson, king of Denmark (1047–74). This account does not mention the earls.

[28] Diana Whaley, *The Poetry of Arnórr jarlaskáld: An Edition and Study* (Turnhout, 1998), 53, 123–8 and 220–68.

king or *Gegenkönig* known from any other source, nor, indeed, a credible name for any Albanian dynast.[29]

Thorfinnr it seems, a little like Cinaed son of Alpín, became retrospectively more significant because he, like Cinaed, was the father of two sons who both established dynastic branches which competed for rulership for several generations. As the apical figure, descent from whom became the *sine qua non* for aspirant earls, it was important that he be made a larger than life figure. His conquest of Scotland served merely to legitimise the bold adventures of Haraldr Maddaðarson, who briefly occupied the lands north of the Mounth in the 1190s. In reality the somewhat vague references in *Thorfinnsdrápa* were probably all the saga-writer had to go on. Attempts by modern historians to make the *saga*'s account of Thorfinnr fit our other sources are almost certainly misguided. Doubtless the Scandinavian polity in the north of Scotland featured in the political calculations of both Alpínids and Moravians, but precisely how it did so is beyond us.

THREE KINGS

Under the year 1031 the 'northern recension' of the *Anglo-Saxon Chronicle* has the following entry:

> In this year King Cnut went to Rome and as soon as he came home he went to Scotland, and the Scots king surrendered to him . . .

The D version continues:

> and became his man, but he observed it but little time.

The E version, on the other hand, follows with:

> Mælcolm and two other kings, Mælbæþe and Iehmarc.

---

[29] Historians have attempted to argue that 'Karl Hundisson' is a Norse pseudonym for some other better known Gaelic ruler but the truth is that the author of *Orkneyinga saga* was pretty good at reproducing Gaelic names without resorting to these kinds of ploys: for example, Brjánn for Brian, Dufgall for Dubgall, Dufníall for Domnall, Dungaðr for Dunchad, Eðna for Eithne, Engus for Oengus, Finnleikr for Findláech, Gilla Oðran for Gilla Odrain, Kjarvalr for Cerbal, Konufogur for Conchobar, Magbjóðr for Macbethad, Margaðr for Murchad, Melbrigði and Melbrikta for Mael Brigte, Melkólmr for Mael Coluim, Melmari for Mael Muire and Myrkjartan for Muirchertach.

This account raises a number of questions regarding both the date of the expedition and the identity of Mael Coluim's companions. Cnut is known to have been in Rome on 26 March 1027 for the imperial coronation of Conrad II of Germany, so our immediate question is, did he return for a second visit or has this annalistic notice been misplaced?[30] It seems that Cnut spent very little time in England between his trip to Rome in 1027 and 1031. He was very much preoccupied by concerns in Scandinavia, particularly conflict with his nephew Önundr, now king of the Svear,[31] and Óláfr Haraldsson, who had seized the opportunity presented by Sveinn Fork-beard's death to take control of Norway in about 1016. In 1028 Cnut drove Óláfr out of Norway and set up Hákon, the son of Earl Eiríkr of Hlaðir, in his place. In 1030, following Eirík's death by drowning in the Pentland Firth, Óláfr, with some backing from Önundr, who was his brother-in-law, entered Trondheim by the overland route from Jämtland but was cut down not far inside the border by local farmers and chieftains who felt that he would bring unnecessary trouble. With Óláfr dead, and the Norwegians apparently reconciled to Danish rule, Cnut could turn his attention back to Britain.

The precise identity of the three kings whom Cnut met is relatively well established. They were almost certainly Mael Coluim son of Cinaed, Macbethad son of Findláech and Echmarcach son of Ragnall. Less certain is the identity of the *regna* that they ruled at this point. Echmarcach was to rule Dublin between 1036 and 1038 and again between 1046 and 1052. In 1061 Echmarcach seems to have been ruling the Isle of Man and at his death in 1065, on his own pilgrimage to Rome, he is described as 'king of the Rhinns', probably of Galloway. Rather than seeing Echmarcach's career as that of a jobbing king who ruled several different kingdoms in the course of his life we should note that there is fairly strong evidence to suggest that Dublin, Man and the Rhinns of Galloway (which in medieval terminology seems to have included the Machars as well as the Rhinns proper, that is, the whole of Wigtownshire) were part of the same kingdom in the early eleventh century. What we are in fact seeing in Echmarcach's career is the gradual conquest of that kingdom by the Leinster king Diarmait mac Maíl na mBó, so that by the time of his death Echmarcach was left with only Wigtownshire.

[30] The fullest discussion of these problems is B. T. Hudson, 'Cnut and the Scottish kings', *English Historical Review* 107 (1992), 350–60.
[31] Önundr had succeeded his father Óláfr in about 1022 and reigned until about 1049. He started minting his own coins from 1026 and this may mark his break with Cnut.

A problem remains, however, in as much as Echmarcach first appears as ruler of this kingdom in 1036. Before this time Sihtric son of Amlaíb Cúarán seems to have ruled this territory (sharing the kingship with his own son Amlaíb for some of the time). If the Iehmarc who met Cnut was Echmarcach, where was he of king at the time? Scholars have disagreed about the identity of Echmarcach's father, Ragnall. Some have argued that he was one of two Ragnalls (father and son) who ruled the Hiberno–Norse *longphort* of Waterford, and who died in 1015 (or 1018) and 1035, respectively. The fact, however, that Echmarcach was already a king somewhere in the north before 1035 (which is also the date of Cnut's death, and thus the latest possible date for the meeting), makes Hudson's suggestion that Echmarcach's father was in fact the Ragnall son of Gofraid, king of Innse Gall, whose death is recorded in the *Annals of Ulster* under the year 1005, far more likely.[32] This Ragnall was the son, and apparent successor of that Gofraid, king of Innse Gall, whose death in 989 we touched upon at the end of the previous chapter. If this Ragnall were Echmarcach's father it seems unlikely that he succeeded directly to the kingship of Innse Gall (the Hebrides), but he may well have done so by the early 1030s. If this interpretation is correct then Echmarcach may have inherited the kingdom of Innse Gall and subsequently, in 1036, embarked upon a conquest of the Irish Sea kingdom that comprised Dublin, Man and parts of Galloway (and perhaps the west of what is now Cumbria). This move on his part may be seen as an attempt to exploit the confusion in England following the death of Cnut in 1035. A Norwegian text from the 1190s claims that between about 1016 and 1030 the Hebrides (*Suðreyjar*) were ruled by Hákon Eiríksson, the son of the Earl Eiríkr whom Cnut had made ruler of Northumbria.[33] Earl Hákon is known to have held an earldom that included, *inter alia*, Worcester under Cnut, and he was briefly installed as ruler of Norway in 1028 before drowning in 1030. If there is any truth to the story of his rule in the Hebrides, which seems unlikely, his death may have initiated Echmarcach's career.

Mælbæðe was almost certainly Macbethad son of Findláech, the Moravian 'anti-king' who was slain in 1020. There have been slight anxieties concerning his presence at this meeting since his cousin, Gilla Comgáin, died with the title of mormaer of Moray in 1032. If, however,

[32] In addition to Hudson's 'Cnut and the Scottish kings', the most important discussions of these matters are S. Duffy, 'Irishmen and Islesmen in the Kingdoms of Dublin and Man, 1052–1171', *Ériu* 43 (1992), 93–133, and C. Etchingham, 'North Wales, Ireland and the Isles: the Insular Viking zone', *Peritia* 15 (2001), 145–87.

[33] *Ágrip af Nóregskonungasögum: a Twelfth-century Synoptic History of the Kings of Norway*, ed. & tr. M. J. Driscoll (London, 1995), 36–7.

the intended date of the chronicle entry is indeed 1031 then this may be
a very minor problem. Cnut may have returned to England in 1031 but
not reached Scotland until some point in 1032 or, alternatively Gilla
Comgáin may actually have been slain in 1031 but news of the killing did
not reach the Irish chronicler until 1032. Minor discrepancies of a few
months are frequent in the chronicle record. More interesting is the
manner of Gilla Comgáin's death:

> *AU* 1032 Gilla Comgáin son of Mael Brigte, mormaer of Moréb,
> was burned together with fifty people.

This is the second house burning that we have encountered; back in
971 Cuilén and his brother Eochaid had been burned in a house by the
Strathclyde Britons. Since Findláech, Macbethad's father, had been slain
by the sons of Mael Brigte (presumably Gilla Comgáin and his brother
Mael Coluim), it seems likely that Macbethad had a hand in the burning
of Gilla Comgáin. After the death of Findláech in 1020, Mael Coluim son
of Mael Brigte seems to have ruled in the north without interruption for
nine years. His own death, in 1029, does not appear to have been violent.
Gilla Comgáin may have been a less effective ruler than his brother and
thus have been more vulnerable; or, alternatively, Macbethad may simply
have only grown to manhood in his time. It is very likely that Macbethad's
survival bears witness to the fact that he had spent the years since his
father's killing in exile. There are no specific hints as to where this might
have been but either Mael Coluim son of Cinaed's court, south of the
Mounth, or the kingdom of Innse Gall are possibilities. Meanwhile Gilla
Comgáin sought to create a dynastic link with the southern dynasty,
begetting a son, Lulach, who would share descent from both lines.
Lulach's mother was Gruoch, daughter of Boete son of Cinaed.
Unfortunately, we cannot be sure whether the Cinaed referred to here
was Mael Coluim's own father (†995), making Gruoch his niece, or the
daughter of his cousin Cinaed son of Dub, whom he had slain in 1005.
On balance the latter seems the more likely scenario. It is possible that this
marriage frightened Mael Coluim enough to risk backing regime change
in Moray.[34] If this was his plan then it backfired, for Macbethad himself
married the widowed Gruoch.

If regime change in Moray did precede Cnut's expedition then we can,
perhaps, assume that it was this instability that prompted him to move

---

[34] The Irish chronicles note, with no further detail, that Mael Coluim slew a grandson
of Boete (but not Lulach) in 1033.

north and enforce peace. Scottish politics in this period was a bit like a game of musical chairs. Every time Cnut appeared on the scene everybody had to stop moving. It has often been noted that the missing fourth king in this narrative was the king of Strathclyde. We last encountered one of these in 1018 when Owain the Bald led the Cumbrians in alliance with Mael Coluim at Carham. Where were they now? If Echmarcach was already king of the Rhinns then the absence of a Cumbrian king would be very strange indeed and might incline us to believe that the kingdom had already been extinguished. We have seen, however, that Echmarcach's realm at this point was probably confined to the islands beyond Kintyre. We are also told by the Chronicle that Cnut went to Scotland, which at this period must have meant the lands north of the Forth. This being the case it seems likely that Cnut's focus was on trouble in Moray and that Echmarcach and Mael Coluim, having kingdoms that bordered Macbethad's, were being bound over to keep the peace.

THE END OF AN ERA

On 25 November 1034 Mael Coluim died, supposedly at Glamis in Strathmore, and the following year Cnut died, on 12 November at Shaftesbury in Dorset. Cnut was not yet forty years old. It is sobering to consider how different British history might have been had he lived to be as old as the Irish kings Brian and Maelsechnaill (both of whom died aged seventy-three). He might still have been king of England and Denmark in 1070. Mael Coluim, on the other hand, was an old man. He had outlived his father by nearly forty years and was succeeded by an adult grandson. We are able to give a precise date to Mael Coluim's death thanks to a Continental chronicler of Irish birth, known to posterity as Marianus *Scotus*. Marianus was really named Mael Brigte and had been born in 1028. His chronicle covered the period from his birth to shortly before his death in 1083, after which it was continued by others. He became a recluse at Fulda in Germany in May 1059 and since the opening portion of the chronicle refers to the fact that he was a recluse it must have been written after this date. It is probable, however, that Marianus/Mael Brigte had written sources before him. It is noteworthy that he refers to Mael Coluim as *rex Scotiae*: this is one of the earliest examples of the use of the term *Scotia* for the kingdom of Alba.[35]

---

[35] The earliest example appears to be in the Life of St Cathróe, from c. 980. This text was also written on the Continent.

THE PROBLEM OF CRÍNÁN

Although Ralph Glaber, the Burgundian chronicler, told us that Cnut had become godfather to Mael Coluim's son he was either mistaken, or, more likely, this boy predeceased his father.[36] In any event Mael Coluim was succeeded by the son of his daughter Bethoc who had married a certain Crínán. There are a number of questions hanging over Crínán's identity. His obituary, under the year 1045, and later king-lists describe him as the abbot of Dunkeld, but he need not have held this office at the time of his marriage. Many churchmen seem to have embraced celibacy only when they entered major orders aged thirty or more. As the senior Columban house in Scotland, Dunkeld may have continued to draw its hierarchy from the Cenél Conaill dynasty of Donegal, from which Columba himself hailed, as Iona had done in the past. If this were the case then Crínán would have been an Irish prince and of appropriate high status to marry the daughter of a king of Alba, but it is possible that a discrete ecclesiastical dynasty had grown up in association with Dunkeld by this time, which, whatever its ultimate origin, was now regarded simply as belonging to that place.

Somewhat more controversial is the possibility that this Crínán was identical with a man of this name who is mentioned in the latter part of *Historia Regum Anglorum* and in the tract we encountered earlier which is known as *De Obsessione Dunelmi*. In these Durham texts we are told that Earl Uhtred of Northumbria gave his daughter Ealdgyth, whom he had begotten upon Ælfgifu the daughter of King Æðelræd, in marriage to a certain Maldred son of Crínán *tein*,[37] to whom she bore a son, Gospatric, who was later, in the 1060s and 1070s, earl of Northumbria under William the Conqueror. Most, though by no means all, historians have tended to accept that Maldred's father was probably the same Crínán who married Mael Coluim's daughter. All we really have to go on, however, are the names and the approximate synchronism. 'Crínán' is certainly a Gaelic name, though not a very common one. 'Maldred' is a name which seems to be localised in northern Northumbria and is only attested in the eleventh and twelfth centuries. Crínán's son appears to be the earliest attested Maldred and the later examples may, for the most part, be from families connected to that of Earl Gospatric. Superficially Maldred looks like an Anglo-Saxon name sharing the

---

[36] Infant mortality would have been relatively high, even among royal kindreds.

[37] The word *tein* is thought to represent the English title 'thegn', meaning a noble retainer of a great lord, usually the king.

same second element, *ræd*,[38] as Uhtred or Æðelræd.[39] If this were the case, however, it is hard to see what the first element is. It is also problematic that, although thousands of Anglo-Saxon names are on record, our man is the only Maldred to predate the Norman Conquest of England. Another possible alternative is that it represents a Gaelic name beginning with the element *Mael*, as in Mael Coluim or Mael Brigte. If this were the case then the best guess would be that it represented an English garbling of the name 'Mael Doraid'. For 'Maldred' to represent Mael Doraid, however, the second 'd' would have to possess the value /ð/. This is not impossible as Anglo-Norman scribes, and even some Anglo-Saxon scribes writing in Latin, regularly used 'd' to represent /ð/. If 'Maldred' does represent a garbled English rendition of 'Mael Doraid', and it remains merely a hypothesis, then it would be of great significance, since this name is particularly closely associated with the Cenél Conaill dynasty, one of whose segments were known as Uí Maíl Doraid. As we have seen, there is a possibility that the abbots of Dunkeld were linked with Cenél Conaill. Caution must be urged, however, and western Northumbria had plenty of noblemen with Gaelic names in the eleventh century, relics of Hiberno-Norse rule.[40] If the two Crínáns were one and the same then it is likely that Maldred's mother was someone other than Bethoc daughter of Mael Coluim, for there is no suggestion that Maldred's descendants, who became powerful men in twelfth-century Scotland, had any claim to the kingship.

According to *De Obsessione* Uhtred was still alive when Maldred married his daughter Ealdgyth: this puts the date no later than 1019 at the very latest. There is a slight problem with this dating in that the same tract tells us that Uhtred's marriage to Ealdgyth's mother, Ælfgifu daughter of King Æðelred, took place after his victory over Mael Coluim, which has been dated to 1006. It is thus extremely unlikely that a daughter of this marriage would have reached marriageable age by the time Uhtred died. It may be, however, that the tract is wrong in presuming Ealdgyth's father, rather than an uncle or brother, gave her in marriage. Ealdgyth and Maldred's son Gospatric could still be

---

[38] 'Counsel', as in Scots *rede* or German *Rat*. This word is also the stem of English 'ready', meaning prepared or well counselled.

[39] G. W. S. Barrow, 'Some problems in twelfth- and thirteenth-century Scottish history: a genealogical approach', *Scottish Genealogist* 25 (1978), 97–112.

[40] Examples include Gilla Michel and Glúniairn. Ongoing research by Fiona Edmonds of Cambridge University is elucidating the Gaelic element in northwest England into the eleventh century.

described as an *adolescens*, although he was clearly a grown man, in 1061 when he was kidnapped by bandits in Italy who mistook him for Earl Tostig of Northumbria.[41] We should probably imagine that he was in his twenties or early thirties at that time, putting his birth in the late 1020s or 1030s, a more realistic range for the son of a woman born in 1007 or later.

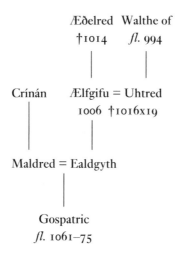

Table 6.5 The descent of Gospatric son of Maldred

A further complication arises with the evidence for a Crínán living in England in the first part of Cnut's reign. Anglo-Saxon pennies as well as bearing the king's name on the obverse, carry a moneyer's name on the reverse. The moneyer was not the man who actually struck the coin but the one who had responsibility for guaranteeing the security of the dies and the quality of the silver. It has long been noted that a disproportionate number of moneyers had foreign names, although most seem to have been burgesses and some were thegns.[42] Oddly, a number have Gaelic names. These may be people from a Hiberno-Norse background but equally they may have been transitory exiles whom the king wished to

[41] *The Life of King Edward who Rests at Westminster*, ed. & tr. F. Barlow (London, 1962), 35–6 and 50. The core meaning of *adolescens* seems to have been 'legally competent but unmarried man'. In early medieval terms this age grade is most likely to have centred on the period between the mid-teens and mid-twenties, but since Gospatric was mistaken for the earl he is likely to have been at the upper end of this range, or a little older, in 1061.

[42] A burgess was a member of an urban corporation, a property holder in a town, and a thegn was a member of the newly emerging gentry class.

provide with an income (gained by taking a percentage of the coin they processed) without granting them lands. Among the moneyers responsible for producing some of Cnut's early coins, belonging to a type current between 1017 and 1023, was one Crínán, who minted coins at Chester, Shrewsbury, Lincoln and York.[43] He would seem a very likely candidate for the father of Maldred, but could he have been the same man who went on to become abbot of Dunkeld? Presuming that individuals with the same name are the same is a dangerous temptation to which historians all too often fall prey; in this case, however, it is strange that the name Crínán, which occurs only in this generation in Britain (and is rare in Ireland) should simultaneously belong to three unrelated individuals. It might also be noted that Crínán the moneyer's *floruit* coincides with the period of warfare between Cnut and Mael Coluim, that is, between Carham and the treaty brokered by Richard of Normandy. Might Crínán have been an exile who returned home after the peace? This is really the stuff of historical novels, but this case study serves to show how complex the evidence for this period really is. When most of our evidence is so fragmentary and laconic it is very easy to combine individuals or erroneously split them into two or three characters. Gospatric son of Maldred was eventually to fall out with William the Conqueror and flee to Scotland where he became the ancestor of the earls of Dunbar. It surely makes a difference if we imagine him to have been a close kinsmen of the royal family (a first cousin of the king at the time) or just another Anglo-Saxon refugee?

DONNCHAD SON OF CRÍNÁN

Mael Coluim son of Cinaed was succeeded as king of Alba by his uterine grandson Donnchad son of Crínán. This man is the king known by the anglicised form of his name as Duncan I; the king who would be slain by Macbethad. It is unlikely, however, that he was an old man as he is portrayed in Shakespeare's play. He was to reign for only five and a half years (1034–40), and since he had succeeded his grandfather he could not have been much more than forty at the outside and was probably a great deal younger in 1034. We know very little of the details of Donnchad's reign, although there are hints of stirrings in the southwest.

---

[43] V. Smart, 'Scandinavians, Celts and Germans in Anglo-Saxon England: the evidence of moneyers' names', in M. A. S. Blackburn, ed., *Anglo-Saxon Monetary History* (Leicester, 1986) 171–85, at 182–3.

Both the *Annals of Ulster* and the *Annals of Tigernach* record, under the year 1034:

> Suibne son of Cinaed, king of Gallgáedil, died.

Gallgáedil is the original Gaelic from which the modern name 'Galloway' derives, although strictly speaking it is a population group name rather than a place-name. It first appears in the Irish chronicles on several occasions in the later 850s and then not again until the notice of Suibne's death in 1034.[44] In the ninth-century accounts the Gallgáedil are clearly a military force operating inside Ireland. By the twelfth century it is clear that the term was used for the dominant group in southwest Scotland and that 'Galloway', at its greatest extent, stretched from the Solway to the Clyde. Although the Lordship of Galloway that emerged in the course of the twelfth century was much more circumscribed and confined more or less to Wigtownshire and Kirkcudbrightshire, ethnic Gaillgáedil still dominated Ayrshire and Dumfriesshire and perhaps some further adjacent areas.[45] This said, our entry for 1034 predates the evidence for 'Galloway' by a century and is separated from the ninth-century Irish entries by nearly two. Where was Suibne's kingdom? Why does he appear in an isolated notice of this sort? One possibility that has tempted historians is that he may have been a brother of Mael Coluim son of Cinaed and that a Gallgáedil 'sub-kingdom' was created for him but did not outlive him. We saw at the beginning of this chapter that one poetic source, the *Prophecy of Berchan*, referred to Mael Coluim as *loingsech* of Islay and Arran, where *loingsech*, literally 'skipper', might imply either 'exile' or 'voyager'. Might Mael Coluim have imposed his authority in the lands around Kintyre and the Outer Clyde and placed a brother as king over the region? This is possible, but once again the only evidence really is the similarity of the names. Against the fact that the two kings were both sons of men called Cinaed it should be noted that Suibne (anglicised as Sweeny), while Gaelic, is not a name otherwise associated with the Alpínids, though it did survive as the name of the progenitor of the Knapdale family of MacSween (as in Castle Sween), but he is thought

---

[44] *AU* 856.3, 856.6 and 857.1, *FA* 856 and 858.

[45] *Gallgáedil* means 'Gaelic-speaking Gaill' and, although the precise interpretation of this is much disputed, the term was probably applied to people who though thoroughly Gaelic in speech, and perhaps descent, behaved more like the Scandinavians, depending to a high degree on a raid-based economy and the use of naval and martial technology derived from Scandinavian practice.

to have lived c. 1200.[46] There is also a Suibhne in the pedigree of Somerled of Argyll (†1164), who, if the pedigree is reliable, might have lived in the mid-eleventh century, but none of the versions of the pedigree give his father's name as anything resembling Cinaed.[47] We should also recall that in this period the Rhinns (roughly corresponding to Wigtownshire) were part of the kingdom ruled by Sihtric son of Amlaíb Cúarán, which also included Dublin and Man, so we must be wary of projecting twelfth-century Galloway back into Suibne's time.

The mystery of Suibne son of Cinaed has also been linked to another problem of the eleventh-century southwest: the disappearance of Strathclyde. Because of the ubiquity of the Gallgáedil in the southwest of Scotland in the twelfth century, and the corresponding absence of the Britons, it has been hypothesised that the Gaillgáedil may have conquered Strathclyde at some point.[48] The *Annals of Tigernach* record a ravaging of the Britons by the Gaill of Dublin and the English under the year 1030, and although this might refer to activities in Wales there is no corresponding account in the, admittedly spare, *Annales Cambriae*, which leaves open the possibility that it was the Cumbrians who had come under attack. The *Anglo-Saxon Chronicle* carries no notice of this conflict, which would lend support to the possibility that the English participants were not royal forces but part of a private venture by a semi-independent ruler such as the Earl of northern Northumbria. This said, it is clear from *Historia Regum Anglorum* that Earl Eadwulf of Northumbria was able to ravage the Britons in 1038 so at least part of their territory is likely to have remained independent at that date.[49] Not knowing where precisely the boundaries of Cumbria lay at this point makes it difficult to interpret such notices. Was Eadwulf simply ravaging the Carlisle area, had he crossed the Solway into Dumfriesshire, or had he gone up Tweeddale and into the heart of Strathclyde?

In 1040, or possibly late 1039, Donnchad son of Crínán invaded Northumbria with a great army and besieged Durham.[50] The defenders,

---

[46] W. D. H. Sellar, 'Family origins in Cowal and Knapdale', *Scottish Studies* 15 (1971), 21–31 at 21.

[47] W. D. H. Sellar, 'The origins and ancestry of Somerled', *Scottish Historical Review* 45 (1966), 123–42.

[48] D. Broun, 'The Welsh identity of the kingdom of Strathclyde, c. 900–1200', *Innes Review* 55 (2004), 111–80 at 136–40.

[49] It is, however, possible that the Gallgáedil were perceived as ruling the Cumbrians and that the English terminology is a little anachronistic.

[50] Symeon of Durham, *Libellus De Exordio*, III.ix. It is widely believed that *De Obsessione*'s account of Mael Coluim's invasion of 1006 was influenced by the events of this war.

however, repulsed the attack and when the Scots went into retreat, followed up with devastating effect. Donnchad, Symeon tells us, fled in confusion. Whether Donnchad had been in some sense trying to avenge the ravaging of Cumbria by Eadwulf or whether he was simply taking advantage of the fact that Cnut's sons were more interested in squabbling amongst themselves than defending their borders is unclear. Symeon reports the sequel laconically:

> Not long afterwards, the king himself, when he had returned to Scotia, was killed by his own men.

Marianus Scotus fills in the detail:

> Donnchad, king of Scotia, was killed in the autumn, on 14 August, by his *dux* Macbethad son of Findláech; who succeeded to the kingdom for seventeen years.

Donnchad's defeat in Northumbria had destroyed confidence in him and finally the division of the kingdom was brought to an end.

MACBETHAD SON OF FINDLÁECH

Marianus refers to Macbethad as Donnchad's *dux*. This word, the source of modern English 'duke', might, at this period, mean either a regional ruler, like a mormaer or an earl, or simply an army commander. The two definitions were probably not so different in meaning in the eleventh century. The main function of an office like that of the mormaer was to lead the army of his province under the king. Germany at this time was divided into 'tribal duchies', such as Saxony, Bavaria and Swabia, which for the most part had evolved from Iron Age ethnic units, yet the title of the local rulers which we translate as duke, is in German, *Herzog*, from the earlier *here*, 'army', plus *tog*, 'something that pulls or leads' (*cf.* English 'tug' and modern German *Zug*).[51] What it tells us about the relationship between Donnchad and Macbethad is that, as far as Marianus was concerned, Macbethad recognised Donnchad's superiority in some sense.

---

[51] Herzogovina, Bosnia's twin province, is named from this German word plus a Slavonic word meaning 'land', and is thus 'The Generalship' or 'The Duchy'. In neighbouring Serbia the name of the northern province of Voivodina is formed in the same way from *voivoda*, Slavonic for 'general'.

This would seem to match up with the *Annals of Ulster*'s claim that Donnchad was killed 'by his own'.

According to the twelfth- and thirteenth-century century king-lists Donnchad was killed at a place called 'Bothgouanan' (with minor spelling variations), which has traditionally been identified with Pitgaveny near Elgin (Morayshire), though places as far apart as Balnagowan (Rossshire) and Govan (Lanarkshire) share second elements of similar appearance. If the Pitgaveny identification is correct then it puts Donnchad's death in the heart of Moray and perhaps bolsters the presumption that Macbethad had some jurisdiction there at the time. Whether Donnchad was attempting to restore his prestige following the Durham debacle by an attack on someone he regarded as a rebel or an over-mighty subject, or whether Macbethad had hitherto been loyal to Donnchad but had been urged to seize power following the king's defeat is unknowable. The royal status accorded *Mælbæþe* by the *Anglo-Saxon Chronicle*, under the year 1031, should encourage us to believe that Macbethad had aspirations to kingship already, and the fact that Marianus, though very nearly a contemporary writer, in fact composed his chronicle in or after 1059, after Macbethad's death, might incline us to be cautious in accepting his views on the relative status of the two men.

Donnchad's own claim to the kingship was explicitly through his mother Bethoc, Mael Coluim's daughter. This was an extremely unusual situation in the early medieval period. As we have seen the Moravian claim to the kingship of Alba may have been dependent upon such a relationship, but if so it is nowhere stated and the weakness of such a link to royalty may have been one reason why Mael Coluim son of Cinaed was able to weather successive challenges from that direction. In Ireland claims of this sort never seem to have been made and even Congalach of Knowth, who in 944 became king of Tara in succession to two maternal uncles and his maternal grandfather, claimed legitimacy through his descent in the male line from the seventh-century king Áed of Slane.

It has been suggested that Donnchad's succession reflected a return to the ancient custom of Pictish matriliny. The evidence for the practice of matriliny among the Picts is, however, not so good as has sometimes been supposed and, in any case, there had been no hint of it in the succession to the kingship of Alba hitherto.[52] It is more likely that two factors influenced the choice of Donnchad as king. First, direct patrilineal descendants of

[52]   See A. Woolf, 'Pictish matriliny reconsidered', *Innes Review* 49 (1998), 147–67, and A., Ross, 'Pictish Matriliny?', *Northern Studies* 34 (1999), 11–22.

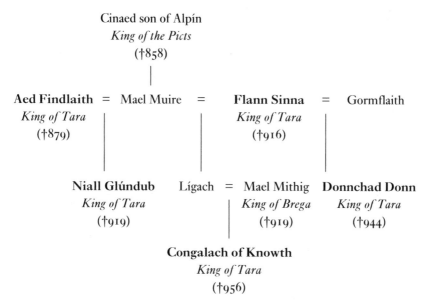

Table 6.6 Congalach of Knowth and the kingship of Tara

Cinaed son of Alpín, who by this date was certainly the apical figure of the royal dynasty, may have been in short supply. The internecine strife of the later tenth century had taken its toll on the dynasty. It has been suggested that Clann Duib, the MacDuffs, who held Fife from at least the twelfth century, may have been descended from Dub son of Mael Coluim who died in 966, but if this were the case we might have expected the family to make more of it.[53] If there was no direct male line descendant of Cinaed available, who should have been regarded as the legitimate heir to the kingship? The success of the dynasty in creating, retrospectively, as we have seen, a new beginning with Cinaed meant that, unlike most Irish ruling kindreds, they could not go further back into the past to locate an earlier apical figure. Had they chosen to do so they might have turned to Aedán son of Gabrán, the sixth-century king of Dál Riata from whom, according to the schema discussed at the beginning of this chapter, the men of Gowrie and Fife were descended. The insistence that Alba was a new kingdom, a continuation of neither Dál Riata nor Pictavia, the essential message of the *Chronicle of the Kings of Alba*, created problems in itself.

---

[53] J. Bannerman, 'MacDuff of Fife', in A. Grant and K. Stringer, eds, *Medieval Scotland: Crown, Lordship and Community* (Edinburgh, 1993), 20–38. Just possibly the only surviving Clann Duib dynast may have been a minor in 1034.

The second factor that may have legitimised Donnchad's succession was the powerful influence of Latin Christendom's leading kingdom, Germany. In 1027 Cnut had attended the imperial coronation of Conrad II at Rome. Three years earlier, in 1024, Conrad had been elected king of Germany. The German kingdom had emerged out of the fragments of the Carolingian empire at about the same time as the kingdom of Alba had appeared. The great dynastic founder (in actual fact the second king) was Henry, previously duke of Saxony, known as Henry the Fowler (919–36). The kingship then passed down from father to son until 1002, via Otto I (936–73), Otto II (973–83) and Otto III (983–1002). Otto III died young and without issue and the kingship stayed within the dynasty but passed to a direct male descendant of Henry the Fowler's younger son, Henry duke of Bavaria. This heir, also Henry duke of Bavaria, became Henry II (1002–24). When he too died without issue there were a number of claimants but, following an assembly at Kamba on the Rhine in early September 1024, Conrad II was elected. Conrad was well connected across much of the kingdom but his dynastic claim was relatively slight; he was the grandson of Otto I's daughter Liutgard. Following the election at Kamba, Henry II's widow, Kunigunde, presented Conrad with the regalia of kingship and by the end of September he had been crowned at Aachen. At Christmas Conrad was in Saxony, at Minden, where he swore to uphold Saxon law and the rights of the Saxons and was, in return, recognised as king by the Saxon nobility. The success of Conrad's kingship, combined with the prestige of the German kingdom, now at its height, opened the doors for uterine succession elsewhere in the Latin West.[54]

An interesting comparative scenario occurred in Denmark in 1042. In that year the last of Cnut's sons died without issue and the Danish royal dynasty came to an end. Two options seem to have presented themselves to the Danes. One was Magnus Óláfsson, king of Norway, who, so far as we know, had no claim to Danish royal blood but was the son of a king and of undoubted royal descent.[55] The other was Sveinn Estriðsson, the son of Cnut's sister. After a brief civil war the Danes opted for Magnus and it was only on his death, once again without issue, that Sveinn, who had been living in exile among the Svear, was deemed acceptable as king. The idea that a claim to the kingship could be transmitted through the female line took a long time to take hold. Civil war broke out in England

[54] For German succession in this period see T. Reuter, *Germany in the Early Middle Ages, 800–1056* (Harlow, 1991), 183–90.
[55] It may have helped that Magnus' father was already being culted as a saint.

over the issue in the 1130s and in the 1150s the same issue led to civil wars in Norway and the Kingdom of the Isles. Donnchad son of Crínán was ahead of his time and perhaps he paid the price for it.

We know nothing of Macbethad's early years but in 1045 the *Annals of Ulster* tell us of:

> *AU* 1045.6 A battle between the Scots themselves in which fell Crínán, abbot of Dunkeld.

Whether Crínán had rebelled, perhaps in favour of one of his grandsons, or whether Macbethad initiated 'anticipatory retaliation' against him is unclear. One of Symeon of Durham's earliest works, known by the title the *Annals of Lindisfarne and Durham*, but in fact a text composed in the twelfth century rather than a true annalistic chronicle, places an invasion of Scotland by Siward (earl of all Northumbria since 1041) in 1046, but this account is so similar to more authoritative accounts of the events of 1054 (treated below) that it is probably misplaced here. By 1050 Macbethad seems to have been secure enough to leave the kingdom, for under that year Marianus Scotus records that:

> Macbethad, king of Scotia, scattered money like seed to the poor at Rome.

It could be argued that Macbethad may not have gone in person to do this, but bearing in mind the fashion at this time for rulers to go to Rome it seems likely that he did. Cnut had gone in 1027, Sihtric son of Amlaíb in 1028, Flaithbertach of Ailech (in the north of Ireland) in 1030: the list goes on. If Macbethad was aiming to spend Easter of 1050 in Rome it is likely that he set off the previous year and he may well have attended one of the great reforming councils which the new pope, Leo IX (1049–54), held north of the Alps that year.[56] The first was held in the ecclesiastical capital of the Western Kingdom at Rheims and although the French king, Henry I, and many of his bishops attempted to boycott the proceedings (the idea that the pope ruled the Church was not widely approved of at this time), the council, combined with a ceremony translating the relics of the city's patron saint, Remigius, was a great success. The event was attended by 'Spaniards, Britons, Franks, *Scotti*, and English'. On his way back to Rome, this time in collaboration with his cousin the German king, Henry III, Leo (his given name was Bruno)

---

[56] I owe this suggestion to Dr Kenneth Veitch.

held a reprise performance at Mainz, the primatial see of *Regnum Teutonicorum*. Macbethad might have attended either of these councils, though that at Mainz is perhaps more likely being held later in the year and on the main route travelled by Gaels and Scandinavians on their way to Italy (Braen, king of Leinster, was to die in Cologne, en route to Rome, in 1052). It may well have been at these great councils that Leo first promulgated the 'Collection in Seventy-Four Titles', the first Roman canon law collection, which began the campaign to enforce clerical celibacy and the freedom of ecclesiastical elections from secular interference. Leo IX and his *curia* were the real architects of the Roman Church as we have traditionally viewed it, and over the next century and a half the aspirations of the 'Seventy-Four Titles' would gradually be achieved throughout western Europe. It is perhaps fanciful, yet intriguing, to imagine that if Macbethad did indeed attend the Council of Mainz he might well have been in the company of the parents of St Margaret (whose mother was related to King Henry), and perhaps even have dangled the infant herself upon his knee.

HOME TO CONFLICT

It is generally assumed that Macbethad must have felt fairly secure at home to be able to go on pilgrimage to Rome. It is just possible that the act of pilgrimage was held in such high esteem that his enemies would have respected a truce while he was away, but this seems unlikely. Probably he had a trusted lieutenant whom he had been able to leave in his place. Often kings left their heirs in charge when they absented themselves from their kingdoms, so Macbethad may have left a son, or perhaps his step-son Lulach, in charge, but somebody without a claim to the kingship might have seemed less of a risk.

Back in Britain the political scene was changing quite radically. The final demise of the Knýtling dynasty in 1042 had cleared the way for Cnut's step-son Edward to assume the throne of his half-brother Harðacnut. The latter, who had clearly sensed his own imminent demise, had invited Edward home from Normandy and associated him in the kingship of the English with him. Immediately upon being consecrated full-king in 1043, Edward seized all the lands and treasures of his mother, Emma. Emma had remained in England in 1016, married Cnut and promoted the interests of her son by Cnut, Harðacnut, over those of her sons by Æðelræd, while the latter, Ælfred and Edward, had fled overseas to Normandy and grown up in exile for nearly a quarter of a century. She was even implicated by some in Ælfred's killing in 1036.[57] From this example we should note that Lulach may not have been on good terms with Macbethad just because his mother, Gruoch, had married him. He may even have been in exile for most of Macbethad's reign.

King Edward had brought many Normans with him when he returned from exile and granted some of them estates and offices in the kingdom. In 1051 he had a falling out with his chief English supporter, his father-in-law, Earl Godwine of Wessex.[58] When reconciliation occurred in 1052 most of Edward's Norman friends were encouraged to leave the kingdom. While the great majority went back to Normandy one group, led by Osbern Pentecost, who had held castles for the king on the Welsh border in Herefordshire, went north and took service with Macbethad.[59] That Osbern and his friend, Hugh, should have chosen to go to Macbethad probably indicates some personal connection and perhaps hints that the Scots king had passed through England on his way to or from Rome.

Osbern and Hugh's move to Scotland was not to be a happy one. In 1054 Earl Siward of Northumbria invaded Scotland on King Edward's orders and, although he sustained heavy casualties, including his own son, another Osbern, and his nephew Siward, he succeeded in routing Macbethad, killing many Scots and all the Normans. The battle took place on 27 July and is recorded in both the *Anglo-Saxon Chronicle* and the Irish chronicles. Curiously, the only casualty noted by the *Annals of Ulster* was one of the English, Dolfinn son of Finntor, unknown from English sources but presumably a leader of the Hiberno-Norse community of western Northumbria in whom the Irish maintained an interest.

The fullest account of Siward's campaign is that in John of Worcester's chronicle from the early twelfth century, which used as its source a version of the 'northern recension' of the *Anglo-Saxon Chronicle*. John tells us that Siward expelled Macbethad and set up in his place 'Mael Coluim, son of the king of the Cumbrians'.[60] William of Malmesbury,

[57] A book, penned on Emma's behalf and intended to exculpate her of these charges, actually survives and is available in a good modern edition: *Encomium Emmae Reginae*, ed. A. Campbell with a supplementary introduction by S. Keynes (Cambridge, 1998). See also P. Stafford, *Queen Emma and Queen Edith: Queenship and Women's Power in Eleventh-Century England* (Oxford, 2001).

[58] Godwine had been created earl of Wessex, previously the preserve of the English kings, by Cnut, probably in 1022 or 1023. While Cnut, with his empire, could sustain the loss of exclusive rights in Wessex, Godwine's control of their heartland put the subsequent kings of England alone in an impossible position.

[59] *The Chronicle of John of Worcester*, vol. II, eds R. R. Darlington and P. McGurk, tr. J. Bray and P. McGurk (Oxford, 1995), 572–3.

[60] *John of Worcester*, 574–5.

writing not long after John, assumed that this Mael Coluim was Donnchad's son, Mael Coluim III, to whose son, David I, William dedicated his history.[61] William's identification of 'Mael Coluim, son of the king of the Cumbrians', with Mael Coluim III has been followed by most subsequent historians. This has led to the attribution of the end of Macbethad's reign to Siward's invasion, as in Shakespeare's play, even though it is clear that he continued to reign until at least August 1057. It has also led to the view that Donnchad must, at some stage, have been king of the Cumbrians, and has thus encouraged historians to date the end of the Cumbrian kingdom to the time of Mael Coluim son of Cinaed. It seems absurd, however, that a son of Donnchad being placed on Macbethad's throne should be alluded to as a 'son of the king of the Cumbrians' when Donnchad was undoubtedly king of Alba. Recently William's presumption and the inferences built upon them by subsequent generations of historians have been seriously questioned.[62]

We should probably recall at this point Symeon of Durham's first attempt at writing history: the *Annals of Lindisfarne and Durham*, in which he placed an invasion of Northumbria by Siward under the year 1046. The result he claims was that:

He expelled King Macbethad and placed another in his place; but after his departure Macbethad recovered the kingdom.

This looks very much as if it is a misplaced account of the events of 1054. Evidently Macbethad was still king in 1057 and so the 1054 regime change must have been short-lived. So who was Edward and Siward's protégé? Were we not influenced by William's reading and the subsequent elaboration of it we should probably infer two things. One, that the king of the Cumbrians alluded to was still alive and reigning, and two, that Mael Coluim, his son, had some claim to Albanian royal blood, probably, like Donnchad, through his mother. The most likely scenario is that Mael Coluim's mother was another daughter of Mael Coluim II. Possibly his father was that Owain the Bald who had fought at Carham in 1018, or his immediate successor. Another question this episode raises, however, is why Edward and Siward would want to affect regime change in Scotland? It may be that local issues regarding northern Northumbria or

[61]   R. A. B. Mynors, R. M. Thomson and M. Winterbottom, ed. & tr., *William of Malmesbury: Gesta Regum Anglorum* (Oxford, 1998), 196.2.
[62]   A. A. M. Duncan, *The Kingship of the Scots, 842–1292: Succession and Independence* (Edinburgh, 2002), 34–41.

Cumbria, that is to says Scots raiding in these areas, had annoyed Siward, or that the king of the Cumbrians had put himself under English protection. The latter hypothesis is lent some support by the fact that the Church of York claimed, in the early twelfth century, that Archbishop Cynsige (1055–60) had consecrated two bishops, 'Magsuen' and Johannes,[63] for Glasgow.[64] Modern historians have tended to be suspicious of claims that Glasgow was already the Cumbrian see this early (because the present cathedral was built by David I (1124–53)), but a stone cross from the site of the cathedral, in eleventh-century Northumbrian style, would seem to lend some weight to the hypothesis.[65] Siward's campaigns have also been seen as a possible context for the return of the Solway Plain (Cumberland and Dumfriesshire) into Northumbrian hands.

THE RETURN OF MAEL COLUIM SON OF DONNCHAD

Marianus Scotus dates the end of Macbethad's seventeenth year, the last complete year of his reign, precisely to the Feast of St Mary on 8 September 1057, the anniversary of Donnchad's killing. He goes on to say that Lulach reigned until St Patrick's Day, 17 March, the following year. Then Mael Coluim son of Donnchad reigned. The *Anglo-Saxon Chronicle* has nothing to say of the fall of Macbethad and Lulach. The Irish chronicles give us some further information:

> *AU* 1058.2 Lulach son of Gilla Comgáin, high-king of Alba, was killed in battle by Mael Coluim son of Donnchad.

> *AU* 1058.6 Macbethad son of Findláech, high-king of Alba, was killed in battle by Mael Sechnaill son of Donnchad.

---

[63] Unfortunately these names give us no real clue as to the linguistic milieu of Glasgow at this time; 'Magsuen' has clearly suffered in transmission (although the Gaelic name Mael Suthain suggests itself) and 'Johannes' is a biblical name.

[64] *Hugh the Chanter: The History of the Church of York, 1066–1127*, ed. & tr. C. Johnson (Oxford, 1990), 52–3.

[65] There has been a tendency to imagine that before David I's time Govan, with its vast collection of Viking Age sculpture, was the episcopal church of Strathclyde. See A. Ritchie, ed., *Govan and its Early Medieval Sculpture* (Stroud, 1994) and S. T. Driscoll, *Govan: from Cradle to Grave* (Govan, 2004). For the 'Northumbrian' cross see K. S. Forsyth, 'Late 12th century cross-head', in S. T. Driscoll, ed., *Excavations at Glasgow Cathedral, 1988–1997*, Society for Medieval Archaeology monograph 18 (2002), 85–7. Forsyth and Driscoll tell me (pers. comm.) that they now favour a mid- to late eleventh-century date for the cross.

AT 1058.1 Lulach, king of Alba, was slain by Mael Coluim son of Donnchad, through treachery (*per dolum*).

AT 1058.5 A fleet was led by the son of the king of Norway, with the Gaill of Orkney, the Hebrides and Dublin, to seize the kingdom of England, but God consented not to this.

AT 1058.6 Macbethad son of Findláech, high-king of Scotland, was slain by Mael Coluim son of Donnchad.

The *Annals of Ulster*'s identification of Macbethad's killer as Mael Sechnaill rather than Mael Coluim is presumably a simple scribal error. More curious is the fact that *AU* and *AT*, at this point seemingly independent witnesses, both place Macbethad's death after Lulach's whereas all the king-lists grant Lulach a reign of several months following Macbethad. Had this apparent mis-ordering occurred in a single chronicle we might have dismissed it as a slip but the coincidence of both making the same slip would seem odd. The simplest solution to this problem is to presume that Macbethad had demitted the kingship to Lulach, willingly or under duress, but was actually still alive when his successor was slain by Mael Coluim. This might explain some inconsistencies in the dating. As well as dating the end of Macbethad's last full year in the kingship to 8 September, Marianus' chronicle also says that he was killed in August. Anderson believed that this meant that Marianus had confused the Nativity of the Virgin, 8 September, with her Assumption, 15 August, but this seems a very unlikely mistake for an eleventh-century reformed monk to make.[66] Similarly the king-lists give Lulach a reign of four, four-and-a-half or five months. Four-and-a-half seems the likeliest approximation since this length might give either of the other two to a scribe rounding the numbers. If Lulach died on St Patrick's Day, this would put the end of Macbethad's reign near the beginning of November 1057. If Macbethad had in fact demitted the kingship this could still leave him alive to be killed by Mael Coluim in August 1058.[67] By this time he may have been quite aged. His father Findláech, you will recall, had been slain by adult nephews as long ago as 1020, suggesting that the generation of Macbethad and the sons of Mael

[66] The marginal notes in Marianus' chronicle were not made by the author himself but by an amanuensis working at his command.

[67] For an alternative attempt to make sense of these confusing and apparently contradictory dates see A. A. M. Duncan, *The Kingship of the Scots, 842–1292: Succession and Independence* (Edinburgh, 2002), 49–51.

Brigte may have been born in the years around 1000.[68] It might also be noted that most, though admittedly not all, rulers who went on pilgrimage to Rome went towards the end of their lives, hoping to atone for sins and gain absolution once they felt that they were unlikely to commit further sins. It would be no surprise if he had entered religion, either willingly or under duress, returning briefly to the world in time of crisis.

The twelfth-century king-list located Lulach's killing at Essie in Strathbogie (between Rhynie and Dufftown), and Macbethad's at Lumphanan in Deeside (Aberdeenshire). If the order of the killings in the Irish chronicles is correct then it would suggest, perhaps, that Mael Coluim was advancing from the north. A northern origin for Mael Coluim's bid for the kingship has been suggested by Professor Duncan. He points to two circumstances that lend support to the hypothesis.[69] First, accepting the identification of the place where Macbethad had killed Donnchad back in 1040 as Pitgaveny near Elgin, and presuming that the king's family had travelled north with him, he suggests that the nearest foreign border across which Donnchad's wife (she is called Suthen, a Gaelic name, in one king-list) and sons might have fled, would have been that which separated Alba from the earldom of Orkney.[70] Secondly, he points to the fact that, according to *Orkneyinga saga*, Mael Coluim's first wife, and the mother of his son Donnchad, who was briefly king in 1094, was Ingibjorg the widow of Thorfinnr of Orkney. To these factors we can add the northern location of the battles. Despite the fact that Macbethad and Lulach's family seem to have had their origins in Moray these battle sites make most sense as a defence from a northern attack. This is particularly the case if the traditional view that the Irish chronicles have the deaths of these two men in the wrong order is correct. A frequent reconstruction of the events has Mael Coluim coming from England, defeating Macbethad as he flees northwards; Lulach then holds out in the dynasty's Moravian stronghold for a few months more. Such a reconstruction fails to explain Lulach's ubiquity in the king-lists. He ruled for only a few months yet he is omnipresent. The only explanation for this must be that he went through the full inauguration ceremony at

---

[68] Gilla Comgáin, Lulach's father, had been slain in 1032 but had probably been an active adult since about 1020. Lulach would probably have been in his late twenties or thirties at the time of his kingship.

[69] A. A. M. Duncan, *The Kingship of the Scots, 842–1292: Succession and Independence* (Edinburgh, 2002), 41–3.

[70] It should be noted that the oft repeated tradition that Donnchad's wife was a cousin of sister of Earl Siward is a late, probably thirteenth-century, addition to the legend, driven by the misinterpretation of the events of 1054.

Scone and was accepted by popular consensus. Had he simply hung on as a resistance fighter north of the Mounth he might easily have been air-brushed out of history (as were the claims of his son Mael Snechtai).

It is on account of this hypothetical Orcadian connection that I chose to include in my citations from the Irish chronicles *Tigernach*'s account of the Norwegian expedition of 1058:

> *AT* 1058.5 A fleet was led by the son of the king of Norway, with the Gaill of Orkney, the Hebrides and Dublin, to seize the kingdom of England, but God consented not to this.

This episode is also noted in other Insular chronicles. *Annales Cambriae* notes:

> Magnus son of Harald laid waste a region of the English in aid of Gruffydd, king of the Britons.

The *Anglo-Saxon Chronicle* states, rather vexingly:

> In this year Earl Ælfgar was banished but he came back forthwith by violence through Gruffydd's help, and a naval force came from Norway. It is tedious to relate fully how things went.

John of Worcester is a little more helpful:

> Earl Ælfgar was outlawed by King Edward for a second time but Gruffydd king of the Welsh helped him and a Norwegian fleet, which came to him unexpectedly, lent support, so that he recovered his earldom.

Ælfgar was the earl of Mercia, the English midlands, and the son of the famous Lady Godiva (Godgifu) and he had, as is clear, a turbulent rela-tionship with King Edward. He had probably been outlawed on this occasion for marrying his sister to King Gruffydd of Gwynedd, who had helped him win back his earldom after his first outlawry. What is clear from John's account is that the Norwegian fleet was not, as the *Annals of Tigernach* suggested, intent on a conquest of England but that they had fallen in with Ælfgar by chance. On the occasion of his first out-lawry Ælfgar had hired eighteen ship-loads of warriors from Murchad king of Dublin (the son of Diarmait mac Maíl na mBó of Leinster, the leading Irish king of the day). Now, in 1058, when he looked to the Irish

Sea for help he found himself negotiating with Magnus Haraldsson of Norway.

Curiously, Magnus Haraldsson's expedition to the west is completely ignored by the Icelandic saga tradition. There is absolutely no mention of it in either *Orkneyinga saga* or any of the sagas of Norwegian kings. This may be partly because Magnus Haraldsson's line had died out long before the sagas came to be written down (he was nobody's glorious ancestor), and perhaps partly because it was easy to confuse or conflate with the two expeditions made to the Irish Sea region by his nephew and name-sake Magnus 'Bare-legs' Óláfsson in the years around 1100. The fact that the sagas were able to completely 'forget' such a major event, the first reliably attested Norwegian royal expedition to the British Isles, serves as a warning about their reliability in general. The death of Magnus the Good, Óláfsson, in 1047 had left Sveinn Estriðsson in undisputed control of Denmark while the Norwegian kingship had passed to Magnus' uncle Haraldr Sigurðsson (1044/7–66). Haraldr was the much younger uterine brother of that Óláfr Haraldsson who had led the Norwegian resistance to Cnut. Although Haraldr belonged to a different lineage from Óláfr, and his father was only a petty chieftain from Ringeríke in the Norwegian interior, he had spent most of the period following Óláf's death as a mercenary captain in Russia and Byzantium and had returned to Norway laden with guile and treasure and accompanied by a retinue of hardened professional warriors who had fought their way around the Mediterranean and the Black Sea with him. After returning to Norway Haraldr had married Thóra the daughter of Thórbergr Árnason and Magnus was the elder of their two sons.[71]

The context for Magnus' expedition should probably be looked for in Orkney. Although his expedition is not mentioned in *Orkneyinga saga* it may well be that it was instigated by Haraldr to take advantage of the death of Earl Thorfinnr. The saga simply tells us that Thorfinnr died 'in the later days of King Haraldr'. Although this phrase is often interpreted very narrowly, and Thorfinn's death is frequently cited as having occurred c. 1065, there is no reason why a date in the late 1050s is not just as credible. Magnus may then have been taking the opportunity of the succession of Thorfinn's young sons, Pál and Erlend, to enforce Norwegian overlordship. Such a hypothesis would fit well with the statement by Adam of Bremen that Haraldr Sigurðsson conquered Orkney. Pál and Erlend's mother, Ingibjorg, was the daughter of Finn Árnason

---

[71] Harald's return to Scandinavia seems to have taken place in 1043 or 1044 so Magnus must have been very young on this expedition.

and was thus a first cousin once-removed of Magnus Haraldsson on both sides of her family. Each was the first cousin of the other's mother.

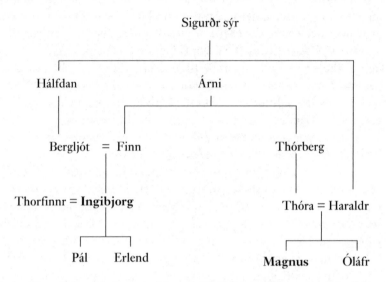

Table 6.7 The relationship between Magnus Haraldsson of Norway and Ingibjorg of Orkney

A successful expedition to Orkney, doubtless helped by the kinship between Magnus and Ingibjorg, may well have been followed up by an expedition through the Hebrides and into the Irish Sea in search of plunder or tribute. Had the expedition to Orkney required fighting then there would have been ample opportunity for Magnus to reward his men with plunder. A diplomatic solution, however, would have left Magnus in a quandary as to how to keep his men satisfied. The opportunity offered by Earl Ælfgar to lay waste one of the richest countries north of the Alps must have seemed like manna from Heaven.

The question we are left with is how this scenario effects Professor Duncan's theory of an Orcadian launch-pad for Mael Coluim son of Donnchad's bid for the Scottish kingship. If Thorfinnr had died in 1057 or 1058 would Ingibjorg have jumped at the chance to marry Mael Coluim and to bank-roll an invasion of Lulach's kingdom? Ingibjorg and Mael Coluim were probably much the same age: certainly the gap would have been less than that between Ingibjorg and Thorfinnr, who was probably older than her mother. If Duncan is correct in suggesting that Mael Coluim may have grown up in Orkney then they might have known each other very well.

A further possible piece of evidence that may be connected with these events is to be found in the Register of Aberdeen Cathedral.[72] This is an inauthentic charter purporting to have been issued by a king Mael Coluim in the sixth year of his reign, endowing an episcopal church at Mortlach (by Dufftown in Banffshire). Although both John of Fordun and the compiler of the Aberdeen Register believed the Mael Coluim in question to be Cinaed's son (†1034), internal evidence makes Mael Coluim son of Donnchad the more likely candidate. What concerns us here is the claim made by the charter that Mael Coluim is making the grant, to God and Saint Moluag, in thanks for a victory won over the Norwegians at the very beginning of his reign. If this is, in any sense, a genuine document, how does it relate to the events of 1058? It should be noted at the outset that Mortlach is close to Essie where Lulach was slain. Indeed, a battle at Essie only makes any sense if one or other of the armies was crossing the highland ridge which separates the Garioch from Speyside (along the route of the modern A941). Kirkton of Mortlach would have been the first place of any significance at the Speyside end of this route. The simplest way of combining the information from the Mortlach foundation charter and our contemporary evidence would be to make Lulach the ally of the 'Norwegians' (who might be either Orcadians or Magnus' forces). If we wish to incorporate the view that Ingibjorg was Mael Coluim's backer then we would have to argue that the Aberdeen account is garbled (which it certainly is in places) and that the later forgers of the charter simply assumed, on nationalist grounds, that the Norwegians must have been the foes, while in fact the battle between Scots and Norsemen was won by Mael Coluim, fighting alongside the Norsemen. If the Mortlach grant was connected to the battle of Essie then it is worth noting that an army approaching Essie from the north would come to Mortlach first. If Mortlach were the last church which Mael Coluim encountered before the battle he may have prayed for victory and made appropriate promises to the patron saint there.

Ultimately the Orkney background to Mael Coluim son of Donnchad's putsch must remain hypothetical. His marriage to Ingibjorg is noted only in a late, not very reliable source. Indeed, the absence of any mention of this marriage in the *Arnmæðlingartal*, an extensive genealogical tract concerning Ingibjorg's family appended to the *Fagrskinna* collection of Norwegian 'Kings' Sagas', should give us cause for

[72] *Aberdeen Registrum*, 3–4. A. C. Lawrie, ed., *Early Scottish Charters prior to 1153* (Glasgow, 1905), no. 4.

caution.[73] The Mortlach foundation legend is later still and less reliable. It makes a good story but it is unverifiable. Before we leave Mael Coluim's accession, however, we should touch on one other category of evidence that makes an English backed regime change unlikely. Symeon of Durham, in his early work, *Annals of Lindisfarne and Durham*, records that in 1059 Mael Coluim was conducted to Edward's court by Archbishop Cynsige, Bishop Æðelwine of Durham and Earl Tostig of Northumbria. Clearly this was an act of submission of some sort. We have to ask ourselves, if he had just left Edward's court would this be a necessary move? Two years later we are also told, in *Historia Regum*, that Mael Coluim took advantage of Earl Tostig's absence in Rome to put Northumbria to fire and sword. Not a very grateful attitude, or a wise one, if his regime had been dependent upon Edward's support.

His attitude to England had not changed in 1065 when he harboured Earl Tostig, who had been outlawed by King Edward. Nor did it change with the Norman Conquest of the following year. Indeed, this latter event created a great opportunity for him to raid the north and to expand his influence. It is in this period that we find the only unambiguous account of the conquest of Strathclyde by the Scots. *Historia Regum Anglorum* while recounting warfare between Earl Gospatric and Mael Coluim in 1070 explains Gospatric's ravaging of Cumbria as revenge for one of Mael Coluim's sallies into England with the words:

> For at that time *Cumbreland* was under the dominion of King
> Mael Coluim, not through just possession, but through violent
> subjugation.

Historians have tended to presume this refers to Cumberland around Carlisle, simply because the name 'Cumberland', an *English* name, survives today in the English province. It was, of course, used in the middle ages for the whole kingdom. The mystery of the disappearance of the Cumbrian kingdom of Strathclyde is explained most easily if we date it to this period. Its ultimate fate has never been in doubt: it was clearly conquered by the Scots. The real mystery is why the event was not noted by chroniclers. The only sensible solution to this problem is that the chroniclers were all distracted at that precise moment by truly momentous events. The Norman Conquest of England and the series of rebellions that followed it create the best context for this distraction. We can be

---

[73] A. Finlay, ed. & tr., *Fagrskinna, a catalogue of the Kings of Norway: a Translation with Introduction and Notes* (Leiden, 2004), 300–2.

fairly certain that Strathclyde was independent of Scotland while Cynsige was Archbishop of York (1055–60), when he consecrated two bishops of Glasgow. The next bishop we hear of, Michael, was conse-crated during the time the future David I was *princeps* of the Cumbrian region, from 1107, but before 1118, when we first encounter Bishop John, his successor.[74] Michael is said to have been appointed after a long inter-regnum, and the fact that David had to hold an inquest to identify what lands belonged to the episcopate suggests that the vacancy in the see had been quite extensive.[75] The final Scottish conquest of Strathclyde can probably be dated fairly securely to the period between 1066 and 1070.

The war between Mael Coluim and Gospatric in 1070 marked a turning point in the king's life in another way. On his second raid into Gospatric's earldom he found himself at Wearmouth and there, on the beach, he met a girl. But that is another story.[76]

[74] For the succession to the see of Glasgow see D. E. R. Watt, *Series Episcoporum Ecclesiae Catholicae Occidentalis, Series VI Britannia,Scotia et Hibernia, Scandinavia*, I *Ecclesia Scoticana* (Stuttgart, 1991), 50–64.

[75] G. W. S. Barrow, *The Charters of David I* (Woodbridge, 1999), 60–1.

[76] For which see R. Oram, *Domination and Lordship: Scotland c. 1070 to c. 1230* (Edinburgh, 2007).

PART TWO

Process

CHAPTER 7

Scandinavian Scotland

THE PROBLEM

In the course of the preceding chapters it has not been possible to obscure the fact that the political narrative for Scotland in the eighth to eleventh centuries has had to be written principally from Irish and English sources. This has led to a southern bias in the story told and we have been able to say almost nothing about either the islands or the mainland north of Ardnamurchan in the west, or the Moray Firth in the east. Even our one native source for this period, the *Chronicle of the Kings of Alba*, has its focus on the Tay basin and gives very little information about the north. The silence here is almost suspicious.[1] In his recent volume dealing with the period before 850 Leslie Alcock chose explicitly to avoid any discussion of the north, arguing that it was still prehistoric at this period and therefore a narrative could not be developed which would bear any meaningful relationship with the text-based political story that could be drawn about the south.[2] A similar argument could be made for the present volume but, unfortunately, it would probably meet with widespread disapproval. The Viking Age, and specifically the settlement of large parts of northern Scotland by Scandinavians in the course of it, marks a major turning point in the country's history. The cultural and linguistic character and the political allegiance of the Western and Northern Isles and the adjacent parts of the mainland were transformed beyond recognition in this period and in some parts of the region, particularly

---

[1] One is tempted to imagine that the original king-list, which was undoubtedly native, may have been augmented by material drawn principally from a Northumbrian source.

[2] Leslie Alcock, *Kings and Warriors, Craftsmen and Priests in Northern Britain, AD 550–850* (Edinburgh, 2003).

Orkney and Shetland, this 'Viking heritage' is still regarded as an important component of modern identities.

Methodologically our major problem is a lack of contemporary written sources. What we can say with some certainty is that by about 1200 most of Scotland north of the Dornoch Firth seems to have been entirely Norse-speaking and that Norse place-names had replaced those which had been in existence before the arrival of the Scandinavians. In the west the evidence is slightly more ambiguous but it seems likely that throughout the Western Isles Norse language and toponymy had replaced the Pictish and Gaelic. Unfortunately, for much of the Western Isles and the adjacent mainland most of our earliest documents date from the very end of the middle ages, or even later, when Gaelic had, in its turn, replaced Norse as the main language of the region, so there remains some debate as to the extent to which Gaelic may have survived in some areas throughout the period. Increasingly, however, place-name scholars are inclined to imagine that at one time the level of linguistic replacement in the west matched that in the north.

Unfortunately, what we cannot tell for certain is the speed at which this linguistic and ethnic replacement took place or the mechanisms which facilitated it. Presumably Scandinavian language is not likely to have begun spreading much before the earliest recorded attacks on Insular church-settlements in the 790s and is quite likely to have reached its maximum extent some time before 1200. Archaeological evidence for the arrival of Scandinavian settlers is hard to pin down to precise dates, such is the nature of archaeology, but on the basis of burials in a Scandinavian style and containing Scandinavian grave goods most scholars would agree that a horizon of between, very roughly, 850 and 950 may well contain all, or nearly all, of the 130 or so 'pagan' Scandinavian burials from Scotland.[3] Narrative sources are even less useful. As we have seen, the Insular chronicles simply ignored events in the far north. Even before the arrival of the Scandinavians few events in this region were noted. The northern parts of the west coast were probably quite poor and politically and culturally insignificant, much like the far west of Ireland or the western coast of Northumbria. There may well have been, indeed almost certainly were, major church-settlements in this region or nearby, at Applecross in Wester Ross, for example. The Northern Isles and the adjacent mainland have produced ecclesiastical sculpture from the later Pictish period but they do not seem to have been well connected to the centres of history

[3] James Graham-Campbell and Colleen E. Batey, *Vikings in Scotland: an Archaeological Survey* (Edinburgh, 1998), pp. 152–4.

writing such as Armagh or the Church of St Cuthbert. The silence of Insular chroniclers thus tells us very little since it predates the coming of the Scandinavians. The Scandinavian communities planted in Scotland in turn have left us no accounts of their own history even after their conversion to Christianity and integration into mainstream western culture in the course of the eleventh to thirteenth centuries.

THE ICELANDIC TRADITION

The one straightforward series of narratives that we do possess are the Icelandic sagas written between the late twelfth and the early fourteenth centuries. One of these, *Orkneyinga saga*, is explicitly a history of the earls of Orkney and this is often treated by modern scholars as if it had been written in Orkney by an Orcadian.[4] It cannot be stressed enough that this text was written in Iceland and that although a version of it was clearly circulating as early as the 1220s the 'complete' form upon which most English translations are based is a product of the later fourteenth century. In terms of its contact with the past its historical value is much the same as that of Fordun's *Chronica Gentis Scottorum* but it has been taken more seriously because, as a genre, Icelandic sagas appear more realist in style and seem to present a grittier image of the past that connects more easily with modern sensibilities. It is certainly a very good read.

Within the broad range of the Icelandic saga literature *Orkneyinga saga* belongs to the same genre as the so-called 'Kings' Sagas', a group of histories of Norwegian kings which survive in several versions, the most famous of which is *Heimskringla* by the chieftain Snorri Sturluson (1178–1241). *Orkneyinga saga*'s main theme, in so far as it can be said to have one, seems to have been to tie in the history of the earldom with that of the kings of Norway and to establish clearly the history of the relationships between the two polities. It claims that the earldom was established by the Norwegian king Haraldr *hárfagri* (†c. 935?), whom it claims was the first king of all Norway. Icelandic writers also claimed that Iceland itself had been settled in the time of Haraldr *hárfagri* and part of their 'project' seems to have been to create a unified origin legend for all

---

[4] The most accessible translation of the saga is the Penguin Classic edition; Hermann Pálsson and Paul Edwards, tr., *Orkneyinga Saga: The History of the Earls of Orkney* (Harmondsworth, 1981), but for those interested in the historical value of the text a more useful version remains A. B. Taylor, tr., *The Orkneyinga Saga* (Edinburgh, 1938). We are badly in need of a new 'student edition' with adequate footnotes and critical discussion.

the territories over which the thirteenth-century Norwegian kings claimed hegemony. The unification of Norway was, in fact, a much longer and more piecemeal process than the story of Haraldr would have us believe and was probably not completed before the eleventh century.[5] For the twelfth century the *Orkneyinga saga* is probably reasonably reliable (though where it can be cross-referenced with contemporary Scottish sources it is often inaccurate in detail) but for the period before this it is largely a work of fiction. Literacy only reached Iceland in the course of the eleventh century and historical writing probably began in the 1130s.[6] The kind of material available to saga writers may have included pedigrees, particularly of Icelandic families, praise poetry and possibly short saga-like narratives composed principally for entertainment and based on a mixture of historical and legendary themes. The Icelanders also seem to have had access to some English sources from the eleventh or twelfth centuries and a small number of other foreign texts. The compilers of the Kings' Sagas and *Orkneyinga saga* thus had a task before them that would not be too dissimilar to trying to create a narrative history of the Second World War on the basis of Hollywood movies. Some of the source material would bear a close relationship to real events, some would get the gist right but make up the detail, and some would simply be telling a universal story set against a broadly familiar historical backdrop. The problem was that the Icelandic historian could not tell which source fell into which category, even if he was aware of all the distinctions.

One major problem with the Icelandic historiography is that the Icelanders had no way of fixing their oral traditions into an absolute chronology. The events of the Viking Age occurred in a non-literate pagan milieu in which even the concept of AD dating was probably unknown. Modern historians have tried very hard to identify characters mentioned in the sagas with individuals appearing in the Irish chronicles and other sources. They have met with varying success. One example of this kind of methodology will serve to illustrate the problem. The earliest surviving piece of Icelandic historiography is *Íslendingabók* written by a man named Ári the Wise in the 1130s or 1140s. It runs to twenty-six pages in the printed edition but this includes extensive footnotes by the modern editor, often taking up a third of the page and sometimes more

[5] For a good review of recent research on this topic see Claus Krag, 'The early unification of Norway', in K. Helle, ed., *The Cambridge History of Scandinavia* (Cambridge, 2003), 184–201.

[6] Runic literacy was, of course, practised by Viking Age Scandinavians but not for the production of lengthy texts.

than half. *Íslendingabók* is a brief history of Iceland from the settlement to the present. At the very end of the book Ári gives his own pedigree:

> These are the names of the long-fathers of the Ynglings and the Breiðfirðings:
> I. Yngvi, king of the Turks. II. Njörðr, king of the Swedes. III. Freyr. IV. Fjölnir, who died at Friðfrodi. V. Svegðir. VI. Vanlandi. VII. Vísburr. VIII. Dómaldr. IX. Dómarr. X. Dyggvi. XI. Dagr. XII. Alrekr. XIII. Agni. XIIII. Yngvi. XV. Jörundr. XVI. Aun the Old. XVII. Egill Vendil Crow. XVIII. Óttarr. XIX. Aðisl at Uppsala. XX. Eysteinn. XXI. Yngvarr. XXII. Braut-Önundr. XXIII. Ingjaldr the Evil. XXIIII. Óláfr Tree-feller. XXV. Halfdann White-leg Uppland king. XXVI. Goðröðr. XXVII Óláfr. XXVIII. Helgi. XXIX. Ingjaldr the son of the daughter of Sigurðr the son of Ragnar loðbrok.[7] XXX. Ólafr the White. XXXI. Thorsteinn the Red. XXXII. Óleifr feilan, the first of them to settle in Iceland. XXXIII. Thorðr bellower. XXXIIII. Eyjolfr, who was baptised in his old age when Christianity came to Iceland. XXXV. Thorkell. XXXVI. Gellir, the father of both Thorkell the father of Brand and of Thorgils my father, and I am called Ári.[8]

This tally recounts thirty-eight generations, including Ári himself, who died in 1148 at the age of eighty. He was thus a slightly older contemporary of David I of Scotland. The earliest ancestor, Yngvi king of the Turks, and many of his immediate descendants are clearly fantasy. The person of real interest to us is number XXX, Óláfr the White. Although Ári did not supply us with any absolute dates there is an alternative methodology available for estimating his *floruit*. We noted above that Ári and David I were near contemporaries and we are lucky enough to know David's pedigree on two sides. The deaths of his ancestors can be securely identified. Thus, we can see how far back they take us when listed in parallel with Ári's. For good measure I have also included the pedigree of Tairrdelbach Ua Conchobhair (Turlough O'Connor) the king of Ireland at the time of Ári's death. All three of these men were quite long lived.

Rather surprisingly this methodology gives us average generation lengths in the thirties rather than the oft-supposed twenties, even for

---

[7] *Loðbrok* has traditionally been interpreted as meaning 'hairy-breeks' but some modern scholars have cast doubt on this.

[8] Jakob Benediktosson, *Íslendingabók, Landnámabók* (Reykjavík, 1986), 27–8.

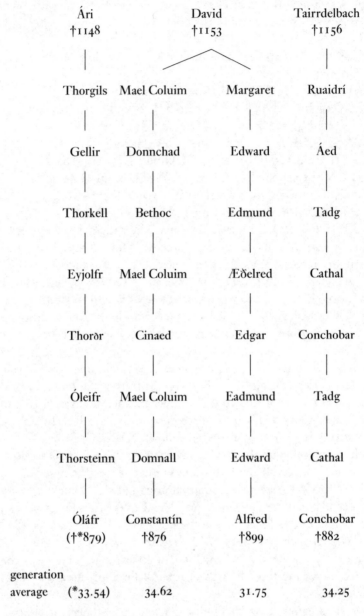

Ári †1148	David †1153		Tairrdelbach †1156
Thorgils	Mael Coluim	Margaret	Ruaidrí
Gellir	Donnchad	Edward	Áed
Thorkell	Bethoc	Edmund	Tadg
Eyjolfr	Mael Coluim	Æðelred	Cathal
Thorðr	Cinaed	Edgar	Conchobar
Óleifr	Mael Coluim	Eadmund	Tadg
Thorsteinn	Domnall	Edward	Cathal
Óláfr (†*879)	Constantín †876	Alfred †899	Conchobar †882

generation
average   (*33.54)   34.62   31.75   34.25

Table 7.1. Comparison of generation lengths in Viking Age dynasties (The *
marks a hypothetical reconstruction)

David's short-lived West Saxon ancestors.[9] I have taken the liberty here of calculating the average generation length between the three well-attested Insular dynasties, which gives *33.5416666^r, and applying it to Ári's pedigree. This gives Óláfr the White a predicted death date of 879. This is, of course, a very crude methodology and should only be expected to return ball-park figures. Caution suggests that we should simply predict his death to have fallen in the second half of the ninth century.

Now Óláfr the White appears elsewhere in Icelandic historiography. The next surviving text we have is *Landnámabók*, the 'Book of Settlements', which purports to tell of the first settler in each district of Iceland and of which kindreds they generated. This was written very shortly after Ári wrote *Íslendingabók* but it survives only in later manuscripts that have been 'updated' slightly on the basis of the later sagas. *Landnámabók* has this to say about Óláfr the White:

> Óleifr the White was the name of a war-king; he was the son of King Ingjald, the son of Helgi, the son of Óláf, the son of Guðroðr the son of Halfdan White-leg, the king of the Upplanders. Óleifr the White harried on the 'west-viking' and he won Dublin in Ireland and Dublin's 'sheath'[10] and made himself king over it. He took to wife Auðr the Deep-minded, daughter of Ketill Flatnose. Their son was called Thorsteinn the Red. Óláfr fell in Ireland in battle, but Auðr and Thorsteinn travelled then to the Western Isles [*Suðreyjar*]. There Thorsteinn married Thuriðr the daughter of Eyvindr the *Austmaðr*,[11] the sister of Helgi the Lean; they had many children. Their son was called Óláfr feilan but their daughters were Gróa, Álöf, Ósk, Thórhildr, Thorgerðr and Vigdís.

> Thorsteinn made himself a war-king; he went into partnership with Sigurðr the Powerful, the son of Eysteinn Glumra. They

---

[9] Since these generation lengths, of about thirty-five years, cover the period between a man's death and that of his father, and since most men will not have become fathers until they were in their twenties at least and may have continued producing sons for as long as they lived the implication is that most of the men in these pedigrees lived past their middle fifties. The low average life expectancies that one often sees quoted include, of course, those who did not live long enough to become parents.

[10] ON *skíði* – literally a sheath of a knife. If this is not a scribal error it may be being used metaphorically for the hinterland of Dublin.

[11] *Landnámabók* explains Helgi's by-name as the result of his having been fostered in Sweden. Since, however, he spent his adult life in Ireland where the Scandinavian's regularly distinguished themselves from the natives by using this term this aetiology is open to question.

won Caithness and Sutherland, Ross and Moray and more than
half of Scotland. Thorsteinn made himself king over it before the
Scots betrayed him and he fell in battle. Auðr was then in
Caithness when she heard of Thorsteinn's fall. She had them
build a *knörr* [a merchant vessel] in the forest secretly and when it
was ready she set out for Orkney. There she married off Gróa,
Thorsteinn the Red's daughter, she was the mother of Grélöðr
whom Thorfinnr Skull-splitter married. After that Auðr
journeyed out to Iceland; she had aboard with her twenty
noble men.[12]

This account seems to contain much of interest to Scottish historians. It
has long been noted that Óláfr the White must be, or at the very least must
draw some of his attributes from the Amlaíb son of the king of Laithlind
who first appears in the Irish sources in 853 and whom the *Chronicle of
the Kings of Alba* seems to say was killed by Constantín son of Cinaed in
Pictavia (c. 871–2).[13] Here, immediately, we are faced with a problem.
Landnámabók claims that Óleifr was slain in battle in Ireland but no such
battle is mentioned in Irish sources and it is fairly clear that *CKA*
describes his death in Pictavia. On one level this may not be such a
problem as it at first appears to be but in providing a solution we under-
mine much of the value of Icelandic literature for the study of Scottish
history.

The solution is as follows. Icelandic literature of the twelfth to fourteenth centuries consistently distinguishes between *Írland* and *Skotland*
when writing about the ninth century, yet never mentions the Picts and
Pictavia. A Norse word for Picts, *Pettar* (a loan from Old English), existed
and appears in at least one Latin history from Norway as well as in some
place-names in Scandinavian Scotland (the best known example is the
Pentland Firth from ON *Pettlandsfjörðr*) but it does not seem to have been
known as an ethnic term in Iceland. As we have seen, before the tenth
century at the very earliest it was impossible to distinguish between Gaels
living in Ireland and those living in northern Britain in any of the vernacular languages or in Latin. The term *Skotar*, like *Pettar*, would seem
to have been borrowed into Norse from English and in the ninth century
would have been used of all Gaels. The term *Írar* would seem to be a back
formation from *Írland* which itself is probably a Norse, or just possibly
English, coinage created out of Gaelic *Ériu* plus Germanic *-land*. The

---

[12] Jakob Benediktosson, *Íslendingabók, Landnámabók* (Reykjavík, 1986), 136–8.
[13] *AU* 853.2: Amlaíb's career is discussed in detail in Chapter 3 above.

distinction displayed by the Icelandic writers reflects developments in English usage since the ninth century and must therefore reflect a rationalisation of whatever terms had come down to them in the tradition. A Norse word did exist that could be used to describe Gaelic-speakers in an undifferentiated sense and this was *Vestmenn* (contrasted with *Austmenn* – 'Norwegians'). It is also possible that the term *Vestmenn* might have been used in an inclusive sense that could have covered other Insular peoples, such as the Picts. According to this hypothesis, early oral narratives concerning Viking activity in the British Isles may have contained numerous references to non-specific *Vestmenn* and *Skotar* which by, or during, the twelfth century became updated, presumably on the basis of educated guesses, to differentiated references to *Skotar* and *Írar* in the written texts. The Icelandic historians of the twelfth and thirteenth centuries were faced with similar problems to those which face us today. They were required to make it clear in modern terms where they meant even when their sources used terms which did not reflect recent historical developments, and the meaning of which were not immediately clear to them.

A similar problem with anachronism appears in the second half of the passage cited above concerning Thorsteinn's conquests with his ally Sigurðr. Here we are told that 'they won Caithness and Sutherland, Ross and Moray and more than half of Scotland'. Clearly in this period 'Scotland' did not exist and Caithness and Sutherland came into existence as two separate provinces only in the course of the twelfth century. What we seem to have here is a 'realistic' interpretation based upon the ambitions of the later earl of Orkney, Haraldr Maddaðsson, who, in the mid-1190s, briefly occupied precisely these territories.[14] It seems likely that the specific names of the provinces are a thirteenth-century interpolation into *Landnámabók*.

Another detail of Thorsteinn's career can also be used to elucidate the problems of saga evidence. In this passage we are told that Thorsteinn was married to Thuriðr the daughter of Eyvindr the *Austmaðr*. Elsewhere in *Landnámabók* we are told that Eyvindr married Rafarta the daughter of Kjarvalr *Írakonungr*. In *Orkneyinga saga* we are told that Earl Hlöðvir married Eðnu the daughter of Kjarvalr *Írakonungr* and that their son was Earl Sigurðr *digri*. This creates a chronological problem. Sigurðr son of Hlöðvir was the earl of Orkney who was slain at Clontarf in 1014 (the first earl of Orkney to appear in a contemporary source) yet we are asked to believe that his mother was the aunt of woman whose husband lived in

[14] For a recent account of this episode see R. Andrew McDonald, *Outlaws of Medieval Scotland, Challenges to the Canmore Kings, 1058–1266* (East Linton, 2003), 39–40.

the late ninth century. At the same time, however, you will recall that Thorsteinn, who was married to a grand-daughter of Kjarvalr, was also allied with a Sigurðr the son of Eysteinn *glumra*. It seems likely that the author of *Orkneyinga saga* knew of a story concerning an Earl Sigurðr and his mother and wrongly applied it to Sigurðr Hlöðvissonr. See Table 7.2.

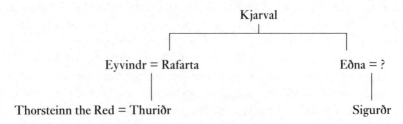

Table 7.2 The relationship of Thorsteinn to Sigurðr

Thorsteinn does not appear in any Insular sources but Kjarvalr is likely to be Cerball of Osraige (847–88)[15] and it is tempting to identify Sigurðr with an individual mentioned in the *Annals of Ulster* under the year 893:

> *AU* 893.4 A great dissension amongst the foreigners of Áth Cliath and they became dispersed, one part following the son of Ímar and another part Sichfrith the Earl.

But if this identification is correct did this episode occur before or after the death of Thorsteinn?

In many ways the remarkable thing is that the Icelandic writers of the twelfth and thirteenth centuries were able to retrieve so much genuine historical information from the oral traditions that came down to them. The problem for us, however, is that they seem to have been wrong, in detail, as often as they were right, as can be seen from this discussion based on one short passage from a single text. Where we can cross-reference their stories with other more reliable sources we can believe them, but since we have the other more reliable sources we then do not need them. Other accurate information is likely to be carried in this literature but cannot be verified and, because so much is clearly wrong or

---

[15]   To continue the theme of longevity explored above it is worth noting that *AU* describes Cerball's death as 'sudden' (*AU* 888.6). Despite the fact he had been king for over forty years his death seems to have been unexpected. For a full account of Cerball's career see C. Downham, 'The career of Cearbhall of Osraighe', *Ossory, Laois and Leinster* I (2004), 1–18.

misunderstood, one can place little reliance upon it. It is best perhaps to think of the Icelandic scholars as colleagues making helpful suggestions rather than as independent witnesses from the period itself. One can fruitfully be inspired upon lines of investigation by this material but until corroborating evidence can be discovered from contemporary sources their information remains 'hearsay' and is inadmissible in court.

Hvítramannaland

An example of the confusion caused by Icelanders trying to match their oral traditions to 'modern' geography is the case of *Hvítramannaland*. In a curious episode tacked on to the end of *Eyrbyggja saga* we are told of how beyond *Írland* there lay a large island called *Írland* the Great, or *Hvítramannaland*, the 'Land of White Men', which is full of rich monasteries the inhabitants of which spoke Irish. Modern scholars have puzzled greatly over this and have either dismissed it as fantasy or claimed that it is an account of America! It is perhaps easier to explain if we recall that in the earlier part of the Viking Age the Insular vernaculars tended not to distinguish between Gaels living in Britain and those living in Ireland. Indeed, in English, the language most accessible to the Norse, *Scotland* might indicate either Ireland or the Gaelic territories in northern Britain. At a slightly later date Latin writers might refer to Alba as *Scotia* and Ireland as *Scotia Magna*. In the light of these observations it seems likely that *Hvítramannaland*, 'Ireland the Great', is in fact Ireland, a large island with many monasteries whose inhabitants spoke Gaelic, and that *Írland*, as it appears in this story, is in fact Dál Riata, the first Gaelic territory encountered by Norwegians sailing to Ireland.[16]

This rather trivial example serves to illustrate the kind of problem Icelandic writers had fitting the oral traditions that had genuinely come down from their Viking Age ancestors into the more scientific understanding of history and geography which they had gleaned from their literary education. It should not be forgotten that the earliest Icelandic historian, whose works sadly do not survive, Sæmundr the Wise, had studied in Paris.

---

[16] What is clear, if this explanation is accepted, is that the story of the journey to 'Ireland the Great' came from a written Latin source and not from Norse oral tradition.

MODELLING THE SCANDINAVIAN SETTLEMENT: CHRONOLOGY

As one might imagine, given the nature of the evidence, scholars have been unable to reach a consensus concerning the character and course of Scandinavian settlement, and are unlikely to do so in the foreseeable future. The two main areas for debate concern chronology and the relations between Norsemen and natives. Both these areas have proved fruitful ground for disagreement.

With regard to the dating of the Scandinavian settlement one popular model might be termed the 'Wave of Advance' model. In this model it is presumed that, generally speaking, people and cultural phenomena spread from their point of origin at a regular rate. Thus, because Shetland, for example, is the nearest part of Scotland to Scandinavia it must have been the part first settled. Proponents of this theory are also quite happy to suggest that Scandinavian settlement of the Northern Isles may have long pre-dated the first appearance of the raiders in Northumbria and Ireland in the 790s. It has even been suggested that the raids on Ireland may have been directed from a Scandinavian kingdom in the north of Scotland and that this was the location of the mysterious Laithlind.[17]

Against this 'Scottish Laithlind' hypothesis we must place the archaeological evidence which would seem to indicate that Scandinavian settlement only became widespread in the second half of the ninth century. For what it is worth this would also fit well with the Icelandic tradition which, as in the extract cited above, tended to claim that Scotland was settled by second generation Scandinavians whose parents had been active in Ireland in the middle of the ninth century. This is made clear by the pivotal role of Óláfr the White and Kjarvalr Írakonungr as the ancestors of Scottish settlers in these traditions. It is certainly the case that by the latter part of the 880s the Irish seemed to have gained the upper hand in their struggle with the Scandinavian invaders and the episodes such as the dispersal of the Dubliners in 893, noted above, may well have provided a context for settlement in Scotland. Elsewhere in the Insular world settlement by Scandinavians seems to be a feature of the last quarter of the ninth century whether this be in England or Man. Prior to this, land-hunger does not seem to have been a motivation for Viking activity.

[17] The most recent and coherent case for this position has been made by Professor Donnchadh Ó Córráin, 'The Vikings in Scotland and Ireland in the ninth century', in *Peritia* 12 (1998), 296–339, and 'Viking Ireland – afterthoughts', in H. Clarke, M. Ní Mhaonaigh and R. Ó Floinn, eds, *Ireland and Scandinavia in the Early Viking Age* (Dublin, 1998), 421–52.

Instead the bulk of attacks from the 790s to the 870s seem to have been focused on acquiring moveable wealth such as church-plate or slaves and although bases like Dublin were established they do not, at first, seem to have acquired extensive rural hinterlands. In these circumstances we might imagine that the Norwegians were frequent visitors to the Northern and Western Isles but mainly en route to more prosperous lands to the south. They may have robbed and enslaved as they went, but equally they may have established a *modus vivendi* with some local communities.

The one exception to this model may be the island portion of Dál Riata, if this was indeed the area referred to by the *Annals of St Bertin* under the year 847:

> the Northmen also got control of the islands all around Ireland
> and stayed there without encountering any resistance from
> anyone.[18]

But the context of this entry was the imposition of tribute upon Ireland, so Islay and its neighbours may well have been seen as bases off the Irish coast – bases which rendered the creation of northern versions of Dublin, Waterford and Limerick unnecessary.

One contemporary textual hint that supports this model for the early relations between the Scandinavians and the Northern Isles is found in the life of St Findan of Rheinau. Findan was an Irishman who ended his career as a leading member of a monastery in the Upper Rhine region. It was in this region that his *vita* was composed not long after his death. When still a young man in Leinster he had been captured by Viking slavers and carried off to the north. While passing through Orkney, his captors, we are told, stopped on a small uninhabited island for water and exercise. Findan managed to hide under an over-hanging rock and eventually, with miraculous help, he floats or swims across to the main island. He is then able to make his way to the household of a bishop who, having trained in Ireland, was able to speak his language.

The most likely interpretation of this story would be that the bishop was located on mainland Orkney and was a native Pictish speaker. The text is not precise on these points, however, and it has been argued by those in favour of an early Scandinavian settlement that either the bishop was a Norseman or that he was located on the mainland of Britain, not Orkney. Based on the later parts of Findan's career this episode is likely

[18] J. L. Nelson, ed., *The Annals of St-Bertin* (Manchester, 1991), 65.

to have taken place in the 840s or 850s.[19] Given the absence of archaeological evidence for early Scandinavian settlement or for Christian Scandinavians in this region before the mid-tenth century the interpretation that Orkney was still Pictish and the bishop a Pict seems the most sensible inference.

This model, which allows for frequent, regular and varied contact between resident natives and itinerant Scandinavians for almost a century before significant Scandinavian settlement (that is, c. 790–875) can explain some evidence which has caused difficulties for scholars studying these issues.[20] These problems focus on what we might term, not unproblematically, 'transitional features' in the archaeological record. These are artefacts or sites which seem to show evidence of both Scandinavian and Pictish cultural input. One example of this category of evidence which has caused some controversy of late are combs made from antlers. In Scandinavia there was a long tradition of making combs from reindeer antlers. In the Northern Isles a similar tradition existed utilising the antlers of the red deer. Though broadly similar the artistic styles in the two regions are clearly distinct. It appears now that a small number of Pictish combs may have been made of reindeer antler. This created an interpretative problem for those who believed that Scandinavian settlement followed on pretty much immediately from first contact. For them the combs indicated that either the Picts had been importing raw materials from Norway before the Viking Age or that the earliest phase of Scandinavian settlement was reflected in a fusion culture which only later re-invented itself as fully Scandinavian.[21] Similarly some archaeologists have argued that the earliest Scandinavian settlers had continued to dwell in Pictish-style houses because objects of Scandinavian provenance were discovered in their ruins. If, however, we recognise that for most of the ninth century the Picts of Orkney and Shetland, and presumably the Western Isles, were in regular contact with Scandinavians but that no significant settlement had occurred then these phenomena cease to be a

---

[19] See C. J. Omand, 'The life of St Findan' and W. P. L. Thomson, 'St Findan and the Pictish-Norse transition', in R. J. Berry and H. N. Firth, eds, *The People of Orkney* (Kirkwall, 1986) at 284–7 and 279–83, respectively.

[20] For an in-depth review of the literature see James Barrett, 'Culture contact in Viking Age Scotland', in J. H. Barrett, ed., *Contact, Continuity and Collapse: The Norse Colonization of the North Atlantic* (Turnhout, 2003), 73–111. The single most influential contribution has probably been Bjørn Myhre, 'The beginning of the Viking Age – some current archaeological problems', in A. Faulkes and R. Perkins, eds, *Viking Revaluations* (London, 1993), 182–203.

[21] Barrett, 'Culture contact', 78–80.

problem. We are simply seeing items acquired from Scandinavians turning up in Pictish settlements.

Those in favour of an early Scandinavian conquest of Orkney have also pointed to a phrase in the life of Findan which they argue supports their case. In this passage Orkney is described as lying *juxta*, 'next to', the land of the Picts. This, they argue, demonstrates that Orkney had already been detached from Pictavia. I suggest this is a specious argument. Who among us, if asked to locate Anglesey or the Isle of Wight would not say that they lay, respectively, off North Wales or the south of England? Does this mean that these islands are not administratively counted as parts of Wales or England?

MODELLING THE SCANDINAVIAN SETTLEMENT: WAR OR PEACE?

The other controversial issue surrounding the Scandinavian settlement in northern Scotland, besides that of dating, concerns the degree to which genocide or population displacement took place.[22] This is part of a much wider debate among archaeologists and historians about migrations and ethnic replacement in the past. Until the last part of the twentieth century traditional historical narratives told of one people arriving and displacing another in various parts of the world, and were accepted unproblematically. To what extent historians and archaeologists actually thought genocide had occurred was unclear. In well attested historical episodes it was often possible to say for certain when a conquest was achieved only by a political elite who displaced a relatively small proportion of the population, as, for example, in the case of the Norman Conquest of England in 1066. Looking at prehistory, when historical data was absent and linguistic data, principally in the form of place-names, gave only very vague indicators, archaeologists tended to follow what has become known as the 'Culture–History' paradigm. According to this model major changes in the material culture, such as the introduction of a new burial rite or a radically new style of pottery, was often presumed to indicate that an invasion and conquest by a new people had occurred. From the late 1960s archaeologists, particularly in England, began to

---

[22] See Brian Smith, 'The Picts and the martyrs or did the Vikings kill the native population of Orkney and Shetland?' and Jessica Bäcklund, 'War or peace? The relations between the Picts and the Norse in Orkney', both published in *Northern Studies* 36 (2001) at 7–32 and 33–48, respectively, for opposing views on the topic.

question this paradigm, pointing out that funerary rites, for example, can sometimes change radically without invasions.[23] The introduction of Christianity to Anglo-Saxon England, for example, led to the decline of burials with grave goods and the disappearance of cremation. Looking at the historical period it was also noted that some invasions and migrations left a clear imprint in the archaeological record while many others did not. Some, such as the Roman conquests in western Europe, led to massive changes in material culture but were probably accompanied by only minimal migration into the conquered provinces from the Roman homeland in central Italy. These observations led archaeologists to lose confidence in their ability to identify invasions, migrations and ethnic change on the basis of archaeological evidence alone. Because of this, they came to accept that questions of ethnicity and migration could not be addressed by the material culture record and should therefore not be asked of material from prehistory.[24] These general observations were apparently bolstered by a development in the archaeology of Greece. In the Bronze Age, at the time of the Trojan War, Greece had been host to a rich literate palace-based society, to which the label 'Mycenaean' was applied. This society had collapsed about 1100 BC and it had been another 400 years or more before similar levels of civilisation emerged in the form of Classical Greek culture. Using the Culture–History paradigm, together with a rationalisation of Greek myths, archaeologists had assumed that northern barbarians, the Dorians, had wiped out the Mycenaean civilisation of the Bronze Age and that these barbarians were the ancestors of the Greeks. At about the same time that the Culture–History paradigm was coming under scrutiny in Britain the enigmatic Linear B script of the Mycenaeans was finally deciphered. To everyone's surprise it turned out that the Bronze Age peoples of the Aegean had already been speaking a form of Greek. Overnight the idea that Dorian invasions from the north had destroyed the palace culture and brought Greek language and identity to the region collapsed.[25]

A combination of the deciphering of Linear B and the deconstruction of the Culture–History paradigm led the next generation of archaeologists,

---

[23] The seminal paper was G. Clark, 'The invasion hypothesis in British archaeology', *Antiquity* 40 (1966), 172–89.

[24] For a reviews of this debate within archaeology see D. Anthony, 'Migration in archaeology: the baby and the bathwater', *American Anthropologist* 92 (1990), 895–914, and T. Champion, 'Migration revived', *Journal of Danish Archaeology* 9 (1990), 214–18.

[25] C. Renfrew, 'Systems collapse as social transformation: catastrophe and anastrophe in early state societies', in C. Renfrew and K. L. Cooke, eds, *Transformations: Mathematical Approaches to Culture Change* (London, 1979), 481–506.

writing principally in the 1980s, not simply to admit that archaeology was too blunt a tool to chart ethnic change and population movement accurately, but that population movement did not happen, or only on a very small scale. This 'immobilist' position argued that most people in history were autochthonous (that is to say aboriginal) and that apparent ethnic change, including linguistic shift, was more likely to be the result of shifting fashion than invasion. Because the collapse of the Culture–History paradigm had denied archaeologists access to migration as a model for explaining cultural change in prehistory they sought to impose this limitation on historical periods even when, to the minds of many historians and linguists, the evidence to the contrary was overwhelming. To complicate matters, in the minds of some scholars, immobilism was charged with a left-wing caché; those who showed too much interest in the ethnic or racial origin of the people they studied, were, it was hinted, guilty of racist tendencies. Thankfully the very polemical debates around these issues which raged in the 1980s and 1990s seem to have calmed down. The subtleties of the critique of the Culture–History paradigm have been absorbed by those who still wish to see a place for migrations in the explanation of culture change, and pictures from Africa and the Balkans on our television screens have convinced all but the most extreme 'immobilists' that genocide and population displacement can sometimes happen.

With regard to Scandinavian Scotland the impact of this debate should be readily apparent. While none can deny that Scandinavian warriors roamed the western sea-ways in this period and imposed their rule on some areas, the extent to which they simply provided an aristocratic elite governing an essentially native population or, alternatively, perpetrated acts of genocide against island populations, is open to question. At first sight the case for genocide would seem overwhelming. Apart from a handful of island-names not a single pre-Norse placename survives in the Northern Isles and there are suggestions that the same may be true for the Outer Isles as well (although the subsequent appearance of Gaelic in this region obscures the quality of the evidence somewhat). The immobilists, however, will point to the fact that we really have no coverage of this area before the thirteenth century and very little until the end of the middle ages. A relatively slow replacement of native culture by Norse might have occurred over several hundred years. For this reason immobilists tend to be keen on putting the Norse conquest as early as possible and seeing the evidence of culture contact in the ninth century, discussed above, as the beginnings of what they call 'elite emulation' – the adoption of the culture of the ruling class by the natives.

The main problem with the 'elite emulation' model is that it was developed specifically to deal with the dissemination of material culture and does not provide a good model for language shift. This is unsurprising since most archaeological theory has been developed by prehistorians who are not required to take language into account. The problem is that elite conquests in the historical period usually result in the conquerors adopting the language of the natives. The Norman Conquest of England is a classic example. Although French remained in use for several centuries amongst the aristocracy the indications are that they had become bi-lingual within a generation or two and the maintenance of French was something of an affectation. The Scandinavian settlement of Normandy in the tenth century seems to have more or less lost its Scandinavian language within a hundred years. With regard to Scottish history it should be noted that a number of Highland clans, Gaelic-speaking until very recently, such as the Frasers and the Grants, were the descendants of Anglo-Norman aristocrats who came into the country in the twelfth century. The replacement of Gaelic by Scots in the eastern lowlands in the later middle ages was not the result of elite immigration but of relatively low status burgesses, or townsmen, being imported from England and the Low Countries. The Highlands, outwith the hinterlands of the burghs, retained Gaelic as the main language into the twentieth century despite the shift of the language of court and government to French, then Scots and eventually English.

The contexts in which native languages have given in to the language of conquerors have, paradoxically, tended not to be those where there was widespread displacement of a native elite but, instead, those areas in which the native elite was incorporated into a bureaucratic government. I am thinking here of the Roman Empire, the Arab Caliphate and modern European colonial empires. One condition of this transformation was generally relatively widespread literacy. It is also the case that in these situations there is rarely a significant impact on the toponymy (place-names). In the Roman Empire a handful of new cities were given Latin names but the vast majority of places retained their native names or combined a native and a Latin element. The same is true for the Arab and colonial empires. The toponymic evidence alone argues very strongly against the elite emulation model in the case of Scandinavian Scotland.

Of course *what* exactly happened to the natives and how long *it* took remains open to debate. Island populations may disappear more easily because flight is easier. An island can be evacuated and the population definitively move away whereas in a large landlocked province refugees are likely to remain within striking distance of their homes and are perhaps more likely to attempt to return. Thus, a relatively small act of genocide may provoke abandonment of a homeland. In the case of the Scottish islands or west coast glens the knowledge that a large, Christian and culturally similar polity (which might offer protection) lay on the adjacent mainland may have made flight more appealing than it might have been in some other contexts. We might also imagine that in an island group like Orkney or Shetland, the Norse may have established themselves on one island first and gradually exerted influence from there, following an apartheid rather than a 'gentry' model of domination. Both natives and Norse may have retained the full social range from chief to slave on their respective islands, but the native chieftain may have been constrained to pay tribute to the Norse one.

If we accepted the model which argues for a lengthy period during which the Scandinavians visiting Ireland, eastern Scotland and England used the islands as a corridor, we might also imagine that sustained, relatively low level raiding and destruction, carried out over several decades may have led to the gradual breakdown of established social and economic patterns and rendered the natives very vulnerable when conquest finally came. This may go some way towards explaining the absence of the more impressive Pictish ecclesiastical monuments from the islands. Late Pictish hoards, like that found buried in the floor of the church at St Ninian's Isle, Shetland, (significantly buried in a box made of Scandinavian larch wood), may reflect such stressful times.[26]

MANX AND THE GALLGÁEDIL

By the late twelfth century some areas which were apparently conquered by Scandinavians in this period appear to have become largely Gaelic-speaking. Some of these areas may have had a significant Gaelic-speaking population before the Scandinavian conquest and this may reflect an elite conquest similar to that which occurred in Normandy. On the other hand, in other areas, most notably Galloway and the Isle of Man, Gaelic seems to have arrived as a significant language in the course of the Viking Age. Since there seem to be no accounts of Irish invasions of these areas it appears most likely that Gaelic was brought to these regions by the Scandinavians. This seems counter-intuitive. The problem is that these regions are among those least represented in the chronicle record. The Isle of Man, formerly British, and perhaps connected dynastically to

[26] S. M. Foster, *Picts, Gaels and Scots* (London, 2004), 63–4 and 68.

Gwynedd, probably fell under Norse rule in the late 870s and, as we saw in Chapter 4, the adjacent coastline of northwest England and southwest Scotland probably came under Scandinavian occupation following the expulsion of the pagans from Dublin in 902.

The toponymy of the Isle of Man and northwest England shows considerable Scandinavian impact and there is some evidence of this in Dumfries and Galloway as well including, for example, Tynwald in Dumfriesshire, from Old Norse *þingvellir* – 'Assembly Fields'.[27] The evidence for Gaelic in the northwest of England is relatively slight but in the twelfth century there were certainly people with Gaelic names living there and there is a small amount of toponymic evidence for Gaelic, as well as a number of settlements bearing the name Ireby or Irby, a Norse construction signifying the residence of an Irishman.[28] It seems quite likely that this Irish Sea region, comprising Man, Dumfries and Galloway and the northwest of England, became, in the course of the tenth century, 'balkanised' from a linguistic perspective. In the Balkans, before the recent break up of Yugoslavija, the various languages, South-Slavic (a.k.a. Serbo-Croat etc.), Vlach (a.k.a. Aroumani and Rumanian) and Albanian, along with smaller amounts of Greek, Italian, Turkish and Hungarian, were the first languages of rural communities scattered across the region. Individual settlements were dominated by speakers of one language but districts were often linguistically diverse. The recent episodes of 'ethnic cleansing' in the 1990s were attempts to make the linguistic map of the region conform more to a western stereotype of what a country 'should look like' (loathe though they would be to admit it, many people have some sympathy with Adolf Hitler's famous dictum: 'one language, one people, one state', and such ideas underlie many less openly aggressive nationalisms). Due to a range of factors the history of the Balkans had not led, until recent times, to the creation of conditions which favoured the development of culturally and linguistically homogeneous countries. The main factors here were probably domination of the region, successively, by the Byzantine and Ottoman empires which shared a long tradition of

[27] G. Fellows-Jensen, 'Scandinavians in Dumfriesshire and Galloway: the place–name evidence', in R. Oram and G. Stell, eds, *Galloway: Land and Lordship* (Edinburgh, 1991), 77–95 and R. Oram, 'Scandinavian Settlement in south-west Scotland with a special study of Bysbie', in B. E. Crawford, ed., *Scandinavian Settlement in Northern Britain* (London, 1995), 127–40.

[28] M. Higham, 'Scandinavian settlement in north-west England, with a special study of Ireby names', in B. E. Crawford, ed., *Scandinavian Settlement in Northern Britain* (London, 1995), 195–205. I am very grateful to Dr Fiona Edmonds for discussing this evidence with me.

polyethnic *imperium* and the separation of bureaucratic and hieratic languages from the vernaculars. It seems quite likely that when the Scandinavian-led groups from Ireland settled in western Northumbria they included at least some Irish who had thrown their lot in with them in Ireland. Perhaps these were people who were native to the immediate hinterland of Dublin who had, over the sixty years or so of the settlement, come to identify with their overlords. Perhaps there were groups of young Irish males who felt that a Viking lifestyle might offer them greater opportunities. Perhaps there were individuals of Irish origin who had, one way or another, ended up living in Dublin. It should also be recalled that the Icelandic authors of the twelfth century seem to have believed that there was considerable inter-marriage between the Irish and the Norse. If this was true, as seems likely, then many 'Scandinavian' households may have been bilingual.

The upshot seems to have been that English, Gaelic, British and Norse appear to have been widely spoken across the region in the tenth and eleventh centuries and that only gradually did one language come to dominate in each district. Unfortunately, the documentary evidence is so poor that we cannot chart this process other than to say it was probably not yet complete by 1200, and it is by no means agreed when Manx, a Gaelic dialect, became the dominant language on Man. For our purposes we probably should imagine that the Irish Sea region remained linguistically balkanised throughout the tenth and eleventh centuries.

Connected to this issue lies the problem of the *Gallgáedil*. The modern provincial name Galloway derives from this term, which means 'Gaelic-speaking Gaill'. Its use for the mainland portion of southwestern Scotland, initially including much of Renfrewshire and Ayrshire as well as Wigtownshire and Kirkcudbrightshire is only securely recorded from the twelfth century. In the ninth century, in 856 and 857, *Gallgáedil* were recorded as being active in Ireland; in alliance with a king of Mide against pagans (*AU* 856.3), in conflict with a king of Ailech (*AU* 856.5), and being routed by Ímar and Amlaíb in Munster (*AU* 857.1). In the latter episode the *Gallgáedil* were said to have been led by one Caittil Find and modern commentators have been quick to see in his name the Norse name Ketill. Many have then gone further and identified him with a figure known from the Icelandic tradition, Ketill Flatnose. According to *Landnámabók* Ketill Flatnose, a Norwegian chieftain from Sogn,[29] was

---

[29] According to some of the later sagas he was from Romsdal, further north. This instability in the tradition is another indication of the problems encountered in using Icelandic literature as an historical source.

sent to subdue the *Suðreyjar* by King Haraldr *hárfagri* of Norway. Having done so, Ketill failed to pay tribute to Haraldr as had been arranged.[30] This looks very much like a story created in later days to legitimise Norwegian claims to sovereignty in the region. The story promotes the idea that establishment of the *Suðreyjar* as a political unit was down to the Norwegian kings and that the only reason they had not been collecting tribute to date was because their first lieutenant in the region, Ketill, broke his promise. Ketill Flatnose's main place in the Icelandic tradition was as the father of a number of the early settlers of Iceland, including Auðr, the wife of Óláfr the White. The identification made between Caittil Find and Ketill Flatnose has encouraged historians to posit a Hebridean origin for the *Gallgáedil* and this has become almost an article of faith in the literature, although the evidence is very weak. Against the identification the following arguments can be laid:

1. Ketill appears to have been a very common Norse name in this period.
2. It is not certain that *Caittil* represents Ketill.
3. *Find* means 'white' not 'flat-nosed'.
4. There is no suggestion in the Icelandic sources that Ketill was active in Ireland.
5. There is no suggestion that the *Gallgáedil* had links with the Isles in the Irish sources.
6. Caittil was an enemy of Amlaíb while Ketill was the father-in-law of Óláfr.

None of these objections is insurmountable but it remains the case that the identification of Caittil Find with Ketill Flatnose is extremely tenuous and has probably been motivated by a desire to tell a more complete story than the sources would allow.

One further factor that may have encouraged the identification of the *Gallgáedil* with Ketill Flatnose's Hebridean subjects was the perception that the Norse impact on the southern Hebrides was somewhat less intense than the impact on the Northern and Outer Isles. This impression is the product of an examination of the toponymic evidence. Early analysis of settlement names in the Outer Isles and the Southern Hebrides, respectively, showed that in the former names of Norse origin made up about seventy per cent of the total, and those of Gaelic only about thirty per cent, while in the latter the proportions were reversed. This created the impression that Norse settlement in Islay and the adjacent islands may have been simply an aristocratic veneer and that the bulk

---

[30] Jakob Benediktosson, *Íslendingabók: Landnámabók* (Reykjavík, 1986), 50.

of the population would have maintained their Gaelic language and identity. This encouraged an interpretation of the *Gallgáedil* as either a hybrid group or as a basically Gaelic group under Norse leadership. Recently more thorough analysis of the place-names of Islay has suggested that in fact as late as the sixteenth century the vast majority of farm names were of Norse origin and that the high proportion of Gaelic names in the modern toponymy of the island are the product of land re-organisation and the establishment of new names in the course of the last 400 years. It seems likely that in the tenth and eleventh centuries Islay was as Norse as Lewis and it seems likely that similar studies of other southern islands, and even Kintyre, might produce similar results.[31] Again, for what it is worth, *Landnámabók* seems to imply that Ketill established himself as ruler of a region that was already inhabited by Scandinavians.

By the middle of the eleventh century, at the latest, the *Gallgáedil* had become the dominant group in much of southwest Scotland and were present in northwestern England. It is notable, however, that no account has survived of early 'Galloway' and no names of its leaders are recorded from before the twelfth century. Likewise its boundaries are very hard to fix. Bearing in mind the suggestion made above that the linguistic situation in the region resembled that in the Balkans one is reminded of the expansion and settlement of the early Slavs in the sixth and seventh centuries. These people, barely if at all recognisable during the height of the Roman era spread rapidly and effectively across much of eastern and southern Europe, replacing or displacing Germanic tribes, like the Goths, and the inhabitants of the imperial provinces. Accounts by Byzantine writers make it clear that one factor which allowed the Slavs to be so successful was that they did not have a centralised political structure and that their raiding and migratory bands were very fluid. Individual chieftains might be identified for specific campaigns but usually two or three leaders might be seen to work in concert. Groups banded together or disbanded as resources and strategic considerations demanded. Some groups were happy to ally themselves with the Byzantines or with the Turkish Avars (who had occupied the Hungarian plain) from time to time. The very success of the Slavs was determined by their fluid political and social structures and the lack of any complex hierarchy that required stability for its maintenance.[32] It seems very likely that the

---

[31] Alan Macniven, *The Norse in Islay: A Settlement Historical Case-Study for Medieval Scandinavian Activity in Western Maritime Scotland* (Edinburgh, 2006), unpublished Ph.D. thesis.

[32] For the early expansion of the Slavs see P. Barford, *The Early Slavs: Culture and Society in Early Medieval Eastern Europe* (London, 2001), particularly 45–66.

Gallgáedil spread across southern Scotland and northern England in much the same way. Their lack of identifiable leaders and enduring dynasties made them practically invisible in an age when chronicles, for the most part, simply recorded the deaths of great men.

POLITICAL STRUCTURES AND HISTORY IN THE *SUÐREYJAR*

The Old Norse term *Suðreyjar* and the Gaelic *Innse Gall* both seem to refer to the Western Isles, but whether either was at any time used in a more restricted or indeed more general sense is unclear.[33] Did Innse Gall, for example, at any time refer to Orkney and Shetland as well as the Hebrides? Was *Suðreyjar* ever restricted in use to one or other part of the Western Isles? It is unlikely that either the Irish writers who used the term *Innse Gall* or the Icelanders who used *Suðreyjar* had themselves a clear sense of the geography of the region. It is only towards the end of our period that a *rí Innse Gall*, 'King of the Islands of the Gaill', is mentioned. The first person to be accorded this title in the Irish chronicles was Gothfrith son of Harald, who is given it in his death notice in 989.[34] He and his brother Maccus first appear in the record, as we saw in Chapter 5, in the 970s. The emergence of a kingdom of *Innse Gall* at this point may, as was suggested earlier, have been linked to the loss of Dublin to Mael Sechnaill of Mide in 980, following the retirement of Amlaíb Cúarán to Iona. Mael Sechnaill had set up his own half-brother, Amlaíb's son Glúniairn, as king of Dublin but the other territories seem eventually to have fallen to Gothfrith, with some help from the *Danair*. From this time onwards a dynasty descended from Gothfrith appears to have competed with one descended from Amlaíb Cúarán for a kingdom comprising both the Irish Sea region and the Hebrides. The question for us is whether the Western Isles had been in Amlaíb's kingdom before 980 or whether some other dispensation had applied.

The only hint we have as to an earlier arrangement is the reference to the 'Lawmen of the Isles' in the entries for 962 and 974 in the *Annals of the Four Masters*.[35] This may possibly suggest that, like Iceland, Gotland and the provinces of the Swedish interior, the Isles comprised one or

---

[33] It is tempting to imagine that the terms *Innse Gall* and *Airer Gáedel* – 'Argyll' 'Coast of the Gael' – emerged as complimentary descriptions during the Viking Age.
[34] *AU* 989.4.
[35] *AFM* 960.14 and 972.13. *AFM* is regularly two years out at this point.

Gofraid mac Fergusa[36]

The pedigrees created for Clann Donald in the later middle ages, like many Gaelic genealogical tracts stretch far back into prehistoric times. The earliest figure in these pedigrees for whom there is secure historical evidence is Somerled son of Gillebrigte who was killed near Renfrew in 1164. One other figure in the pedigree has been possibly identified as an historical figure however. This is Gofraid son of Fergus who appears at six, seven or eight places above Somerled in different versions of the pedigree. The seventeenth-century compilation of Irish chronicles known as the *Annals of the Four Masters* contains two references to this man who is otherwise absent from the chronicles. They appear under the years 835 and 851 and read:

Gofraid son of Fergus, chief of the Oirghialla, went to Alba, to strengthen Dál Riada, at the request of Cinaed son of Alpín.

And

Gofraid son of Fergus, chief of Innsi Gall, died.

These entries are problematic on a number of counts. First, Gofraid is a Norse name and Fergus a Gaelic name. This would seem to suggest a man of mixed descent with some authority in a landlocked territory Oirghialla (roughly Fermanagh, Tyrone and Monaghan) already in the early ninth century. This seems remarkably early for such close Norse–Irish relations. It is also rather earlier than we should expect Cinaed to be active since the first entry predates the battle of 839 in which Áed son of Boanta, king of Dál Riata was slain. It should also be noted that the second entry contains the term 'Innsi Gall', not otherwise attested before 989 and almost certainly anachronistic at this period.

The rest of the pedigree makes it clear that Gofraid's father Fergus was the son of one 'Erc', which makes it likely that he was imagined as Fergus mór mac Erc, the legendary fifth-century founder of Dál Riata. In sum the pedigrees look very much like the product of fourteenth-century propagandists from Clann Donald who sought to make the Lords of the Isles kinsmen of the kings of Scots and the annalistic entries later concoctions produced with the same aim. A more detailed examination than we have space for here puts this beyond doubt.

---

[36] Alex Woolf, 'The origins and ancestry of Somerled: Gofraid mac Fergusa and 'the Annals of the Four Masters', *Mediaeval Scandinavia* 15 (2005), 199–213.

more 'farmer republics' in which a number of small-scale chieftains constantly competed for clients. The kings of the Irish Sea zone may have gradually established a loose sort of hegemony over them as did the kings of Norway over Iceland and Jämtland, and as the kings of the Svear did over provinces like Gotland and Värmland. Presumably the *Suðreyjar* lay on the trade route between Scandinavia and Ireland and the leading men of this region would have become thegns of the rulers in Man and Dublin, or in Orkney, when they travelled into their kingdoms to engage in commerce. Gradually such king's men would have formed a core of support which would have encouraged the kings to claim sovereignty over their homelands.

It seems likely that each island or group of small islands would have had its own assembly or *þingr*, but it is less clear whether we should imagine there to have been a single *alþingr* or 'general assembly' for the Isles, or whether intermediate sized groupings, such as the Outer Isles, and the Islay group were the largest functional units. Unfortunately, none of these assembly sites have so far been identified.

THE EARLDOM OF ORKNEY

A particularly thorny problem lies in the early history and origins of the earldom of Orkney. In the twelfth century, this earldom operated as a semi-autonomous unit of the Norwegian kingdom, although it was under increasing pressure from Scottish kings to switch allegiance. The earliest contemporary reference to the earldom comes in the Irish chronicles' notice of the dead at the battle of Clontarf, near Dublin:

> *AU* 1014.2 . . . and of the Gaill there fell there Dubgall son of Amlaíb, Siucraid son of Loduir, jarl of *Innsi Orc*, and Gilla Ciaráin son of Glúniairn, *rígdamna* of the Gaill, and Oittir the Black and Suartgair and Donnchad son of Erulb and Griséne and Luimne and Amlaíb son of Lagman and Brotor and six thousand who were slain or drowned.

Siucraid son of Loduir is the man who appears in Icelandic literature as Sigurðr *digri* Hlöðvisson. Tracing the history of the Orkney earldom beyond this relies almost entirely upon the saga literature and there are good reasons for distrusting this, in detail at least. Even the saga literature does not tell of the Scandinavian colonisation of the islands since it claims that the earldom was established by Haraldr *hárfagri* to pacify the

Vikings who were raiding Norway from Orkney. Probably the earliest account that survives of the foundation of the earldom is in the *Historia Norvegiae*. This is a Latin history, probably written in Norway in the third quarter of the twelfth century. In contrast to the saga literature this account does link the coming of the comital family with the conquest of the Picts. It contains the following passage:

> In the days of Harald Long-hair, king, that is, of Norway, certain pirates descended from the stock of that most robust *princeps* Rog[n]wald, with a great fleet crossing the Solund Sea [between Norway and Scotland] totally destroyed these people [*Peti* – 'Picts'] after stripping them of their long established dwellings and made the islands subject to themselves. When they had gained safety and security by building winter residences, they went off in summer on tyrannical expeditions against the English and the Scots and sometimes the Irish. The result was that in England they brought Northumbria, in Scotland Caithness and in Ireland Dublin and all the other maritime towns under their dominion. One of this band, Rodulf – known to his friends as Göngu Hrólfr, because he was unable to ride on horseback owing to his enormous physical size and therefore always walked[37] – captured the city of Rouen in Normandy . . . Now this Rodulf, after acquiring control of that domain, married the widow of the deceased count. By her he sired William Longsword, the father of Richard, who in turn produced a son of the same name. This younger Richard had a son, Robert, who was father to William the Bastard, who conquered the English.[38]

If we were to try and link this account into the narrative derived from contemporary Insular sources, without reference to the Icelandic material, it would be tempting to identify the 'most robust *princeps*' Rögnvaldr with Ragnall grandson of Ímar who restored Scandinavian fortunes in the Irish Sea region, establishing his dynasty in Dublin and conquering Northumbria, before dying in 921 (see Chapter 4). The chronological markers here would be Ragnall's *floruit* in the Insular sources (914–21),

---

[37] *Göngu Hrólfr* means, literally 'walking Hrólfr'.
[38] I. Ekrem and L. B. Mortensen, eds, and P. Fisher, tr., *Historia Norwegie* (Copenhagen, 2003), 67. I have made minor emendations to Fisher's translation. A translation of this fascinating text can also be found in C. Phelpstead, ed., and D. Kunin, tr., *A History of Norway and the Passion and Miracles of the Holy Óláfr* (London, 2001).

Harald's death (c. 935) and the career of Rollo, the first Norman ruler of Rouen and father of William Longsword, who is obviously the prototype for Göngu Hrólf, and who died c. 928. There are also verbal echoes between this account which talks of the kindred of Rognwald advancing *cum magna classe* – 'with a great fleet' – and *Historia de Sancto Cuthberto* which describes how *Regenwaldus rex uenit cum magna multitudine nauium* – 'King Ragnall came with a great multitude of ships'. No Insular source mentions the grandsons of Ímar having dominion in Orkney, but then they do not mention Orkney at all in this period. The link with Normandy is also absent from either British or Continental sources (which give Rollo a vague Danish origin) but it is consistently maintained by all Scandinavian accounts.[39]

When we turn to the Icelandic literature, however, an alternative identification is offered for Rögnvaldr. In a variety of sources, including both *Landnámabók* and *Orkneyinga saga*, the earls of Orkney and the Normans are traced back to Rögnvaldr Mœrajarl who, according to Snorri Sturluson's *Heimskringla* and *Orkneyinga saga* had been made ruler of North Mæri and Romsdal by King Haraldr.[40] Rögnvaldr Mœrajarl's most important place in the Icelandic material was as the father of the Icelandic settler Hrollaug[41] who established a great chieftaincy at Siða in the southeast of the island and who was an ancestor of both the powerful *Siðumenn* kindred and, significantly, of Snorri Sturluson's mother Guðný. One possibility is that Icelandic writers encountering Insular traditions of Ragnall grandson of Ímar simply equated him with their own ancestor figure in order to bask in his reflected glory. There are, however, other links between these two characters. First, according to the Icelandic material, Rögnvaldr was the son of Eysteinn *glumra* who was himself the son of Ívarr Upplendingajarl. This makes Rögnvaldr jarl a grandson of an Ívarr, just like Ragnall. Secondly, Snorri tells us that Rögnvaldr jarl was given Orkney by King Haraldr as compensation after his son Ívarr was slain in battle during an expedition to Scotland. Here we are reminded that, prior to Ragnall's appearance in 914, we had last heard of a grandson of Ímar

---

[39] A related story, but different in almost all its details, save the foundation of Normandy, can be found in the Cambro-Latin text *Vita Griffini Filii Conani*, edited and translated by Paul Russell (Cardiff, 2005), at 54–7.

[40] The most accessible version of *Heimskringla* is Lee M. Hollander, tr., *Heimskringla, History of the Kings of Norway* (Austin, 1977). The critical edition of the text is Bjarni Aealbjarnarson, ed., *Heimskringla* (Reykjavík, 1941–51), three vols.

[41] It has always struck me that Hrollaug would be the best guess for a genuine Norse name lying behind the Franco-Latin 'Rollo'. Perhaps medieval Icelanders were also struck by this similarity.

when Ímar grandson of Ímar was slain in battle by the men of Fortriu in 904.[42] All this could be coincidence but it seems quite likely that the Icelandic account has been reconstructed, not very accurately, on the basis of traditions, and perhaps even Irish or English textual accounts, of the exploits of the grandsons of Ímar in the early tenth century. If this is true it tells us a great deal about how the saga traditions were developed but, perhaps, not very much about early tenth-century Orkney.

Yet another curious element in the early history of Orkney is the patronymic of Earl Sigurðr *digri* who was slain at Clontarf and who has walk-on parts in a number of sagas. His father's name is consistently given as Hlöðvir by the Icelandic sources and the form 'Loduir' appearing in the *Annals of Ulster* would seem to confirm that this is correct. This is a curious name. Sigurð's father would appear to have been the only Norseman to have borne this name yet it is not unknown elsewhere in Norse literature. 'Hlöðvir' is the form consistently used by Icelandic writers to represent the Continental name which we conventionally represent with the modern French form 'Louis'. This name, which came from an original early Germanic *Chlodowecas, gives the modern personal names Ludwig, Louis and Lewis. In twelfth-century Latin texts the name, when used for French kings, for example, was spelled *Ludouicus*, but this was an archaic spelling and in Old French the 'c' was already unvoiced, the compositional vowel 'o' syncopated and the medial 'd' lenited. In simple terms the name would have been pronounced something like /Luðwih/. This brings us very close to the Norse form, for the final 'r' of Hlöðvir is simply a nominative case ending which would normally not be present (the reader will have noted above that I have written 'Sigurðr' but 'Sigurð's'; the 'r' is only present in uninflected forms). Had the common Germanic form of the name descended directly into Icelandic we should not have expected the 'c' (*ludouic*) to disappear. As in German 'Ludwig', it would have remained a hard consonant. What this shows is that the form Hlöðvir actually derives from the French name which we write 'Louis' and not from its Scandinavian or German cognates. Since this name is otherwise unattested among Norsemen it is very suggestive of a specific link between Sigurð's father and France.

A further point worth considering is the nature of the Orkney earldom. The earls, in the twelfth century at least, ruled Orkney, Shetland and Caithness (which included Sutherland) and they seem to have felt that they had some claim to overlordship in at least parts of the Western Isles. This is a vast area, comparable in size to kingdoms elsewhere. The

[42] *AU* 904.4. This episode has been discussed in detail in Chapter 4 above.

earls certainly appear to have been richer than the kings of the Isles by that time. Why was their domain simply an earldom? The Scandinavian term *jarl*, from which modern English 'earl' derives, meant specifically a deputy to a king. It first appears not in a Scandinavian source but in the Irish chronicles where, in the ninth century, the killing is recorded of *Tomrair erell, tanise righ Laithlinne* – 'Thórir jarl, deputy of the king of Laithlind'.[43] Usually the term seems to have been used for a king's man holding vice-regal authority over a territory with its own traditional ethnic or regnal identity. Thus, Cnut ruled formerly independent kingdoms within the kingdom of the English, like Wessex, Mercia and Northumbria, through earls and when in England appointed an earl over Denmark and one over Norway. Earls were rarely, if ever, of royal blood. Royal princes granted vice-regal status usually took the kingly title, as, towards the end of his reign, Cnut's sons did in Norway (Sveinn) and Denmark (Harðacnut). When, in 1262, the Icelanders fully recognised the sovereignty of the Norwegian king he appointed one of their chieftains, Gizur Thorvaldsson, to the office of earl. Generally speaking, earls were supposed to gather tribute, administer justice and lead the provincial levies on behalf of the king. There is some suggestion that the title earl might sometimes be given to a nobleman who acted as regent or 'prime minister' with authority throughout the kingdom. In the second half of the twelfth century Birgir jarl in Sweden and Erling Skakke in Norway seem to have held this kind of earldom. Earldoms were, therefore, territories which either had been, or were imagined to have been, independent lands with their own established communities and the earls replaced local kings or representative officers such as law-speakers or lawmen. Whereas the authority of his predecessors ascended to them from the community the earl's authority descended to him from the king.

Both Snorri, in *Heimskringla*, and the author of *Orkneyinga saga* (who may not be independent of one another), credited the establishment of the earldom of Orkney to King Haraldr *hárfagri*. He was believed to have ruled for about seventy years in the period running up to c. 935. Haraldr was also given credit for uniting Norway and for expelling the Norwegian chieftains who were to establish the colonies in Iceland and the Insular world, and to found the duchy of Normandy. Modern scholars think that Harald's achievements may have been more limited and that his rule may well have been confined to western Norway, the lands which by the central middle ages accepted the *Gulatingslag*, with its general assembly on the island of Gula near modern Bergen. The *Gulatingslag* stretched

---

[43] *AU* 848.5.

from Egðerness, the southernmost point of Norway, to Staðir, a little south of the modern city of Ålesund. Even if it were somewhat more extensive than this, perhaps penetrating Trønderlag to the north, it was far more limited than the Icelanders claimed.[44] It is also unlikely that a king who reigned until c. 935 could really have been responsible for expelling men who settled in Iceland in about 870. Clearly Haraldr, like Cinaed son of Alpín, having become the apical figure of a dynasty, was credited with all the subsequent achievements and aspirations of that dynasty. When compared with Harald's original Westland kingdom, the Orkney earldom was a sizeable territory of significant agricultural capacity. The likelihood that Haraldr really did establish the earldom is small. Indeed, in his earlier work *Óláfs saga ins helga*, which was later incorporated into *Heimskringla*, Snorri gave a different account of how Orkney came under the Norwegian kings:

> So it is said, that in the days of Haraldr *hárgfagri*, king of Norway, Orkney was settled. Before that it was a lair of pirates. Sigurðr was the name of the first earl in Orkney, he was the son of Eysteinn *glumru* and the brother of Rögnvaldr Mœrajarl, then, after Sigurðr, his son Guþormr for one year. After him Torf-Einarr took the earldom, Earl Rögnvald's son, and he was earl for a long time and a powerful man. Hálfdan *háleggr*, son to Haraldr *hárfagri*, went against Einarr and drove him away from Orkney. Then Einarr returned and slew Hálfdan, on Ronaldsay. After that King Haraldr went with an army to Orkney. Einarr fled then, up into Scotland. King Haraldr ordered the Orcadians to swear away all their *óðöl* rights.[45] After that the king and the earl made peace and the earl became his man and took the land as a fief from him, but did not have to pay tax for it because it was much harried. The earl paid the king sixty gold marks.[46] Then the king harried in Scotland as is told in *Glymdrápu*.[47] After Torf-Einar, his sons ruled over the land: Arnkell, Erlendr, and Thorfinnr *hausakljúfr*. In their days Eiríkr Blood-Axe came from Norway and the earls were in vassalage to him. Arnkell and Erlendr fell in battle and Thorfinnr ruled the land and grew old. His sons were Arnfiðr,

[44] Claus Krag, 'The early unification of Norway', in K. Helle, ed., *The Cambridge History of Scandinavia* (Cambridge, 2003), pp. 184–201.

[45] ON *Óðöl* was used to denote both inalienable inherited property and the rights that went with it.

[46] Presumably as wergild for his son.

[47] A poem.

Hávarðr, Hlöðvir, Ljótr and Skúli. Their mother was Grélöð, the daughter of Dungaðr [Donnchad or Dúnchad], earl of Caithness.[48] Her mother was Gróa, the daughter of Thorsteinn the Red. Towards the end of Earl Thorfinn's days Blood-Axe's sons came from Norway, when they fled before earl Hákon. They were a great burden on Orkney. Earl Thorfinnr died of sickness. After them his sons ruled and there is a great deal said about them. Of them Hlöðvir lived the longest and ruled the land undivided. His son was Sigurðr *digri*, who took the earldom after him. He was powerful and a great warrior.[49]

An interesting feature of this story is the joint rule of brothers on two occasions. A real earldom, a vice-regal ministry, should not have been divided in this way. Indeed, here it looks very much as if Orkney itself is being treated as *óðöl*: a free inheritance than can be divided like any landed property. In the twelfth century the kingdom of Norway was several times shared in this way between brothers but it was rarely a happy arrangement. It seems at least in part to have been the product of the kingdom being a recently constructed composite with the different provinces each claiming the right to elect their own king. This recalls similar arrangements in tenth-century England. It is possible that each island in Orkney thought of itself as a community in this way but it seems unlikely given the physical centrality and wealth of Mainland. If we try and explain this as a constructed narrative explaining something about the nature of Orkney in the later twelfth or early thirteenth centuries then we might consider the possibility that we are being presented with an origin legend. Orkney and Shetland had a class of leading men with whom the earls needed to consult on matters of importance. They were known as the *gæðingar*. One possibility is that the kindreds which supplied the *gæðingar* claimed to be a nobility of descent as well as one of property and that these kindreds were presented as kinsmen of the earls. If that were the case the brothers of Earl Hlöðvir may represent the apical figures of such kindreds attached to the earls' pedigree at a convenient point. This brings us to the question of the *óðöl* rights of the Orcadians. In the passage above from *Óláfs saga hins helga* we are told that the Orcadians lost their rights in the

[48] Dungaðr, certainly, and Grélöð, probably, are representations of Gaelic names. If this information were reliable then it would imply that Caithness was under Gaelic rule in the mid-tenth century. This would seem to imply a Gaelic phase between the Pictish and the Norse.

[49] Bjarni Aðalbjarnarson, ed., *Heimskringla* (Reykjavík, 1941–51), II, 158–9 (my translation).

days of Torf-Einarr. In *Orkneyinga saga* we are told the same story with the additional information that they were granted back to the farmers by Earl Sigurðr Hlöðvisson. Thus, the 'modern constitution' of Orkney dated to the days of Earl Sigurðr (†1014), the first generation subsequent to the, hypothetical, apical brethren.

The complete absence of contemporary textual references to the north in the key period between the mid-ninth and the late tenth centuries will always limit our ability to provide answers to these questions. This said one might at least offer an alternative hypothesis. Adam of Bremen, writing in the 1070s, ascribes the conquest of Orkney to Haraldr *harðraði*, king of Norway (c. 1043–66), and it has been argued that many of Haraldr *hárfagri*'s attributes may have been projected back from his later name-sake.[50] Let us, for a moment, consider the possibility that the first histor-ically attested earl, Sigurðr *digri*, was in fact the first earl? He died in 1014 but was succeeded by a number of adult sons and had adult grandsons by the 1030s. He may well have been an active leader since the 980s. In the extract just cited we are told that Orkney was oppressed by the sons of Erik Blood-Axe when they were driven from Norway by Earl Hákon. Hákon Sigurðsson, the Hlaðajarl, was not operating on his own. He acted in alliance with the Danish king Haraldr Blue-tooth (c. 958–87). This king is best known for the monument he erected at Jelling in Jutland which incorporates the following runic inscription:

> King Haraldr commanded this monument to be made in memory of Gorm, his father and in memory of Thorvi, his mother – that Haraldr who won the whole of Denmark for himself and Norway and made the Danes Christian.[51]

Haraldr Blue-tooth was the grandfather of Cnut and in many ways the architect of the Danish kingdom. He maintained his independence from an expanding German kingdom through a mixture of diplomacy and warfare and as part of this process adopted Christianity. He also expanded

---

[50] Indeed, even the epithet *hárfagri* may have originally belonged to the eleventh-century king. See J. Jesch, 'Norse historical traditions and the *Historia Gruffud vab Kenan*', in K. L. Maund, ed., *Gruffudd ap Cynan: A Collaborative Biography* (Woodbridge, 1996), 117–48, and P. H. Sawyer, 'Harald Fairhair and the British Isles', in R. Boyer, ed., *Les Vikings et leur civilisation: problèmes actuels* (Paris, 1976), 105–9. Haraldr *harðraði* was, of course, a contemporary of the Orkney earl Rögnvaldr Brusason who is said to have obtained his inheritance with Norwegian aid.

[51] B. Sawyer, *The Viking-Age Rune-Stones: Custom and Commemoration in Early Medieval Scandinavia* (Oxford, 2000), 158–66.

his *imperium* in Scandinavia and it was he who was responsible for expelling the Eiríkssons in c. 970, the point at which they are supposed to have fled to Orkney. He then placed the native magnate Hákon Sigurðsson, from Trønderlag, as earl over all of Norway north of Egðerness. In the east he seems to have been happy to rule through a number of local kinglets. Haraldr also expanded his influence into the Baltic and seems to have established control over the town of Wolin, a sort of Polish equivalent of Dublin known to the Scandinavians as Jómsborg, placing it under an earl named Sigvaldi. This Haraldr of Denmark was an expansionist ruler who exercised his authority through semi-regal earls. He may well be a prime candidate for the founder of the earldom of Orkney. It should perhaps be noted, in this light, that it is at the every end of his reign, in 986, that we first hear of *Danair* in the Irish annals.[52] According to Adam of Bremen Harald's reign ended in rebellion and exile: perhaps the *Danair* who sacked Iona in 986 were dogs let off the leash. Certainly they seem to have come from the north, the direction of Orkney.

To summarise. The alternative hypothesis put forward here to explain the appearance of the earldom of Orkney is that it was a creation of the Danish empire of Haraldr Bluetooth. Under this hypothesis, as in the *Orkneyinga saga*, the first earl was named Sigurðr and received his earldom from a king called Haraldr, but the event took place c. 980 rather than c. 880 and Haraldr was a Dane and not a Norwegian. Before this there may have been no central authority on Orkney, which might explain the ease with which Eiríkr, and later his sons, were said to have been able to impose themselves. Orkney, as I have suggested for the Western Isles, may, like Iceland and the forest provinces of Sweden, have been a land where small-scale chieftains competed for influence among farmer clients. Individuals from the islands may have served as king's men at the courts of kings in Norway, the Irish Sea or further afield, but any hegemony exercised by rulers may have been fleeting. After the death of Cnut the earldom eventually passed into the hegemony of the Norwegian king Haraldr *harðraði* with whose predecessors, Óláfr Tryggvason (c. 995–9) and Óláfr Haraldsson (c. 1016–30), some of the earls may have flirted (particularly during the disputed succession following Earl Sigurð's death at Clontarf). If there were no earls in Orkney before Sigurð's time it might help to explain the islands' low profile in the annals since these, for the most part, record only the deaths of great men.

[52] *AU* 986.2, 986.3, 987.1 and 987.3.

EARL THORFINNR

All the twelfth-century and later earls of Orkney claimed descent from Sigurðr *digri*'s son Thorfinnr. His reign seems to have been the time at which a bishopric was established in the islands, and *Orkneyinga saga* has a detailed and generally credible (if not always perfect) narrative after his time. His lengthy period of rule probably marked the effective historical horizon for Orcadians of the twelfth and thirteenth centuries. According to the saga he was the youngest of Sigurð's sons and his grandfather was a Scottish king named Melkólmr. This may have been either Mael Coluim son of Cinaed (1005–34) or the Moravian Mael Coluim son of Mael Brigte (1020–9) or it may be that, as elsewhere in Icelandic literature, Melkólmr was used as a stereotypical Scottish royal name. Like Hlöðvir and the earlier Thorfinnr *hausakljúfr*, we are told, Thorfinnr Sigurðsson started out as one of a group of brothers and ended up as the sole survivor. In his case, however, we are told of the conflict between him and his kinsmen in detail.

Unfortunately, the detail is vague on hard facts and, as we saw in Chapter 6, hard to coordinate with our other sources. The saga claims that Thorfinnr died in the later days of Haraldr *harðráði* and, as I have suggested above, his death may have provoked the expedition of Harald's son Mágnus into the west in 1058. Other than that his conflict with his nephew Rögnvaldr seems to have taken place during the reign of Magnus the Good in Norway (c. 1034–47) and he is said to have gone on pilgrimage to Rome following the death of Rögnvaldr. Prior to this conflict he also fought at least one battle in Orkney, near Deerness, against a rival called Karl Hundason, whom the saga identifies as a Scottish king. At this point, however, as pointed out in the previous chapter, the saga writer seems to be entirely dependent upon the poem *þorfinnsdrápa*, which does not

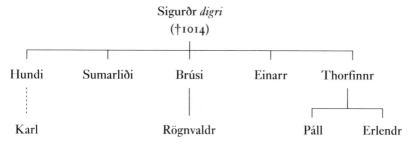

Table 7.3. Thorfinnr the Mighty and his kinsmen (the dotted line marks a hypothetical link)

identify Karl as a king of Scots. It is more likely that he was another nephew, the son of Thorfinn's eldest brother, Hundi, whom the saga claims was taken to Norway as a hostage by Óláfr Tryggvason and died there.

THE CONVERSION OF SCANDINAVIAN SCOTLAND

There is no contemporary account of the conversion of Scandinavian Scotland from Norse paganism to Christianity. Among the sagas *Fagrskinna* attributes the conversion of Orkney and Shetland to Óláfr Tryggvason and both *Heimskringla* and *Orkneyinga saga* expand this simple statement into a story in which Óláfr surprises Sigurðr *digri* and forces him to accept baptism. Otherwise we have to rely upon silence and the archaeological evidence. As we have seen accompanied burials, which are usually assumed to indicate pagan or recently converted communities, disappear from Scotland in the middle of the tenth century and not long after this, in the Western Isles at least, some explicitly Christian sculpture begins to appear.[53] The cross slab from Cille Bharra (Barra), dated on art historical grounds to c. 1000 and related to monuments from the Isle of Man, is explicitly Norse as it bears a runic inscription reading:

After Thorgerðr, Steinar's daughter, this cross was raised.

At Iona another runic inscription, on an Irish-style grave slab, reads:

Kali Olivsson laid this stone over his brother Fugl.

Other sculpture with stylistically Scandinavian features appears in the inner Hebrides, the Outer Clyde and Galloway. The Northern Isles are not so closely linked with the Manx tradition but do have a number of eleventh-century hogback grave markers. This type of monument seems to have its origins in the Cumbrian kingdom with centres at Penrith in Cumberland, and at Govan on the Clyde in the tenth century. The four Orkney examples and the single example from Shetland, like those in southeast Scotland, are thus slightly later and it is tempting to see them as the grave markers of men who had been in service with the kings of the Cumbrians.

---

[53] For a survey of pagan burials see J. Graham Campbell and C. Batey, *Vikings in Scotland: an Archaeological Survey* (Edinburgh, 1998), 113–54, sculpture is discussed at 248–52.

The absence of dramatic conversion narratives may reflect the fact that the Scandinavians in the Insular world were always a minority surrounded by richer Christian polities. Many individuals may have converted on entering the service of Christian kings in England, Denmark or the Celtic-speaking world, and mixed marriages and political submissions would probably have required baptism as a *sine qua non*. The absence in much of Scotland of long established dynasties and ritual landscapes may have meant that major cult centres associated with political and ethnic identity, such as those described by Thietmar of Merseburg at Leire in Denmark and Adam of Bremen at Uppsala in Svealand never developed.[54] An intricate relationship between kingship and pagan ritual seems to have existed in ancient Scandinavia. Swedish kings in particular seem to have had great difficulty in persuading their people to abandon such rituals even after they had converted and more than one seems to have been expelled from the kingdom on this account. In dispersed communities with little overt hierarchy, as in the Scottish islands, pagan ritual may have been largely domestic and not dissimilar from the many folkloric practices which, while not approved of by the Church, were rife throughout medieval Christendom. Scandinavian Scotland slipped, without drama, into Christendom.

[54] D. A. Warner, tr., *Ottonian Germany: The Chronicon of Thietmar of Merseburg* (Manchester, 2001), 80, and F. J. Tschan, tr., *Adam of Bremen: A History of the Archbishops of Hamburg-Bremen* (New York, 2002), 207–8.

CHAPTER 8

Pictavia to Albania

SCOTLAND (750–1050): CONTINUITY AND CHANGE

Having reached the end of our chronological survey it remains to review what had changed in Scotland between the mid-eighth and the mid-eleventh centuries. In many ways, particularly in the area of daily life, little had changed. There were still no towns and the vast majority of the population lived in scattered dwellings or small hamlets and engaged in a mixture of arable and pastoral farming. Coinage was still not produced in the country, nor widely circulated, although in the areas of Scandinavian settlement coin from England, and further afield, appears in the archaeological record with increasing frequency. Northern Britain was still fundamentally rural and occupied by kin-based societies.

Changes had occurred, however. North of the Forth something had happened to the great church-settlements of the eighth and ninth centuries. In the areas of most intense Scandinavian settlement, such as the Northern Isles, we can be in no doubt that the majority of such sites were abandoned; perhaps destroyed by the invaders, perhaps simply decaying through lack of support from a non-Christian local community. In much of the country, however, such an explanation will not do. Many of the churches survived, although some, as we have seen, moved location, generally inland. None the less, they seem to have had access to fewer resources. The high-quality religious sculpture that defines the later Pictish period (c. 700–900) disappears and for most of the tenth and eleventh centuries little sculpture seems to have been produced and what survives is generally of lower quality. Some sites, which the Pictish sculpture would suggest were major churches in the ninth century, such as Meigle and St Vigeans all but disappear from the record. At others, such as St Andrews, it seemed necessary for twelfth-century rulers to re-grant the original endowments.[1]

Not unconnected to this transformation in the fortunes of ecclesiastical centres seems to have been the apparent change in character of royal sites. The chronology of this change is not entirely clear but the fortified citadels, which were such a marked feature of the early Christian period, sites like Dunadd, Dundurn and Burghead may have been abandoned. What little evidence we have suggests that the most important royal sites came to be located in low-lying land and were often associated with major churches. The *Chronicle of the Kings of Alba* links both the sons of Alpín with Forteviot in Strathearn and an early version of the St Andrews origin legend seems to have been composed at the royal *villa* of King Wrad at Meigle.[2] An account of the foundation of Cennrígmonaid (St Andrews), written c. 1120, also makes it clear that there was a royal *aula*, or hall, located there.[3] The increasingly close association of kingship with the Church in the course of the period is probably reflected in the imagery associated with the Biblical king David which appears so frequently in later Pictish sculpture. It may be the case, however, that as the Viking Age progressed some, at least, of these *Klosterpfalzen*, or 'monastic palaces', became increasingly secular with resources redirected towards royal rather than religious projects.

The precise fate of the Pictish church-settlements is far from clear but it is paralleled across the Insular world. Writing of the Norman conqueror Robert fitzHamon's appropriation of the ancient south Welsh monasteries of Llancarfan and Llantwit Major (Llanilltud Fawr) in order to endow the new reformed monastic foundations at Gloucester and Tewkesbury, respectively in the years around 1100, Christopher Brooke has claimed that 'it is reasonably clear that there was nothing in these [Welsh] monastic houses which the Normans (or anyone else) would have recognised as regular or monastic'.[4] Much the same argument might be

---

[1] I am thinking here particularly of Alexander I's endowment of St Andrews recorded in the register of St Andrews priory. This is published, without translation, by W. F. Skene in *Chronicle of the Picts and Scots* (Edinburgh, 1867), 183–93. A new edition, with translation, is being prepared by Simon Taylor and Dauvit Broun. Alexander's endeavours in this field are discussed by Kenneth Veitch in ' "Replanting Paradise": Alexander I and the reform of religious life in Scotland', *Innes Review* 52 (2001), 136–66.

[2] Skene, *Picts and Scots* at 188.

[3] M. O. Anderson, *Kings and Kingship in Early Scotland* (Edinburgh, 1973), 260.

[4] C. L. N. Brooke, 'The archbishops of St David's, Llandaff and Caerleon-on-Usk', in N. K. Chadwick, ed., *Studies in the Early British Church* (Cambridge, 1958), 201–42, at 223.

applied in Scotland. When King William founded Arbroath Abbey, dedicated to Thomas Becket and staffed by Tironensian monks in the late 1170s, the core endowment of 'Aberbrothoc (Arbroath) and all its shire' was probably the land originally associated with St Vigeans. Indeed, the name Aberbrothoc was almost certainly originally applied to the church-settlement at St Vigeans and the church there was included in William's grant to the monks of Tiron.[5] Although Brooke's interpretation of these sorts of grants is quite typical of modern historians we must be wary of the danger that the language of the twelfth-century reformers might blind us to contrary evidence. Llancarfan, the ancient church granted to Gloucester Abbey, produced in the late eleventh and early twelfth centuries, two first-class scholars, Llifris and Caradog, capable of writing major works of hagiography.[6] These writers also tell us that in their own day Llancarfan possessed both a bell and a gospel book said to have been produced by the sixth-century St Gildas.[7] It is unlikely that these relics really did date back to the sixth century but it is very likely that they had survived from the eighth or ninth century, the golden age of Insular art when most of the sculpture at places like Meigle and St Vigeans was also produced. If Llancarfan had been able to produce educated and well-read men like Llifris and Caradog, and had retained possession of valuable relics, like the Book and Bell of Gildas, then it is hard to believe that it was not a thriving ecclesiastical establishment.

In fact, what seems to have happened in Wales, Ireland and much of Scotland is that within the major church-settlements a distinction had come to be drawn between the community as a whole and the hard-line ascetics, known in Gaelic as the *Céli Dé* or 'Friends of God'. The *Céli Dé* practised extreme abstinence and their presence in small numbers (usually twelve monks and an abbot, it would seem, reflecting Christ and the apostles) at many major churches may have legitimised the relaxation of monastic standards for many of the other members of the community.[8]

[5] The charter announcing the foundation is printed in G. W. S. Barrow, *Regesta Regum Scottorum II: The Acts of William I, King of Scots, 1165–1214* (Edinburgh, 1971), 250–2. I am grateful to Simon Taylor for discussing the relationship between St Vigeans and Aberbrothoc with me.

[6] For Llifris and Caradog see Brooke, 'Archbishops', and A. W. Wade-Evans, ed., *Vitae Sanctorum Britanniae et Genealogiae* (Cardiff, 1944).

[7] Llifris mentions the bell in his 'Life of St Cadoc', Wade-Evans, *VSB*, at 84–7, Caradog mentions the gospel book in his 'Life of Gildas', printed with translation in Hugh Williams, *Two Lives of Gildas* (London, 1899 and Felinfach, 1990), at 95–7.

[8] A brief but very perceptive summary of the values of the *Céli Dé* can be found in T. O'Loughlin, *Celtic Theology: Humanity, World and God in Early Irish Writings* (London, 2000), 178–80, for a longer exposition see P. O'Dwyer, *Céli Dé: Spiritual*

Because the *Céli Dé* eschewed the world, many of the office holders within these communities, those who had to deal with the world, were not members of the *Céli Dé* cell and did not observe strict vows. Often a single family seems to have dominated a particular church (Llifris of Llancarfan, for example, was the son of the local bishop) giving the appearance of hereditary office-bearing. When the reform-minded clergy arrived in the eleventh and twelfth centuries they failed to understand the nature of these institutions and observed instead two separated communities, one pious but apparently poor and excluded from power, and another, apparently made up of laymen enjoying the fruits of the church estates. From a native perspective these two bodies would probably have seen themselves as two parts of a single community maintaining one another symbiotically. The apparent laymen were, in fact, clergy living according to the rules of their tradition.[9] This clash of perspectives is not really a concern for our period, but much of what we know about the Church of the tenth and eleventh centuries is gleaned from texts written by the Continental reformers of the twelfth and we must be wary of this.

Whereas in Ireland the *Céli Dé* seem always to have remained a minority movement, in Scotland, where they have become known as 'Culdees' (a spelling not in evidence in the middle ages), they appear by the twelfth century to have become ubiquitous. To some extent this is due to the failure of most of our sources to recognise the existence of the communities, or those portions of communities, which did not adhere to strict monastic standards, but such an explanation may not in itself be sufficient. Thomas Clancy has argued that the prominent role in the *Céli Dé* movement of Diarmait, abbot of Iona from 814 to some point in the 830s, may perhaps have led to, or reflected, a greater commitment to the movement amongst the Columban clergy.[10] This may be a contributing factor but it is hard to believe that the Albanian Church was entirely

Reform in Ireland, 750–900 (Dublin, 1981). Many of the original texts relating to the *Céli Dé* are printed in W. Reeves, *The Culdees of the British Islands as they Appear in History with an Appendix of Evidences* (Dublin, 1864 and Felinfach, 1994).

[9] For a recent discussion of this clash of perspectives in Ireland see Martin Holland, 'Were early Irish church establishments under lay control?', in D. Bracken and D. Ó Riain-Raedel, eds, *Ireland and Europe in the Twelfth Century: Reform and Renewal* (Dublin, 2006), 128–42. Holland's arguments may as easily be applied to the Scottish evidence. For a good general account of the church in the Insular world in this period see Huw Pryce, 'The Christianization of Society', in W. Davies, ed., *From the Vikings to the Normans* (Oxford, 2003), 139–68.

[10] 'T. O. Clancy, 'Iona, Scotland and the Céli Dé', in B. E. Crawford, ed., *Scotland in Dark Age Britain* (St Andrews, 1996), 111–30.

Columban by affiliation, despite the undoubted importance of Columba and Dunkeld.[11]

If we consider the apparent popularity of the *Céli Dé* movement in Scotland alongside the evidence for the increased royal presence on ecclesiastical sites then a possible explanation for the transformation of the Church in Scotland which would be in line with the experience of other western European countries presents itself. Across much of the west the response to the attacks of Vikings, Magyars and Slavs was largely similar. Tenurial patterns that had developed to support ecclesiastical institutions (initially springing from the fact that churches accumulated land generation upon generation without the constant pressure to divide inheritance, and from the necessity for ecclesiastical institutions to have access to large quantities of goods, such as wine and oil, that were not locally available in all regions), were adapted to endow a military class answerable, first and foremost, to the king or provincial ruler rather than to their kindred. In many regions the beginnings of this policy of creating benefices or fiefs/feus seems to have lain in the actual appropriation of the lands of the great monasteries themselves. Kings had for a century and a half been engaged in developing a symbiotic relationship with the Church and this seems to have enabled the appropriation of Church property, for the defence of Christendom, to be achieved with little opposition.

In some areas, notably in Munster in the southwest of Ireland and in Germany, the response to the international crisis was for kings explicitly to adopt sacerdotal status. Elsewhere the doctrine of the three orders, those who pray, those who fight and those who labour was promoted in contradistinction to the older division of Christian society, much in evidence in Gaelic penitentials, which saw the fighters as completely beyond the pale; presumably because in the seventh and eighth centuries those whom they fought were also supposed to be Christians. Robin Fleming has argued that in the south of England Alfred the Great and his successors appropriated monastic lands to endow a military class and that even as late as the Domesday survey of the 1080s much, if not most, of the land in royal and comital hands could be shown to have been previously granted to churches in the period leading up to the Viking Age.[12] This phenomenon was certainly not confined to the West Saxon *imperium*. In 980 Emperor Otto II appointed his old tutor Gerbert of Aurillac to the

[11] Many Scottish churches were dedicated to saints who, while Irish, were not Columban; for example, Brigit of Kildare (at Abernethy and the various Kilbrides) and Féchín of Fore ('St Vigean').

[12] R. Fleming, 'Monastic lands and England's defence in the Viking Age', *English Historical Review* 100 (1985), 247–65.

abbacy of that greatest of Gaelic foundations, the monastery of Bobbio in the Apennines. In receipt of royal patronage from the days of its founder, St Columbanus and his patron Queen Theudelinda in the early seventh century onwards Bobbio was, on parchment, one of the richest land-holders in Italy, but the rather unworldly intellectual, Gerbert, was hor-rified at what he found there on his arrival. Two letters written in the summer of 982 will serve to exemplify his situation:

Letter 9 from Bobbio, May–June 982.

> Likewise to the Same Otto,
> I prefer to carry joyful rather than sad news to the most serene ears of my lord. But, when I see my monks wasting away from hunger and suffering from nakedness, how can I keep silent? This evil might be endurable, however, if, at the same time, the hope for improved conditions here was not also being snatched away. The whole sanctuary of God has been stripped bare by some sort of documents which they call *libelli*; the money which was collected is nowhere to be found; the storehouses and granaries have been emptied, in the purses there is nothing. What, therefore, am I, a sinner, doing here? If it could be done at the pleasure of my lord, I would prefer to be the only one in need among the Franks rather than to be begging with so many in need among the Italians.[13]

Letter 19 from Bobbio, August–September 983.

> To Hugh the Chaplain,
> To his Hugh, from Gerbert, formerly a teacher. In proportion to the greatness of my mind my lord has enriched me with very extensive properties. For what part of Italy does not contain blessed Columbanus' possessions? This, indeed, our Caesar's generous benefice provided. But fortune decreed otherwise. For in proportion to the greatness of my mind, she has honoured me with enemies everywhere. For what part of Italy does not contain my enemies?
> My military strength is unequal to Italy's. The terms of peace are these: if, after being robbed, I am subservient, they

---

[13] H. P. Lattin, ed. & tr., *The Letters of Gerbert, with his Papal Privileges as Sylvester II* (New York, 1961), 49.

will cease from striking. An inflexible man, owning so much as a suit of clothes, they will pursue with swords.

When they are unable to strike with the sword, they assail him with the darts of words. The imperial majesty is despised, not only through me but also in its very self by their spoliation of God's sanctuary. Because I refuse to comply with the book-leases, executed under their special laws, I am called faithless, cruel, tyrannical. The scoundrels compare Caesar himself, the most superior of all men, to an ass.[14]

Gerbert, who became Pope Sylvester II, stands at the head of the reform movement that would ultimately result in the rise of the papal supremacy and of reformed orders such as the Cistercians who were to play such a major role in the transformation of Scotland in the twelfth century. As the last remaining pagan nations of Europe were pacified or transformed them-selves into full members of western Christendom, so church rulers and reformers turned to their ancient muniments and rediscovered the lands that had been appropriated during the crisis of the ninth and tenth cen-turies. The eleventh and twelfth centuries are thus characterised, wherever records survive, by complex court cases prosecuted to regain these lands or to receive compensation. In Scotland the absence of pre-twelfth-century charter material makes this process harder to trace but in at least one case, that of the *Cursus Apri* or Boar's Rake, at St Andrews we seem to see the record of a successful reclamation in an act of Alexander I which appears to grant to the Church lands which it had already received from Onuist son of Wrguist 300 years before.[15] Another classic example of this phenomenon may be seen at Forteviot. In the ninth century this was a leading *Klosterpfalz* of the Pictish kingdom. Its bounds seem to have been marked out by the crosses at Dupplin and Invermay and architectural fragments, including the splendid Forteviot arch now on display in the Royal Museum of Scotland, have been recovered from the site itself. The *Chronicle of the Kings of Alba* records the death of Cinaed son of Alpín there and Forteviot was also where Cinaed's brother Domnall met with the 'the Gaels and their king'. By the middle of the twelfth century, however, it has every appearance of being simply a royal *villa*. Then, in the 1170s, at about the same time as the foundation of Arbroath Abbey, King William granted the church at Forteviot to the Augustinian abbey at Stirling (Cambuskenneth), founded by David I. In return for this grant King William recovered the tenth of

---

[14]   Lattin, *Letters of Gerbert*, 57–8. Hugh was the Emperor Otto's chaplain.
[15]   Veitch, 'Replanting paradise'.

royal revenues from the burgh of Stirling, Stirlingshire and Calatria (a small shire in the region of Falkirk) with which the abbey had previously been endowed. The value of these teinds indicates the wealth associated with the church of Forteviot and that it, rather than the royal residence, had the first claim on the estate.[16] The Alpínid kings may have been happy to

Abernethy

Abernethy in Perthshire, close to the confluence of the Earn and the Tay, was clearly at one time one of the leading churches of the kingdom. Geoffrey Barrow has reconstructed its original territory which stretched from Exmagirdle in lower Strathearn to Coultra near Balmerino (Fife) taking all the lands between the Tay and the Ochil watershed. In the fifteenth century it was claimed that the bishops of Alba had been based at Abernethy before relocating to St Andrews. Today it remains one of only two places in Scotland where an Irish-style round tower (a bell tower) has been preserved. In 1072 it was the place chosen by Mael Coluim son of Donnchad for his submission to William the Bastard. A record of a land grant kept in St Andrews notes the names of some of the clerical personnel at Abernethy in the late eleventh century, Ness and Cormac sons of Mac Bethad and Mael Snechta son of Beólán, priests of Abernethy, Mael Brigte the altar priest and Tuathal and Augustín, priests of the Céli Dé and Berbead, rector of the school of Abernethy. This clearly indicates a thriving community and Thomas Clancy has suggested that it was here, in the third quarter of the eleventh century that the Gaelic translation of the ninth-century Cambro-Latin text *Historia Brittonum*, known as *Lebor Bretnach*, was made.[17] Yet we also know that the abbacy was at a date not much later than this held by a family closely associated with the *mormaír* of Fife and identified by the reformists as laymen. By the end of the twelfth century the 'lay-abbot' succumbed to the pressures of the reform movement and granted his own abbatial share of the revenues along with half the tithes and the advowson of the Church (the right to nominate its priests) to King William the Lion's new reformed monastery at Arbroath.

[16] N. Aitchison, *Forteviot: A Pictish and Scottish Royal Centre* (Stroud, 2006), 25–6. King William's charter is printed in G. W. S. Barrow, *Regesta Regum Scottorum II: The Acts of William I, King of Scots, 1165–1214* (Edinburgh, 1971), at 228.

[17] T. O. Clancy, 'Scotland, the "Nennian" recension of the *Historia Brittonum*, and the *Lebor Bretnach*', in S. Taylor, ed., *Kings, Clerics and Chronicles in Scotland, 500–1297* (Dublin, 2000), 87–107 at 100–2.

promote the *Céli Dé* and their reformist tendencies in return for greater freedom to exploit the temporal wealth of the churches of Albania for their own purposes.

PICTS AND SCOTS

Of course, the most obvious change in the political landscape of northern Britain in the period under discussion was the disappearance of the Picts and their replacement as the dominant people of the region by the Scots. As we have seen, no contemporary source describes the events surrounding this transformation, but they do seem fairly consistent in describing Cinaed son of Alpín's sons as rulers of the Picts (862–78) and his grandsons as rulers of the Scots (889–943). The appropriation of the term Alba to signify the Alpínid kingdom seems to coincide very closely with this change.[18] Without an explicit account of the end of the Picts we are forced to speculate. Later medieval writers focused on Cinaed son of Alpín because he was the common ancestor of all the tenth-century kings, but the chronology suggests that the key period was the problematic era between the death of Áed son of Cinaed (878) and the accession of Domnall son of Constantín (889), for which the Irish chronicles note no king of Picts or of Alba. It is to this period that the *Chronicle of the Kings of Alba* assigns the reign of Eochaid, grandson of Cinaed through his daughter, while all other versions of the Scottish king-list ascribe this period to the reign of Giric son of Dúngal, who does not appear to have belonged to the Alpínid dynasty.[19]

We seem, simultaneously, to be presented with evidence that suggests both, on the one hand, a Scottish conquest of Pictavia and, on the other, dynastic continuity through this period. A Scottish king-list compiled in the mid-twelfth century extends back through the Pictish king-list, suggesting that kings of that period saw themselves as heirs of the Pictish kings.[20] The link between Cinaed son of Alpín's alleged Dál Riatan ancestry and the idea that the kingship of Alba itself was a continuation of that of Dál Riata seems to have been fully formulated only in the late eleventh or twelfth centuries.[21] It is even possible that this revised stance was the

---

[18]   It first appears as the name for the kingdom in the *Annals of Ulster* under the year AD 900.

[19]   See Chapter 3 above.

[20]   See D. Broun, *The Irish Identity of the Kingdom of the Scots in the Twelfth and Thirteenth Centuries* (Woodbridge, 1999),168–74.

[21]   A list of the kings of Dál Riata was placed before a list of Cinaed son of Alpín and his successors in this king-list only as late as the reign of William (1165–1214), Broun,

work of partisans of Macbethad or Lulach whose claims to patrilineal kinship with the royal house were to be sought in Dál Riatan times.[22] Likewise, the major churches of the kingdom, such as St Andrews, Dunkeld and Abernethy, together with lesser churches such as Deer, Culross and Loch Leven, seem to have promoted the idea that they had a continuous history originating in Pictish times and their origin legends appear to regard the kingdom ruled by the Picts as the same kingdom as that ruled by the more recent kings. The idea, well known today, that there was a union of the Picts and Scots is a very late development, originating in the period after the Union of Scotland and England in 1707, a classic example of writing the past in the image of the present. The contemporary and near contemporary evidence would seem to suggest that the Pictish kingdom suffered a political takeover by a Gaelic-speaking group but retained its integrity – much as England remained England despite the Norman Conquest. Against this interpretation seems to the incontrovertible evidence that the Alpínid dynasty provided both the last Pictish and first Scottish kings.

One possible explanation for the political transformation of Pictavia into Albania would be to attribute a Scottish, that is to say Gaelic, conquest of Pictavia to Giric son of Dúngal. We have seen (in Chapter 3) that later versions of the king-list include the statement that Giric 'first gave liberty to the Scottish church, which, up to that time, had laboured under the customs and *mores* of the Picts', and this may bear witness to popular or ecclesiastical beliefs about his role. Although after his death, or expulsion, the Alpínid dynasty he had supplanted returned, it may be that the nature of his 'regime change' had been such that certain aspects of it were irreversible. We might compare the situation of Edward the Confessor who ruled the kingdom of the English from 1042 to 1066. Although Edward was the son of Æðelræd, a member of the West-Saxon dynasty, who had ruled the kingdom from 979 to 1014, and the brother of Æðelræd's successor Eadmund (1014–16), England had been conquered by Cnut in the intervening period and ruled by him and his sons for twenty-six years (1016–42). When Edward came to the throne, following the death without issue of Cnut's sons, he was not in a position to evict all of the Scandinavian office-holders and land-holders whom the previous regime had promoted, even had he wished to do so. Indeed, for the first nine years of his reign he even maintained the Scandinavian

---

144–64. Curiously a similar, though not identical linkage of Dál Riatan and Albanian king-lists had occurred in Ireland c. 1100, Broun, 153, n. 106.

[22] Broun, *The Irish Identity of the Kingdom of the Scots*, 173.

mercenary fleet that Cnut had established. Cnut's earls, men like Siward and Godwine, remained in power and the kingdom of Edward and his successor Harold II continued to be Anglo-Danish in character despite the demise of the Danish dynasty.[23] Although Giric's reign was considerably shorter than the period of Danish rule in England it is quite likely that Cinaed's grandsons may have spent their exile in Ireland where their aunt Mael Muire had been married to two kings of Tara in succession, Áed Findlaith (865–79) and Flann Sinna (879–916), and mother to a third, Niall Glúndub (916–19). If this was the case then Domnall and Constantín may have returned to Britain, having spent their childhood and teenage years in Ireland, culturally Gaelic themselves despite their Pictish heritage.[24] If the grandsons of Cinaed were to all intents and purposes Gaels but, nonetheless, heirs to the last Pictish kings, they may have been ideally suited to the task of reconciliation between Picts and Scots within the kingdom.

LANGUAGE AND CULTURE IN THE SCOTO-PICTISH KINGDOM

When we consider early medieval conquests and invasions one important issue is the linguistic outcome: in the long run is it the language of the conquerors or the conquered which prevails? Elite conquests, such as those of the Normans in southern Italy, England, Wales and Ireland did not lead to these places becoming French-speaking any more than the influx of French (largely Norman) nobility turned Scotland into a French-speaking land. Certainly the nobility maintained French as the language of court for a few generations, and loan-words from French entered the native languages, but before long they had adopted the local vernacular and it was this, albeit slightly modified, which survived.[25] It is easy to understand why this happens. In medieval societies without mass literacy or state education the bulk of the population simply had no access to the language of the nobility – they rarely met nobles and were certainly not in a position to demand language lessons from them. The nobility, on

[23] The standard account of Edward's reign and regime remains Frank Barlow's *Edward the Confessor* (London, 1970 and subsequent editions).

[24] To extend the comparison with Edward the Confessor, the situation envisaged for the Alpínids would be analogous to that which would have arisen had Edward spent his exile in Scandinavia (as his nephews did) rather than in France.

[25] In Scotland one can think of families like the Frasers and the Grants who, though of Norman stock, became quintessential Highlanders.

the other hand, were thinly scattered among the poor of society and many, if not most, of their servants, including nursery maids and kitchen staff, would have been speakers of the native language and well placed to pass it on. At the opposite end of the extreme we can think of other invasions in which the native language disappeared completely such as the Anglo-Saxon invasions of eastern Britain or the Slavic invasions of the Balkans. In both these cases the languages of the invaders replaced Latin and pre-Roman native languages. Such linguistic replacement is usually accompanied by a complete disruption of settlement patterns and other aspects of social organisation. We have seen that in parts of Scandinavian Scotland this latter form of linguistic replacement took place. Although in such cases the evidence for what precisely happened is usually pretty meagre, it is fairly clear that these kinds of invasions seem to have been carried out by peoples whose own society was less hierarchical and who did not possess the social infrastructure to produce either a gentry class or a literate elite capable of recording their actions.

In Albania, it seems, neither of these models fits precisely. The British dialects, which place-names and personal names suggest were widespread among the Picts, do not appear to have survived, certainly not into the modern era and probably not into the later middle ages. Instead it is widely believed that by the twelfth century all of the Scottish mainland between the Forth and the Oykel, together with substantial tracts south of the Forth, seems to have been inhabited almost exclusively by speakers of dialects of Gaelic, which the later medieval sources refer to as *lingua Scotica*. None the less, a considerable number of place-names survived this transformation; those containing the British element *Aber* meaning a river mouth (as opposed to Gaelic *Inver*) being most easily recognised. Examples include Aberfeldy, Abernethy, Abernyte, Aberdeen and Aberchalder. This component is also the second element in the place-name *Cupar*, in which British **cum* replaces the *a* of *aber*, giving the meaning 'confluence'. The most familiar Pictish British place-name element is the word *pett* which survives as the component *Pit-* in names like Pitgavenny, Pitsligo, Pitlochry and Pitlessie. This element is, however, found almost exclusively in combination with Gaelic second elements, suggesting that it was a word which remained in currency and generated place-names after the use of Gaelic began to predominate. Indeed, it is not found as a toponymic (place-name) element in other British-speaking areas, such as Wales (where as *peth* it is the modern Welsh word for 'thing'), so its meaning may perhaps have been modified within Gaelic. Its use in place-names seems to suggest that it had a similar semantic range to Gaelic *baile*, Old English *tún*, Welsh *tref* and French *ville* meaning a

substantial farm or 'estate' centre.[26] All these words seem to have implied
a household which was responsible for paying universal dues, such as *cáin*
and *coinnmed*, directly rather than through an intermediate lord. Albania,
of course, contained names with *baile* (such as Balbirnie or Balmerino) and
with *pett*, and one might be tempted to see this as evidence of Gaelic- and
British-speaking settlements, respectively, but since the *pett* names usually
have a Gaelic second element this is clearly not the case. It may, none the
less, indicate some sort of cultural horizon. The *pett* element is rare south
of the Forth, north of the Oykel or west of the central Highlands and thus
its distribution map seems to reflect the boundaries of Pictavia or Albania
in the period before the mid-eleventh century.[27] A note of caution should,
perhaps, be sounded with regard to this use of the absence of *pett* south of
the Forth. Nicholaisen's distribution map shows six *pett* names south of
the Forth. Three of these are in Lothian and two near Stirling. The sixth
example is a real outlier in north Ayrshire. The area in which *pett* names
are absent but which none the less have significant numbers of Gaelic
place-names is thus principally Ayrshire, Clydesdale, Dumfries and
Galloway; all districts to which Gaelic was introduced, either certainly or
possibly, by Gallgáedil rather than by Albanians. The Gallgáedil are
unlikely to have had many Pictish British loan-words in their dialects.[28]

It is also the case that in some places *pett* seems to alternate with *baile*
in the same settlement names in early recorded forms. Thus, Baldinny
(Angus) appeared as 'Petdynny' in the sixteenth century, and Pitroddie
(Perthshire) has appeared as 'Baltrody'. Simon Taylor has convincingly
argued that *pett* and *baile* were not absolute equivalents and that while the
former has a principal meaning 'parcel of land' the latter, like Old English
tún, had a primary meaning of 'enclosed settlement', thus Pitroddie
originally meant 'Lands of Trodin', while Baltrody originally meant
'Steading of Trodin'.[29] It is easy to see how the two forms could be used

[26] Subsequently all these words have come to mean 'town' in their respective languages;
an interesting case of parallel development.

[27] Provisional maps showing the distribution of the elements *pett* and *baile* in Scottish
place-names can be found in W. F. H. Nicolaisen, *Scottish Place-Names, their Study and
Significance* (London, 1976), at 153 and 137, respectively, and in P. G. B. McNeill and
H. L. MacQueen, eds, *Atlas of Scottish History to 1707* (Edinburgh, 1996). These
distribution maps remain provisional and highly subjective due to the absence of any
systematic survey of Scottish place-names. Toponymic study is an area in which
Scotland lags far behind its neighbours.

[28] A full and systematic survey of Scottish place-names might allow us to definitively
define the boundaries between Albanian and Gallgáedil settlement.

[29] S. Taylor, 'Generic element variation, with special reference to eastern Scotland',
Nomina 20 (1997), 5–22.

interchangeably. It is presumably significant that *pett* had ceased to be productive of new place-names by c. 1100 while *baile* continued to be so after that date (as both charter evidence and the distribution maps suggest). In Ireland, where *baile* is very common but *pett* unknown, our earliest references to the former element also date to the eleventh century.[30] Clearly there its appearance is not linked to the introduction of Gaelic, which had been spoken on the island for centuries. It is possible that this horizon reflects a change in the nature of our documentation. Most secular settlements mentioned in the Irish chronicle record were royal sites and not simple steadings so it is not surprising that *baile* rarely appears in the chronicle record and becomes more visible in both Scotland and Ireland when charters recording the transfer of agricultural estates begin to appear from c. 1100.[31] Alternatively it may reflect changing tenurial practice. The need for Gaelic-speakers in Albania to adopt a British word, *pett*, may mean that they had no readily understood word for the concept which it described. Whether this would have been a problem specifically for the Gaelic dialects introduced into Albania (presumably from Dál Riata, where the landscape, and thus the economic structures, were somewhat different from those of lowland Pictavia), or a problem for the whole of the Gaelic-speaking world, including eastern Ireland, which more closely resembled Pictavia, is unclear. It may be that *baile* developed in Ireland simultaneously with *pett* in Albania but that the cultural dominance of Ireland within Gaeldom led to its introduction to Scotland, initially with a slight semantic difference. One might compare the way that British English and American English developed separate words for 'motorised goods-wagon', *lorry* and *truck*, but that the cultural dominance of America has led to the gradual expansion of the use of *truck*, at the expense of *lorry*, in Britain.

The 'motorised goods-wagon' was clearly a technological innovation which was developed after the American republic gained its independence from the British empire and, therefore, it is not surprising that the two nations developed different words for the vehicle. If *pett* does describe an innovation in Gaelic society that developed after the conquest of the Picts in the 870s and 880s, what was it? Clearly it has something to do with land-holding but it cannot simply be 'land-holding' *per se*, since sedentary agriculture had been a part of Insular life for centuries and we

[30] L. Price, 'A note on the use of the word *baile* in place-names', *Celtica* 6 (1963), 119–26; D. Flanagan, 'Common elements in Irish place-names: *baile*', *Bulletin of the Ulster Place-Name Society*, 2nd series, 1 (1978), 8–13.
[31] The earliest reference to *baile* is, however, a chronicle notice at *AU* 1011.6. This notice is discussed by Taylor in 'Generic element variation' at 11.

know from Irish law-codes dating from c. 700 that land was held and inherited by individuals.

It may be that the tenth and eleventh centuries saw similar developments in Albania to those which were occurring in much of western Europe at the time. In Gerbert's letters from Bobbio, which we read earlier in this chapter, he refers to 'some sort of documents which they call *libelli*', and later on to 'book-leases, executed under their special laws'. The problem that Gerbert encountered was that a warrior class had been 'sub-let' the monastic lands of Bobbio and that they held *libelli* or 'book-leases', which demonstrated this. It is clear from his language that this was an unfamiliar innovation which he had not encountered before. These were neither rich men living off their ancestral lands and their local client-base, nor members of the royal retinue temporarily occupying royal villas. A new class had been created by devolving rights to the extraction of tribute and other dues which had originally been a preserve of kings and then, increasingly, included in the endowment of churches. What was new in the tenth century was the creation of relatively small parcels of lordship which were not subject to the traditional demands of partible inheritance and were sufficient to support warrior tenants who could leave most of the responsibility for the daily running of the agricultural work to others. These lordships had some features previously confined to the extensive lordship of kings and great churches and some features which more closely resembled allodial (that is, private) land tenure. This transformation happened across Europe at about this time, though the date of its inception, the speed at which it developed and the degree to which it became the dominant mode of organising the landscape varied enormously from region to region. The exact details of this transformation are also the subject for some of the hottest debates and controversies among medieval historians. Some French historians have argued that this was a sudden revolution which occurred a decade or two on either side of the year 1000.[32] Others are more sceptical and cautious and question whether we are observing the spread of a coherent cultural package or merely a general trend.[33] Tied up with the development of the

[32]   There is a huge literature on this topic but some key texts in support of the revolutionary model are: G. Duby, *The Early Growth of the European Economy: Warriors and Peasants from the Seventh to the Twelfth Century* (Ithaca, 1974), P. Bonnassie, *From Slavery to Feudalism in South-Western Europe* (Cambridge, 1991), and G. Bois, *The Transformation of the Year One Thousand: the Village of Lournand from Antiquity to Feudalism* (Manchester, 1992).

[33]   See, for example, S. Reynolds, *Fiefs and Vassals: The Medieval Evidence Reinterpreted* (Oxford, 1994).

gentry was, necessarily, the development of a peasantry (you cannot have the one without the other). The development of the peasantry was in itself connected to a decline in slavery.[34] The fundamental division in society ceased to be that between the free and the unfree and instead became that between the noble and the base.

It is quite clear that Scotland and Ireland did not go very far down this road, the continued importance of the 'Common Army' performing what was known as 'Scottish Service' into the late middle ages indicates that the free farmer retained his honour in a way that he did not in parts of Europe where the 'feudal revolution' ran its full course.[35] Slave raiding also remained a Scottish concern into at least the middle of the twelfth century. The increasing distinction drawn, however, between the behaviour of the men of Galloway and the men of 'Scotia Proper', benorth the Forth in the twelfth and thirteenth centuries, reflects the fact that the *Gallgáedil*, unreconstructed barbarians that they were, had not even begun to travel this road. It seems most likely that the emergence of *pett* and *baile* as useful terms in tenth- and eleventh-century Albania reflects, in a rather modest and unpretentious way, the beginnings of a social transformation similar to that experienced elsewhere in Europe.[36]

The fact that Scottish Gaelic initially borrowed a Pictish British word, *pett*, to describe this new tenurial phenomenon suggests one of two things: either the institution was already in existence among the Picts before the Scottish conquest or, alternatively, British dialects were still fairly widely spoken when the institution was being developed. Since the tenurial revolution of the central middle ages seems to have been largely a phenomenon of the tenth and eleventh centuries the latter is possible (and we have seen in a previous chapter that the British word *albid-*,

---

[34] A phenomenon which has provoked something of a 'chicken or egg' controversy. See D. A. E. Pelteret, *Slavery in Early Mediaeval England, from the Reign of Alfred until the Twelfth Century* (Woodbridge, 1995), especially 24–37 and 251–9.

[35] For 'Scottish service' see G. W. S. Barrow, *The Kingdom of the Scots*, 2nd edn (Edinburgh, 2003), 273.

[36] For a very useful account of the similarly tentative 'first footsteps into feudalism' in Anglo-Saxon England see J. Gillingham, 'Thegns and knights in eleventh-century England: who was then the gentleman?' *Transactions of the Royal Historical Society*, 6th series, 5 (1995), 129–53. For a broad account of the transformation of lordship and the development of the peasantry in England see R. Faith, *The English Peasantry and the Growth of Lordship* (London, 1999). Studies such as these are not possible for Scotland due to the dearth of documentary evidence but it is very important that Scottish historians and those interested in interpreting what little evidence we have should familiarise themselves with them in order that they may develop their own interpretative frameworks.

which appears in Latinised from in the *Chronicle of the Kings of Alba*, survived into the tenth century), although one might postulate the *pett* had already developed some sort of specialised meaning in relation to the management of ecclesiastical estates within the Pictish period.

The relationship between Scottish Gaelic and Pictish British remains poorly understood. A number of questions remain unanswered. It would be particularly useful to know when British dialects ceased to be spoken north of the Forth. In the Introduction to this volume we encountered Henry of Huntingdon's assertion that the Pictish language had disappeared without trace by his time, that is, in the 1140s. Henry may well have been right but it is just possible that, even were he reflecting the views of great men like David I, pockets of British speech might have hung on in isolated areas. It is also not impossible that Henry was merely misled by labels. When the English first began to refer to the inhabitants of Albania as *Scottas* in the early tenth century it is extremely unlikely that Gaelic was the universal language of the kingdom, none the less in English usage the 'Scottish tongue' was presumably the language spoken by *Scottas*. Just as in the later middle ages the 'Scottish language' came to be used to designate the Scottish dialects of English[37] rather than Gaelic, so it is just possible that in Henry's time dialects descended from Pictish British might have been designated 'Scottish' by the English. Bald statements like Henry's may tell us far less than at first appears.

Place-names and personal names provide the best evidence that Gaelic was the dominant language in Albania in the twelfth century but these are limited in the information that they can give us. Language is made up of not just words but of grammar and syntax as well. Modern Scottish Gaelic, while very close to Irish Gaelic is none the less distinct in a number of ways, some of them quite significant. Some of these distinctive features do bear at least a superficial resemblance to Welsh, although this is not an area that has been exhaustively researched.[38] It should also be remembered that most of our evidence for modern Scottish Gaelic is drawn from an analysis of the language of the Highlands and Islands and not from areas that were in the heartlands of either Pictavia or Albania. We now tend to think of islands like Lewis and Islay as the heartland of

[37] For some people the identification of Scots as a language rather than a dialect is a political concern. In reality there are no hard linguistic distinctions between languages and dialects and here Scots is identified as an English dialect merely with respect to its origin and early development.

[38] For a preliminary study see D. Greene, 'Gaelic: syntax, similarities with British syntax', in D. S. Thomson, ed., *The Companion to Gaelic Scotland* (Oxford, 1983), 107–8.

Scottish Gaelic but in the tenth and eleventh centuries Norse rather than Gaelic was probably the language of the Western Isles, and it is not known for certain when or from where Gaelic was introduced into these areas. Inevitably this means that the study of modern Scottish Gaelic is of limited value in understanding the linguistic situation in the eastern lowlands in the middle ages. Our earliest written Gaelic from this area, some short records of land grants to the church of Deer (Aberdeenshire) copied into the Gospel book of that church, dates from the mid-twelfth century.[39] At about the same time that these notes were being written into the Book of Deer the administrative language of the kingdom was rapidly becoming Latin and although a number of twelfth- and thirteenth-century tracts make reference to sources that may have been written in Gaelic nothing of significance survives.[40] It is also the case that the Gaelic notes in the Book of Deer and most subsequent texts produced in Gaelic in medieval and early modern Scotland followed literary standards set in Ireland. Indeed, many of the poets who composed for Scottish chiefs were themselves Irish born. The distinctiveness of Scottish Gaelic only really becomes apparent in written form after the collapse of the patronage networks that supported a professional literary class in the eighteenth century. Study of the distinctive features of modern Scottish Gaelic and of the few slips in medieval and early modern texts which betray the vernacular usage of the authors is still in its infancy. Just as nineteenth-century Scottish writers tended to express themselves in the language of the middle classes of the English home counties, rather than the language of the people, so medieval writers of Gaelic aspired to the language of educated scribes in the scriptoria of Irish church-settlements such as Glendalough and Clonmacnoise.

[39] The standard account of these appears in K. Jackson, *The Gaelic Notes in the Book of Deer* (Cambridge, 1972). A collection of essays on different aspects of the Book of Deer and the texts contained within it, *This Splendid Little Book: Studies on the Book of Deer*, is currently being produced under the editorship of Katherine Forsyth (Dublin, forthcoming).

[40] It is uncertain whether references to books written in the 'Scottish style', and similar phrases, denote books in Gaelic or simply written in an Insular script, for the Norman conquest of England and the twelfth-century renaissance also brought with them a major transformation of handwriting styles. Kathleen Hughes, in her article 'Where are the writings of early Scotland', in D. Dumville, ed., *Celtic Britain in the Early Middle Ages: Studies in Scottish and Welsh Sources by the late Kathleen Hughes* (Woodbridge, 1980), 1–21, argued that the lack of a rich vernacular literature surviving from Albania, in contrast to the situation in Ireland and Wales, was due to the cultural transformation of the twelfth century which forestalled the production of great codices in native monasteries.

The only real evidence that survives for the nature of the language in Albania lies in the thousands of place-names recorded in charters of the twelfth and thirteenth centuries. At the time of writing a systematic survey of the material has not been published, although several projects are now belatedly underway which will make some contribution in this area.[41] Superficial observation of both place-names and personal names appears to indicate that they are largely Gaelic in character but that a significant number of British forms survived or remained in use. There are difficulties in making this assessment, however. As was noted at the beginning of this volume Gaelic writers were able to Gaelicise the British names of Pictish rulers unproblematically, turning Wrguist into Fergus and Onuist into Oengus, for example. Doubtless they were also able to do this with place-names, for when St Andrews is first mentioned it appears, in the *Annals of Tigernach*, as *Cind righ monaigh*, a Gaelic form.[42] While the second element of the name *rigmonaid* would have been pronounced almost identically in British (the modern Welsh form would be **rhifynydd*) the first element, *Cind* (modern Gaelic *ceann*), 'head', would produce an expected *penn* in British (thus the whole name would be **Penrhifynydd* in Welsh). It is very likely that even if the church-settlement at St Andrews had been founded by Irish clerics (as its notice in the Irish chronicles perhaps suggests), it would have had a local British name. The ease with which a name such as this, and indeed the personal names, could be converted from British to Gaelic forms means that many other names preserved in the landscape of Scotland might have originated as British names but have subsequently been converted into Gaelic forms.

If we keep in mind the parallel of modern Scots and Standard English we can imagine how such 'code-switching' could work. It is debateable whether, in the ninth to eleventh centuries, Pictish British and Scottish Gaelic were as close to one another as Scots and English are today and our lack of clear information on either language will probably mean that it will remain so. None the less, it may be that when looking for a parallel in modern times for the replacement of Pictish British by Scottish Gaelic that of Scots by Standard English is more appropriate than that of modern Gaelic by either Scots or, more recently, English. The decline of Scots since the Union of 1707 has been gradual and almost imperceptible. Most people in Scotland today speak dialects that are somewhere on

[41] Volume 1, at least, of Simon Taylor's *The Place-Names of Fife*, in 4 vols, (Donington, 2006 ff.), is available. There is also a major project underway on the history of Gaelic in Scotland, funded by the Arts and Humanities Research Council, under the auspices of Professor Thomas Clancy of the University of Glasgow.

[42] *AT* 747.

a continuum between relatively broad Scots (particularly in the rural northeast) and Standard English with a slight Scottish accent (particularly among the privately educated). Many people can code-switch between forms, perhaps using more Scots forms among friends and family and more English forms at work. Most of the people of Scotland, and particularly the middle classes, speak what linguists term 'Scottish Standard English'. This is fundamentally Standard English but with Scottish phonology (that is, accent) and a small number of distinctly Scottish words or turns of phrase: words such as 'outwith', 'dram', 'pieces' (to mean 'packed lunch') and 'messages' (used to mean 'shopping') spring to mind.

Scots stems from the dialects of English brought to Scotland by settlers in the burghs from the twelfth century onwards. Most of these settlers probably came from eastern England. A contribution was also made by the native speakers of English in the far southeast of Scotland and by settlers from Flanders, for in the twelfth century Flemish and English were still very close. Once 'Inglis' (as it was called) had become established in the Scottish kingdom, it went its own way and Scots and English developed on parallel lines, not necessarily borrowing the same words from foreign language nor choosing to abandon or retain the same words from the common inheritance. In many ways Scots appears to be more conservative and to retain more of the speech forms of late Anglo–Saxon than English does. From the time of the Union of the Crowns in 1603, and particularly after the parliamentary Union of 1707, the educated classes in Scotland began to adopt southern English forms and, from the nineteenth century, when universal education began to spread this conformity to the population at large, southern standards became more widespread. The broadest and most distinctive Scots was probably that spoken in the early seventeenth century about 500 years after the first settlers brought the language to the country and when it had had time to develop its own features but before reconvergence with Southron dialects began. The divergence, and reconvergence of Scots and English can thus provide a model for linguistic histories in the past. It is potentially useful when looking at the decline of Pictish British because the decline of Scots was not the product of an act of ethnic cleansing. What happened was possible, however, because a high degree of mutual intelligibility survived between Scots and English. Scots speakers were able, gradually, to filter anglicisms in to their speech without having to learn an entirely new language and the development of Scottish Standard English has been gradual and incremental. This kind of relationship between closely related languages is actually quite common, Norwegian, for example, drifted towards Danish during the colonial period (1536–1814), and various dialects of northwestern Germany might just as easily become Dutch as German had the political situation been different.

If we are to adopt this model for explaining the disappearance of Pictish British then the fundamental question is: what degree of mutual intelligibility existed between it and Scottish Gaelic? This is, of course, an impossible question to answer conclusively. Even between modern languages it is hard to get observers to agree upon degrees of intelligibility since to some extent it depends upon the aptitude, hearing and local dialect of the individual. The relationship between modern Scottish Gaelic and modern Irish is a case in point. Sometimes the relationship is not reciprocal. It is often said, for example, that Spanish-speakers find it relatively easy to understand Portuguese but that Portuguese-speakers cannot understand Spanish. This seems, on the face of it, implausible but it should be remembered that Spain is a large country with a great deal of dialect variation within it (not to mention in its former colonies) whereas Portugal is not. The Spanish are, perhaps, more used to making a bit more effort to understand people who speak differently from themselves and can thus accommodate, or 'put up with', the 'oddities' of Portuguese. In cases like this, of course, we are talking about degrees of mutual intelligibility, not the ability to understand every word or idiom.

Pictish British and Scottish Gaelic were both Celtic languages. Celtic had spread across much of Europe (and even established outlying communities in western Asia) in the first millennium BC and had gradually developed distinctive dialects across this vast region.[43] It seems likely that by the tenth century only those dialects which had developed in the Insular world had survived, although at least one of these had been re-exported to the Continent where it laid the foundation for the development of Breton.[44] It is conventional to divide the Insular Celtic dialects into two families, British, or Brittonic, and Irish, or Goidelic (Gaelic). When Celtic first came to the Insular world it was relatively undifferentiated. After it became established, the Irish Sea and the North Channel created a barrier to communication which meant that dialects on one side of the sea shared innovations which distinguished them from dialects on the other. Recently Ewen Campbell has suggested, somewhat controversially, not unreasonably, that in the north the central Highlands

[43] The date at which Celtic itself first became a distinct language is hotly debated and probably unknowable. It is possible that the beginnings of the Celtic diaspora pre-dated 1000 BC.

[44] Some linguists have considered the possibility that Breton, or some dialects thereof, represent a reconvergence of Continental Celtic and British Celtic.

would have posed a greater barrier to communication than the North Channel and that the dialects of some parts of the western Scotland may have shared innovations with Irish dialects, rather than other British dialects, from the start.[45] Campbell's observation, however, draws attention to the overall crudeness of the model. Presumably his general point, that the sea is not a consistent barrier between Ireland and Britain, could be extended. Bearing in mind that in ancient and early medieval times there was no state education, very limited literacy and not even a centralised royal court in either Britain or Ireland, it seems likely that there was considerable regional variation in dialects across the Insular Celtic world. The effect of open sea and extensive highland areas upon communication might have varied from region to region depending upon the breadth or roughness in each case. In the pre-Roman era we might have expected the dialects of Cornwall, Galloway and the western peninsulas of Wales to share linguistic features with the eastern areas of Ireland which separated them from those of eastern Britain, and at the same time separated the eastern Irish dialects from those of the Atlantic coast. The Roman occupation of Britain may have been a fundamental factor in the creation of the Irish (or Gaelic) language, as most dialects of British Celtic began to be transformed by contact with Latin and as diplomatic and commercial links between Ireland and her eastern neighbour were increasingly dominated by Latin speakers. Medieval Welsh contained between 600 and 900 words borrowed from Latin and may also have undergone some grammatical changes as a result of widespread bilingualism between speakers of British and Latin in the Roman and immediately post-Roman period.[46]

Viewed in this way questions are inevitably raised about the nature of Pictish British. In the pre-Roman period the topographical constraints on communication would almost certainly have meant that the dialects of eastern Britain from Aberdeenshire to East Anglia (at least) are likely to have maintained a degree of closeness. The creation of a Roman frontier, which fluctuated between the Gask Ridge (just south of Perth) and Hadrian's Wall (Cumberland and Northumberland), would have upset this dynamic.

The more northerly dialects of British will have escaped much of the impact which Latin imposed on the dialects spoken within the frontier and this may have been a factor in Pictish ethnogenesis. It may also have

---

[45] E. Campbell, 'Were the Scots Irish?', *Antiquity* 75 (2001), 285–92.
[46] D. Greene, 'The making of Insular Celtic', *Proceedings of the Second International Congress of Celtic Studies* (Cardiff, 1966), 121–36.

meant that the hard linguistic frontier that was gradually developing between Welsh and Irish may not have been so pronounced in the north. Something more like a gradually differentiated dialect continuum stretching from northeast to southwest may have continued to exist (or developed) among the un-Romanised Insular Celtic speakers. This is something of a controversial suggestion but it is widely agreed that many of the main features which distinguished medieval and modern Welsh and Gaelic were themselves the result of divergent development in Late Antiquity (c. 300–700).[47] Thus, for example, many Roman period personal names would have been indistinguishable in Irish and British form. *Caratacos*, the name of the famous British king who opposed the Romans, is not diagnostically British and it is not until the end of the sixth century that the developed forms in Irish and Welsh, *Carthach* and *Ceredig*, would have emerged. One of the reasons Gaelic and British are often distinguished as 'Q' and 'P' Celtic, respectively, is because the alternation between these two sounds (the 'q' later becoming /k/) was one of the few diagnostic differences which preceded this Late Antique 'neo-Celtic transition'. Before this British words which did not have a 'p' in them were, for the most part, indistinguishable from Gaelic.[48] It seems very likely that before the fifth or sixth century there was a relatively high degree of mutual intelligibility between most British and Irish dialects of Celtic. One might speculate that beyond the Roman frontier in northern Britain this divergence of the two dialect clusters may have been more gradual. While it is clear that Pictish British did share many innovations with Welsh it seems almost certain that there were others it did not share, particularly those which were the product of interference from Latin whether these were loan-words, the semantic shift of Celtic words or morphosyntactical features (such as grammatical inflexion and word order). Both the geographical factors to which Campbell has drawn attention and the absence of Roman control may have meant that the linguistic frontier between Irish and British was not so clearly defined in the northern parts of Britain and Ireland as it was in the southern. If this were

---

[47] See Patrick Sims-Williams, 'Dating the transition to neo-Brittonic: phonology and history, 400–600', in A. Bammesberger and A. Wollman, eds, *Britain, 400–600: Language and History* (Heidelberg, 1990), 217–61.

[48] Patrick Sims-Williams in his *The Celtic Inscriptions of Britain: Phonology and Chronology, c. 400–1200* (London, 2003), at 9–10, was forced to devise his categories of 'British', 'Possibly Irish' and 'Probably Irish' personal names appearing on the earliest inscriptions on the basis of other locatable attestations of the names rather than on any purely linguistic criteria. The absence of a 'Certainly Irish' category in his schema serves to emphasise the problem.

the case it may have facilitated reconvergence of the two languages in the Alpínid era.

A parallel and contemporary example of this phenomenon can be found in parts of northern and eastern England. Much of this area was conquered and settled by Danes at precisely the same time that the Gaels seem to have conquered Pictavia in the 870s and 880s. Here the evidence of place-names seems to suggest that for some time, perhaps several generations, communities of English speakers and communities of Old Norse speakers dwelt alongside one another.[49] Eventually these regions of the Danelaw, as they became known, developed homogeneous dialects which contained elements drawn from both Norse and English. Now the relationship between Old Norse and Old English was broadly comparable to that between Irish and British. Both Norse and English represent branches of the Germanic language group. Germanic spread across Europe somewhat later than Celtic and it is traditionally divided into three major sub-groups: North Germanic; West Germanic; and East Germanic. East Germanic originally developed in regions such as Poland and the Ukraine and need not concern us here. West Germanic is the name given to the cluster of dialects that were spoken in western Germany and the Low Countries while North Germanic was ancestral to the Scandinavian languages. Just as the Irish Sea provided the defining boundary between the Irish and British groupings of Celtic dialects so the Baltic separated North and West Germanic populations from one another. Denmark was, to some extent, the Dál Riata, in this analogy – the Danes occupying the islands which separated *Scandza* from Continental Germany and the peninsula of Jutland which, Kintyre-like, protruded into this island group. Jutland, together with the southern Danish islands, provided the boundary zone where dialects exhibited both North Germanic and West Germanic features.[50]

The ancestors of the Anglo-Saxons had migrated from northern Germany and Jutland, and indeed some scholars believe that their migration contributed to the split between the North and West Germanic dialect groupings. The earliest English settlers had come from among a

---

[49] L. Abrams and D. N. Parsons, 'Place-names and the history of Scandinavian settlement in England', in J. Hines, A. Lane and M. Redknap, eds, *Land, Sea and Home: Proceedings of a Conference on Viking-Period settlement, at Cardiff, July 2001*, Society for Medieval Archaeology Monograph 20, (Leeds, 2004), 379–431.

[50] For a more detailed yet accessible discussions of this topic see H.-F. Nielsen, *The Germanic Languages: Origins and Early Dialectal Interrelations* (Tuscaloosa, 1989) and O. W. Robinson, *Old English and its Closest Relatives: a Survey of the Earliest Germanic Languages* (London, 1992).

number of different Germanic-speaking tribes, notably, though not exclusively, the Angles, Saxons and Jutes, each speaking its own dialect. The Jutish dialect seems to have shared many of the diagnostic features of North Germanic while the Saxon seems to have been part of West Germanic grouping. Anglian may have lain somewhere between the two, perhaps leaning more toward the northern grouping. Within Britain, however, the various dialects mixed, converged and re-diverged so that although Old English had distinct dialects which to some extent reflected the original tribal dialects brought from the Continent, they also all shared innovations common to what we might term 'Insular Germanic',[51] but is better known as Old English or Anglo-Saxon.[52] Just as with the Insular Celtic languages it was the Late Antique period that saw a clear parting of the ways between West Germanic and North Germanic and by the ninth century, while Old English was still barely distinguishable from its nearest West Germanic Continental neighbours, such as Flemish, Frisian, Old Saxon and, to some extent, Old Franconian, there were significant differences between Old English and Old Norse. This can be illustrated with reference to the Anglo-Saxon heroic poem *Beowulf* which, though composed in Old English, was set in Scandinavia. A number of tribes and individuals are mentioned in this text who also are known from the Scandinavian tradition. These include the hero Beowulf's own people who are the *Geatas* in Old English but the *Gautar* in Old Norse, the Danes, *Dene* in OE but *Danir* in ON, the Danish kings *Healfdene* and *Hroðgar* who are *Halfdan* and *Hroðgeirr* (later *Hróarr*) in ON and their dynasty known as the *Scyldingas* in OE but *Skjöldungar* in ON. Common nouns can also be used to illustrate this, including OE *wulf* as opposed to ON *ulfr* and OE *stede* as opposed to ON *staðr*. Some words are less obviously the same, such as OE *eoh*, 'war-horse,' and ON *jór*, 'stallion'. In this example we see a slight semantic shift as well as a phonological one. Sometimes this can be quite extensive. Thus, *dóm*, phonologically identical in both languages means a 'law' or 'judgement' in Old English but a 'court of law' in Old Norse, which used the word *lag* (whence our word 'law'), a word not found in Old English or the other West Germanic dialects (in which the cognate word gives us modern English 'lay'), to mean 'law'.

[51] This is not a term widely used by historical linguists.

[52] J. Hines, 'The becoming of the English: identity, material culture and language in early Anglo-Saxon England', *Anglo-Saxon Studies in Archaeology and History* 7 (1994), 49–60, and D. N. Parsons, 'The language of the Anglo-Saxon settlers', in H.-F. Nielsen and L. Schøsler, eds, *The Origins and Development of Emigrant Language*, NOWELE supplement 17 (Odense, 1996), 141–56.

There is a great deal of debate about whether or not Anglo–Saxons and Scandinavians would have been able to understand one another in the Viking Age.[53] In reality the question is a little naive. Even people speaking different dialects of the same language have difficulty understanding each other fully when they first meet (most southern English people, for example, find the Geordie dialect of Newcastle-upon-Tyne completely impenetrable upon first encountering it). The appropriate question should be 'would it have been *relatively* easy for speakers of Old English to understand Old Norse?', in which case the answer is certainly 'yes'. If three Anglo-Saxons from the same social and educational background were sold in to slavery and one was bought by a Norse household, another by a Gaelic household and another by a British-speaking household one could be certain that the slave owned by the Norse would master the language of his new home first, even though he thought himself a *þeow* and his owners thought him a *þræll*.

In England, the Scandinavian conquests of the ninth century led to the establishment of Old-Norse-speaking communities alongside Old-English-speaking communities. These communities seem to have maintained their separate identities for a generation or two, perhaps even longer in some places, but eventually they came together and new dialects of English emerged which displayed significant Scandinavian influence. In the course of the later middle ages, long after the end of the Viking Age, these dialects in turn influenced the development of Standard English (some of the distinctive features of Scots derive from the fact that it descends, in the main, directly from these very dialects of early Middle English). The influence of Scandinavian on English was extremely extensive. Loan-words are frequently used to fill gaps in languages and accompany technological or conceptual developments from one nation to another, thus words like 'television' or 'croissant' have become international. In English many of the words borrowed from Scandinavian, however, replaced very basic ideas. Thus, our word 'take' is derived from Old Norse *taka* instead of from the Old English word *niman*, and the word 'law' was a Norse word carrying much the same meaning as Old English *dom* which survives only as 'doom'.[54] Common English words of Norse origin include such basic items as 'though', 'they', 'them', 'their', 'till', 'again', 'give', 'run', 'thrive' and 'get'.[55] Middle English also derived

[53] The most recent major contribution is Matthew Townend, *Language and History in Viking-Age England: Linguistic Relations between Speakers of Old Norse and Old English* (Turnhout, 2002).
[54] R. Lass, *Old English: A Historical Linguistic Companion* (Cambridge, 1994), 186–9.
[55] S. G. Thomason and T. Kaufman, *Language Contact, Creolization, and Genetic Linguistics* (Berkeley, 1988), 291.

up to twenty per cent of its grammatical features from Old Norse.[56] Sometimes the Scandinavian and English forms of the same word were both retained to allow more subtle distinctions to be made, as in the case of 'skirt' and 'shirt'. Thomason and Kaufman summarise their study of what they call the 'Norsification' of English thus:

> The Norse influence on English was pervasive, in the sense that its results are found in all parts of the language; but it was not deep except in the lexicon [that is, vocabulary]. Norse influence could not have modified the basic typology of English because the two were highly similar in the first place . . . What Norse did was to add a few subtleties of meaning and a large number of new ways of saying old things, often by replacing an English item of similar but not identical sound. The hundreds of semantically basic lexical borrowings from Norse assured that in Norsified English one could hardly speak a sentence in English without using a Norse-origin element. In many ways Norse influence on English was a kind of prestige borrowing that took little effort to implement.
>
> The fact that Norse and English at the time of their contact were structurally and lexically so similar meant that:
> (a) it was relatively easy to learn the other language; and
> (b) it was relatively easy to learn to understand the other language without learning to speak it. Nevertheless, one could never have been in doubt which language was being spoken . . .[57]
>
> That Norse influenced Danelaw English more than French did English generally [after 1066] is due to the closer genetic relationship and (hence) greater typological similarity of Norse and English.[58]

The case of the Old Norse impact on English language history is well studied and depends upon relatively clear evidence surviving in significant quantities. While specialists may disagree about the details and minimalists and maximalist views can be taken, the broad analysis has achieved a consensus. Debate tends to focus on which truly innovative features of Middle English, not in evidence in Old Norse nor Old

---

[56] Thomason and Kaufman, *Language Contact*, 263–304, at 292.

[57] This is the situation currently existing between Danish, Norwegian and Swedish, speakers of which languages almost never bother learning the others but merely modify their own language slightly when speaking to one another.

[58] Thomason and Kaufman, *Language Contact*, 302–3.

English, might or might not have happened without Norse influence. The reason for dealing with this case-study in some detail here is that it touches upon a contemporary and analogous situation to that which may have occurred in Scotland and with languages which were spoken in early medieval Scotland. Principally, however, it may provide us with a way to start thinking about the relationship between Gaelic and the British dialects of Pictavia.

Broadly speaking the relationship between British and Gaelic was similar to that between Old Norse and Old English. We have also seen that many, though by no means all, of the sharp distinctions that can be drawn between Gaelic and British have been observed through a comparison of Irish and Welsh. In the north sustained geographical proximity and the absence of Roman and Latin influence may well have meant that the dialects of Gaelic and British spoken were less clearly differentiated than the dialects of the south. Following a Gaelic conquest of Pictavia, we might expect several generations in which Gaelic-speaking communities lived alongside British-speaking communities. In this situation there would have been a great deal of influence of one language on the other and some linguistic convergence would have occurred. Gaelic, though initially spoken by a smaller proportion of the population, may have had some advantages as the language of the dominant class, as the language of the Columban Church, and also as the language of Argyll, parts of which may have been considered to have been within the kingdom. Gaelic also had an advantage which Norse had lacked in England. While 'Norsification' was still taking place England was conquered by the Normans (1066). This event not only introduced French as a new elite language but also changed the whole cultural and commercial trajectory of England away from Scandinavia. Eleventh-century England had been very much a part of the Scandinavian world with strong links particularly to Denmark and the Irish Sea. Had these remained the main cultural ties of the English through the twelfth century, it seems likely that the English language would have undergone even greater levels of Norsification. In Albania links with Ireland did continue into the twelfth century and when Norman French influence came it was more gradual and less overwhelming than it had been in England. The decline and disappearance of other British-speaking areas in Scotland would also have had an effect. English as a whole underwent significant Norsification even though a substantial part of England, in the south and west, received almost no Scandinavian settlement. The relative purity of these dialects in the late Anglo-Saxon period provided a brake to Norsification as the dialects converged. The situation in Albania was

such that there were no neighbouring British provinces of any significance whose dialects could reinforce the British of Pictavia. Strathclyde
was small and geographically quite discreet and after its apparent re-
expansion in the tenth century much of its population probably spoke
languages other than British. Among these elements the Gallgáedil, who
spoke a form of Gaelic, seem rapidly to have become the most numerous.

To summarise: the Gaelic and British dialects of Albania probably
influenced one another enormously during the course of the tenth
century and probably began to converge into a single Albanian language.
The continued influence of purer forms of Gaelic through the standard
literary language used by the Church together with cultural and political
ties with Ireland and the west coast, and the absence of similar factors
reinforcing British led, ultimately, perhaps by the middle of the eleventh
century, to the apparent dominance of the Gaelic elements in the language. Had significant samples of the vernacular dialects spoken in
Albania in the eleventh and twelfth centuries survived, however, it seems
likely that the British elements in them would be readily apparent.[59]

THE GAELIC CONQUEST OF PICTAVIA:
A HYPOTHESIS

We have seen that the most likely period for a Gaelic conquest of the Picts
was the 870s after the deaths of Constantín son of Cinaed (876) and his
brother Áed (878). Constantín was remembered in the Irish historical
tradition as the last king of the Picts (and was also the last king in the
Pictish king-list) but his brother, Áed, who reigned for little more than a
year, was the last ruler to be styled *rex Pictorum* in the chronicles.
Constantín's reign had been characterised by ceaseless Scandinavian
attacks on the heartland of the kingdom, directed from both northern
England and Dublin (and perhaps also from the north). The disruption
caused by these attacks should not be underestimated. Much of the debate
about early medieval warfare focuses on the relatively small size of armies
and it has been suggested that they could never have killed or displaced
significant numbers of natives in the kingdoms they attacked. One must
remember, however, that in destroying crops, driving off live-stock and
requisitioning stored foodstuffs, not to mention the simple disruption of
the agricultural cycle, they were condemning thousands to starvation and
disease in the months following their departure. The occupation of

[59] It is possible that a systematic survey of place-names might demonstrate this.

Fortriu by Amlaíb for two or three years in the late 860s (discussed in Chapter 3) must have placed an insupportable burden of supply upon the kingdom. Malnutrition and disease would also have been accompanied by psychological trauma. Kin- and neighbourhood-based collaborative labour would have suffered from a shortage of manpower and if the priesthood also suffered from the depredations of the Norsemen then parts of the population may well have been denied access to the sacraments and Christian burial. Whereas Cinaed son of Alpín had led campaigns deep into Northumbria burning Melrose and Dunbar, his sons were fighting for their very survival in the heartland of their own kingdom. While Cinaed's armies would have fed themselves by foraging in enemy territory, those of Constantín and Áed, maintained to combat the Norsemen, would have added to the strain put on domestic agrarian production.

It seems likely that Dál Riata, the Gaelic polity in Argyll, which had been subject to Pictish hegemony for most of the previous century and a half, had already suffered similar depredations in the earlier part of the ninth century. This, as we have seen, was the probable context for the establishment of the Columban *familia* at Dunkeld. We might imagine that that period had seen an influx of Gaelic refugees into Pictavia of the sort with which we are familiar from conflicts in modern Africa. It is possible that the compact made between Domnall son of Alpín (858–62) and 'the Gaels and their king' at Forteviot reflected an accommodation reached in response to this crisis: either the re-affirmation of Pictish protection over what remained of Dál Riata or the settlement of the Dál Riata within Pictavia proper. Displaced Gaelic warriors may well have provided willing recruits to Alpínid war-bands. The killing of Áed by Giric son of Dúngal in 878 may thus, viewed from one perspective, have been a coup d'état carried out by a faction, albeit a Gaelic one, within the kingdom (much as the Congolese civil war of the 1990s was to some degree prosecuted by Rwandan refugees).

The genealogical tract which we examined at the beginning of Chapter 6 appeared to map the *cenéla* of Dál Riata on to the provinces of Albania, and on the basis of this, together with provincial names, we were able to place Cenél Loairn in Moray, Cenél nOengusa in Angus, Cenél Comgaill in Strathearn, and Cenél nGabráin in Gowrie and Fife. This may reflect, perhaps at a little distance, the accommodation of the Gaels in Pictavia in the later ninth century. This said, we should not imagine that the Gaelic *cenéla* replaced the native population at a stroke. Instead, we should imagine the leaders of the kindreds taking tribute from the territories they had come to dominate, with their relatively small numbers of followers settling on land made available in a number of ways. Given the disruption and destruction caused by the Scandinavian depredations some redistribution of land was probably relatively easily accomplished and, as we have seen, much land held by the Church may have been made available for the maintenance of Christian warriors engaged in the struggle against the pagans.

ALBANIAN SOCIETY IN THE TENTH AND ELEVENTH CENTURIES

By the tenth century the leading man in each of the Albanian provinces was known by the title *mormaer* (pl. *mormaír*). The origins of this word have been the subject of some debate.[60] By the twelfth century the term was regularly Latinised as *comes*, the term used for English 'earl' and from which, via French, the word 'count' derives. The office of earl in later medieval Scotland was derived from the Albanian *mormaer* and, indeed, as late as the fifteenth century Irish sources use *mormaer* for Scottish earls, despite using the Norse loan-word *iarla* for earls in Ireland and England. The scholarly disputes concerning the word relate to its ultimate etymology. There is no doubt that the second element is the word for 'steward' (it is also the stem of the district name Mearns, from Gaelic *Maoirne*, meaning 'Stewartry'). This was in origin a Latin loan, from *maior*, but borrowed early into both British and Gaelic. The identity of the first element, however, is ambiguous. This element *mor* might represent either Gaelic *már* or *mór*, 'great', or the genitive of *muir*, 'sea', which was *moro* or *mora*. The only phonological difference we should expect between these two possibilities would be the length of the vowel, indicated here by the accent or length-mark, thus *mórmaer* means 'great-steward' and *mormaer* 'sea-steward'. Unfortunately, mediaeval scribes were less consistent in their use of diacritics than modern academics and the fact that the vast majority of attested forms of this word do *not* carry length-marks is not conclusive. The fact that this term was not widely used in Ireland, save of Albanian nobles, has led scholars to speculate that the term may be Pictish in origin. This makes little difference as far as etymology is concerned since the British forms of the three words under discussion were very similar, *már* (Modern Welsh *mawr*) being 'great', *mor* (MW *môr*) being 'sea' and *maer* (MW *maer*) being 'steward'.[61] Jackson

---

[60] The lengthiest discussion remains Jackson's in *The Gaelic Notes in the Book of Deer* (Cambridge, 1972), 102–10.

[61] This example serves once more to indicate how easily Gaelic and British might have converged.

observed that a number of Scottish earldoms of the twelfth century or later have no sea-coast and therefore argues that *mormaer* cannot mean 'sea steward'. In arguing thus he perpetrates what is known as the 'etymological fallacy', the idea that a word's original meaning controls its subsequent use. To demonstrate the flaw in such reasoning one need only take the example of the modern English word 'fee'. This derives from an early Germanic word meaning 'live-stock', yet how many of us today would insist that any fees we might be owed should be paid in cattle or sheep? To use a more pertinent example the Latin word *comes*, which translates *mormaer*, 'earl' and 'count', originally meant 'companion' and came to be used for 'ruler of a province or district' when such offices were temporarily held by members of the king or emperor's retinue. The fact that these offices eventually, became, hereditary and could be held by men who had never 'accompanied' the king did not mean that people stopped using the word *comes*. Similarly the word *dux*, whence 'duke', originally meant 'general', yet many dukes have never commanded armies. So while it is clear that *mormaer* was not thought of as literally meaning 'seasteward' by the later middle ages this does not mean that it had never meant that. Indeed, the modern Scottish Gaelic *morair* (from *mormaer*), meaning simply 'lord', is pronounced in such a way as to indicate that the first element was indeed 'sea' rather than 'great'. One possible context for the development of 'sea steward' as a title might lie in Dál Riata. There is a strong likelihood that in the seventh century Dál Riata comprised several kingdoms loosely unified in a fluctuating hegemony.[62] Under Pictish domination in the later eighth and ninth centuries, if not before, it seems to have developed into a unitary kingdom. The individual *prímchenéla*, 'chief kindreds', survived, as we have seen, into the later ninth century but they seem not to have been ruled by kings. One of the few texts to survive from Dál Riata is a document describing the naval levy of the kingdom.[63] This levy was organised by *cenéla*, so it may be that by the ninth century the chiefs of the kindreds of Dál Riata were chiefly known as admirals in the service either of their own king or the Pictish overlord. If this was the case the title of 'sea steward' may have been brought to the east by the leaders of the *cenéla* in the ninth century. Alternatively, it may have originated either as 'great steward' or 'sea steward' as an indigenous Pictish term.

[62] See most recently, J. E. Fraser, 'Strangers on the Clyde: Cenél Comgaill, Clyde Rock and the bishops of Kingarth', *Innes Review* 56 (2005), 102–20.
[63] J. Bannerman, *Studies in the History of Dalriada* (Edinburgh, 1974), 41–62 and discussion at 148–54.

Whether the *mormaír* originated as provincial rulers in pre-conquest Pictavia or as the leaders of immigrant Gaelic *cenéla* they formed, by the eleventh century at least and probably by the mid-tenth century, the highest ranking category of laymen outwith the royal family. Their absolute status and power is unclear, however. Because of the equation *mormaer* = *comes* = 'earl' it is easy to imagine them as the direct equivalents of eleventh-century English earls who controlled whole provinces (often former kingdoms) with vice-regal power. Surviving twelfth-century sources give cause to question this equation. The *mormaer* of Fife seems to have been regarded as the premier magnate in the kingdom, possibly because of his Cenél nGabráin descent, yet he seems to have held relatively little land in his own right.[64] Once one subtracts the lands held by great churches such as St Andrews and Dunfermline, lands still in royal hands and lands granted out to secular vassals, including the *mormaer*, by the crown, or held by great men other than the earl, it is hard to see what the hereditary estates of the *mormaer* might have been.[65] His main function seems to have been to lead the men of the province in war and to enforce the king's justice, but within local society he may have been more of a *primus inter pares* than a ruler. This view of the *mormaer* is at odds with the traditional assumption that he was in some sense descended from previously independent Pictish provincial kings and retained much of their character.

The Gaelic notes in the Book of Deer[66]

The Book of Deer is a small workaday gospel book from the monastery of Deer (now Old Deer) in Aberdeenshire. Written into some of its blank pages are records of a series of land grants, probably originally made in the eleventh and early twelfth centuries. The grants appear to

[64] John Bannerman has argued that the comital family of Fife descended from the tenth-century king Dub in 'MacDuff of Fife', in A. Grant and K. Stringer, eds, *Medieval Scotland: Crown, Lordship and Community, Essays Presented to Geoffrey Barrow* (Edinburgh, 1998), 20–38. The eleventh-century genealogical tract discussed in Chapter 6 describes the men of Fife as descendants of Conall Cerr son of Eochaid Buide, a seventh-century king of Dál Riata. It is, of course, possible than descendants of Dub displaced descendants of Conall in the course of the eleventh century.

[65] A glance through the collected acts of Malcolm IV makes this abundantly clear; see G. W. S. Barrow, ed., *Regesta Regum Scottorum* I, *The Acts of Malcolm IV* (Edinburgh, 1960). It would be interesting to undertake a more systematic analysis of the landholding in the province.

[66] Dauvit Broun, 'The property-records in the Book of Deer as a source for early Scottish society', in K. Forsyth, ed., *This Splendid Little Book: Studies on the Book of Deer* (Dublin, forthcoming).

have been copied into the book in the mid-twelfth century. The first note is brief, legendary, account of the foundation of the Church of Deer by St Drostán in the days of St Columba. The second note is as follows;

> Comgall son of Aed gave from the Oirdie as far as Púiréne to Columba and to Drostán.
> Muiredach son of Morgann gave the *pett* of Gartnait's son and the field of Toiche Teimne; and he was mormaer and was toísech.
> Matain son of Cairell gave a mormaer's portion in Altrie and Cú Lí son of Baíthín gave a toísech's portion.
> Domnall son of Giric and Mael Brigte son of Cathal gave the *pett* of the mill to Drostán.
> Cathal son of Morgann gave the field of the clerics to Drostán.
> Domnall son of Ruaídrí and Mael Coluim son of Cuílen gave Biffie to God and Drostán.
> Mael Coluim son of Cinaed gave a king's portion in Biffie and in the *pett* of the son of Gobrách, and two *dabaig* of the uplands of *Rois an Baird*.
> Mael Coluim son of Mael Brigte gave the deer trap.
> Mael Snechta son of Lulach gave Mael Duib's *pett* to Drostán.
> Domnall son of Dubucán extinguished all church-lands in favour of Drostán in return for giving him his goodwill.
> Cathal extinguished his toísech's portion on the same terms, and gave a feast for a hundred every Christmas and Easter to God and to Drostán.
> Cainnech son of the son of Dobarchon and Cathal gave the Altrie on this side, from the well of the bend as far as the birch tree between the two Altries.
> Domnall and Cathal gave Ednie to God and Drostán.
> Cainnech and Domnall and Cathal extinguished all church-lands in favour of God and of Drostán from beginning to end, free from mormaer and toísech till Domesday.

Some of these donors are identifiable, such as Mael Coluim son of Cinaed was king from 1005 to 1034, and his rival Mael Coluim son of Mael Brigte (†1029), and Mael Snechta son of Lulach who died as 'king of Moray' in 1085, but most are unknown individuals, presumably members of the local aristocracy. The 'extinguishing' of lands, presumably, refers to the granting of relief from universal dues.

Such a minimalist view of the *mormaer* is also supported by a legal text which, though only surviving in later manuscripts, probably reflects conditions in the Albanian kingdom in the tenth or eleventh centuries. This text is known to scholarship as the *Leges inter Brettos et Scottos*, almost certainly a misapplied title originally belonging to another tract which does not survive. It is preserved in French, Latin and Scots recensions. None of the manuscripts is earlier than the later thirteenth century.[67] The tract lists the compositional payments required for killings, woundings and breakings of the peace. As with other early medieval law codes the amount to be paid varies in accordance with the status of the injured party. The payments were listed in cattle with monetary equivalents. Since cash was neither produced nor widely circulated in Scotland before the twelfth century, the monetary equivalents may well be a later addition. The payments due following a killing, termed *cro* in this tract, can be summarised, in kine, as follows:

1,000 kine	King			
150 kine	King's son	*comes*		
100 kine		son of a *comes*	Thane	
66.66 kine			Thane's son	
44.44 kine			Thane's grandson	*ógtigern*
16 kine				*rusticus*

This brief table allows us to reconstruct the basic structure of Albanian society. The fundamental division in society, as in all early medieval societies, was between noble and base. Here that division is represented by the thane and the *rusticus*. The justification for it was probably based principally upon landed wealth, the thane being a man who could afford to entertain the king and his retinue in his own house. In England at this time a *thegn* (Scots 'thane') (whose monetary wergild was very similar to the monetary equivalent presented in the *Leges*) had to own five hides of land to maintain his noble status.[68] It should be noted that the thane, as

---

[67] Printed in *The Acts of the Parliament of Scotland*, vol. 1, 663–5. There is an important note on the interpretation of the text by F. W. L. Thomas, 'Proposed correction of the text of "Leges inter Brettos et Scottos" ', *Proceedings of the Society of Antiquaries of Scotland* 19 (1884–5), 73–4. The key portions of the text are also reprinted and discussed in F. Seebohm, *Tribal Custom in Anglo-Saxon Law* (London, 1911), 307–18. The title was applied to it by John Skene in the seventeenth century and was probably used originally to describe another tractate (a treaty between Albanians and Cumbrians?) which has not survived.

[68] A number of late Anglo-Saxon law tracts deal with property and status, they have been usefully translated and presented alongside one another in D. Whitelock, *English Historical Documents* I, *500–1042* (London, 1955), n. 52, 431–4.

he appears in this law tract, is certainly not the royal officer envisioned by many commentators.[69] Whether such 'official' thegns existed, or are a product of the desire among historians to see the early Scottish 'state' as a more bureaucratic polity than is justified, is a moot point. In England the 'hide', the basic unit of land assessment, reflected productivity but was notionally 120 acres and thus noble status was accrued with a land-holding of about 600 acres.[70] Since, in the Scottish tract, the *cro* of the *rusticus* was a little under a sixth of that of the thane we might imagine that his minimum landholding would be a little under a 100 acres (or its equivalent).[71] These figures are, of course, 'round' numbers and represent the minimum qualifications so it is probably sensible to imagine *rustici* with holdings of between about 100 and 500–600 acres and thanes with holdings of over about 500–600 acres. These figures must remain extremely notional and serve only to give a general impression of the relative wealth of the different classes of society. It is possible that the unit of land assessment, widespread benorth the Forth, known as the *dabach* (pl. *dabaig*), Anglicised as 'davoch', was related in some way to these calculations.[72] The appearance of specific *cro* payments for the son and grandson of a thane reflect the fact that noble status was to some extent hereditary. The son and grandson received some reflected glory on

[69] It should be noted that the interpretation of the thane presented here is in line with that advocated by John Skene in the seventeenth century and W. F. Skene in the nineteenth, see W. F. Skene, *Celtic Scotland: The History of Ancient Alban*, vol. 3, (Edinburgh, 1880), 239, n. 62. For the alternative view, in which the thane is a royal official rather than wealthy freeholder, see G. W. S. Barrow, *The Kingdom of the Scots* (Edinburgh, 1973 & 2003), 7–56, A. Grant, 'Thanes and thanages from the eleventh to the fourteenth centuries', in A. Grant and K. Stringer, eds, *Medieval Scotland: Crown, Lordship and Community, Essays Presented to Geoffrey Barrow* (Edinburgh, 1998), 39–81, and, by the same author, 'The construction of the early Scottish state' in J. R. Maddicott and D. M. Palliser, eds, *The Medieval State: essays presented to James Campbell* (London, 2000), 47–72.

[70] The definitive study of the hide probably remains F. W. Maitland, *Domesday Book and Beyond: Three Essays in the Early History of England* (Cambridge 1897), 357–520. The hide was, in the early Anglo-Saxon period, the notional holding of a single household. By the time of Domesday Book (1086) the common peasant holding seems to have been a yardland or virgate, measuring one-quarter of a hide. For the relevance and relationship of the hide to Celtic institutions see T. M. Charles-Edwards, 'Kinship, status and the origins of the Hide', *Past and Present* 56 (1972), 3–33.

[71] This ratio of roughly 1:6 which separates the thane's worth from that of the rustic suggests that in Albania, in contrast to England, nobility may have required six rather than five times the average land holding.

[72] For a recent review of the scholarship concerning *dabaig* see A. Ross, 'The Dabhach in Moray: a new look at an old tub', in A. Woolf, ed., *Landscape and Environment in Dark Age Scotland* (St Andrews, 2006), 57–74.

account of their father but if they failed to acquire the appropriate property qualification, through inheritance or rewards for service, then the fourth generation, the thane's great-grandsons, would become *rustici*. Indeed, the tract explicitly states that 'all that are lower than this, in the kindred, are *rustici*'. As in the rest of early medieval Britain and Ireland, social 'exfoliation' was the norm, or, as Mac Firbhisigh put it:

> It is customary for great lords that, when their families and kindreds multiply, their clients and their followers are oppressed, injured and wasted.[73]

The identity of the *ógtigern* is unclear. Literally the term means 'young lord' and it appears occasionally in Irish law tracts indicating the lowest status noble. It may be that it is his lordship itself that is 'young', and that the *ógtigern* is a man of 'rustic' stock who has acquired the property qualification of a thane. If this were the case then his descendants had the opportunity of travelling the same road as the thane's son and grandson but in the opposite direction, gaining full noble status after two or three generations.[74]

Having come to terms with the basic classes of land-holder we can return to the *mormaer*. His *cro*, at 150 kine, is, in relative terms, only fifty per cent higher than that of the thane while the thane's *cro* is 625 per cent higher than that of the *rusticus*. This is in great contrast to the situation in Northumbria where the earl's *wergild* was valued at four times that of the *thegn*.[75] Bearing in mind that some at least of the added value of the *mormaer*'s *cro* must accrue from his office then his property qualification must have been broadly within the same parameters as that of the thane. In some ways this should not surprise us. In this pre-feudal society large estates, as we have seen, were largely confined to the Church. While the *mormaer* may have had access to hypothecated royal tribute while in office it is likely that he was recruited from the thanely class and that his inherited family lands would have been on much the same scale as those of other thanes. In this sense he was very much the *primus inter pares* of his

---

[73] Cited and discussed in T. M. Charles-Edwards, *Early Irish and Welsh Kinship* (Oxford, 1993), at p. 121.

[74] *Cf.* the Irish law of status, *Críth Gablach*, ed., D. A. Binchy (Dublin, 1941), summarised in F. Kelly, *A Guide to Early Irish Law* (Dublin, 1988), 28, and the English tracts translated in Whitelock, n. 52.

[75] *Norðleoda laga*, one of the tracts presented by Whitelock in *EHD* 1, n. 52, rates an earl at 8,000 *thrymsas*, a *hold* or *heah-gerefa* at 4,000 and a *thegn* at 2,000. The *ceorl*, this tract's equivalent of the *rusticus*, is rated at 266 *thrymsas*.

kindred, who will, doubtless, have generated the bulk of the thanes and many of the *rustici* of his province. The unexceptional nature of the man who would be *mormaer* is paralleled in the case of the king' son. While the king has a *cro* of 1,000 kine, comparable with the king of Gwynedd in North Wales, whose *galanas* (the Welsh term used for the concept termed *cro* in the *Leges*)[76] amounted to 100 kine from every cantref he ruled (the core territory of Gwynedd comprised nine *cantrefi*),[77] the king's son, like the *comes*, is worth only 150. This may reflect the conditions created by the prevalent succession practice in which several sons of several kings may have been active at one time without any individual being heir apparent. It may also reflect the possibility that some *mormaers* were recruited from among the royal kindred, although there is no firm evidence that this ever happened.

This interpretation of the evidence is somewhat at odds with the prevailing view of a precocious Scottish 'state' best summed up in Professor Duncan's claim that Scotland at the beginning of the 'high middle ages' was 'the only Celtic realm with well formed and independent political institutions'.[78] It seems unclear that as early as the middle of the eleventh century such an argument could be made at all. To some extent it is a product of the fact that in this period we see in the kingdom of Alba a polity that is clearly the direct ancestor of modern Scotland. Indeed, the Anglo-Saxons were already calling it Scotland. Yet, while modern Scotland, at 30,405 square miles, is roughly the same extent as Ireland, at 32,062 square miles, and considerably larger than Wales, at 8,016 square miles, the kingdom of Alba comprised little more than a third of the modern country, and much of that was sparsely populated when compared with Ireland. Alba, as we have seen, was divided into two interlocking *regna*, north and south of the Mounth, and the larger of these, based around the Tay basin, was little larger than the modern province of Northern Ireland. Irish writers of the central middle ages regarded the *rí Alban* as the equal of a provincial king, such as the king of Munster, Connaught or Leinster, and, in terms of access to resources they probably had it about right. These Irish 'provincial kingdoms' were, like Alba, sometimes bifurcated, in Leinster, for example, the Uí Cheinnselaig of the south competed for dominance with the Uí Dúnlainge of the north.

[76] The term *galnes*, presumably a variant of *galanas*, is actually cited in the *Leges* as a synonym for *cro*, though whether this represents Cumbrian or Pictish British terminology is unclear.

[77] D. Jenkins, ed. & tr., *The Law of Hywel Dda: Law Texts from Medieval Wales* (Llandysul, 1986), 5–6.

[78] A. A. M. Duncan, *Scotland: the Making of the Kingdom* (Edinburgh, 1975), 111.

These divisions were often ancient, as they were in Alba, going back to the division of the Picts into northern and southern groupings noted by Bede. The kings of Alba, as Pictish kings had done before them, itinerated around their kingdom staying sometimes on their own estates, sometimes in the great church-settlements and sometimes in the houses of their thanes. These thanes, however, were not a well developed ministerial class but, for the most part, simply wealthy landowners fulfilling their obligation to provide *coinnmed*. In each province one among these thanes bore the title of *mormaer* and responsibility for leading the military levy and enforcing justice, owing his position, presumably, to a combination of inherited status and royal patronage. In its fundamental structures the Scottish kingdom was not so different from the kingdoms which had dominated northern Britain in the eighth century. Scotland was, eventually, to outstrip Ireland in the race to statehood but, in the mid-eleventh century, this was a race which had barely begun.

Table of Events

900	Constantín son of Áed succeeds
902	Scandinavians expelled from Ireland
903	Ímar grandson of Ímar occupies the Tay basin
904	Constantín slays Ímar
906	The oath-swearing at Scone
910	Anglo-Danish dynasty wiped out at Tettenhall
913	Death of Eadwulf, king of Northumbria
914	Ragnall grandson of Ímar first appears in the Irish Sea zone
917	Sihtric grandson of Ímar reoccupies Dublin
918	Battle of Corbridge, Ragnall defeats Constantín and the Northumbrians
920	Constantín, the Cumbrians and Ragnall meet with Edward of Wessex
921	Death of Ragnall
926	Death of Sihtric
927	Æðelstan of Wessex annexes Northumbria and meets the northern kings at Eamont Bridge
934	Æðelstan invades Scotland
937	The Battle of Brunanburh
939	Death of Æðelstan and the Hiberno-Norse conquest of Northumbria
943	Abdication of Constantín, retirement to St Andrews
945	Eadmund *lets* Cumbria to Mael Coluim
c. 948–54	Amlaíb Cúarán and Eric Haraldsson struggle for Northumbria
954	Mael Coluim succeeded by Ildulb
962	Dub succeeds and struggles with Cuilén
966	Cuilén secures the kingship
971	Cuilén slain and Cinaed son of Mael Coluim succeeds
973	Cinaed and the other kings submit to Eadgar at Chester
980	Battle of Tara, Amlaíb Cúarán retires to Iona
986	Danes in the Hebrides
989	Gofraid, first known king of Innse Gall, dies
995	Murder of Cinaed
997	Murder of Constantín son of Cuilén
1005	Mael Coluim son of Cinaed succeeds
1006	Failed Scots attack on Durham
1014	The battle of Clontarf, first mention of the Orkney earldom
1018	The battle of Carham, Scots conquest of Lothian?
1020	Death of Findláech son of Ruaídrí, 'king of Alba'
1029	Death of Mael Coluim son of Mael Brigte
c. 1030	Cnut visits Scotland
1034	Death of Mael Coluim son of Cinaed, last of the Alpiníds
1040	Donnchad son of Crínán slain by MacBethad after failed attack on Durham
1050	Macbethad on pilgrimage to Rome
1054	Earl Siward's invasion of Scotland
1057	MacBethad overthrown
1058	Lulach treacherously slain by Mael Coluim son of Donnchad and probable death of Thorfinn of Orkney
1066	Norman Conquest of England
1070	Mael Coluim annexes Cumbria and meets St Margaret

Guide to Further Reading

I. GENERAL SURVEYS

The modern study of early medieval Scotland really began with W. F. Skene's *Celtic Scotland: A History of Ancient Alban*, published in three volumes between 1876 and 1880. Although much of Skene's work has been superseded in the century and a quarter since he wrote he has cast a long shadow over the subject and is well worth revisiting. Among modern works pride of place is probably still held by A. A. M. Duncan's *Scotland: the Making of the Kingdom* from 1975. This book covers the whole period from the Romans to 1286 and necessarily deals more briefly with some topics than it might otherwise have done. It also came out just before the great leap forward in the criticism of early Celtic sources which occurred in the late 1970s and 1980s. The first text book of Scottish history to benefit from this revolution was Alfred Smyth's *Warlords and Holy Men*. This is an exciting book which stimulated a generation of students and scholars but it is also something of a curate's egg, Smyth pursuing his own interests, on the one hand, and under researching other areas. To some extent this is a danger for all history books and will doubtless be a criticism of the present volume. Mention should also be made of Ben Hudson's *Kings of Celtic Scotland*, published in 1994. Hudson is a leading scholar in this field as frequent mentions of his work in the present text make clear. Curiously, however, his best work are his shorter articles in which he really gets to grips with specific knotty problems. In his longer works, however, he often succumbs to the temptation to fill out the narrative with stories drawn from much later literary texts, an approach which has been largely eschewed in this volume.

2. VIKINGS IN SCOTLAND

Barbara Crawford's *Scandinavian Scotland* remains a good introduction to the study of Scandinavian settlement and Viking activity in Scotland. A more recent archaeological survey, James Graham-Campbell and Colleen Batey's *Vikings in Scotland* is extremely thorough and brings together much new work that has been done in the last twenty years. Archaeological fieldwork in the Northern and Western Isles is continuing to turn up new finds on a regular basis and our picture of social and economic life in Scandinavian Scotland is improving all the time, but this material is unlikely to contribute much to our understanding of the political narrative of the era and the precise dating of many sites remains open to debate. James Barrett's edited collection, *Contact, Continuity and Collapse: the Norse Colonization of the North Atlantic*, reflects the growing trend to place Scandinavian Scotland in the context of Norwegian settlement in other colonies such as Iceland, Greenland and the Faeroes.

3. EARLY INSULAR SOCIETY

The paucity of source material makes it impossible to study the social history of Scotland in this period. There is not even much archaeological evidence published from the eastern lowlands. To a large extent we are left to presume that the situation in Scotland was broadly similar to that in Ireland and to some extent Anglo-Saxon England. Because of the copious legal material surviving from early medieval Ireland scholars have been able to make a great deal of progress is reconstructing the rhythms of daily life there. Perhaps the most useful works of synthesis in this area are Thomas Charles-Edwards' *Early Irish and Welsh Kinship* and Fergus Kelly's *Early Irish Farming*. The comparative approach to early Insular social history is exemplified by the various contributions to *After Rome*, edited by Thomas Charles-Edwards, and *From the Vikings to the Normans*, edited by Wendy Davies, the first two volumes of the *Short Oxford History of the British Isles*.

4. THE IRISH SEA WORLD IN THE LATER VIKING AGE

In the tenth and eleventh centuries the lands around the Irish Sea came to be dominated by communities living a Viking lifestyle but drawing much of their cultural heritage from native societies and particularly from Gaelic Ireland. In the last quarter of a century the study of this 'Insular Viking Zone' has become one of the more exciting areas of Dark Age historical writing. This 'sub-discipline' owes its genesis to Alfred Smyth's two-volume work *Scandinavian York and Dublin*, covering the period up to the West Saxon annexation of Northumbria. Ben Hudson has recently brought out two volumes dealing with this area, one *Irish Sea Studies, 900–1200*, is a collection of papers previously published in academic journals and contains some excellent pieces. His other volume, *Viking Pirates and Christian Princes: Dynasty and Empire in the North Atlantic*, provides a sequel to Smyth's work and charts the history of the dominant dynasties in the region from the mid-tenth to the early twelfth century and is, at times, perhaps, more speculative than one might have hoped. A leading figure in this area of study is Sean Duffy but he has yet to produce a monograph on the topic although his articles have proved very influential. The most important recent work on the Irish Sea in this period is probably Colmán Etchingham's 'North Wales, Ireland and the Isles: the Insular Viking Zone', published in the journal *Peritia* in 2001.

5. NORTHUMBRIA AND THE EXPANSION OF WESSEX

The scholarly literature on later Anglo–Saxon England is vast and this is not the place to undertake an in depth survey. Some readers will doubtless feel that this book has already said more than enough about the English. The most recent survey of Northumbrian history is David Rollason's *Northumbria, 500–1100: Creation and Destruction of a Kingdom*, this is an ambitious book which attempts to pull together half a century of scholarship and a wide range of primary sources. For the later period, however, Rollason's analysis is perhaps a little skewed by his rather uncritical acceptance of Symeon of Durham's early twelfth-century views. None the less, this remains an important work that cannot be ignored. For the deeds and dealings of Æðelstan and his kinsmen and the making of England two good starting points would be Pauline Stafford's *Unification and Conquest: a Political and Social History of England in the Tenth and Eleventh Centuries*, and David Dumville's collection of essays *Wessex and England, from Alfred to Edgar*. An invaluable reference work that can lead one to further reading is *The Blackwell Encyclopaedia of Anglo-Saxon England* edited by Michael Lapidge and a host of other luminaries.

6. THE SCOTTISH SOURCES

The sources from Scotland itself, mostly preserved in later copies and in a fragmentary and emended state, are extremely hard to interpret or place a value upon. In the early twentieth century Alan Orr Anderson attempted to collect together all the sources for Scottish history before 1286 and present them in translation for the student. His great work remains an invaluable first port of call but in the century since he began his labours our understanding of the complexity of the sources has increased enormously and, at the same time, the extent of our residual ignorance has become clearer. There is, to date, no single work which can replace Anderson's nor is there likely to be in the near future and instead a great many detailed and closely argued articles have dealt with the fragments with which we must work. Of late the leading scholars in this field are probably Dauvit Broun, David Dumville and Ben Hudson and the reader is advised to look under their names in the bibliography for specific works.

The Principal Medieval Chronicles used in this Volume

AC =   *Annales Cambriae*: a family of chronicles maintained in South Wales. The core recension dates from the mid-tenth century. The best edition to date is D. N. Dumville, ed. & tr., *Annales Cambriae*, AD *682–954: texts A–C in Parallel* (Cambridge, 2002). Various other editions and translations are available in print and on the internet.

AFM = *Annals of the Four Masters*: a composite chronicle of Irish history put together in the seventeenth century but compiled, to a very great extent, from contemporary chronicles. This chronicle was published with a translation in the nineteenth century: J. O'Donovan, ed., *Annala Rioghachta Eireann, Annals of the Kingdom of Ireland by the Four Masters from the earliest period to the year 1616*, 7 vols (Dublin, 1856). This edition is also available at www.ucc.ie/celt/.

ASC = *The Anglo-Saxon Chronicle*: a group of closely-related chronicles kept in England from the late ninth century to the mid-twelfth century. They are based on a common stock composed in late ninth-century Wessex and covering the period from the English settlement of the fifth century. The individual manuscripts, which vary significantly in places, are being edited without translations as a series of volumes by Cambridge University Press under the general editorship of D. N. Dumville and S. Keynes. The best translation, giving the various manuscripts in parallel, remains D. Whitelock (with D. C. Douglas and S. I. Tucker), ed. & tr., *The Anglo-Saxon Chronicle* (London, 1961), which is a slightly updated and expanded version of the translation which appears in her *English Historical Documents* (London, 1955). Various other translations and editions are available in print and on the web.

AT =   *Annals of Tigernach*: a chronicle kept at the monastery of Clonmacnoise in the Irish midlands. The entries up to 911 in this chronicle, as in the *Annals of Ulster*, derive from an otherwise lost chronicle kept at or near Armagh which historians have labelled the *Chronicle of Ireland*. It has been published with a partial translation by W. Stokes in *Revue Celtique* 16 (1895), 374–419, 17 (1896), 6–33, 119–263 and 337–420, 18 (1897), 9–59, 150–97, 268–303 and 374–90. This edition has been reprinted as W. Stokes, ed., *The Annals of Tigernach*, 2 vols, (Felinfach, 1993). It is also accessible at www.ucc.ie/celt/.

AU =   *Annals of Ulster*: a chronicle based on the *Chronicle of Ireland* kept in the north of Ireland until the late fifteenth century. For the present purposes the best edition is S. mac Airt and G. mac Niocaill, eds & tr., *The Annals of Ulster*, vol. I, *(to* AD *1131)* (Dublin, 1983). The entire chronicle is also available on www.ucc.ie/celt/.

CKA =   *Chronicle of the Kings of Alba* (also known as the *Older Scottish Chronicle* or the *Scottish Chronicle from the Poppleton Manuscript*): this is a complicated text surviving in a fourteenth-century manuscript copy of a late twelfth-, or very early thirteenth-, century compilation of Scottish historical texts. It tells the story of Cinaed son of Alpín and his descendants into the later tenth century. This chronicle is based at least in part on a mid-tenth-century king-list, but it has had additional material added in both the tenth and the twelfth centuries. The most accessible edition is B. T. Hudson, ed. & tr., 'The Scottish Chronicle', *Scottish Historical Review* 77 (1998), 129–61. It is the only chronicle source that emanates from Scotland in the period covered by this book.

CS =   *Chronicum Scotorum* (also sometimes called *Chronicon Scotorum*): is an Irish chronicle very closely related to the *Annals of Tigernach*. Published with a translation in the nineteenth century by W. M. Hennessy, ed. & tr., *Chronicum Scotorum: A Chronicle of Irish Affairs from earliest times to 1135* (London, 1866). This edition is accessible on www.ucc.ie/celt/.

HRA = *Historia Regum Anglorum*: a composite chronicle made up of a number of otherwise known or unknown sources in a series of stages. The final editor was Symeon of Durham writing c. 1110, and he was formerly credited with its compilation and authorship. His role is now considered to have been over-rated. This text is a major source for northern English history of the period after Bede. The only published translation is not entirely reliable. It was originally published in 1858 but has been reprinted as J. Stephenson, tr., *Simeon of Durham: A History of the Kings of England* (Felinfach, 1987).

HSC = *Historia de Sancto Cuthberto*: an account of the history of the Church of St Cuthbert at Chester-le-Street (and later Durham). Its exact date of production is in doubt but it appears to have a core put together in the 940s, although it survives only in an updated version from the reign of Cnut (1016–35). It has recently been published as T. Johnson South, ed. & tr., *Historia de Sancto Cuthberto: a History of Saint Cuthbert and a Record of his Patrimony* (Woodbridge, 2002).

LDE = *Libellus de Exordio atque Procursu istius hoc est Dunhelmensis Ecclesie*: this is genuinely the work of Symeon of Durham written c. 1120, and based upon *HSC*, *HRA* and other sources no longer surviving. This *libellus*, or little book, tells the story of the Church of St Cuthbert in far more detail than *HSC*. Some of the additional detail, however, may have been fabricated, or massaged, to suit the needs of twelfth-century Durham. It has been published as D. Rollason, ed. & tr., *Symeon of Durham: Libellus de Exordio atque Procursu istius hoc est Dunhelmensis Ecclesie* (Oxford, 2000).

Bibliography

Abrams, L., and D. N. Parsons, 'Place-names and the history of Scandinavian settlement in England', in J. Hines, A. Lane and M. Redknap, eds, *Land, Sea and Home: proceedings of a conference on Viking-Period Settlement, at Cardiff, July 2001*, Society for Medieval Archaeology Monograph 20, (Leeds, 2004), 379–431.

Airlie, S., 'The view from Maastricht', in B. E. Crawford, ed., *Scotland in Dark Age Europe* (St Andrews, 1994), 33–46.

Aitchison, N., *Forteviot: A Pictish and Scottish Royal Centre* (Stroud, 2006).

Alcock, L., and E. A. Alcock, 'The context of the Dupplin Cross: a reconsideration', *Proceedings of the Society of Antiquaries of Scotland* 126 (1996), 455–7.

Alcock, L., *Kings and Warriors, Craftsmen and Priests, in northern Britain, AD 550–850* (Edinburgh, 2003).

Anderson, A. O., *Early Sources of Scottish History*, 2 vols (Edinburgh, 1922 and Stamford, 1990).

Anderson, M. O., 'Scottish materials in the Paris Manuscript, Bib. Nat., Latin 4126', *Scottish Historical Review* 28 (1949), 31–42.

Anderson, M. O., *Kings and Kingship in Early Scotland* (Edinburgh, 1973).

Anderson, M. O., 'Dalriada and the creation of the kingdom of the Scots', in D. Whitelock, R. McKitterick and D. N. Dumville, eds, *Ireland in Early Medieval Europe: Studies in Memory of Kathleen Hughes* (Cambridge, 1982), 106–32.

Anthony, D., 'Migration in archaeology: the baby and the bathwater', *American Anthropologist* 92 (1990), 895–914.

Bäcklund, J., 'War or peace? The relations between the Picts and the Norse in Orkney', *Northern Studies* 36 (2001), 33–48.

Bannerman, J., 'Notes on the Scottish entries in the early Irish annals', *Scottish Gaelic Studies* 11:2 (1968), 49–70.

Bannerman, J., *Studies in the History of Dalriada* (Edinburgh, 1974).

Bannerman, J., 'MacDuff of Fife', in A. Grant and K. Stringer, eds, *Medieval Scotland: Crown, Lordship and Community* (Edinburgh, 1993), 20–38.

Bannerman, J., 'The Scottish takeover of Pictland and the relics of Columba', *Innes Review* 48 (1997), 27–44.

Barford, P., *The Early Slavs: Culture and Society in Early Medieval Eastern Europe* (London, 2001).

Barlow, F., ed. & tr., *The Life of King Edward who Rests at Westminster* (London, 1962).

Barlow, F., *Edward the Confessor* (London, 1970 and subsequent editions).

Barrett, J., 'Culture contact in Viking Age Scotland', in J. H. Barrett, ed., *Contact, Continuity and Collapse: The Norse Colonization of the North Atlantic* (Turnhout, 2003), 73–111.

Barrow, G. W. S., ed., *Regesta Regum Scottorum I: The Acts of Malcolm IV* (Edinburgh, 1960).

Barrow, G. W. S., ed., *Regesta Regum Scottorum II: The Acts of William I, King of Scots, 1165–1214* (Edinburgh, 1971), 250–2.

Barrow, G. W. S., 'Some problems in twelfth- and thirteenth-century Scottish history: a genealogical approach', *Scottish Genealogist* 25 (1978), 97–112.

Barrow, G. W. S., *The Anglo-Norman Era in Scottish History* (Oxford, 1988).

Barrow, G. W. S., *The Charters of David I* (Woodbridge, 1999).

Barrow, G. W. S., *The Kingdom of the Scots*, 2nd edn (Edinburgh, 2003).

Bernhardt, J. W., *Itinerant Kingship and Royal Monasteries in Early Medieval Germany, c. 936–1075* (Cambridge, 1993).

Binchy, D. A., ed., *Críth Gablach* (Dublin, 1941).

Bjarni Aðalbjarnarson, ed., *Heimskringla* (Reykjavík, 1941–51).

Bois, G., *The Transformation of the Year One Thousand: the Village of Lournand from Antiquity to Feudalism* (Manchester, 1992).

Bonnassie, P., *From Slavery to Feudalism in South-Western Europe* (Cambridge, 1991).

Brooke, C. L. N., 'The archbishops of St David's, Llandaff and Caerleon-on-Usk', in N. K. Chadwick, ed., *Studies in the Early British Church* (Cambridge, 1958), 201–42.

Brooks, N., *The Early History of the Church of Canterbury* (Leicester, 1984).

Broun, D., 'Dunkeld and the origin of Scottish Identity', *Innes Review* 48 (1997), 112–124.

Broun, D., 'The birth of Scottish history', *Scottish Historical Review* 76 (1997), 4–22.

Broun, D., 'Pictish kings 761–839: integration with Dál Riata or separate development', in S. M. Foster, ed., *The St Andrews Sarcophagus and its International Connections* (Dublin, 1998), 71–83.

Broun, D., *The Irish Identity of the Kingdom of the Scots in the Twelfth and Thirteenth Centuries* (Woodbridge, 1999).

Broun, D., 'The Church of St Andrews and its foundation legend in the early twelfth century: recovering the full text of version A of the foundation legend', in S. Taylor ed., *Kings, Clerics and Chronicles in Scotland, 500–1297* (Dublin, 2000), 108–14.

Broun, D., 'The Church and the origins of Scottish independence in the twelfth century', *Record of the Scottish Church History Society* 31 (2001), 1–35.

Broun, D., 'The Welsh identity of the kingdom of Strathclyde, c. 900–c. 1200', *Innes Review* 55 (2004), 111–80.

Broun, D., '*Alba*: Pictish homeland or Irish offshoot?', in P. O'Neill, ed., *Exile and Homecoming: Papers from the Fifth Australian Conference of Celtic Studies* (Sydney, 2005), 234–75.

Broun, D., 'The property-records in the Book of Deer as a source for early Scottish society', in K. Forsyth, ed., *That Splendid Little Book: Studies in the Book of Deer* (Dublin, forthcoming).

Campbell, A., *The Battle of Brunanburh* (London, 1938).

Campbell, A., ed. & tr., *Encomium Emmae Reginae*, with a supplementary introduction by S. Keynes (Cambridge, 1998).

Campbell, E., 'Trade in the Dark Age west: a peripheral activity?', in B. E. Crawford, ed., *Scotland in Dark Age Europe* (St Andrews, 1996), 79–92.

Campbell, E., 'Were the Scots Irish?', *Antiquity* 75 (2001), 285–92.

Carver, M. O. H., 'An Iona of the east: The early-medieval monastery at Portmahomack, Tarbat Ness', *Medieval Archaeology* 48 (2004), 1–30.

Cavill, P., S. Harding and J. Jesch, eds, *Wirral and its Viking Heritage* (Nottingham, 2000).

Cavill, P., S. Harding and J. Jesch, 'Revisiting *Dingesmere*', *Journal of the English Place-Names Society* 36 (2004), 25–38.

Champion, T., 'Migration revived', *Journal of Danish Archaeology* 9 (1990), 214–18.

Charles-Edwards, T. M., 'Kinship, status and the origins of the hide', *Past and Present* 56 (1972), 3–33.

Charles-Edwards, T. M., *Early Irish and Welsh Kinship* (Oxford, 1993).

Charles-Edwards, T. M., *The Early Medieval Gaelic Lawyer* (Cambridge, 1999).

Charles-Edwards, T. M., ed., *After Rome* (Oxford, 2003).

Clancy, T. O., 'Iona, Scotland and the Céli Dé', in B. E. Crawford, ed., *Scotland in Dark Age Britain* (St Andrews, 1996), 111–30.

Clancy, T. O., ed., *The Triumph Tree. Scotland's Earliest Poetry AD 550–1350* (Edinburgh, 1998).

Clancy, T. O., 'Scotland, the "Nennian" recension of Historia Brittonum and Lebor Bretnach', in S. Taylor, ed., *Kings, Clerics and Chronicles in Scotland, 500–1297* (Dublin, 2000), 87–107.

Clancy, T. O., 'Iona in the kingdom of the Picts: a note', *Innes Review* 55 (2004), 73–6.

Clark, G., 'The invasion hypothesis in British archaeology', *Antiquity* 40 (1966), 172–89.

Colgrave, B., ed. & tr., *Two Lives of Saint Cuthbert* (Cambridge, 1940 and 1985).

Cowan, E. J., 'The Scottish chronicle in the Poppleton manuscript', *Innes Review* 32 (1981).

Crawford, B., *Scandinavian Scotland* (Leicester, 1987).

Darlington, R. R., and P. McGurk, eds, and J. Bray and P. McGurk, tr., *The Chronicle of John of Worcester* (Oxford, 1995).

Davidson, M. R., 'The (non-)submission of the northern kings in 920', in N. J. Higham and D. H. Hill, eds, *Edward the Elder, 899–924* (London, 2001), 200–11.

Davies, W., ed., *From the Vikings to the Normans* (Oxford, 2003).

Downham, C., 'An imaginary Viking-raid on Skye in 795?', *Scottish Gaelic Studies* 20 (2000), 192–6.

Downham, C., 'The career of Cearbhall of Osraighe', *Ossory, Laois and Leinster* 1 (2004), 1–18.

Downham, C., 'Eric Bloodaxe – axed? The mystery of the last Scandinavian king of York', *Medieval Scandinavia* 14 (2004), 51–78.

Driscoll, M. J., ed. & tr., *Ágrip af Nóregskonungasögum: a Twelfth-Century Synoptic History of the Kings of Norway* (London, 1995).

Driscoll, S. T., 'Church archaeology in Glasgow and the kingdom of Strathclyde', *Innes Review* 49 (1998), 95–114.

Driscoll, S. T., *Govan, from Cradle to Grave* (Govan, 2004).

Duby, G., *The Early Growth of the European Economy: Warriors and Peasants from the Seventh to the Twelfth Century* (Ithaca, 1974).

Duffy, S., 'Irishmen and Islesmen in the kingdoms of Dublin and Man, 1052–1171', *Ériu* 43 (1992), 93–133.

Dumville, D. N., 'A note on the Picts in Orkney', *Scottish Gaelic Studies* 12 (1976), 266.

Dumville, D. N., 'The West Saxon genealogical regnal list: manuscripts and text', *Anglia* 104 (1986), 1–32.

Dumville, D. N., *Wessex and England from Alfred to Edgar* (Woodbridge, 1992).

Dumville, D. N., 'Ireland and Britain in Táin Bó Fráich', *Études Celtiques* 32 (1996), 175–87.

Dumville, D. N., 'Cethri Prímchenéla Dáil Riata', *Scottish Gaelic Studies* 20 (2000), 170–91.

Dumville, D. N., 'The Chronicle of the Kings of Alba', in S. Taylor, ed., *Kings, Clerics and Chronicle in Scotland, 500–1297* (Dublin, 2000), 73–86.

Dumville, D. N., 'St Cathróe of Metz and the hagiography of exoticism', in J. Carey, M. Herbert and P. Ó Riain, eds, *Studies in Irish Hagiography: Saints and Scholars* (Dublin, 2001), 172–88.

Dumville, D. N., 'Ireland and north Britain in the earlier Middle Ages: contexts for the *Miniugud Senchusa Fher nAlban*', in C. Ó Baoill and N. R. McGuire, eds, *Rannsachadh na Gàidhlig, 2000* (Aberdeen, 2002),185–212.

Dumville, D. N., ed. & tr., *Annales Cambriae, AD 682–954: texts A–C in Parallel* (Cambridge, 2002).

Duncan, A. A. M., *Scotland: the Making of the Kingdom* (Edinburgh, 1975).

Duncan, A. A. M., 'The battle of Carham, 1018', *Scottish Historical Review* 55 (1976), 20–8.

Duncan, A. A. M., *The Kingship of the Scots, 842–1292: Succession and Independence* (Edinburgh, 2002), 34–41.

Ekrem, I., and L. B. Mortensen, eds, and Peter Fisher, tr., *Historie Norwegie* (Copenhagen, 2003).

Etchingham, C., *Viking Raids on Irish Church Settlements in the Ninth Century* (Maynooth, 1996).

Etchingham, C., 'North Wales, Ireland and the Isles: the Insular Viking zone', *Peritia* 15 (2001), 145–87.

Faith, R., *The English Peasantry and the Growth of Lordship* (London, 1999).

Fellows-Jensen, G., 'Scandinavians in Dumfriesshire and Galloway: the place-name evidence', in R. Oram and G. Stell, eds, *Galloway: Land and Lordship* (Edinburgh, 1991), 77–95.

Finlay, A., ed. & tr., *Fagrskinna, a Catalogue of the Kings of Norway: a Translation with Introduction and Notes* (Leiden, 2004).

Flanagan, D., 'Common elements in Irish place-names: *baile*', *Bulletin of the Ulster Place-Name Society*, 2nd series, 1 (1978), 8–13.

Fleming, R., 'Monastic lands and England's defence in the Viking Age', *English Historical Review* 100 (1985), 247–65.

Fletcher, R., *Bloodfeud: Murder and Revenge in Anglo-Saxon England* (London, 2002).

Forbes, A. P., *Kalendars of Scottish Saints* (Edinburgh, 1872).

Forsyth, K. S., 'The inscription on the Dupplin Cross', in C. Bourke, ed., *From the Isles of the North. Early Medieval Art in Ireland and Britain* (Belfast, 1995), 237–44.

Forsyth, K. S., 'Late 12th century cross-head', in S. T. Driscoll, ed., *Excavations at Glasgow Cathedral, 1988–1997*, Society for Medieval Archaeology monograph 18 (2002), 85–7.

Forsyth, K. S., ed., *This Splendid Little Book: Studies on the Book of Deer* (Dublin, forthcoming).

Foster, S. M., *Picts, Gaels and Scots* (London, 2004).

Fraser, J. E., *The Roman Conquest of Scotland: The Battle of Mons Graupius, AD 84* (Stroud, 2005).

Fraser, J. E., 'Strangers on the Clyde: Cenél Comgaill, Clyde Rock and the bishops of Kingarth', *Innes Review* 56 (2005), 102–20.

Fraser, J. E., *From Caledonia to Pictland* (Edinburgh, 2007).

Gillingham, J., 'Thegns and knights in eleventh-century England: who was then the gentleman?' *Transactions of the Royal Historical Society*, 6th series, 5 (1995), 129–53.

Graham-Campbell, J., and Colleen E. Batey, *Vikings in Scotland: an Archaeological Survey* (Edinburgh, 1998).

Grant, A., 'Thanes and thanages from the eleventh to the fourteenth centuries', in A. Grant and K. Stringer, eds, *Medieval Scotland: Crown, Lordship and Community, Essays Presented to Geoffrey Barrow* (Edinburgh, 1998), 39–81.

Grant, A., 'The construction of the early Scottish state', in J. R. Maddicott and D. M. Palliser, eds, *The Medieval State: Essays Presented to James Campbell* (London, 2000), 47–72.

Greenaway, D. ed., *Henry Archdeacon of Huntingdon: Historia Anglorum* (Oxford, 1996).

Greene, D., 'The making of Insular Celtic', *Proceedings of the Second International Congress of Celtic Studies* (Cardiff, 1966), 121–36.

Greene, D., 'Gaelic: syntax, similarities with British syntax', in D. S. Thomson, ed., *The Companion to Gaelic Scotland* (Oxford, 1983), 107–8.

Grierson, P., and M. Blackburn, *Medieval European Coinage: 1, The Early Middle Ages (5th–10th centuries)* (Cambridge, 1986), 298–303.

Halloran, K., 'The Brunanburh campaign: a reappraisal', *Scottish Historical Review* 84 (2005), 133–48.

Hamilton Thompson, A., ed., *Liber Vitae Ecclesiae Dunelmensis: A Collotype Facsimile of the Original Manuscript*, Records of the Surtees Society 136 (1923).

Hart, C. R., 'Athelstan "Half-king" and his family', *Anglo-Saxon England* 2 (1973), 115–44, reprinted in C. R. Hart, *The Danelaw* (London, 1992), 569–604.

Henderson, L., and E. J. Cowan, *Scottish Fairy Belief: a History* (East Linton, 2001).

Herbert, M., *Iona, Kells and Derry: the History and Hagiography of the Monastic Familia of Columba* (Oxford, 1988).

Hermann Pálsson and Paul Edwards, tr., *Orkneyinga Saga: The History of the Earls of Orkney* (Harmondsworth, 1981).

Higham, M.,'Scandinavian settlement in north-west England, with a special study of Ireby names', in B. E. Crawford, ed., *Scandinavian Settlement in Northern Britain* (London, 1995), 195–205.

Hill, D. H., *An Atlas of Anglo-Saxon England* (Oxford, 1981).

Hill, P., *Whithorn and St Ninian: The Excavation of a Monastic Town, 1984–91* (Stroud, 1997).

Hines, J., 'The becoming of the English: identity, material culture and language in early Anglo-Saxon England', *Anglo-Saxon Studies in Archaeology and History* 7 (1994), 49–60.

Holland, M., 'Were early Irish church establishments under lay control?', in D. Bracken and D. Ó Riain-Raedel, eds, *Ireland and Europe in the Twelfth Century: Reform and Renewal* (Dublin, 2006), 128–42.

Hollander, L. M., tr., *Heimskringla, History of the Kings of Norway* (Austin, 1977).

Hollister, C. W., *Anglo-Saxon Military Institutions on the Eve of the Norman Conquest* (Oxford, 1962 and 1998).

Hudson, B. T., '*Elech* and the Scots in Strathclyde', *Scottish Gaelic Studies* 15 (1988), 145–9.

Hudson, B. T., 'Cnut and the Scottish Kings', *English Historical Review* 107 (1992), 350–60.

Hudson, B. T., 'Kings and Church in early Scotland', *Scottish Historical Review* 73 (1994), 145–70.

Hudson, B. T., *Kings of Celtic Scotland* (Westport, 1994) 26–33.

Hudson, B. T., *Prophecy of Berchan: Irish and Scottish High-Kings in the Early Middle Ages* (Westport, 1996).

Hudson, B. T., *Viking Pirates and Christian Princes: Dynasty and Empire in the North Atlantic* (New York, 2005).

Hudson, B. T., *Irish Sea Studies, 900–1200* (Dublin, 2006).

Hughes, K., *Early Christian Ireland. Introduction to the Sources* (London, 1972).

Hughes, K., 'Where are the writings of early Scotland', in D. N. Dumville, ed., *Celtic Britain in the Early Middle Ages: Studies in Scottish and Welsh Sources by the late Kathleen Hughes* (Woodbridge, 1980), 1–21.

Jackson, K. H., *The Gaelic Notes in the Book of Deer* (Cambridge, 1972).

Jakob Benediktsson, *Íslendingabók, Landnámabók* (Reykjavík, 1986).

Jenkins, D., ed. & tr., *The Law of Hywel Dda: Law Texts from Medieval Wales* (Llandysul, 1986).

Jesch, J., 'Norse historical traditions and the *Historia Gruffud vab Kenan*', in K. L. Maund, ed., *Gruffudd ap Cynan: A Collaborative Biography* (Woodbridge, 1996), 117–48.

Johnson, C., ed. & tr., *Hugh the Chanter: The History of the Church of York, 1066–1127* (Oxford, 1990).

Jones, T., ed. & tr., *Brut y Tywysogyon or the Chronicle of the Princes: Peniarth MS. 20* (Cardiff, 1952).

Jones, T., ed., *Brut y Tywysogyon or the Chronicle of the Princes, Red Book of Hergest Version* (Cardiff, 1955).

Kapelle, W., *The Norman Conquest of the North: the Region and its Transformation, 1000–1135* (Chapel Hill, 1979).

Karras, R. M., *Slavery and Society in Medieval Scandinavia* (New Haven, 1988).

Kelly, F., *A Guide to Early Irish Law* (Dublin, 1988).

Kelly, F., *Early Irish Farming* (Dublin, 1997).

Keynes, S., *An Atlas of Attestations in Anglo-Saxon Charters, c. 670–1066* (Cambridge, 1998).

Keynes, S., 'King Alfred and the Mercians', in M. Blackburn and D. Dumville, eds, *Kings, Currencies and Alliances: History and Coinage of Southern England in the Ninth Century* (Woodbridge, 1998), 1–46.

Keynes, S., 'Kingston-upon-Thames', in M. Lapidge, J. Blair, S. Keynes and D. Scragg, eds, *The Blackwell Encyclopaedia of Anglo-Saxon England* (Oxford, 1999), 272.

Keynes, S., 'Wulfstan I', in M. Lapidge, J. Blair, S. Keynes and D. Scragg, eds, *The Blackwell Encyclopedia of Anglo-Saxon England* (Oxford, 1999), 492–3.

Keynes, S., and M. Lapidge, eds & tr., *Alfred the Great: Asser's Life and other Contemporary Sources* (Harmondsworth, 1983).

Kirby, D. P., 'Hywel Dda: Anglophile?', *Welsh History Review* 8 (1976–77), 1–13.

Koch, J. T., with J. Carey, ed., *The Celtic Heroic Age: Literary Sources for Ancient Celtic Europe and Early Ireland and Wales* (Aberystwyth, 2000).

Krag, C., 'The early unification of Norway', in K. Helle, ed., *The Cambridge History of Scandinavia* (Cambridge, 2003), 184–201.

Laing, D., ed. & tr., *Andrew of Wyntoun: Orygynale Cronykil of Scotland*, 2 vols, *Historians of Scotland II & III*, (Edinburgh, 1872).

Lane, A., 'Trade, gifts and cultural exchange in Dark-Age western Scotland', in B. E. Crawford, ed., *Scotland in Dark Age Europe* (St Andrews, 1994), 103–15.

Lane, A., and E. Campbell, *Dunadd, an Early Dalriadic Capital* (Oxford, 2000).

Lapidge, Michael, J. Blair, S. Keynos and D. Saragg, eds, *The Blackwell Encyclopaedia of Anglo-Saxon England* (Oxford, 1999).

Lass, R., *Old English: A Historical Linguistic Companion* (Cambridge, 1994).

Lattin, H. P., ed. & tr., *The Letters of Gerbert, with his Papal Privileges as Sylvester II* (New York, 1961).

Lawrie, A. C., ed., *Early Scottish Charters prior to 1153* (Glasgow, 1905).

McDonald, R. A., *Outlaws of Medieval Scotland, Challenges to the Canmore Kings, 1058–1266* (East Linton, 2003).

McNeill, P. G. B., and H. L. MacQueen, eds, *Atlas of Scottish History to 1707* (Edinburgh, 1996).

Macniven, A., *The Norse in Islay: A Settlement Historical Case-Study for Medieval Scandinavian Activity in Western Maritime Scotland* (Edinburgh, 2006), unpublished Ph.D. thesis.

Maitland, F. W., *Domesday Book and Beyond: Three Essays in the Early History of England* (Cambridge, 1897).

Miller, M., 'The last century of Pictish succession', *Scottish Studies* 23 (1979), 39–67.

Miller, M., 'Amlaíb Trahens Centum', *Scottish Gaelic Studies* 19 (1999), 241–5.

Morris, C. J., *Marriage and Murder in Eleventh Century Northumbria: a Study of the 'De Obsessione Dunelmi'*, Borthwick Papers no. 82, (York, 1992).

Murphy, D., ed., *The Annals of Clonmacnoise* (Dublin, 1896 and Felinfach, 1993).

Myhre, B., 'The beginning of the Viking Age – some current archaeological problems', in A. Faulkes and R. Perkins, eds, *Viking Revaluations* (London, 1993), 182–203.

Mynors, R. A. B., R. M. Thomson and M. Winterbottom, eds & tr., *William of Malmesbury: Gesta Regum Anglorum* (Oxford, 1998).

Nelson, J. L., ed. & tr., *The Annals of St-Bertin* (Manchester, 1991).

Nielsen, H.-F., *The Germanic Languages: Origins and Early Dialectal Interrelations* (Tuscaloosa, 1989).

Nicolaisen, W. F. H., *Scottish Place-Names, Their Study and Significance* (London, 1976).

Ó Córráin, D., 'The Vikings in Scotland and Ireland in the ninth century', in *Peritia* 12 (1998), 296–339.

Ó Córráin, D., 'Viking Ireland – afterthoughts', in H. Clarke, M. Ní Mhaonaigh and R. Ó Floinn, eds, *Ireland and Scandinavia in the Early Viking Age* (Dublin, 1998), 421–52.

O'Dwyer, P., *Céli Dé: Spiritual Reform in Ireland, 750–900* (Dublin, 1981).

O'Loughlin, T., *Celtic Theology: Humanity, World and God in Early Irish Writings* (London, 2000).

Ó Riain, P., 'St Finnbarr: a study in a cult', *Journal of the Cork Historical and Archaeological Society* 82 (1977), 63–82.

Omand, C. J., ed. & tr., 'The life of St Findan', in R. J. Berry and H. N. Firth, eds, *The People of Orkney* (Kirkwall, 1986), 284–7.

Oram, R., 'Scandinavian settlement in south-west Scotland with a special study of Bysbie', in B. E. Crawford, ed., *Scandinavian Settlement in Northern Britain* (London, 1995), 127–40.

Oram, R., *Domination and Lordship: Scotland c.1070 to c.1230* (Edinburgh, 2007).

Parsons, D. N., 'The language of the Anglo-Saxon settlers', in H.-F. Nielsen and L. Schøsler, eds, *The origins and Development of Emigrant Language*, NOWELE supplement 17, (Odense, 1996), 141–56.

Parsons, D. N., *The Vocabulary of English Place-Names* (vol. 3), *Ceafor – Cock-pit* (Nottingham, 2004).

Pelteret, D., *Slavery in Early Mediaeval England, from the Reign of Alfred until the Twelfth Century* (Woodbridge, 1995).

Phelpstead, C., ed., and D. Kunin, tr., *A History of Norway and the Passion and Miracles of the Holy Óláfr* (London, 2001).

Phythian-Adams, C., *Land of the Cumbrians: A Study in British Provincial Origins, AD 400–1120* (Aldershot, 1996).

Powel, D., *The history of Cambria, now called Wales: A part of the most famous Yland of Brytaine, written in the Brytish language above two hundred years past: translated into English by H. Lloyd Gentleman: Corrected, augmented and continued out of Records and best approued Authors by David Powel Doctor in Diuinitie* (London, 1584, reprinted 1697 and 1774).

Price, L., 'A note on the use of the word *baile* in place-names', *Celtica* 6 (1963), 119–26.

Pryce, H., 'The Christianization of society', in W. Davies, ed., *From the Vikings to the Normans* (Oxford, 2003), 139–68.

Radner, J., ed., *The Fragmentary Annals of Ireland* (Dublin, 1978).

Randsborg, K., *The Viking Age in Denmark* (London, 1980).

Renfrew, C., 'Systems collapse as social transformation: catastrophe and anastrophe in early state societies', in C. Renfrew and K. L. Cooke, eds, *Transformations: Mathematical Approaches to Culture Change* (London, 1979), 481–506.

Reeves, W., *The Culdees of the British Islands as they Appear in History with an Appendix of Evidences* (Dublin, 1864 and Felinfach, 1994).

Reuter, T., 'Plunder and tribute in the Carolingian Empire', *Transactions of the Royal Historical Society*, 5th series, 35 (1985), 75–94.

Reuter, T., *Germany in the Early Middle Ages, 800–1056* (Harlow, 1991), 183–90.

Reynolds, S., *Fiefs and Vassals: The Medieval Evidence Reinterpreted* (Oxford, 1994).

Ritchie, A., ed., *Govan and its Early Medieval Sculpture* (Stroud, 1994).

Rivet, A. L. F., and C. Smith, *The Place-Names of Roman Britain* (London, 1979).

Robinson, O. W., *Old English and its Closest Relatives: a Survey of the Earliest Germanic Languages* (London, 1992).

Rollason, D., *Northumbria, 500–1100: Creation and Destruction of a Kingdom* (Cambridge, 2003).

Ross, A., 'Pictish matriliny?', *Northern Studies* 34 (1999), 11–22.

Ross, A., 'The Dabhach in Moray: a new look at an Old Tub', in A. Woolf, ed., *Landscape and Environment in Dark Age Scotland* (St Andrews, 2006), 57–74.

Russell, P., ed. & tr., *Vita Griffini filii Conani* (Cardiff, 2005).

Sawyer, B., *The Viking-Age Rune-Stones: Custom and Commemoration in Early Medieval Scandinavia* (Oxford, 2000).

Sawyer, P. H., 'Harald Fairhair and the British Isles', in R. Boyer, ed., *Les Vikings et leur civilisation: problèmes actuels* (Paris, 1976), 105–9.

Sawyer, P. H., *The Making of Sweden* (Alingsås, 1988).

Sawyer, P. H., 'The last Scandinavian kings of York', *Northern History* 31 (1995), 39–44.

Seebohm, F., *Tribal Custom in Anglo-Saxon Law* (London, 1911).

Sellar, W. D. H., 'The origins and ancestry of Somerled', *Scottish Historical Review* 45 (1966), 123–42.

Sellar, W. D. H., 'Family origins in Cowal and Knapdale', *Scottish Studies* 15 (1971), 21–31.

Sharp, S., 'The West Saxon tradition of dynastic marriage with special reference to the family of Edward the Elder', in N. J. Higham and D. H. Hill, eds, *Edward the Elder, 899–924* (London, 2001), 79–88.

Sims-Williams, P., 'Dating the transition to neo-Brittonic: phonology and history, 400–600', in A. Bammesberger and A. Wollman, eds, *Britain, 400–600: Language and History* (Heidelberg, 1990), 217–61.

Sims-Williams, P., *The Celtic Inscriptions of Britain: Phonology and Chronology, c. 400–1200* (London, 2003).

Skene, W. F., ed., *Chronicle of the Picts and Scots* (Edinburgh, 1867).

Skene, W. F., *Celtic Scotland: A History of Ancient Alban*, 3 vols (Edinburgh, 1876–80).

Smart, V., 'Scandinavians, Celts, and Germans in Anglo-Saxon England: the evidence of moneyers' names', in M. A. S. Blackburn, ed., *Anglo-Saxon Monetary History* (Leicester, 1986), 171–84.

Smith, B., 'The Picts and the martyrs or did the Vikings kill the native population of Orkney and Shetland?', *Northern Studies* 36 (2001), 7–32.

Smyth, A. P., *Scandinavian Kings in the British Isles* (Oxford, 1977).

Smyth, A. P., *Scandinavian York and Dublin*, 2 vols (Dublin and New Jersey, 1975 and 1979).

Smyth, A. P., *Warlords and Holy Men: Scotland AD 80–1000* (London, 1984).

Stacey, R. C., *The Road to Judgment: From Custom to Court in Medieval Ireland and Wales* (Philadelphia, 1994).

Stafford, P., *Unification and Conquest: a Political and Social History of England in the Tenth and Eleventh Centuries* (London, 1989).

Stafford, P., *Queen Emma and Queen Edith: Queenship and Women's Power in Eleventh-Century England* (Oxford, 2001).

Taylor, A. B., tr., *The Orkneyinga Saga* (Edinburgh, 1938).

Taylor, S., 'Generic element variation, with special reference to eastern Scotland', *Nomina* 20 (1997), 5–22.

Taylor, S., *The Place-Names of Fife*, 4 vols, (Stamford, 2006 ff.).

Thomas, F. L. W., 'Proposed correction of the text of "Leges inter Brettos et Scottos"', *Proceedings of the Society of Antiquaries of Scotland* 19 (1884–5), 73–4.

Thomason, S. G., and T. Kaufman, *Language Contact, Creolization, and Genetic Linguistics* (Berkeley, 1988).

Thomson, W. P., 'St Findan and the Pictish–Norse transition', in R. J. Berry and H. N. Firth, eds, *The People of Orkney* (Kirkwall, 1986), 279–83.

Thornton, D. E., 'Edgar and the eight kings, AD 973', *Early Medieval Europe* 10 (2001), 49–80.

Thornton, D. E., 'Hey Mac! The name Maccus, tenth to fifteenth centuries', *Nomina* 20 (1997), 67–98.

Townend, M., *Language and History in Viking-Age England: Linguistic Relations between Speakers of Old Norse and Old English* (Turnhout, 2002).

Tschan, F. J., tr., *Adam of Bremen: History of the Archbishops of Hamburg-Bremen* (New York, 1959 and 2002).

Veitch, K., ' "Replanting Paradise": Alexander I and the reform of religious life in Scotland', *Innes Review* 52 (2001), 136–66.

Wade-Evans, A. W., ed. & tr., *Vitae Sanctorum Britanniae et Genealogiae* (Cardiff, 1944).

Wainwright, F. T., 'Ingimund's invasion', *English Historical Review* 247 (1948), 145–67.

Wainwright, F. T., 'The battles at Corbridge', *Saga-Book of the Viking Society* 13 (1950), 156–73.

Wainwright, F. T., 'The submission to Edward the Elder', *History* 37 (1952), 114–30.

Wainwright, F. T., and H. P. R. Finberg, eds, *Scandinavian England* (Chichester, 1975).

Warner, D. A., ed. & tr., *Ottonian Germany: The Chronicon of Thietmar of Merseburg* (Manchester, 2001).

Watson, W. J., *Scottish Place-Name Papers* (Edinburgh, 2002).

Watt, D. E. R., *Series Episcoporum Ecclesiae Catholicae Occidentalis ab initio usque ad annum MCXCVIII, Series VI, Britannia, Scotia et Hibernia, Scandinavia, vol I Ecclesia Scoticana* (Stuttgart, 1991).

Whaley, D., *The Poetry of Arnórr jarlaskáld: An Edition and Study* (Turnhout, 1998).

Whitelock, D., ed., *English Historical Documents*, vol. I, *AD 500–1042* (London, 1955, 2nd edn, 1979).

Williams, A., 'An outing on the Dee: King Edgar at Chester, *AD* 973', *Medieval Scandinavia* 14 (2004), 229–44.

Williams, H., ed. & tr., *Two Lives of Gildas* (London, 1899 and Felinfach, 1990).

Wilson, P. A., 'On the use of the terms "Strathclyde" and "Cumbria" ', *Transactions of the Cumberland and Westmoreland Antiquarian and Archaeological Society* 66 (1966), 57–92.

Woolf, A., 'Erik Bloodaxe revisited', *Northern History* 34 (1998), 189–93.

Woolf, A., 'Pictish matriliny reconsidered', *Innes Review* 49 (1998), 147–67.

Woolf, A., 'The "Moray Question" and the kingship of Alba in the tenth and eleventh centuries', *Scottish Historical Review* 79 (2000), 145–64.

Woolf, A., 'Amlaíb Cuarán and the Gael, 941–81', in S. Duffy, ed., *Medieval Dublin III* (Dublin, 2002), 34–42.

Woolf, A, 'The origins and ancestry of Somerled: Gofraid mac Fegusa and "the Annals of the Four Masters" ', *Mediaeval Scandinavia* 15 (2005), 199–213.

Woolf, A., 'Dún Nechtáin, Fortriu and the geography of the Picts', *Scottish Historical Review* 85 (2006), 182–201.

Woolf, A., 'Reporting scotland in the Anglo-Saxon Chronicle', in A. Jorgensen, ed., *Studies in the Anglo-Saxon Chronicle* (Woodbridge, forthcoming).

Index